FERRARI
1960–1965

Published in November 2022

ISBN 978-1-910505-81-6

Published by Evro Publishing

Westrow House, Holwell, Sherborne, Dorset DT9 5LF, UK

Translated by David Waldron
Edited by Mark Hughes
Designed by Richard Parsons

Printed and bound in Bosnia and Herzegovina by GPS Group

www.evropublishing.com

PHOTOGRAPHY

The photographs in this book were mainly
taken by Bernard Cahier, one of the greatest
racing photographers of all time. His son,
Paul-Henri, also a racing photographer, curates
the best of his father's work at *f1-photo.com*.

A small number of photographs are from other sources as follows: Archivio Ferrari — pages 11, 130 bottom, 191,
227 top; *barcboys.com* (Dave Nicholas) — pages 23, 91 top/bottom, 130 top; Archives Maurice Louche — pages 227
bottom, 228 top/bottom, 293 bottom, 294; Motorsport Images — pages 230, 236, 281, 291 top/bottom, 303, 304, 358,
359; *sebringrace.com* (William A. Jordan) — page 131.

TRANSLATOR

David Waldron began a long-time role as English commentator at the Le Mans 24 Hours in 1988. That year brought
Jaguar's first 'modern-era' victory and for Waldron it formed a pleasing link to childhood in his native Ireland
when he followed this classic race on the radio in 1951, the year of Jaguar's first Le Mans success. Resident in
France since 1974, he has written three books about F1, including one about Ferrari, and continues to apply his
deep knowledge of motorsport to translations of books.

JACKET PHOTOGRAPHS

All photographs on the jacket of this book were taken by Bernard Cahier. Front cover: top — Lorenzo Bandini,
Ferrari 250 P, Sebring 12 Hours, 1963; bottom — John Surtees, Ferrari 158, German Grand Prix, Nürburgring, 1964.
Back cover: Wolfgang von Trips and Phil Hill, Belgian Grand Prix, Spa-Francorchamps, 1960; Willy Mairesse,
Ferrari 156, German Grand Prix, Nürburgring, 1961; John Surtees, Ferrari 158, Monaco Grand Prix, Monte Carlo,
1964; flat-12 engine, Belgian Grand Prix, Spa-Francorchamps, 1965.

FERRARI
1960–1965
The hallowed years

EVRO
PUBLISHING

William Huon
Photographs by Bernard Cahier

CONTENTS

INTRODUCTION 6

1960 **THE TURNAROUND** 8

1961 **TRIUMPH AND TRAGEDY** 72

1962 **DOUBT CREEPS IN** 124

1963 **THE MESSIAH ARRIVES** 176

1964 **A DREAM FULFILLED** 238

1965 **RUNNING OUT OF STEAM** 300

TECHNICAL SPECIFICATIONS 364

INDEX 366

◀ The epitome of the famous Ferrari V12 engine: it is seen in 3-litre form in the 250 GTO raced by Umberto Maglioli/Gotfrid Köchert in the Nürburgring 1,000Km of 1962.

INTRODUCTION

Yet another book on Ferrari, I hear you sigh, and probably with good reason as those who write about Maranello — the man himself, his cars, his successes, his setbacks — are legion. However, I should like you to indulge me.

I lived the story of the period covered in these pages, through magazines and the rare radio or televised broadcasts of the time, but the fact that I was born in Reims gave me the opportunity to live some moments of it with rare intensity. As I write this, I suddenly recall the memory of Fangio's Maserati passing close to my father's motorcycle as we approached *Thillois*, where I caught my first glimpse of cars that I had previously seen only in magazines. The year was 1958 and Fangio was taking part in his last race. And the cry 'It's Fangio' uttered by the spectators massed in the viewing zone at that corner as the great Argentine driver came round on his first lap still resonates inside me. I not only remember Fangio, of course, but also Peter Collins, Mike Hawthorn, Wolfgang von Trips and Luigi Musso… all drivers whose destinies were to be so brutally cut short, in Musso's case that very weekend.

My memories of subsequent years in Grand Prix paddocks, or even in the pits when I managed to sneak in, are enriched by the human aspect. It was an era when you could easily get near your heroes to ask for autographs that were signed with care and respect. When Bruce McLaren signed an autograph for me in 1960, he added 'NZ' after his name as a reminder of his country of origin, not to be confused with his famous team-mate Jack Brabham's native Australia. Tony Brooks gave me an autograph just when he was about to set off in his sluggish Vanwall. There was an added thrill when Innes Ireland, my favourite, signed for me and later I kept his photo in my wallet, something that earned me a grimace from Denis Jenkinson when I showed it to him at Reims a few years later.

Helped by my father's travels for his work, my autograph book began to fill up with precious signatures after visits to Pau and Albi as well as regular return trips to Reims to see my family. Unfortunately, I was never able to obtain the signatures of Ricardo Rodríguez or Lorenzo Bandini as they were inaccessible from my place in a grandstand at the 1962 Pau Grand Prix. But at Reims in 1963 I was able to add the names of Masten Gregory, Richie Ginther, Graham Hill, Jo Bonnier, Jo Schlesser, Jo Siffert and Jim Clark. I not only met Clark in the Champagne region but also in practice for the Formula 2 Albi Grand Prix in September 1964, this time for a photo taken with me in the paddock while we exchanged a few words. I also have photos where I'm with Denny Hulme snapped in the sun

The author (left) met many of his racing heroes during this 1960–65 era, including a shirtless Jim Clark at the Formula 2 Albi Grand Prix in 1964.

as he was seated in his Brabham and with Tony Maggs installed in his Lola while a few adjustments were carried out. These were unforgettable moments and I bored my friends with them at the time because, then as now, I wanted to share what I had seen.

Nowadays, racing heroes have their images curated by marketing people and are all but inaccessible to the fans without whom there would be no gilded livelihoods. Without drowning in nostalgia for a bygone past, I do not think I am taking any risks in saying that Jack Brabham, Phil Hill, Graham Hill, Jim Clark and John Surtees — to mention only the World Champions of the 1960–65 era — were of a higher calibre when they tackled circuits designed around natural layouts in cars of wider diversity that enhanced the breadth of their talents. The debate between the old and the new never goes away.

My unflagging passion as time passed and my desire to tell this story led me to meet photographer Paul-Henri Cahier, whose father, Bernard, took exquisite photographs that play a huge part in the perpetuation of my memories, and translator David Waldron, whose texts I read long before he turned my French manuscript for this book into an English one. They were my rocks during the adventure that writing this book represented, the first for tirelessly searching out the exact images I wanted for each race, and above all for the right portraits of drivers, the second for having consulted me unceasingly as he sought *le mot juste* and occasionally corrected my errors.

Working down the page from the top, these are the signatures of Jo Siffert, Maurice Trintignant, Phil Hill, Jo Schlesser, Tony Brooks, Jackie Stewart, Masten Gregory, Allen Grant, Bruce McLaren, Innes Ireland, Chris Amon, Jim Clark, Denny Hulme, Tony Maggs, Bob Bondurant, Jack Brabham and Jo Bonnier. The author gathered most of them at Reims, the high-speed track just outside the city where he grew up and became a life-long Ferrari enthusiast.

Le Mans 24 Hours. Paul Frère at the wheel of the victorious 250 TR 59/60 he shared with fellow Belgian Olivier Gendebien. Due to a major error by the Scuderia, the sister cars of Wolfgang von Trips/Phil Hill and Ludovico Scarfiotti/Pedro Rodríguez ran out of fuel before making their first scheduled pitstops.

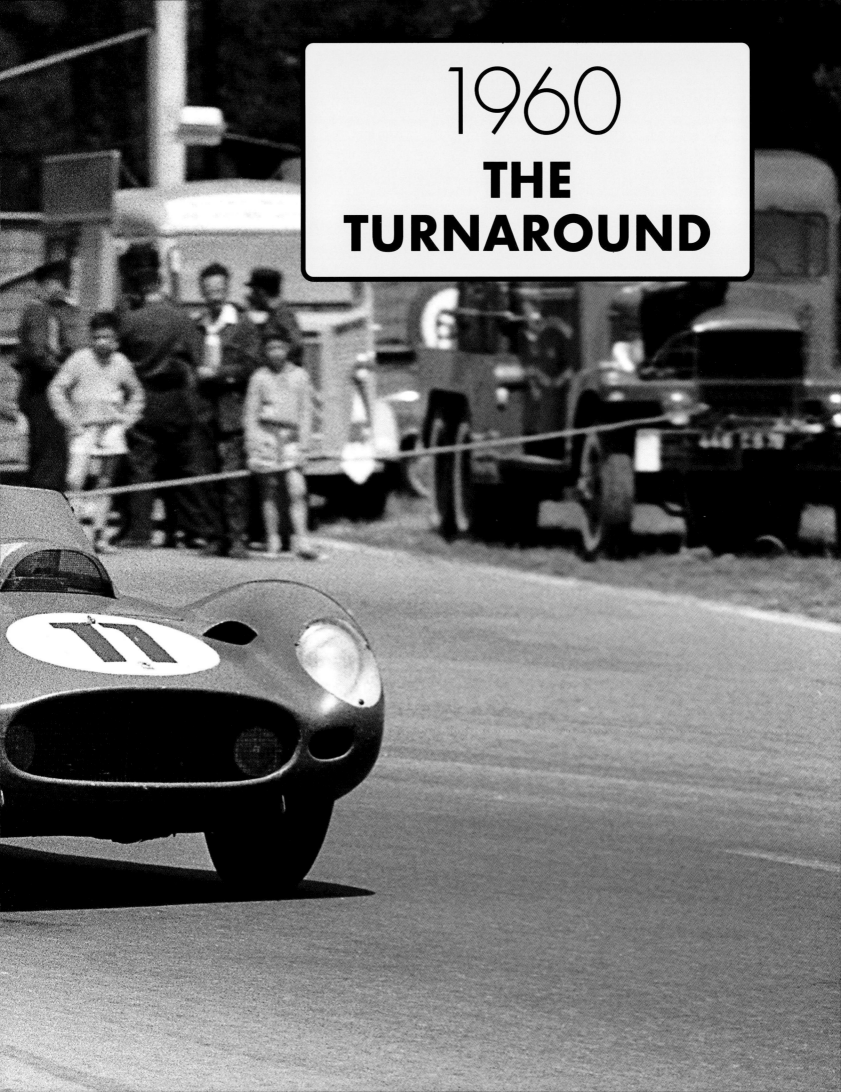

1960
THE TURNAROUND

At the beginning of 1960, the Grand Prix community was in a state of uproar. This was the last season for the existing Formula 1 regulations, which allowed normally aspirated engines of 2,500cc (or supercharged ones of 750cc), and the proposed new rules, first announced at the end of 1958, would reduce maximum capacity to 1,500cc. This prospect had created considerable strife among the constructors. Numerous meetings had ended in the same acrimonious conclusions — nobody agreed on anything — even though the main elements of change had been common knowledge since 1957, because the new rules were essentially identical to those that had governed Formula 2 since that date. This is an important point of perspective about the debate and helps throw light on the positions of the various adversaries.

Ferrari and Porsche had already gathered considerable experience of Formula 2 and were broadly in favour of the changes, whereas the British constructors, led by Cooper, were now doing well in Formula 1 and were very much against upsetting the status quo. One argument advanced by those who wanted to preserve the 2.5-litre Formula 1 had been to leave things unchanged for circuits with an average lap speed above 180kph (112mph) but to introduce the new 1.5-litre rules for slower tracks, but this had been dismissed. Apart from reducing maximum weight from 500kg to 450kg (from 1,102lb to 992lb), the *Commission Sportive Internationale* (CSI) had turned a blind eye to partisan interests and would not budge. And even if the introduction of the new Formula 1 was not yet done and dusted, cracks began to appear in the ranks of its opponents because they were afraid of falling behind as their rivals, particularly Ferrari, honed their weapons for the new era.

Sports car racing appeared much calmer, at least on the surface. While the maximum engine capacity of 3 litres set by the CSI's Appendix C regulations was still in force for the World Sports Car Championship, there were new requirements that were intended to bring the cars a little closer to everyday vehicles. These details variously raised people's hackles or just made them smile. Annoyance arose about the CSI's imposition, supposedly for safety reasons, of the need for the 'protective height' of a car's cockpit to be 85cm (33.5 inches), to which was added a windscreen height of 25cm (10 inches) that obliged some drivers to use a cushion to see over the top when vision became compromised, because of splattered insects, low sun or rain. As for smiling, this was one reaction to the new requirement for a rudimentary luggage compartment that could accommodate a suitcase measuring 65 x 40 x 20cm (25.5 x 16 x 8 inches). As for the Grand Touring cars that now had increasing appeal for more and more manufacturers, they did not yet supplant the sport cars. In the meantime, while waiting for this idea to gain traction, the CSI tried to entice potential entrants with the creation of a cup for each of the cubic-capacity categories from 500cc to over 2,000cc. These cups would be contested in the classic races and in events specially created for them.

'We won't die of starvation'

The 1960 season looked busy. In January, Raymond Miomandre of *L'Automobile* asked Enzo Ferrari if he intended to take part in 'all the sports car, F1 and F2 races on the calendar'. The response was clear: 'Certainly not! This year we have three works drivers who will share the events between them. The calendar is really tightly packed and for us at Ferrari it's impossible to compete in all the events because they clash.' He specifically mentioned the Monaco and Dutch Grands Prix, which now fell on consecutive weekends, causing preparation headaches, especially if cars had been damaged at the street race. 'There's no question of competing for the world title, either in sport cars or in single-seaters,' Ferrari added. Was this an admission of weakness or an objective analysis of his resources? He went on to state some of his intentions without really clarifying details: 'The Nürburgring 1,000Km: we have big commercial interests in Germany where we have a large client base so that's pretty much on the cards. The Targa Florio: it's our home race; we're still waiting for the regulations, which will be modified this year… In any case, we'll have a number of clients taking part in the grand touring and sports car categories, but only as privateers. The 24 Hours of Le Mans: It's the greatest race in the world so we must take part, but there are regulations that give an advantage to certain cars; we're still in discussion. No cars in the Tourist Trophy: lapping a 2.4-mile circuit [Goodwood] for hours on end isn't sport; it's a circus!' He was also very circumspect about Formula 2, awaiting the decision of the *Fédération Internationale de l'Automobile* (FIA) to find out if the category would evolve into Formula 1 for 1961.

He summed up: 'What's important at present is to continue. And for that winning isn't always necessary, but above all it's necessary to persevere. We won't die of starvation because of a defeat and we have to find the right balance: *Il mezzo juste*.'

➤ Although this photo has nothing to do with the interview cited in the text, it is proof that for Enzo Ferrari gestures counted as much as what was said. He liked to find just the right word and also to speak French, in particular with Raymond Miomandre, someone he had known for a long time.

A name that became a legend

In sports cars, Ferrari persevered with the 250 Testa Rossa, the championship-winning car in 1958 and runner-up to the Aston Martin DBR1 the following year. In fact, its origins went back to 1955, when Ferrari wanted to breathe new life into the four-cylinder 500 Mondial because it had become outclassed by the Maserati A6GCS in the very important — from a commercial viewpoint — 2-litre category. During the winter of 1955/56, Vittorio Bellentani and Alberto Massimino revamped the chassis and suspension and also modified the in-line four-cylinder engine, reinforcing the lower part of the block and raising the compression to give an improved power output of 306bhp at 7,000rpm. The cylinder head covers were painted bright red and the finished car was called the 500 Testa Rossa ('Red Head'), the first of a line of cars that would achieve legendary status. Let's see how.

The Le Mans disaster in 1955 cost Pierre Levegh and 84 spectators their lives when his Mercedes-Benz 300SLR went into the crowd. Two years later came the accident in the Mille Miglia in which Alfonso de Portago and Ed Nelson died when their Ferrari 335 S crashed and killed both of them as well as nine spectators. This tragedy not only ended the Mille Miglia for good but also brought to a close a sports car category in which the battle for power had led to a frantic escalation in engine size. In order to limit performance, the FIA asked its CSI subsidiary to impose a 3-litre limit for cars competing for the manufacturers' title of the 1958 World Sports Car Championship. For Enzo Ferrari, either better informed or more perspicacious, this regulation change came as only a minor surprise. In 1956, a reduction in cubic capacity and the harmonisation of regulations to increase the number of title contenders had prompted the FIA to create a Grand Touring category, which led to the birth of the Ferrari 250 GT Competizione.

While waiting for his rivals to reveal their intentions, Enzo Ferrari unveiled his own 3-litre sports car in May 1957 with the entry for the Nürburgring 1,000Km, via Scuderia Temple Buell, of a conventional-looking 'hybrid' prototype comprising a 290 MM chassis powered by a 3-litre single-overhead-camshaft engine. Masten Gregory and Wolfgang von Trips were originally nominated as drivers, but after the up-and-coming German ace injured himself in a practice accident at the wheel of a 250 GT, a little-known Italian driver, Olinto Morolli, replaced him; the car finished the race in 10th place. The following month, a second prototype, this time with a 3.1-litre engine installed in a lengthened 500 TRC chassis, was entered for Le Mans. Its bodywork by Sergio Scaglietti stood out from the first prototype by having cutaway sections on the nose either side of the air intake, making the fenders appear separate. This 'pontoon-fender' shape was said by some to upset the stability of the car and was replaced by a more conventional front end on works Ferraris soon after the start of the 1958 season. Entrusted to Olivier Gendebien and Maurice Trintignant, this second prototype was a podium contender at Le Mans until its retirement soon after nightfall due to a blown piston. The car's performance, combining speed and fuel economy, was enough to reassure Enzo Ferrari and Carlo Chiti, an engineer who had only recently arrived in Maranello, that they had made the right decision.

From 1958 onwards, the 250 TRs were all powered by the 3-litre V12 engine whose original design, by Gioacchino Colombo, went back to the early years after the Second World War. Having begun life at 1,497cc, it had been progressively enlarged to reach 2,953cc in 1952. Baptised the *Tipo* 128, it first powered the 250 S and later the 250 GT Competizione. By 1958, its power output was 250bhp, increasing to around 280bhp two years later. Depending on where a Testa Rossa was to be sold and the nature of its racing, various modifications were possible, such as having a gearbox with five speeds (instead of four) and incorporating independent rear suspension. For 1960, the tubular chassis, which had already been tweaked the previous year to accommodate an engine canted to the left, was revised to improve weight distribution and to meet other requirements demanded by the CSI. As in 1959, Dunlop supplied the disc brakes and Medardo Fantuzzi made the bodywork to Pinin Farina's design.

Dino forever

In the 2-litre category, Ferrari was counting on a new version of the 196 S that had won the previous year's Coppa Sant'Ambroeus driven by Giulio Cabianca. Compared with its older sister, this right-hand-drive car's tubular chassis had thinner transverse tubing incorporating a space for luggage at the rear as required by the revised regulations. The engine was a Dino, a powerful and reliable V6 whose origin was the 65-degree double-overhead-camshaft unit designed by Vittorio Jano in 1956 for Formula 2 on the initiative of Alfredino Ferrari. From its initial 1,489cc, it had been enlarged in stages to over

➤ An unusual view of a Testa Rossa V12 fed by six Solex carburettors instead of the usual six twin-choke Webers. This experiment was tested on the Gino Munaron/Wolfgang Seidel 250 TR in the 1958 Targa Florio but not continued.

▼ Luigi Musso heads to victory in the 1958 Targa Florio at the wheel of the 250 TR he shared with Olivier Gendebien. The cutaway wings previously seen on the Testa Rossa had given way to a more conventional design because Ferrari's Carlo Chiti reckoned that stability was preferable to a hypothetical benefit to brake cooling.

▲ Even if the Dino 246 was becoming an endangered species, it still proved to be a winner in 1958, helping Mike Hawthorn to that year's Formula 1 World Championship title. Here he is at Spa that year on his way to second place in the Belgian Grand Prix.

◄ Beautiful though it was, the Dino 246 V6 engine already belonged to the past. Here it is in Wolfgang von Trips's car during practice for the 1960 Belgian Grand Prix.

2.4 litres (246 F1) and nearly 2.5 litres (256 F1) in the Formula 1 versions that had helped Mike Hawthorn to become World Champion in 1958 and Tony Brooks to fill the runner-up spot behind Jack Brabham in 1959.

A 1,998cc 60-degree single-overhead-camshaft version of this engine, putting out around 200bhp at 8,000rpm according to Enzo Ferrari himself, equipped the 196 S that débuted in Nassau in December 1959. Entered by the North American Racing Team (NART) for Ricardo Rodríguez, it finished fourth in the preliminary heat of the Governor's Trophy for 2-litre cars and then achieved second place in the final. Although it was beaten by the benchmark in the category, Bob Holbert's Porsche RSK, this was an encouraging result against a decent field. Two days later, however, it was a non-starter for the Nassau Trophy because of a gearbox failure while it was being pushed to its place on the starting grid.

Even though Enzo Ferrari had stated that he would not be drawn into taking part in all World Championship Grands Prix, Formula 1 was certainly not neglected. The Dino 246 did not look radically different from the previous version but it differed in several ways. Returning to that interview by Raymond Miomandre, let us allow Mr Ferrari to outline the main differences: 'The car is transformed. The chassis is new

and lighter; the cockpit is slightly narrower; it has independent rear suspension. The engine-gearbox unit hasn't changed. We've abandoned the De Dion axle. We've resited the fuel tanks on the sides as in 1956 on the Squalo. We think we have found a more equitable weight distribution.'

A 'normal' victory

Buenos Aires 1,000Km, 31st January

After a year's break, the Temporada series in Argentina was back as the international season opener in the year the country celebrated the 150th anniversary of its independence. As before, the series comprised three races on consecutive weekends, beginning on 31st January with the Buenos Aires 1,000Km (the first round of the World Sports Car Championship) and continuing with the Argentine Grand Prix (the first round of the Formula 1 World Championship) and the Buenos Aires Grand Prix (a race for 'allcomers' run to *Formule Libre* rules). As the Autodrómo Oscar Alfredo Gálvez offered a selection of layouts, the 1,000Km combined part of the official track with a straight section of dual carriageway, the Avenida General Paz,

➤ **Buenos Aires 1,000Km.** This photo of Phil Hill (left), Cliff Allison (centre) and Dan Gurney is a little misleading because Gurney was no longer racing for Ferrari. After one brief season, the politics at Maranello had got to him, so now he was driving for Maserati in sports cars and BRM in Formula 1.

Buenos Aires 1,000Km. At the Autódromo Oscar Alfredo Gálvez, which hosted the first round of the World Sports Car Championship, Masten Gregory's Maserati *Tipo 61* (shared with Dan Gurney) leads Cliff Allison's Ferrari 250 TR 59/60 (shared with Phil Hill). The Maserati failed to last the distance; the Ferrari won.

Buenos Aires 1,000Km. From this angle, Wolfgang von Trips's 250 TR 59/60 shows clearly how the CSI now required the windscreen to be of increased height. As he was tall, the German was almost able to see over the top, but diminutive Richie Ginther needed a cushion.

➤ **Buenos Aires 1,000Km.** Phil Hill makes his way towards his first victory of the season. For co-driver Cliff Allison, the race brought the only win of his Ferrari career.

to form a 5.888-mile (9.476km) circuit while the other two races took place on the 2.430-mile (3.912km) 'circuit no. 2'.

Maranello put on a show of strength right from the start by entering three cars. Two were tried-and-tested 250 TR 59/60s complying with the new regulations; one of them, 0770 TR, had raced for the entire 1959 season while the other, 0774 TR, had only been seen at Le Mans and in the Tourist Trophy. The third entry was a 246 S that bore an external resemblance to its bigger sisters but was powered by the 2,417cc double-overhead-camshaft V6 Dino borrowed from Formula 1. Two 250 GT LWB (long-wheelbase) models and an 'interim' 250 GT beefed up Ferrari's presence in the race.

There was a surprise in the driver line-ups even if there was nothing new about the pairings in the two Testa Rossas, with Phil Hill/Cliff Allison in 0774 TR and Richie Ginther/Wolfgang von Trips in 0770 TR. However, the 246 S was shared by an Italian coming man, Ludovico Scarfiotti, and one of the greats of the recent past, none other than José Froilán González. Aged 38, the Argentine driver had history with Maranello, having achieved Ferrari's first Formula 1 World Championship victory in the British Grand Prix of 1951, and had also triumphed at Le Mans with Maurice Trintignant in 1954 after a nail-biting finish. That same year, González scored his second British Grand Prix victory for Ferrari although this was also a period in which his

career went downhill, prior to this return that was announced as his swansong.

Ferrari's main opposition in the race came from Porsche and Maserati. Of nine Porsche starters, the factory entered three RSKs with windscreens that 'just about met the requirements', due to a lack of time, and a 356 B Carrera. The German cars were driven by top-class line-ups comprising Olivier Gendebien/ Edgar Barth, Maurice Trintignant/Hans Herrmann and Jo Bonnier/Graham Hill, the aim, with just 160bhp available from these 1.6-litre spyders, being to play a waiting game and see how the race panned out for their 3-litre rivals from Maranello. As for the Carrera, its objective was to get to the chequered flag without being too far behind the Ferrari GTs — in itself an ambitious target.

Maserati presented a new 3-litre *Tipo* 61, which was a redoubtable rival in several ways, along with a mixture of 200 S and 300 S models to make up numbers. The *Tipo* 61 retained the 2-litre *Tipo* 60's multi-tubular chassis (the famous 'Birdcage'), the rigidity and lightness of which had been a major factor in the model's success in 1959, but had a 2,980cc double-overhead-camshaft four-cylinder engine with twin-plug ignition delivering 250bhp at 6,800rpm, an increase of 50bhp over the 2-litre model. In the driving seat of this car, entered by American Lloyd 'Lucky' Casner's Camoradi (Casner Motor

BUENOS AIRES 1,000KM

Buenos Aires, 31st January 1960, 106 laps (5.888 miles/9.476km), 624.161 miles/1,004.490km • Starters 23, classified finishers 11

1st	Phil Hill/Cliff Allison	Ferrari 250 TR 59/60 (0774 TR)	6h 17m 12.1s
2nd	Richie Ginther/Wolfgang von Trips	Ferrari 250 TR 59/60 (0770 TR)	105 laps
3rd	Jo Bonnier/Graham Hill	Porsche 718 RSK	101 laps
4th	Celso Lara Barberis/Christian Heins	Maserati 300 S	101 laps
5th	Pedro von Döry/Anton von Döry/Juan-Manuel Bordeu	Porsche 718 RSK	100 laps
6th	Christian Goethals/Curt Delfosse	Porsche 718 RSK	100 laps
9th	'Madero'/Nino Todaro	Ferrari 250 GT Interim	92 laps
11th	Ugo Tosa/Silvano Turco	Ferrari 250 GT LWB	83 laps
DNF	Ludovico Scarfiotti/José Froilán González	Ferrari Dino 246 S (0778)	38 laps (ignition)
DNF	Carlo Mario Abate/Alberto Rodríguez-Larreta	Ferrari 250 GT LWB	2 laps (brakes)
DNS	Cesar Reyes/Julio Guimarey	Ferrari 750 Monza	–
DNS	Carlo Mario Abate/Casimiro Toselli	Ferrari 250 GT LWB	–

Fastest practice lap: Hill, 3m 23.1s, 104.372/167.970kph **Fastest race lap:** Dan Gurney (Maserati Tipo 61), 3m 22.4s, 104.735mph/168.554kph
Winner's average speed: 99.283/159.780kph **FIA World Sports Car Championship:**[1] 1st Ferrari 8, 2nd Porsche 4, 3rd Maserati 3

[1] Scoring system for the top six places was 8–6–4–3–2–1; only the manufacturer's highest-placed car scored points

Racing Division) team, were Dan Gurney and Masten Gregory, who were as quick as they were consistent. They showed their out-and-out speed in practice by separating the Testa Rossas at the top of the timesheets, just one second short of Phil Hill's pole-position time of 3m 23.1s, while the Ferrari 246 S lined up fourth.

The race, or at least the first third of it, confirmed the indications provided in practice. Gurney set off like a scalded cat, quickly sliced past Phil Hill and pulled away. Was Hill playing a waiting game and betting on the unreliability of the Maserati? Was he worried about the reliability of his Ferrari? Whatever, when Gregory got behind the wheel of the Maserati, it was leading the second-placed TR, now driven by Allison, by nearly two minutes, with von Trips/Ginther fourth. But then Gregory became handicapped by failing shock absorbers and Allison closed in, eventually taking the lead. When Gurney got back in the car, he threw everything at the task of reclaiming the advantage, twice breaking the lap record, but also spun and fell back to third before being forced out of the race with gearbox failure just after half distance. Despite this, the threat from Maserati that had been feared before the race was not an illusion.

With no rivals left, the two Testa Rossas slackened to a leisurely pace and Hill/Allison beat Ginther/von Trips by a lap. In the works Dino, González was as feisty as ever in the early stages, but the car's race came to an end on lap 38 with ignition failure.

The second half of the race was bereft of excitement as each of the drivers waited for a mistake on the part of the man in front to move up the order. This was the case for the Porsche of Bonnier/Hill, who took advantage of the Trintignant/Herrmann Porsche running out of fuel towards the end to clinch their place on the podium only 12 seconds in front of the Maserati 300 S of Brazilians Celso Lara Barberis/Christian Heins.

'A defeat leads to changes'

Argentine Grand Prix, 7th February

Enzo Ferrari had seen too much, done too much and lived through too much to let himself be fooled by what looked like a pretty easy victory in the Buenos Aires 1,000Km. 'This win was normal; it was down to teamwork,' he told Raymond Miomandre shortly afterwards. He added: 'Success is success. One day you win, the next day you lose. What you have to try and achieve is to always be the best. A defeat leads to changes while victory brings complacency in its wake.'

Words of wisdom? They were in any case words of a pragmatic man of action for whom only the result counted. Or prophetic words? Proof was provided the following weekend at the Argentine Grand Prix. A quick look at the results, with second place for Cliff Allison and fifth for Wolfgang von Trips,

> **Argentine Grand Prix.** To counter the growing threat from English cars, Ferrari raced an experimental Dino 246 with its V6 moved backwards to improve weight distribution. Phil Hill put it on the second row alongside Wolfgang von Trips and Cliff Allison in their regular versions.

▾ **Argentine Grand Prix.** Phil Hill stayed in the wake of Jack Brabham's Cooper from the 14th to the 32nd lap of the 80-lap race. The Australian went out with gearbox failure while Hill struggled home in eighth place.

◄ Argentine Grand Prix.
Wolfgang von Trips found himself stuck mid-field until half distance and finished an unconvincing fifth, a lap behind Bruce McLaren's winning Cooper. At least Cliff Allison upheld Ferrari honour by coming home second after repulsing Stirling Moss's assaults.

showed that while Ferrari's performance was not exactly catastrophic, it was misleading, especially as the fastest of the four Dinos 246s, driven by von Trips, had qualified only fifth. For Maranello, the race could be summed up as being under the yoke of the various rear-engined Coopers entered by the factory (Jack Brabham and Bruce McLaren) and by Rob Walker (Stirling Moss and Maurice Trintignant), all of which found themselves lagging behind Jo Bonnier when he led the race for

57 laps in his front-engined BRM P25. And this was without mentioning Innes Ireland's stunning demonstration at the wheel of his rear-engined Lotus 18, a car as radical as it was promising, making its first appearance and holding second place for a long time.

So the story of the encounter from Ferrari's point of view was that the cars driven by Allison and von Trips took advantage of their rivals' retirements to finish in the points, while Phil Hill,

ARGENTINE GRAND PRIX

Buenos Aires, 7th February 1960, 80 laps (2.431 miles/3.912km), 194.464 miles/312.960km • Starters 22, finishers 14

RACE				PRACTICE	
1st	Bruce McLaren	Cooper T51 Climax S4	2h 17m 49.5s	13th	1m 41.8s
2nd	**Cliff Allison**	**Ferrari Dino 246 V6**	**+26.3s**	**7th**	**1m 39.7s**
3rd	Maurice Trintignant/Stirling Moss	Cooper T51 Climax S4	+36.9s	8th	1m 39.9s
4th	Carlos Menditéguy	Cooper T51 Maserati S4	+53.3s	12th	1m 41.8s
5th	**Wolfgang von Trips**	**Ferrari Dino 246 V6**	**79 laps**	**5th**	**1m 39.3s**
6th	Innes Ireland	Lotus 18 Climax S4	79 laps	2nd	1m 38.5s
8th	**Phil Hill**	**Ferrari Dino 246 V6**	**77 laps**	**6th**	**1m 39.5s**
10th	**José Froilán González**	**Ferrari Dino 246 V6**	**77 laps**	**11th**	**1m 41.0s**

Pole position: Moss, 1m 36.9s, 90.308mph/145.337kph **Fastest race lap:** Moss, 1m 38.9s, 88.482mph/142.398kph
Winner's average speed: 84.636mph/136.208kph **Drivers' championship:**[1] 1st McLaren 8, 2nd Allison 6, 3rd Menditéguy 3, 4th von Trips 2
Constructors' championship:[2] 1st Cooper-Climax 8, 2nd Ferrari 6, 3rd Cooper-Maserati 2

[1] Scoring system for the top six places was 8–6–4–3–2–1 [2] Scoring system for the top six places was 8–6–4–3–2–1; only the manufacturer's highest-placed car scored points

suffering from cooling problems, came home eighth and Jose Froilán González tenth in his last-ever race.

In the end, victory went to McLaren, the youngest driver in the field, who triumphed after a flawless drive during which he handled his Cooper with kid gloves. It was difficult to know whether the driver dominated the car or vice versa. Taking into account his success at Sebring in the final Grand Prix of 1959, it was his second victory on the trot and it shook Ferrari to the core. Was it still possible to reject the success of a school of thought — the 'rear-engined revolution' — that an entrepreneur as daring and innovative as Colin Chapman had just joined, to striking effect? Because behind Enzo Ferrari's refusal to put the cart before the horse ('they pull but don't push,' he liked to quip) a battle was going on behind the scenes as to who would conquer the reticence in Maranello about embracing the new way of thinking.

Easier than expected

Sebring 12 Hours, 26th March

American petrol companies were sticklers about their prerogatives and Amoco was certainly a prickly official sponsor of the 12 Hours of Sebring. It had a problem with competitors that were under contract to other fuel suppliers and in 1959 a clash had been narrowly avoided. This year it flared up again and prevented Ferrari and Porsche — supported respectively by Shell and BP — from formally being works entrants, so the championship contenders had to race by proxy.

In the Ferrari camp, it was no surprise to see Luigi Chinetti's NART operation given the 250 TR that had won in Argentina (to be driven by Richie Ginther/Chuck Daigh) and the Dino 196 S seen in Nassau (for the Rodríguez brothers), while another 250 TR run by Jack Nethercutt (for him to share with Pete Lovely) completed Maranello's presence in the sports car category. They were backed up by major reinforcements, the 250 GTs, whether in the form of Californias or Short Wheelbase Berlinettas, the latter racing for the first time after starring at the 1959 Paris motor show but placed in the sports car category because the new model, best known as the famous SWB, was still undergoing homologation. In total, seven Ferraris lined up on the grid.

As for Porsche, Jo Bonnier now had a private team that was suddenly boosted by the presence of two RS 60 spyders. They were tended by Stuttgart mechanics — who were coincidentally 'on holiday' in Florida! — and driven by crews whose names

needed no introduction, namely Bonnier himself with Graham Hill, and Olivier Gendebien with Hans Herrmann. A third works RS 60 spyder was entrusted to a strong American team, Brumos Porsche, for Bob Holbert/Roy Schechter/Howard Fowler.

Their main opposition came from Maserati, which entered four *Tipo* 61s, two via Camoradi for Carroll Shelby/Masten Gregory and Stirling Moss/Dan Gurney, one for local lad Dave Causey (Dave Causey/Luke Stear) and the fourth belonging to Briggs Cunningham (Walt Hansgen/Ed Crawford). Without belittling the rest of the 65 competitors, Maserati seemed to have the upper hand provided its representatives avoided inter-team scraps, and the pairing of Moss and Gurney was formidable.

▼ **Sebring 12 Hours.** Ricardo Rodríguez rests after his exertions at the wheel. The 'niño prodigy', two years younger than brother Pedro, had just turned 18. At the time *los hermanos Rodríguez* were little known outside the Americas but were soon to prove on the European scene that Luigi Chinetti's choice owed more to their precocious talents than to their father's fortune.

◄ **Sebring 12 Hours.** Richie Ginther extricates himself from the NART-entered 250 TR 59/60, the most competitive Ferrari in the race, to hand over to fellow countryman Chuck Daigh. For more than five hours the all-American duo held on to second place sandwiched between the Maserati *Tipo* 61s of Dan Gurney/ Stirling Moss and Walt Hansgen/ Ed Crawford, but then retired with a blown cylinder head gasket.

▼ **Sebring 12 Hours.** Ricardo Rodríguez took over from his brother in the Dino 196 S, a car already familiar to him after racing it at Nassau the previous December. After four hours, the young Mexicans were lying fourth but clutch failure ended their thrilling display.

Stirling, who loved driving for Maserati (just as Maserati loved him), had fallen for the 'Birdcage' ever since first trying it at Modena the previous May, finding the car very nimble and easy to drive. As for his co-driver, he regarded Gurney as his best-ever team-mate other Fangio — a huge compliment.

Moss's prospects in the race received a setback at the Le Mans-style echelon start, with cars arranged in order of engine capacity. As usual, he was just about the quickest to sprint across the track but was then delayed by a recalcitrant starter motor, and he was only 23rd when he finally got going. At the end of the lap, though, he had the *Tipo* 61 in fifth place, and by the third lap he was in the lead! When, two hours later, it was time to hand over to his co-driver, the white-and-blue Maserati was 50 seconds in front of the Ginther/Daigh Ferrari. Dan was not actually ready to take over but the time lost at the pitstop did not pose a problem, for the Maserati was soon in front again and at half distance had two laps in hand over the NART-run 250 TR. At this stage, the Gendebien/Herrmann Porsche lay third and the Lovely/Nethercutt 250 TR fourth, nine laps adrift of the leaders.

Although the race was far from over, it was looking good for Maserati, even if the Shelby/Gregory *Tipo* 61 had retired very early on with an overheated engine and the Hansgen/Crawford car had been severely delayed after an excursion into sand at the hairpin, where Crawford, who had no shovel, had to dig his way out using his hands, followed by a 45-minute spell in the pits sorting out frontal damage. But so often things went wrong for Maserati. With four hours left, Gurney stopped to hand over to Moss. A change of brake pads seemed to go on forever because the team could not find the right tool. When Stirling did finally rejoin, he had to return to his pit almost immediately because the transmission, which had been making strange noises, gave up the ghost. After more than 130 laps in the lead, the *Tipo* 61 was pushed away, gifting victory to the Bonnier-entered Porsche of Gendebien/Herrmann, with the Brumos Porsche in second place, nine laps down.

Only one of the three quasi-works Ferraris finished, the Nethercutt one, in third place, followed by a splendid clean sweep of 250 GTs all the way down to eighth place. In their first outing on the world stage, the 250 GT SWBs had certainly lived up to expectations, with three of them in the top-seven placings, the best being the car of Ed Hugus/Augie Pabst just one lap shy of the podium. After lacklustre showings, NART's pair of works Ferraris retired within three laps of each other during the second half of the race, the 250 TR with a failed cylinder head gasket, the Dino with clutch failure.

➤ **Sebring 12 Hours.** While Porsches finished 1–2, the Pete Lovely/Jack Nethercutt 250 TR 59/60 saved face for Ferrari with third place. Behind it, 250 GT SWBs put on a marvellous performance on their first major international appearance by taking three of the next four places.

SEBRING 12 HOURS

Sebring, 26th March 1960, 196 laps (5.200 miles/8.369km), 1,019.199 miles/1,640.243km • Starters 65, classified finishers 41

1st	Olivier Gendebien/Hans Herrmann	Porsche RS 60	12h 0m 3.3s
2nd	Bob Holbert/Roy Schechter/Howard Fowler	Porsche RS 60	187 laps
3rd	Pete Lovely/Jack Nethercutt	Ferrari 250 TR 59/60 (0768 TR)	186 laps
4th	Ed Hugus/Augie Pabst	Ferrari 250 GT SWB	185 laps
5th	George Reed/Alan Connell	Ferrari 250 GT California	185 laps
6th	Bill Sturgis/Fritz D'Orey	Ferrari 250 GT SWB	183 laps
7th	George Arents/Bill Kimberly	Ferrari 250 GT SWB	183 laps
8th	Giorgio Scarlatti/Fabrizio Serena/Carlo Mario Abate	Ferrari 250 GT California	179 laps
10th	Robert Publicker/George Constantine/Dean McCarthy	Ferrari 250 GT California	174 laps
DNF	Pedro Rodríguez/Ricardo Rodríguez	Ferrari Dino 196 S (0776)	126 laps (clutch)
DNF	Richie Ginther/Chuck Daigh	Ferrari 250 TR 59/60 (0774 TR)	123 laps (engine)
DNF	Gianni Balzarini/Carlo Mario Abate	Ferrari 250 GT	28 laps

Fastest practice lap: Masten Gregory (Maserati Tipo 61), 3m 19.0s **Fastest race lap:** Stirling Moss (Maserati Tipo 61), 3m 17.06s, 94.996mph/152.881kph

Winner's average speed: 84.927mph/136.677kph **FIA World Sports Car Championship:** 1st= Ferrari & Porsche 12, 3rd Maserati 3

The results left Ferrari and Porsche equal in the championship standings on 12 points. The Maserati debacle and the Lovely/Nethercutt third place had saved Ferrari's bacon. There was no doubt a sigh of relief in Maranello.

Defeat on home turf

Targa Florio, 8th May

A great deal was at stake in Sicily. With the World Sports Car Championship only allowing points to count from three of the five rounds, and Porsche now equal with Ferrari at the top of the table, another defeat would be a disaster for Maranello, especially as Porsche had recent form on the Targa Florio as winners of the previous year's race. Each of these protagonists honed their weapons to a razor-sharp edge.

To take up the gauntlet, the Prancing Horse counted on four works sports cars — two Testa Rossas with independent rear suspension and two Dino 246 S models with different rear suspensions — supplemented by a Dino 196 S entered under the NART banner for the Rodríguez brothers but looked after by the factory. But what was Ferrari's strategy? In the single official practice session, the Scuderia seemed to prove the old adage 'grasp all, lose all'. After several days' practice on open roads, Richie Ginther wrecked the team's four-cylinder Monza 'training' mule against a house near the spot where Phil Hill had gone off two years earlier and crushed a bystander's motor scooter. Cliff Allison had a high-speed left-front tyre blow-out that destroyed the 250 TRI he was supposed to share with Hill, prompting one of the driver reshuffles that team manager Romolo Tavoni always seemed to enjoy. So it was that Allison and Ginther were put together in the surviving 250 TRI, while Hill joined Wolfgang von Trips in the Dino with independent rear suspension and Willy Mairesse/Ludovico Scarfiotti, as planned, crewed the sister car with de Dion rear axle. Just to complete the story of damaged Ferraris, one of the Rodríguez brothers, who were both learning the ropes on their first visit to the Sicilian classic, stoved in the rear of their Dino during practice, but the car was repairable for the race.

Porsche's hopes, meanwhile, rested on three works RS 60s for five drivers. Hans Herrmann was earmarked to share with both Olivier Gendebien and Jo Bonnier, doing shorter stints than each of the team's stars, while Edgar Barth and Graham Hill were assigned the other car. With the addition of four 356Bs, including a Carrera Abarth, Stuttgart had seven cars for its campaign to keep Ferrari out of the points. There was only one Maserati *Tipo* 61 on the entry list, a Camoradi version that had been experimentally beefed up by the factory in various ways — rear hubs, gearbox, back axle, chassis and crankshaft — to assess their effect before taking them further. At the wheel were Umberto Maglioli and Palermo-born Nino Vaccarella, a schoolteacher who liked to race and had unrivalled knowledge of his local roads.

As usual, the cars started this 10-lap test of endurance and concentration one by one, with the small-capacity tiddlers setting off first, followed by the GTs and then the pukka sports cars. As ever, it was obvious that agility not power was what would really make the difference. Giorgio Scarlatti led the GTs in his Scuderia Sant'Ambroeus Ferrari 250 GT LWB and covered the first lap in 49m 5s, followed by Barth's Porsche in 49m dead. Then Bonnier stunned everybody with a lap in 45m 4s after passing both Porsche team-mate Gendebien and Ricardo Rodríguez's Dino, despite the mountain roads being slippery after a sudden downpour. Maglioli, suffering from a cold but nonetheless driving the Maserati more quickly than all the Ferrari men through the mountain sections, did the second-best opening lap at 45m 27s. Von Trips at this stage lay sixth after pushing in his Dino's right-front fender against a rock, so a pitstop was required at the end of the lap to have the bodywork straightened and the damaged wheel changed. After resuming, the German did the best lap of the Ferrari camp at 45m 49s.

Bonnier's next two laps were carbon copies of his first and his advantage over Maglioli increased to 2m 5s, with Allison flying the Ferrari flag in third place. The end of the fourth lap brought the first stops to change drivers and refuel, Herrmann taking over from Bonnier with 2m 44s in hand over the Maserati. Maglioli continued for another lap, either because that was part of the Camoradi team's strategy or a decision taken because of the way the race was unfolding. During that lap he gobbled up Herrmann, who seemed to have problems getting up to speed. By the time Maglioli pulled in at the end of the lap — half distance — the Maserati was 1m 21s ahead of the Porsche.

Suddenly the whole of Sicily fell silent. Why? Because after local hero Vaccarella restarted the Maserati's engine, it cut out.

▾ **Targa Florio.** Having needed the bent front end to be straightened out, the result of contact on lap 1, Wolfgang von Trips rejoins in sixth place in the Dino 246 S that he shared with Phil Hill. Both drivers pushed hard and managed to close the gap to the Olivier Gendebien/Hans Herrmann Porsche, but not enough to prevent it from winning.

A host of helpers swarmed over the car — Porsche considered lodging a protest — but the big four-cylinder engine came back to life without too much delay. On his very first lap, Vaccarella used all his knowledge of the roads to rebuild the Maserati's margin over Herrmann to 1m 55s and next time round increased it to 3m 12s. With that, Herrmann was brought in again to hand the Porsche back to Bonnier and to snatch a chance to draw breath before a spell in Gendebien's third-placed car. In fourth and fifth places were the works Dinos, with Hill now driving in place of von Trips while Scarfiotti occupied the other car, but Hill moved up to third when the Porsche refuelled. By now, Ferrari's hopes rested with the Dinos because the 250 TRI had

TARGA FLORIO

Piccolo Madonie, 8th May 1960, 10 laps (44.7 miles/72.0km), 447.4 miles /720.0km • Starters 69, classified finishers 37

1st	Jo Bonnier/Hans Herrmann	Porsche RS 60	7h 33m 8.2s
2nd	**Wolfgang von Trips/Phil Hill**	**Ferrari Dino 246 S (0784)**	**7h 39m 11.0s**
3rd	Olivier Gendebien/Hans Herrmann	Porsche RS 60	7h 41m 46.0s
4th	**Willy Mairesse/Ludovico Scarfiotti/Giulio Cabianca**	**Ferrari Dino 246 S (0778)**	**7h 44m 49.0s**
5th	Edgar Barth/Graham Hill	Porsche RS 60	7h 59m 11.0s
6th	Herbert Linge/Paul Ernst Strähle	Porsche Carrera Abarth	8h 10m 6.0s
7th	Pedro Rodríguez/Ricardo Rodríguez	Ferrari Dino 196 S (0776)	8h 16m 52.0s
9th	Elio Lenza/Antonio Maglione	Ferrari 250 GT SWB	8h 22m 27.0s
10th	Edoardo Lualdi/Giorgio Scarlatti	Ferrari 250 GT LWB	8h 26m 38.0s
12th	Gerino Gerini/Salvatore La Pira	Ferrari 250 GT SWB	8h 31m 27.3s
18th	Pietro Ferraro/Armando Zampiero	Ferrari 250 GT SWB	8h 54m 7.0s
DNF	Domenico Tramontana/Giuseppe Alotta	Ferrari 750 Monza	–
DNF	**Cliff Allison/Richie Ginther**	**Ferrari 250 TRI 60 (0772 TR)**	**5 laps (accident)**
DNS	**Cliff Allison/Richie Ginther**	**Ferrari 250 TRI 60 (0780 TR)**	**– (practice accident)**

Fastest race lap: Bonnier, 42m 26.0s, 63.260mph/101.807kph **Winner's average speed:** 59.237mph/95.334kph
FIA World Sports Car Championship: 1st Porsche 20, 2nd Ferrari 18, 3rd Maserati 3

crashed out, Ginther the culprit shortly after taking over from Allison.

Bonnier covered the eighth lap in 43m 59s on what was now an entirely dry track. Little did he know that the threat from behind had disappeared because the Maserati's fuel tank had been pierced by a wayward stone. Initially the car stopped at the trackside and Sicilian solidarity immediately kicked in as spectators formed a line passing bottles full of petrol from hand to hand to help the stricken *Tipo* 61 get back in the race, which it did, but to no avail because it ran dry again, this time while Vaccarella was charging down a fast descent and about to change down a gear, leaving him unable to avoid clouting a bank. On lap 9, Bonnier went for the kill with a time that was only 8.5 seconds slower than the lap record of 42m 17.5s set by Stirling Moss back in 1958 in an Aston Martin DBR1, a car with an engine twice the size of the fleet-footed Porsche's.

Once Bonnier learned of the Maserati's demise, he lifted off. Even so he took the chequered flag with six minutes in hand over von Trips, who consolidated his second place for Ferrari with a 43m 38s final lap in front of the Gendebien/Herrmann Porsche, with the other Dino in fourth place, now driven by Giulio Cabianca after he had been summoned to relieve Mairesse and Scarfiotti for two laps.

Edoardo Lualdi/Giorgio Scarlatti won the over-2.5-litre GT category for Ferrari with tenth place, but that did not mean too much considering that the Porsche Carrera Abarth of Herbert

Linge/Paul Ernst Strähle had completed the race 15 minutes earlier to claim the up-to-2.5-litre GT honours. For Maranello, the homologation of the Short Wheelbase Berlinettas, announced for the week before the Le Mans 24 Hours, could not come soon enough.

Lords of the Ring

Nürburgring 1,000Km, 22nd May

The contrast in the weather between the Mediterranean and the Eifel could hardly have been more striking. It was raining and fog shrouded places in the gloomy forests as melting snowflakes — a possibility that a complacent weather forecast 'forgot' to mention — fluttered down through the pine trees. As Porsche was racing on home ground as well as leading the championship with 20 points against 18 for Ferrari, the Stuttgart firm went for broke and entered three RS 60 spyders for Jo Bonnier/Olivier Gendebien, Hans Herrmann/Maurice Trintignant and Edgar Barth/Graham Hill. Backing them up and classified in the sports car category because they were considered experimental vehicles were a Super 90 (Helmut Schulze/Wittigo Einsiedel) and a Carrera Abarth (Sepp Greger/Herbert Linge) equipped with factory disc brakes. In total, no fewer than 17 works and private Porsches lined up on the grid.

➤ **Nürburgring 1,000Km.** A new 250 TRI 60, Phil Hill as teammate, the will to shine on home soil — all the ingredients were in the mix for 'Taffy' von Trips to be #1. But it was not to be. A V12 that quickly became sluggish and rear suspension that proved to be too independent shattered the dashing German's dreams, while the Maserati *Tipo* 61 of Stirling Moss and Dan Gurney romped away from all rivals.

Nürburgring 1,000Km. Initially driven by Willy Mairesse (pictured) and Cliff Allison, the #2 250 TR 59/60 managed to snatch third place from the Hans Herrmann/Maurice Trintignant Porsche thanks to a hard-charging stint from Phil Hill, who had become available after his own car's retirement. Despite Hill's skills, the red car was unable to close the gap to the second-placed Jo Bonnier/Olivier Gendebien Porsche, which finished just 71 seconds ahead.

In terms of numbers and variety, Ferrari came close to its German rival. There were four LWB 250 GTs including those of Carlo Mario Abate/Colin Davis and Jo Schlesser/Lucien Bianchi plus a short-chassis Berlinetta entered by Ecurie Francorchamps for 'Beurlys'/Pierre Noblet. The factory turned up with four sports cars: this time Wolfgang von Trips/Phil Hill shared a brand-new 250 TRI 60; Cliff Allison/Willy Mairesse were at the wheel of a 250 TR 59/60 with de Dion rear axle and four-speed gearbox as seen in Buenos Aires; and Richie Ginther/Ludovico Scarfiotti and Giorgio Scarlatti/Giulio Cabianca crewed the two Dino 246 Ss that had raced in Sicily. The Rodríguez brothers were at the wheel of their fully repaired Dino 196 S entered in their own name.

Maserati, which had flattered only to deceive in the first three rounds, ran two cars under the Camoradi banner once again for a couple of very quick driver pairings, Stirling Moss/Dan Gurney and Masten Gregory/Gino Munaron, under the strict management of a former winner of the race, Piero Taruffi. This time Modena would not disappoint — or at least that was the plot before the start.

Practice was anything but a doddle for Maserati although not as tough as Moss made out in his memoirs. Things went badly on Friday for him and Gurney as they were hamstrung by overly short gear ratios and chronic instability under braking. On Saturday an oil line ruptured after only two laps with Gurney at the wheel. Nonetheless, the Maserati finished second in practice (9m 50.10s) between the Porsches of Bonnier/Gendebien (9m 43.6s) and Herrmann/Trintignant (9m 51.8s). Ferrari would have been quite happy with this result as the quickest of the Testa Rossas in the hands of von Trips/Hill was fifth, 3.3 seconds behind Jim Clark/Roy Salvadori in their Aston Martin DBR1/300.

The winter weather that arrived shortly before the start did little to soothe jangled nerves in the Ferrari camp when it came to tyre choices. In the end, Hill opted for a risky choice of dry-weather rubber while Maserati went for a discreet mix of Goodyears at the front and Pirelli at the rear, as the tyres provided by the more experienced Italian supplier offered better grip. Just to add a further touch of uncertainty, snow was in the offing when the 67 cars roared off at 9am to tackle the Eifel circuit after a Le Mans-type getaway.

It is well known that Moss liked nothing better than having the odds stacked against him provided he had a car capable of taking up the challenge and, should it be necessary, a team-mate of the necessary calibre. When he handed over to Gurney after a 14-lap stint on a slippery track — just what he loved — he was 2m 30s ahead of the von Trips/Hill Ferrari. Rivals like Bonnier and Clark tried to match Stirling's pace, the Swede getting to within 44 seconds of the Maserati after four laps following a catastrophic start, while Clark, before retiring with a blown engine after six laps, displayed the multiple facets of a talent that would soon become a benchmark. In the sports car category, the other Scuderia drivers were already either running out of steam, with Allison only fourth when he handed over to Mairesse, or out of the race altogether. While Ginther went out with a blown cylinder head gasket on lap 13, Scarlatti avoided disaster by the skin of his teeth just one lap later. He was still in the Dino 246 S during refuelling and had to leap out of it when a fire broke out, with catastrophe prevented only by timely intervention by the

safety services in putting out, in the words of Denis Jenkinson, 'a blaze that was one of the biggest ever witnessed in motor racing'. The Rodríguez brothers were still in the fight and in their usual style posed a major threat to competitors in the 2-litre category.

After the three races in Argentina, Florida and Sicily in which Maserati had not lived up to expectations, would the marque's familiar unreliability again prove fatal to its hopes? During the Moss/Gurney driver change, the four-cylinder engine's oil pressure was on the low side and it was necessary to clean up the cockpit after the oil had been topped up. The most vocal of the Cassandras pointed this out and prophesied a ruptured oil line in the very near future. They looked to be proved right when, on lap 20, Gurney stopped with his overalls soaked in lubricant. Repairs seemed to go on forever and Taruffi contemplated a driver swap with the Gregory/Munaron *Tipo* 61, which was lying sixth, but decided against it. When the American rejoined the fray after a 4m 35s stop, Hill's Ferrari led from Gendebien's Porsche and Mairesse's Ferrari.

It looked like it was all over bar the shouting. But no! When the fog was at its thickest, with visibility down to 150 metres according to Phil Hill, Gurney put in a stunning performance. He obliterated his rivals and on lap 24 he was 1m 23s behind his fellow American. Next time round he cut the gap to 47 seconds. Then came a pitstop for von Trips to replace Hill but it proved sluggish because refuelling had to rely on gravity due to a lack

NÜRBURGRING 1,000KM

Nürburgring, 22nd May 1960, 44 laps (14.173 miles/22.810km), 623.633 miles/1,003.640km • Starters 67, classified finishers 41

1st	Stirling Moss/Dan Gurney	Maserati Tipo 61	7h 31m 40.5s
2nd	Jo Bonnier/Hans Herrmann	Porsche RS 60	7h 34m 32.9s
3rd	**Cliff Allison/Willy Mairesse/Phil Hill**	**Ferrari 250 TR 59/60 (0770 TR)**	**7h 35m 44.1s**
4th	Hans Herrmann/Maurice Trintignant	Porsche RS 60	7h 37m 57.7s
5th	Masten Gregory/Gino Munaron	Maserati Tipo 61	43 laps
6th	Heini Walter/Thomas Losinger	Porsche 718 RSK	42 laps
8th	Carlo Mario Abate/Colin Davis	Ferrari 250 GT LWB (1333 GT)	41 laps
11th	Jo Schlesser/Lucien Bianchi	Ferrari 250 GT LWB (1509 GT)	40 laps
15th	'Beurlys' (Jean Blaton)/Pierre Noblet	Ferrari 250 GT SWB (1811 GT)	40 laps
23rd	Carlo Peroglio/Piero Frescobaldi	Ferrari 250 GT LWB	38 laps
DNF	**Wolfgang von Trips/Phil Hill**	**Ferrari 250 TRI 60 (0782 TR)**	**34 laps (engine)**
DNF	Pedro Rodríguez/Ricardo Rodríguez	Ferrari Dino 196 S (0776)	31 laps (engine)
DNF	**Giorgio Scarlatti/Giulio Cabianca**	**Ferrari Dino 246 S (0778)**	**14 laps (fire)**
DNF	**Richie Ginther/Ludovico Scarfiotti**	**Ferrari Dino 246 S (0784)**	**13 laps (oil pressure)**
DNF	Gerino Gerini/Alfonso Thiele	Ferrari 250 GT California	7 laps (accident)

Fastest practice lap: Jo Bonnier (Porsche RS 60), 9m 43.6s, 87.431mph/140.706kph **Fastest race lap:** Stirling Moss (Maserati Tipo 61), 9m 37.0s, 88.319mph/142.135kph **Winner's average speed:** 82.842mph/133.322kph **FIA World Sports Car Championship:** 1st Porsche 26, 2nd Ferrari 22, 3rd Maserati 11

of pump pressure, added to which the 250 TRI 60's engine was now losing its edge and its independent rear suspension was becoming a little too independent. All this allowed both Gurney and Bonnier to shoot past the ailing Ferrari on lap 28. Six laps later it was all done and dusted. While Moss was back behind the wheel taking advantage of less capricious weather and exceeding even his formidable limits, the von Trips/Hill Ferrari joined the Dino 196 S of the Rodríguez brothers in the dead car park where it had been laid to rest three laps earlier. On Tavoni's orders, Hill took over the Allison/Mairesse 250 TR 59/60 and put on a final charge to try to snatch second place from the Bonnier/Gendebien Porsche and bag the precious points that went with it, but he could not quite manage to do so. Moss and Gurney therefore took the top-most step of the podium, congratulating each other and silencing the doomsayers, backed up by the fifth-placed sister *Tipo* 61 of Gregory/Munaron.

Ferrari was relatively satisfied with the GT victory achieved by Abate/Davis, in eighth place overall, although they were still behind the experimental Porsche Carrera Abarth of seventh-placed Greger/Linge. Other notable performances were those of Schlesser/Bianchi (11th) and a young English engineer called Michael Parkes who raced in his leisure time in a Lotus Elite and set the fastest lap in the 1.3-litre GT class in 10m 47.9s compared with 10m 44.4s for the quickest of the Carreras.

Driving lessons

Monaco Grand Prix, 29th May

Less than a week after the chills and thrills of the Eifel, yesterday's team-mates became today's rivals in the Monaco Grand Prix. Stirling Moss returned to Rob Walker Racing and its recently acquired Lotus 18. Dan Gurney was back with Jo Bonnier and Graham Hill in the Owen Racing Organisation's BRM P48s. Gino Munaron and Giorgio Scarlatti rejoined Scuderia Castellotti and its Ferrari-engined Coopers while Maurice Trintignant and Masten Gregory returned to Scuderia Centro-Sud's Cooper-Maseratis. The bulk of the British entries were completed by the works Coopers of Jack Brabham and Bruce McLaren, the works Lotuses of Innes Ireland, Alan Stacey and John Surtees, and the Yeoman Credit Coopers of Tony Brooks and Roy Salvadori.

Ferrari had finally capitulated, as proved by the presentation of a rear-engined Dino 246 P in addition to the three Dino 246s with their horses at the front for Cliff Allison, Phil Hill and Wolfgang von Trips. The main distinguishing features of the new car compared with its elder sisters was its five-speed gearbox on the rear axle, clutch coupled to the differential, in-board rear brakes and independent rear suspension; front suspension was similar to that of the Dino 246. After being tested in Modena on the Sunday prior to the Grand Prix, the new model was entrusted to Richie Ginther, a driver known for his mechanical sensitivity.

Due to the constraints and length of the circuit, the number of starters was limited to 16 out of the 24 entries, with Munaron having withdrawn, so the Principality was agog with activity on Thursday for the first of three practice sessions. Salvadori was credited with a time well under the 1m 40s barrier and then Brooks was given a rather startling 1m 34.4s before Moss clocked a completely implausible 1m 32.3s, at which point the session was interrupted because it was very clear that the timekeeping equipment had gone on the blink and was giving times that were optimistic by as much as six seconds. In the Ferrari camp, Ginther, who was stationary at his pit for a long time while gear ratios were changed, just went out to bed in the car. Allison, Hill and von Trips, overwhelmed by the effort required to manhandle their front-engined beasts around the circuit's twists and turns, simply racked up the laps, their cars floundering around like beached whales.

On Friday morning, the Scuderia suffered a blow when Allison changed down from fifth to second gear by mistake and hit the chicane on the harbourside, injuring himself badly enough when thrown out of the car to put an end to his season. By the end of Saturday's session, von Trips (1m 38.3s) shared the third row with Ireland and Graham Hill, while Ginther and Phil Hill were both credited with 1m 38.6s and shared the fourth row. All were a long way off Moss's pole time of 1m 36.3s.

The race reflected these results. Bonnier emerged first from the *Gazomètre* hairpin and stayed locked in battle with Moss as they swapped the lead over 78 laps apart from a brief interlude when Brabham hit the front. The Swede, though, was ill-rewarded for his efforts and ceded second place to McLaren before quitting on lap 83. While this was going on, Ferrari simply had to take a back seat.

A second-lap pitstop for von Trips to extinguish a fire caused by oil spurting onto the exhaust pipes dropped him to 14th place and during his recovery he was sandwiched between Salvadori and Gurney for a long time and then between the two Hills and Ginther in a battle for sixth place. The German finally bowed out on lap 70 when his clutch cried enough. Ginther spent the afternoon playing a walk-on role at the back of the field in a car that lacked track time but moved up the timesheets as those in front of him fell by the wayside. When he retired on lap 70, only

➤ **Monaco Grand Prix.** Wolfgang von Trips's smile looks a little strained. Although he pushed his Dino 246 to the limit, the best he could extract from the car during practice put him eighth quickest. The clutch let him down in the race while lying sixth.

➤ **Monaco Grand Prix.** The 246 P was the star attraction in the paddock and it did more than just play a walk-on role. In the hands of Richie Ginther, it was as quick in practice as the conventional Dino driven by Phil Hill and almost matched the pace of Hill's car for two-thirds of the race.

five cars were left strung out around the short circuit, although the little Californian had done enough to be classified sixth.

So what about Phil Hill? His day could be summed up by comparing photos of a dominant Moss relaxed behind the wheel of his Lotus with those of the American's distorted face as he wrestled his recalcitrant Dino through the snaking Monaco streets. It was easy to see who had the easier ride. And yet Hill drove one of the best races of his career that day. Despite starting

▾ **Monaco Grand Prix.** Free from the threat of Graham Hill with whom he battled for the first two-thirds of the race, Phil Hill struggles to stay ahead of Bruce McLaren's Cooper. With exhaustion setting in, he was only able to keep the New Zealander at bay for four laps and had to settle for third place.

tenth on the grid, he was fifth second time round and held that position for the next 28 laps behind Brooks before a shower transformed the track into a skating rink on which the cars waltzed gaily all over the tarmac. At half distance (lap 50), after the rain had stopped but before the sun showed its face again, Hill was back in fifth place following an 'off' at the *Gazomètre* hairpin behind the other Hill. Two laps later he was in front of the BRM with McLaren now in his sights.

There followed a fierce cut-and-thrust scrap in which neither the New Zealander nor the American managed to gain the upper hand. But on lap 67, just when Moss was on the point of snatching the lead from Bonnier after a fleeting stop to replace a plug lead, Hill's constant pressure paid off, causing McLaren to lose control of his Cooper on the run-in to the *Gazomètre*. Phil avoided him by going round the outside while Graham tried to

MONACO GRAND PRIX

Monaco, 29th May 1960, 100 laps (1.954 miles/3.145km), 195.4 miles/314.5km • Starters 16, finishers 7

RACE				PRACTICE	
1st	Stirling Moss	Lotus 18 Climax S4	2h 53m 45.5s	1st	1m 36.3s
2nd	Bruce McLaren	Cooper T53 Climax S4	+52.4s	11th	1m 38.6s
3rd	**Phil Hill**	**Ferrari Dino 246 V6**	**1m 1.9s**	**10th**	**1m 38.6s**
4th	Tony Brooks	Cooper T51 Climax S4	99 laps	3rd	1m 37.7s
5th	Jo Bonnier	BRM P48 S4	83 laps	5th	1m 37.7s
6th	**Richie Ginther**	**Ferrari Dino 246P V6**	**70 laps**	**9th**	**1m 38.6s**
DNF	**Wolfgang von Trips**	**Ferrari Dino 246 V6**	**62 laps (clutch)**	**6th**	**1m 38.3s**

Pole position: Moss, 1m 36.3s, 73.055mph/117.570kph **Fastest race lap:** McLaren, 1m 36.2s, 73.132mph/117.694kph
Winner's average speed: 67.480mph/108.599kph **Drivers' championship:** 1st McLaren 14, 2nd Moss 8, 3rd Allison 6, 4th Phil Hill 4,
7th von Trips 2, 9th Ginther 1 **Constructors' championship:** 1st Cooper-Climax 14, 2nd Ferrari 10, 3rd Lotus-Climax 8

go through on the inside but went too wide and demolished a radio commentator's cabin — that really gave the man a close-up view of the action! — and ended his race under a deluge of wooden boards with the nose of his BRM missing.

McLaren quickly recovered and resumed his duel with the Ferrari driver. On lap 71, he got past the red car with Hill putting up only token resistance and at the chequered flag less than 10 seconds separated them. Had Phil thrown in the towel as Denis Jenkinson made out, using the adjective 'demoralised', or was it a wise move? 'If I hadn't been so exhausted near the end I might have been able to pass Bruce into second,' confessed Hill to William F. Nolan, author of *Phil Hill, Yankee Champion*, adding that taming the Ferrari had drained all his energy. It was an admission by a driver who had made amends for a performance a year earlier on the same circuit that had made him seriously doubt his ability to extract the best from a Formula 1 car. And that was probably the most important thing.

Caution thrown to the wind

Dutch Grand Prix, 6th June

At Zandvoort, the slippery slope on which Maranello had embarked from the start of practice on Saturday morning seemed to go on and on. At the outset, Stirling Moss set a benchmark time of 1m 33.8s in his Lotus while at Ferrari the rear anti-roll bar used to try to correct the understeer of the Dinos seemed only to make things worse. Proof that the Scuderia needed to

search for other solutions came during the afternoon when Phil Hill set the team's best time in 1m 36.4s, which was way off the quickest rear-engined cars. The next day it was unclear whether the Scuderia had resigned itself to its unhappy situation or if it was satisfied with the times set and was looking to the future as the drivers spent most of the day testing the 246 P before giving up when it oozed oil.

Final positions on the starting grid showed that Ferrari's performance in practice had been a disaster, with all three Dinos quite close to the back: Ginther (1m 36.3s) was 12th, Hill (1m 36.4s) 13th and von Trips (1m 36.7s) 15th. What was just as serious as being over three seconds adrift of Moss's pole time (1m 33.2s), with Jack Brabham's Cooper (1m 33.4s) and Innes Ireland's Lotus (1m 33.9s) alongside him on the front row, was that von Trips owed his starting money to the withdrawal of Chuck Daigh's Scarab. Lance Reventlow, Scarab's owner, vehemently contested the timing that bumped his driver out of the 15 paid starters and retaliated by withdrawing his two cars. And just to underline how far Ferrari had slipped, the Dinos were behind the BRMs and all the Coventry Climax-powered cars except Carel Godin de Beaufort's Formula 2 Cooper in last place.

On Monday when the flag fell at 3.15pm to unleash the pack, there was a big surprise. Although nobody knew it at the time, Moss deliberately fluffed his start. He was fed up with all the negative comments in the press accusing him of being a car breaker. In agreement with team owner Rob Walker, he wanted to prove that he could win a race without going hell for leather from the outset, so he let Brabham and Ireland race off into the distance. Phil Hill, however, set off like a scalded cat from his 13th spot and after passing several cars on the outside through the corners he roared past the pits in fifth place first time round,

▲ Dutch Grand Prix. Soon after the start, Wolfgang von Trips in the #2 Ferrari trails this group after starting from second-last position on the grid. Jim Clark's Lotus is on the left while the Yeoman Credit Coopers of Tony Brooks (#9) and Henry Taylor (#10) occupy the middle of the track.

◄ Dutch Grand Prix. After getting off to a flying start, Phil Hill's charge soon petered out. Richie Ginther and Wolfgang von Trips got past him on lap 17 and he remained behind them until lap 40 before falling back and retiring with engine trouble on lap 55.

> **Dutch Grand Prix.** Wolfgang von Trips is very visibly hard at work while Richie Ginther looks more at ease. They were at each other's throats for most of the race before the German came out on top, finishing fifth with his team-mate sixth.

before slipping to sixth and becoming locked in battle with Bruce McLaren's Cooper. This performance rather showed up his team-mates, for Ginther was ninth and von Trips, who had made a poor getaway, was 15th, just where he started.

Up front, Moss was, to use his own word, 'religiously' locked onto Brabham's tail waiting for the Australian to make a mistake. By lap 10, the next two, the Ireland and Stacey Lotuses welded

together, were already 17 seconds behind the duelling leaders, followed by the Gurney and Hill BRMs. In the Ferrari camp, worry was vying with hope: Hill was now seventh, Ginther eighth and von Trips 11th. Suddenly two incidents turned the race on its head.

On lap 12, Gurney's BRM suffered rear brake failure approaching the *Tarzan* hairpin, hit the bank and overturned

DUTCH GRAND PRIX

Zandvoort, 6th June 1960, 75 laps (2.605 miles/4.193km), 195.406 miles/314.475km • Starters 17, finishers 8

RACE					PRACTICE	
1st	Jack Brabham	Cooper T53 Climax S4	2h 1m 47.2s		2nd	1m 33.4s
2nd	Innes Ireland	Lotus 18 Climax S4	+24.0s		3rd	1m 33.9s
3rd	Graham Hill	BRM P48 BRM S4	+56.6s		5th	1m 35.1s
4th	Stirling Moss	Lotus 18 Climax S4	+57.7s		1st	1m 33.2s
5th	**Wolfgang von Trips**	Ferrari Dino 246 V6	74 laps		15th	1m 36.7s
6th	**Richie Ginther**	Ferrari Dino 246 V6	74 laps		12th	1m 36.3s
DNF	Phil Hill	Ferrari Dino 246 V6	55 laps (engine)		13th	1m 36.4s

Pole position: Moss, 1m 33.2s, 100.638mph/161.961kph **Fastest race lap:** Moss, 1m 33.8s, 99.994mph/160.925kph
Winner's average speed: 96.268mph/154.929kph **Drivers' championship:** 1st McLaren 14, 2nd Moss 11, 3rd Brabham 8, 6th Allison 6, 8th= von Trips 4, 8th= Phil Hill 4, 15th Ginther 2 **Constructors' championship:** 1st Cooper-Climax 22, 2nd Lotus-Climax 15, 3rd Ferrari 12

on top of its driver, who was most fortunate to escape with superficial hand injuries. Five laps later, Brabham's Cooper grazed a granite corner marker, breaking off a piece that hit and deformed the right-hand front wheel of Moss's Lotus. The time it took Stirling to get round to his pit and change the wheel for a borrowed replacement from Team Lotus cost him two laps and he rejoined 12th. Now he threw caution to the winds. For the rest of the race, Stirling put on a demonstration of brio behind the wheel that brought him up to fourth place by the chequered flag.

Phil Hill endured a nightmarish slide down the timesheets due to his capricious engine before finally stuttering to a halt on lap 55. Twenty laps later, Jack Brabham scored the third Grand Prix victory of his career to which he added the pleasure of lapping von Trips and Ginther as they circulated in tandem to finish fifth and sixth.

A day of mourning

Belgian Grand Prix, 19th June

The next two tracks on the World Championship trail — Spa-Francorchamps and Reims-Gueux — had such similarly high average speeds that they basically shared the claim to be the fastest in Europe, with the Belgian track in the lush valleys of the Ardennes having a slight edge. Compared with Monaco and Zandvoort, both circuits favoured sheer power and were usually happy hunting grounds for Ferrari. At Spa, the Scuderia entered three Dino 246s with independent suspension for Phil Hill, Wolfgang von Trips and Willy Mairesse, the Belgian hotshoe replacing Richie Ginther for the simple commercial reason that Belgium had always provided good clients for Maranello in the form of Equipe Nationale Belge and Ecurie Francorchamps. In addition, Enzo Ferrari had never had any complaints about Belgian drivers of the calibre of Jacques Swaters, Paul Frère, Olivier Gendebien, 'Beurlys' (Jean Blaton), André Pilette and Lucien Bianchi, all of whom who had served and continued to serve his interests in competition. In addition, familiarity with a circuit was always a strong advantage at Spa and Mairesse knew the place like his own back yard.

Although Hill did not share this local knowledge, the layout whetted his appetite for stringing together curves and vertiginous downhill sections, but in the opening session on Friday it was Jack Brabham who stunned everybody. After patiently getting to grips with the circuit, lapping at around the four-minute mark, he stopped the clock near the end of practice with a time of 3m 50.0s (137.133mph), over two seconds

quicker than the 3m 52.5s achieved by Tony Brooks (Cooper), the previous year's winner. Maybe Maranello regretted the fact that it did not have Olivier Gendebien in its ranks as the Belgian set the fourth-quickest time in his Cooper at 3m 53.5s. Despondency reigned in the Ferrari camp, especially as the team had arrived with high hopes. Von Trips, who was unhappy with his Dino, could do no better than 3m 58.9s in Mairesse's car and Hill was unable to get close to the four-minute mark.

The next day, however, brought times that were more in keeping with the Scuderia's expectations. Hill had the bit between his teeth and lapped in 3m 53.3s while von Trips managed 3m 57.8s. The American's time put him on the front row alongside Brabham and Brooks, neither of whom improved on their efforts of the previous day, while von Trips lined up on row four alongside Jim Clark (3m 57.5s). Mairesse (3m 58.9s), who had spent the entire session racking up laps, was a row further back between Dan Gurney (3m 58.3s) and Bruce McLaren (4m 0.0s).

Unfortunately, these times were set against a sombre backdrop. Shortly after the start of practice, Stirling Moss crashed at the bottom of the downhill section leading to the village of Burnenville. He was at full chat just before the *Malmedy* esses when his Lotus 18's left-rear hub, which was under maximum load in this right-hand corner, suddenly broke and the wheel flew into the air. The Lotus went into a triple spin and ended up against the left-hand bank, throwing out its hapless passenger at the moment of impact. Hill, one of the first to arrive on the scene, remembered seeing Moss lying 'in the foetal position coughing up blood and begging us not to move him till the doctor arrived as he was afraid his back was broken'. Stirling was finally carried away with a broken nose, ribs and kneecaps.

On the same lap as Moss's crash, the steering column on Mike Taylor's Lotus 18 broke in the curve at *La Carrière*, sending him flying off the track. He suffered burns to his face and hands and although his life was not in danger he joined his fellow Englishman in hospital in nearby Malmedy. Colin Chapman immediately stopped the three works Lotuses of Innes Ireland, Jim Clark and Alan Stacey from going out for any more practice laps. After dismantling the cars and examining their hubs with Magnaflux, he had new hubs flown in from England that arrived three hours before the start of the race, just in time for the cars to make the grid.

Hill had always been a brave driver and told William F. Nolan: 'I'd never driven at Spa prior to this 1960 Belgian Grand Prix, but I felt at home on the circuit once I learnt it.' Indeed, he felt so much at home that when the race started, with Brabham leading the field up the climb after *Eau Rouge*, he glued his Ferrari to second-placed Gendebien's gearbox with Graham Hill (BRM)

> **Belgian Grand Prix.** Phil Hill and Wolfgang von Trips have every reason to look perplexed. After practice, Hill was on the front row but a full 3.3 seconds behind Jack Brabham's Cooper while von Trips was 7.8 seconds adrift on the fourth row.

> **Belgian Grand Prix.** Inseparable in the early stages of the race, Wolfgang von Trips, visibly on the limit, leads Chris Bristow's Cooper before ceding position due to the transmission trouble that caused his retirement. Bristow lost control and crashed fatally on lap 25.

and Innes Ireland following. Next time round, Ireland was second with Phil in his wake. By lap 4, Hill had got past Ireland and was all over Brabham, who responded by upping the pace and setting a new lap record at 3m 53.5s. It was obvious that the battle for victory would be fought out between these two drivers, who were now so closely matched that they were literally neck and neck on the run down to the *Masta* kink. However, despite his brilliance and sheer grit, Hill could not sustain his challenge and gradually Brabham pulled away. On lap 10, when the Australian posted another record at 3m 51.9s, the gap between

them was 6.5 seconds. Five laps later it had grown to 12 seconds and now Gendebien, Graham Hill and McLaren were homing in on the Ferrari.

In total contrast, the other two Ferrari drivers languished in the middle ranks, although not yet completely outdistanced. Early on, they had run together, von Trips ahead of Mairesse, but by half distance the German was having to cope with a sticky clutch and his Belgian team-mate was ahead. At different stages, both men had battles with Chris Bristow (Cooper), a rising British star, and as the race passed the halfway mark Mairesse and Bristow were locked in a high-risk duel. On lap 20, Bristow had just got ahead when he approached the right-hander near *Burnenville* a little too quickly. Mairesse saw the Cooper 'drift further and further to the exterior on the left' then clip the verge and go out of control. The Belgian, lucky not to be collected by the Cooper, shot through on the right and escaped the unfolding tragedy.

▼ **Belgian Grand Prix.** From the outset, Phil Hill occupied second place behind Jack Brabham's Cooper and posed a sustained threat until a fuel leak in the cockpit caused him to stop first at the trackside and then at the pits. Fourth place was a well-deserved outcome.

BELGIAN GRAND PRIX

Spa-Francorchamps, 19th June 1960, 36 laps (8.761 miles/14.100km), 315.408 miles/507.600km ≙ Starters 17, finishers 6

RACE				PRACTICE	
1st	Jack Brabham	Cooper T53 Climax S4	2h 21m 37.3s	1st	3m 50.0s
2nd	Bruce McLaren	Cooper T53 Climax S4	+1m 3.3s	13th	4m 00.0s
3rd	Olivier Gendebien	Cooper T51 Climax S4	35 laps	4th	3m 53.5s
4th	**Phil Hill**	**Ferrari Dino 246 V6**	**35 laps**	**3rd**	**3m 53.3s**
5th	Jim Clark	Lotus 18 Climax S4	34 laps	9th	3m 57.5s
6th	Lucien Bianchi	Cooper T45 Climax S4	28 laps	14th	4m 00.6s
DNF	**Willy Mairesse**	**Ferrari Dino 246 V6**	25 laps (transmission)	12th	3m 58.9s
DNF	**Wolfgang von Trips**	**Ferrari Dino 246 V6**	23 laps (transmission)	6th	3m 57.8s

Pole position: Brabham, 3m 50.0s, 137.134mph/220.696kph Fastest race lap: Innes Ireland (Lotus 18 Climax S4), Hill & Brabham, 3m 51.9s, 136.010mph/218.887kph Winner's average speed: 133.625mph/215.049kph Drivers' championship: 1st McLaren 20, 2nd Brabham 16, 3rd Moss 11, 5th Phil Hill 7, 7th Allison 6, 9th von Trips 4, 16th Ginther 2 Constructors' championship: 1st Cooper-Climax 30, 2nd Lotus-Climax 17, 3rd Ferrari 15

Bristow's car climbed a bank and took off, ejecting its driver into barbed wire. The 22-year-old had no chance of survival.

Mairesse and von Trips retired within the next five laps, both through transmission failures, von Trips coming to rest at *Stavelot* while Mairesse was able to crawl back to the pits. Up at the front, meanwhile, Brabham now led Phil Hill by eight seconds, with Gendebien and Graham Hill running wheel to wheel behind them, and McLaren in fifth place playing a waiting game.

Just 20 minutes after Bristow's crash, tragedy struck again. A long way back in sixth place, Stacey was rounding the *Malmedy* curve when he suddenly lost control of his Lotus, which slid off to the outside of the track, hit the bank, overturned and caught fire. When the dead driver's goggles were found to be covered with feathers, it became clear that the 26-year-old had been hit in the face by a bird. Britain had lost two of its most promising young drivers in a single afternoon.

Ferrari's hopes of victory were dashed on lap 29. Fuel had begun to spurt onto Hill's left leg from the capillary tube feeding the fuel-pressure gauge and when it caught alight he stopped in panic at the trackside on a downhill slope. What followed was almost like a scene from a Mack Sennett silent comedy film. He had hardly vacated the cockpit to put out the flames when the Ferrari began to roll forward. After trying in vain to block one wheel with his foot, he had just enough time to vault aboard and bring the car to a halt against a concrete abutment. He managed to drive to the pits where it took the mechanics 1m 38s to repair the leak, which was enough for the leader to lap him and end any lingering prospect of victory. Hill came home fourth behind Brabham, McLaren and Gendebien, the latter owing

his place on the podium to Graham Hill's retirement after his BRM's engine let him down on the penultimate lap while lying second. Gendebien, with only two of his Cooper's five gears still operative, came home third after wisely stopping just before the finish line, waiting for the winner to pass and then crossing the line to secure his position without having to risk one more lap.

McLaren's second place put him ahead of the reigning World Champion in the drivers' standings with 20 points to 16. Ferrari really could not care less by now. The team's scorecard read seven points for Hill and four for von Trips, so Maranello's ambitions could only lie elsewhere. 'There's no question of fighting for the world title either in sports cars or in F1,' Enzo Ferrari had said at the beginning of the season. In F1 the situation was already pretty clear, but what about sports cars, with Le Mans coming next and a world title still a possibility? It all depended on victory in the Sarthe classic provided Porsche did not finish the race in second or third place, either of which would have left the two marques equal on points, thus requiring recourse to the more obscure clauses of the regulations to decide the outcome as the rule of the best three results dictated.

A Belgian tale

Le Mans 24 Hours, 25th–26th June

Le Mans had its own specific requirements and a car had to be powerful and reliable in equal measure to emerge victorious. So it was that Maranello opted for a Testa Rossa mix that combined conservatism and daring by entering two 250 TR 59/60s with de Dion axles and two 250 TRI 60s with independent rear suspension. Similarly distinct choices were reflected in their respective driver line-ups with a combination of hardened long-distance specialists Wolfgang von Trips/Phil Hill and Olivier Gendebien/Paul Frère in the older models and drivers who were theoretically more accustomed to shorter distances, Willy Mairesse/Richie Ginther and Ludovico Scarfiotti/Pedro Rodríguez, in the newer ones. In addition, Ferrari expanded its cooperation with NART by entrusting the American squad with a 250 TR 59 with de Dion axle to a blend of youth and experience in the form of 18-year-old Ricardo Rodríguez and 42-year-old André Pilette. The Mexican prodigy had hoped to race a Testa Rossa at Le Mans two years earlier, when only 16, but the organisers had ruled it out on the grounds that he was too young, so he had tried again in 1959 and this time they had allowed him to take part but only in a little OSCA. Eight 250 GTs (seven short-chassis Berlinettas and a California) run by private teams completed an armada of Ferraris.

Porsche's burning determination to secure the title was stronger than ever and the works team brought along three RS 60 spyders, two of them 1,606cc versions for Jo Bonnier/Graham Hill and Maurice Trintignant/Hans Herrmann, the other a 1,498cc machine for Edgar Barth/Wolfgang Seidel. Their aim was to take advantage of any chinks in Maranello's armour by betting on bodywork that was as streamlined as possible from nose to tail including a cockpit configuration that turned the German cars into 'roofless coupés'. Although Maserati was now, mathematically speaking, eliminated from the title race, it entered three *Tipo* 61s under the Camoradi banner, a remarkable effort given the cash-strapped situation of both manufacturer and team. In addition, even if the three cars were by now a well-known quantity, one of them stood out from the other two because of its elongated windscreen, which began at the front axle line. As Stirling Moss was recovering from his Spa injuries

> **Le Mans 24 Hours.** While Jim Clark in his Aston Martin DBR1 has already disappeared in the direction of the Dunlop curve, we see a swathe of the field at the getaway. Nearest the camera are two Jaguars, the Ron Flockhart/Bruce Halford D-type (#5) followed by the Walt Hansgen/Dan Gurney E2A (#6). The Aston Martin DBR1 (#8) driven by Ian Baillie/Jack Fairman leads the 250 TRs of Wolfgang von Trips/Phil Hill (#9), Willy Mairesse/Richie Ginther (#10), Olivier Gendebien/Paul Frère (#11), Ludovico Scarfiotti/Pedro Rodríguez (#12) and Ricardo Rodríguez/ André Pilette (#17). The 250 GT of Fernand Tavano/'Loustel' (#16) brushes the fencing while the similar cars of Graham Whitehead/Henry Taylor (#15) and George Arents/Alan Connell (#18) have yet to move.

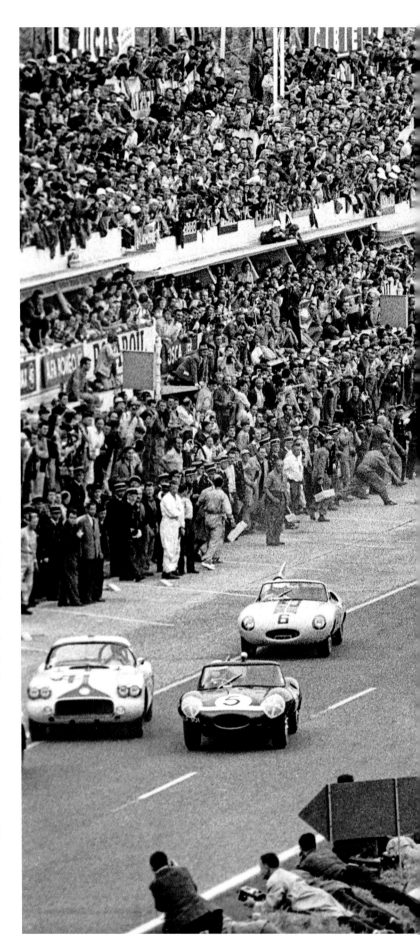

and Dan Gurney was driving for Jaguar, this car was entrusted to Masten Gregory/Chuck Daigh while the regular examples were driven by Gino Munaron/Giorgio Scarlatti and Lloyd Casner/Jim Jeffords.

Jaguar? There was a daring entry in the form of Briggs Cunningham's experimental E2A, powered by a new 3-litre six-cylinder engine said to produce 293bhp, but its status as an untried singleton entry did not prevent it from setting the fastest lap in practice with a time of 4m 4.5s (123.155mph). Alongside Jaguar's calculated risk with E2A, the company completed its line-up with a D-type in the colours of Ecurie Ecosse for Ron Flockhart/Bruce Halford. And lastly, and discreet almost to the point of anonymity, Border Reivers entered the Aston Martin DBR1/300 seen at the Nürburgring for Jim Clark/Roy Salvadori while owner/driver Ian Baillie ran his similar car for himself and Jack Fairman.

On lap 22 of the race, Ferrari team manager Romolo Tavoni called in the #11 Ferrari with Gendebien at the wheel for, in co-driver Frère's words, 'safety reasons'. As refuelling stops were scheduled every 24–25 laps, the decision came as a surprise, all the more so as Clark, after a brief fireworks display at the start, had fallen back into line and the Ferrari was lying second behind Gregory's Maserati. Was it indeed for 'safety reasons' — or a strategic change by Tavoni after chewing over a mistake he had made that was about to bring disgrace?

As the drivers did their handover, Gendebien asked Frère to use the electric pump to restart the engine because on the car's last lap it had been hiccupping since *Maison Blanche* due to fuel starvation. Refuelling completed, Frère followed his team-mate's advice and rejoined. What happened next was extraordinary. After completing his 22nd lap, von Trips found himself stranded at *Tertre Rouge* in his #9 Ferrari because it had run out of petrol. At the same time and just a few hundred yards further down the track, Scarfiotti was crawling along in the #12 Ferrari and about to coast to a halt for the same reason. In one lap, the Scuderia had lost two of its cars before Phil Hill and Pedro Rodríguez had even had a chance to drive them.

There had been a major screw-up. The capacity of the fuel tanks was fixed at 31.7 gallons by the CSI and the teams had calculated their refuelling needs according to the consumption of their cars. Had Tavoni, working with long-time Ferrari stalwart Luigi Bazzi, based his calculations on inaccurate data? If so, perhaps he had been misled by the way drivers at Le Mans often 'sandbagged' during the April test weekend and official practice in order to conceal their true pace, especially as there was never any imperative to 'go for a time' during practice because starting positions for the 24 Hours in this era were allocated according to

engine capacity, so that the cars with the biggest engines headed the echelon line-up. Frère put forward another hypothesis, stating that since the test weekend there had been a significant specification change: 'The positioning of the exhaust system exiting on the sides of the chassis to comply with the ground clearance of 4.7 inches imposed by the regulations had led to a big increase in fuel consumption in the mid-rev range.' This explanation seems to be all the more plausible as the #10 Ferrari of Mairesse/Ginther had its exhaust system positioned slightly differently and was not afflicted by unexpected fuel thirst. What can be of little doubt was that Enzo Ferrari's anger on learning of the debacle would have resounded in Tavoni's ears for a very long time.

Shortly after the two Ferrari retirements on the 23rd lap, the team's signalling pit at *Mulsanne* told Frère he was in the lead. Gregory's Maserati had been much quicker, as proved by its best lap of 4m 4.0s, which would remain the fastest of the race, but the car was now stuck in its pit because a broken wire had left its starter motor inoperative at its first refuelling stop and the task of tracing and repairing the fault took half an hour. So, three incidents handed Gendebien and Frère a lead they would hold to the finish. Their racing know-how and intelligence helped them cope with the storm that hit the circuit in the early evening followed by a wet and gloomy night.

Their pursuers were never in a position to pose a threat. The Mairesse/Ginther Ferrari suffered a broken universal joint in the 16th hour, gifting second place to the Rodríguez/Pilette 250 TR 59, while the Clark/Salvadori Aston Martin finished third. None of the Maseratis saw the flag: after fighting their way back up from 46th place to 21st, Ginther/Daigh went out with engine failure in the eighth hour; the Munaron/Scarlatti car was unable to restart after a spin; and Casner/Jeffords were sidelined by gearbox failure after an incursion into the *Mulsanne* sand trap. The Jaguar E2A, troubled soon after the start by ignition gremlins, quit in the ninth hour with a broken injector, while the D-type reached an excellent fourth place by half distance only to retire shortly afterwards with engine failure. The Baillie/Fairman Aston Martin, whih ran in the top third of the field for a long time, finished ninth behind the John Fitch/Bob Grossman Chevrolet Corvette.

And what about Porsche? It was a race to forget for Stuttgart as two of its RS 60s went out with engine failures, Trintignant/Herrmann in the fifth hour and Bonnier/Hill after 17 hours, the Swede having driven rapidly during his stints, the Englishman less so, declaring the car to be 'frankly undriveable'. The RS 60 that saw the finish was the Barth/Seidel example in 11th place, just behind the Herbert Linge/Hans Walter Carrera

➤ **Le Mans 24 Hours.** The Dick Thompson/Fred Windridge Chevrolet Corvette is in front on the entry to the Dunlop curve while three other Corvettes are obviously holding up the quicker cars among them, including the Ferraris of Olivier Gendebien/ Paul Frère (#11) and Fernand Tavano/'Loustel' (#16). The other cars are the Jaguar pair of Ron Flockhart/Bruce Halford (#5) and Walt Hansgen/Dan Gurney E2A (#6) and the Aston Martin DBR1 (#8) of Ian Baillie/Jack Fairman.

⌄ **Le Mans 24 Hours.** Paul Frère crosses the finishing line and wins the 28th running of the Sarthe classic. In this all-Ferrari scene, he is followed by the second-placed Ricardo Rodríguez/André Pilette 250 TR 59 and the 250 GT SWBs of Fernand Tavano/'Loustel' and Pierre Noblet/'Elde'.

LE MANS 24 HOURS

Le Mans, 25th–26th June 1960, 313 laps (8.364 miles/13.461km), 2,620.649 miles/4,217.527km • Starters 55, classified finishers 20

1st	Olivier Gendebien/Paul Frère	Ferrari 250 TR 59/60 (0772/0774 TR)	313 laps
2nd	Ricardo Rodríguez/André Pilette	Ferrari 250 TR 59 (0766 TR)	309 laps
3rd	Jim Clark/Roy Salvadori	Aston Martin DBR1/300	305 laps
4th	Fernand Tavano/'Loustel' (Pierre Dumay)	Ferrari 250 GT SWB (2001 GT)	301 laps
5th	George Arents/Alan Connell	Ferrari 250 GT SWB (1931 GT)	299 laps
6th	'Elde' (Léon Dernier)/Pierre Noblet	Ferrari 250 GT SWB (2021 GT)	299 laps
7th	Ed Hugus/Augie Pabst	Ferrari 250 GT SWB (1759 GT)	298 laps
DNF	Bill Sturgis/Jo Schlesser	Ferrari 250 GT California (2015 GT)	258 laps (engine)
DNF	Henry Taylor/Graham Whitehead	Ferrari 250 GT SWB (2009 GT)	258 laps (engine)
DNF	**Willy Mairesse/Richie Ginther**	**Ferrari 250 TRI 60 (0780 TR)**	**204 laps (gearbox)**
DNF	'Beurlys' (Jean Blaton)/Lucien Bianchi	Ferrari 250 GT SWB (1811 GT)	29 laps (accident)
DNF	**Wolfgang von Trips/Phil Hill**	**Ferrari 250 TR 59/60 (0770 TR)**	**22 laps (out of fuel)**
DNF	**Ludovico Scarfiotti/Pedro Rodríguez**	**Ferrari 250 TRI 60 (0782 TR)**	**22 laps (out of fuel)**
DNS	Carlo Mario Abate/Gianni Balzarini	Ferrari 250 GT SWB (1999 GT)	– (practice accident)

Fastest practice lap: Dan Gurney (Jaguar E2A), 4m 4.5s, 123.155mph/198.199kph **Fastest race lap:** Masten Gregory (Maserati *Tipo* 61), 4m 4.0s, 123.407mph/198.605kph **Winner's average speed:** 109.194mph/175.730kph **FIA World Sports Car Championship:** 1st Ferrari 22 (30)[1], 2nd Porsche 22 (26)[1], 3rd Maserati 11, 4th Aston Martin 4

[1] *Figure in brackets indicates all points scored; only the best three results counted towards the championship*

◄ **Le Mans 24 Hours.** Ninth at the end of the first hour, sixth at half distance and fourth at the finish, the 250 GT SWB driven by Fernand Tavano/'Loustel' won the GT category in impressive fashion.

➤ **Grand Prix de l'ACF.** Graham Hill (left), Richie Ginther (back to the camera), Jo Bonnier (partially hidden) and Dan Gurney all have something in common: at one time or another during their careers they drove a Ferrari. Here at Reims, however, Ginther had found a temporary berth at Scarab while Hill, Bonnier and Gurney were all in BRMs.

Abarth. When it came to totting up the points, Porsche's failure to add to its tally narrowly gave Ferrari the title. Both ended up with the same score, 22, but Maranello came out on top thanks to having accumulated the higher number of points before deductions.

Ferrari's satisfaction was enhanced by the successes achieved by the short-wheelbase 250 GTs. The model fulfilled all its promise with four of the six starters grouped together just shy of the podium, with only three laps separating the fourth-placed entry (Fernand Tavano/'Loustel') from the seventh (Ed Hugus/Augie Pabst).

A short-lived storm!

Grand Prix de l'ACF, 3rd July

Less than a week after his Le Mans let-down, Phil Hill was back at the Reims-Gueux circuit where he had made his Formula 1 début two years earlier. The placesuited him down to the ground. It was quick, demanding and required more skill than its triangular shape implied because it had two major challenges:

the *Gueux* curve, which the bravest took without lifting, and the *Thillois* corner, which lay between two rapid sections that favoured slipstreaming.

As Grands Prix were now following one another in quick succession, with this one — run by the Automobile Club de France (ACF) and still officially named in its honour — taking place only two weeks after the Belgian round, Maranello entered the drivers and cars seen at Spa. The decision to keep Mairesse in the team liberated Richie Ginther for a one-off ride with Lance Reventlow's Scarab team only for the car to be withdrawn before the race. There were three practice sessions and Jack Brabham underlined his championship credentials in cloudy and windy conditions on the Wednesday by going quicker and quicker with every lap and eventually posted a time of 2m 17.0s, astounding rivals who were still just finding their feet. At the end of the session the atmosphere in the Ferrari camp mimicked the weather — gloomy and overcast — as its best men were much slower, Phil Hill by 2.0s and Wolfgang von Trips by 2.9s. Next day, the Aussie twisted the knife with apparent nonchalance by setting a time of 2m 16.8s and Hill, searching for a response, had to use ballast to find the correct balance on his Dino but at least got closer and set the second fastest time at 2m 18.2s, just

◄ **Grand Prix de l'ACF.** On the sprint down from *Thillois* towards the pits and main grandstands, Jack Brabham's Cooper speeds along ahead of the Ferraris of Wolfgang von Trips and Phil Hill.

► **Grand Prix de l'ACF.** Phil Hill has just accelerated past Jack Brabham's Cooper on the exit from *Thillois* but their battle ended soon after half-distance when the Ferrari's transmission failed.

▼ **Grand Prix de l'ACF.** Phil Hill (#2) and Wolfgang von Trips (#4) hotly pursue Jack Brabham's Cooper on the entry to *Thillois*. The nose of Hill's car bears damage from contact with the back of the Cooper, proof of the intensity of the battle.

ahead of Graham Hill's BRM on 2m 18.4s. A stroke of luck saw Mairesse start on the second row (2m 19.3s), one place in front of von Trips (2m 19.4s), but it turned out that the timekeepers had credited Mairesse with a time set by von Trips and in fact his best was only 2m 21.6s, which would have put him 13th.

The secret of winning at Reims was to master the art of slipstreaming and wait for the right moment to go for the kill after exhausting one's opponents. This is what Mike Hawthorn did in his epic duel with Juan Manuel Fangio in 1953 when he pipped his rival on the line. Now, seven years later, Brabham and Phil Hill gave spectators a scintillating demonstration of this art. In the meantime, Graham Hill was the victim of a messy start. When Phil roared off in front of Brabham while Mairesse drew level with von Trips, Graham's BRM remained glued to the spot and got clobbered by Maurice Trintignant's Cooper starting from the back row, eliminating the BRM on the spot.

Under braking for *Thillois*, Brabham got the jump on Hill and led the pack as the cars flashed past the pits at the end of the first lap. Next time round it was von Trips in second place, then Hill reclaimed the position a lap later, then the American got back in

front on lap 4. The pace was so frenetic that the lap record fell twice in those first four laps, to von Trips (2m 19.6s) on lap 2, then Brabham (2m 18.8s) on lap 4. The raucous, colourful gaggle also included Innes Ireland's Lotus and Jo Bonnier's BRM, while a little further back the Coopers of Olivier Gendebien and Bruce McLaren fell into a duel that would last the whole race.

It was thrilling racing. Hill remembered Brabham glued to his tail to the point of using him for a tow in his 'big beast', until the moments when the roles were briefly reversed at *Thillois*. Barrelling down the long straight towards that corner, the Cooper would stay hidden from view behind the Dino before pulling out to overtake under braking, only for the more powerful Ferrari to draw level again under acceleration and nose ahead in front of the grandstands. For 17 laps Hill and Brabham went at it hammer and tongs, with von Trips close behind in third place, but then the Ferraris began to falter. First to go was Mairesse, who had lacked the pace to mix it at the front and had remained stuck in the middle of the field until his transmission let him down. Then Hill found it increasingly difficult to deal with Brabham, such that on lap 21, when Brabham had led for

GRAND PRIX DE L'ACF

Reims-Gueux, 3rd July 1960, 50 laps (5.158 miles/8.301km), 257.931 miles/415.100km • Starters 20, finishers 9

RACE				PRACTICE	
1st	Jack Brabham	Cooper T53 Climax S4	1h 57m 24.9s	1st	2m 16.8s
2nd	Olivier Gendebien	Cooper T51 Climax S4	+48.3s	11th	2m 20.0s
3rd	Bruce McLaren	Cooper T53 Climax S4	+51.9s	9th	2m 19.6s
4th	Henry Taylor	Cooper T51 Climax S4	49 laps	13th	2m 22.8s
5th	Jim Clark	Lotus 18 Climax S4	49 laps	12th	2m 20.3s
6th	Ron Flockhart	Lotus 18 Climax S4	49 laps	8th	2m 19.5s
11th	**Wolfgang von Trips**	**Ferrari Dino 246 V6**	**31 laps (transmission)**	**6th**	**2m 19.4s**
12th	**Phil Hill**	**Ferrari Dino 246 V6**	**29 laps (transmission)**	**2nd**	**2m 18.2s**
DNF	**Willy Mairesse**	**Ferrari Dino 246 V6**	**15 laps (transmission)**	**5th**	**2m 19.3s**

Pole position: Brabham, 2m 16.8s, 135.749mph/218.467kph **Fastest race lap:** Brabham, 2m 17.5s, 135.058mph/217.354kph
Winner's average speed: 131.805mph/212.119kph **Drivers' championship:** 1st= Brabham 24, 1st= McLaren 24, 3rd Moss 11, 6th Phil Hill 7, 8th Allison 6, 10th von Trips 4, 18th Ginther 2 **Constructors' championship:** 1st Cooper-Climax 38, 2nd Lotus-Climax 19, 3rd Ferrari 15

three laps, he had to take to the *Thillois* escape road and resumed in third place.

This was the moment when Brabham chose to show who was boss and pushed even harder, setting another lap record on lap 25 — exactly half distance — with a time of 2m 17.5s, which equated to an average speed of 135.017mph. The Aussie led von Trips by five seconds when Hill, who had fallen slightly behind, suddenly slowed with broken transmission just in front of the timekeeping box as he completed his 29th lap and freewheeled along in front of the grandstands to a crackle of applause before coming to rest at the end of the pitlane. Two laps later von Trips limped into *Thillois* at a snail's pace hamstrung by the same problem. It was all over for Ferrari.

Now without any real opposition, Brabham claimed his third consecutive win, one of his finest and certainly the best constructed. In the championship standings he now level-pegged with McLaren while Hill and von Trips failed to add to their tally.

All the luck in the world

British Grand Prix, 16th July

For quite some time, all eyes in Maranello had been scanning horizons that stretched much further than the next Grand Prix, all the more so in the case of Silverstone because the British circuit did not suit the Ferraris. Two months earlier, on 14th May, the Scuderia had found this out the hard way in the BRDC

International Trophy, run over 150 miles at the same circuit. Phil Hill was Ferrari's only representative and in practice he had soon discovered the Dino's shortcomings when it proved to be more than four seconds slower than Stirling Moss's runaway pole position in his Cooper at 1m 50.4s, with the BRMs of Jo Bonnier and Dan Gurney also superior. While Moss waltzed away until a suspension failure gifted victory to Innes Ireland (Lotus), Phil's race boiled down to a scrap with Masten Gregory (Cooper) before he dropped down the timesheets and retired.

Much more serious was that Harry Schell died in practice. In wet weather at Abbey curve, Schell lost control of his Cooper, which then hit a wall and slid along it for several hundred yards, throwing him out to instant death. Of French origin but American by choice, he was a big man both in terms of talent and size, and with his passing motor racing lost one of its outstanding players. He was a strong character whose serious approach to racing was in striking contrast to his constant good humour in daily life.

He was always ready for a laugh and during the evening before the 1958 Grand Prix de l'ACF at Reims he was the butt of one of the best practical jokes in the history of motor racing. Bernard Cahier, the esteemed photographer whose work graces this book, and a few other jesters — believed to be Mike Hawthorn, Luigi Musso and Maurice Trintignant — managed to get Schell's little Vespa 400 car up to the first floor in the Hôtel du Lion d'Or

▾ **British Grand Prix.** The factory Coopers of Bruce McLaren (#2) and Jack Brabham (#1) head the field at the start with the Ferrari pair of Wolfgang von Trips (#11) and Phil Hill (#10) visible between them and the BRMs of Jo Bonnier (#6) and Dan Gurney (#5) nearby. There are two Lotuses in line astern at the left, Jim Clark (#8) heading Innes Ireland, the latter with his trademark chequered helmet, while John Surtees's third works Lotus is at far right. Graham Hill's BRM had been on the front row of the grid but got swallowed up after stalling.

◄ ∧ **British Grand Prix.** Never in contention for victory, Phil Hill (#10) and Wolfgang von Trips (#11) spent most of the race locked in a battle that ended when the German got the better of his team-mate on lap 66 and went on to finish sixth, with Hill seventh.

BRITISH GRAND PRIX

Silverstone, 16th July 1960, 77 laps (2.927 miles/4.711km), 225.401 miles/362.747km • Starters 24, finishers 16

RACE				PRACTICE	
1st	Jack Brabham	Cooper T53 Climax S4	2h 4m 24.6s	1st	1m 34.6s
2nd	John Surtees	Lotus 18 Climax S4	+49.6s	11th	1m 38.6s
3rd	Innes Ireland	Lotus 18 Climax S4	+1m 29.6s	5th	1m 36.3s
4th	Bruce McLaren	Cooper T53 Climax S4	76 laps	3rd	1m 36.0s
5th	Tony Brooks	Cooper T51 Climax S4	76 laps	9th	1m 37.0s
6th	**Wolfgang von Trips**	**Ferrari Dino 246 V6**	**75 laps**	7th	1m 37.0s
7th	**Phil Hill**	**Ferrari Dino 246 V6**	**75 laps**	10th	1m 37.8s

Pole position: Brabham,1m 34.6s, 111.398mph/179.277kph **Fastest race lap:** Graham Hill (BRM P48 BRM S4), 1m 34.4s, 111.623mph/179.640kph
Winner's average speed: 108.690mph/174.920kph **Drivers' championship:** 1st Brabham 32, 2nd McLaren 27, 3rd= Moss 11, 3rd= Ireland 11, 7th
Phil Hill 7, 8th Allison 6, 11th von Trips 5, 19th Ginther 2 **Constructors' championship:** 1st Cooper-Climax 46, 2nd Lotus-Climax 25, 3rd Ferrari 16

where most of the drivers were staying. When its baffled owner found it the next morning, he had to round up some of the hotel personnel to bring it downstairs as those responsible had long since vanished into thin air.

For the British Grand Prix, the Scuderia entered two Dinos for Phil Hill and Wolfgang von Trips. Compared with previous appearances, their only distinguishing feature was chrome-plated extractors at the end of the exhausts. British-built cars were in their element on home turf and Jack Brabham's Cooper proved to be the best yet again by clinching pole in 1m 34.6s in the first session while Ferrari was still trying to find its bearings. Next day, Hill and von Trips gave it their all but it did not change anything. Brabham shared the front row with Bruce McLaren's Cooper and the BRMs of Graham Hill and Jo Bonnier. Von Trips was only seventh quickest (1m 37.0s) while Phil Hill was just tenth (1m 37.8s).

Brabham made it four victories on the trot although Graham Hill was in the running for glory until he made a mistake at Copse corner that led to his retirement. The race was dismal for the Scuderia with von Trips and Hill finishing sixth and seventh, both two laps behind the winner. Perhaps the most startling achievement, however, was multi-talented John Surtees's second place on only his second Formula 1 World Championship appearance after a long and celebrated career on motorcycles, where his career had begun at the age of 16 as the 'monkey' in his father's racing sidecar combination before he moved up to solo riding a year later. His result was all the more convincing because he was also finishing his two-wheel season before devoting himself full-time to four-wheel competition and did that in style by securing his seventh world title and his fourth in the premier 500cc category.

Tomorrow's winners

Solitude Grand Prix, 24th July

Of course, one swallow does not make a summer and a victory does not make a season, but before considering the Formula 2 Solitude Grand Prix, let us go back to the Syracuse Grand Prix run on 19th March. Against a field of Formula 2 top guns, including the Porsche of Stirling Moss, the Coopers of Jack Brabham, Olivier Gendebien and Maurice Trintignant, and the Lotus of Innes Ireland, Wolfgang von Trips won in style in his front-engined Dino 156. After setting the fifth-quickest time in practice and starting on the second row, his task was made easier by the retirements of Brabham and Moss, the latter having led until half distance with the Ferrari eight seconds behind. Thereafter, von Trips paced his race until the chequered flag, fending off attacks from Trintignant and Gendebien. After the finish he was given credit for his mastery and maturity, attributes that previously had been questioned.

In this context, the Solitude Grand Prix took on particular significance as it gave a foretaste of what the future 1.5-litre Formula 1 might be like. The race was held on a circuit nestling in a heavily wooded area near Stuttgart in West Germany and resembled Spa-Francorchamps thanks to its length (7.1 miles), its triangular shape and its variety of hairpins and fast corners.

Porsche was determined to shine on home ground and entered no fewer than four factory cars for Jo Bonnier, Hans Herrmann, Graham Hill and Dan Gurney. John Surtees was another reinforcement for Porsche in Rob Walker's private entry, which the injured Stirling Moss would normally have driven.

Il Grande John
From two wheels to four

Goodwood, October 1959. Tony Vandervell wanted to assess John Surtees at the wheel of a Vanwall after the motorcycle ace's previous brief runs in Aston Martins arranged by Reg Parnell, first a DBR1, then a DBR4. Of course, John immediately went for it and tried to find his limits, so the test was an action-packed one that involved a few spins. He was eager to explore new horizons after describing his motorcycle career as 'having done the same thing for many years' and he had every intention of making his mark on four wheels.

To obtain an international racing licence, he had to take part in seven British national events, so for the 1960 season he bought a Formula 2 Cooper-Climax, which he never actually raced, and a Formula Junior Cooper-Austin. His maiden outing came at Goodwood on 19th March at the circuit's first meeting of the year. He posted the fastest time in practice and then had a long battle with Jim Clark's Lotus in the race before settling for second place. On 2nd April at Oulton Park, he again finished second, this time behind Innes Ireland's Lotus. Colin Chapman, the Lotus boss, saw

that a new talent was about to explode on the scene and offered Surtees a Formula 1 seat in the non-championship International Trophy at Silverstone, where he got as high as fourth before a burst oil line put paid to his display. That same day, Surtees also took in the Formula Junior race, once more finishing second to Clark. Chapman was already convinced and put the motorcycle racer in a third works Lotus at the Monaco Grand Prix.

Surtees arrived the day before practice and that evening dined with Chapman and new team-mates Ireland and Alan Stacey. After his fellow drivers had chatted away about their afternoon on the beach, he announced that he had spent his time walking round the track and described the gear ratios that he wanted on his car for the next day. 'To top it all,' said Chapman to Colin Hornsey, who noted his words, 'he was right and the ratios he'd chosen were absolutely spot on.' Half measures were not part of Surtees's make-up: this story shows how demanding he was on a professional level and how his uncompromising approach could also raise a few hackles.

Jack Brabham was Cooper's only official representative but the marque supplied two-thirds of the field. Lotus entered Jim Clark and Innes Ireland.

As proof that Ferrari was there not just to make up the numbers, Phil Hill was down to drive the Syracuse-winning Dino 156 while von Trips had a completely revamped version of the 246 P seen in Monaco and at Zandvoort, now fitted with a 1,484cc (2.87 x 2.32 inches) 65-degree V6 putting out around 180bhp at 9,000rpm. The clutch linkage was now on the left-hand rear of the gearbox, which was still placed at the extreme end of a tubular chassis modified to accommodate it. The redesigned and reinforced suspension wishbones were repositioned. From an aesthetic point of view, the very slim rear was topped by a now-horizontal air intake. In short, Maranello's latest brainchild, without being at all radical compared with its rivals, looked surprisingly slim and compact for a Ferrari.

Practice was held in rainy conditions. While this limited the opportunity to fully assess the 246 P, the car could at least be compared with the other runners and measured against Hill's Dino. Clark gave another stunning display of his virtuosity to take pole position at 4m 23.6s while von Trips created a sensation by clinching second place on the grid at 4m 24.1s. The rest, led by Herrmann on 4m 28.3s, were way back. Clark, as fast as his talent was vast, won the Formula Junior race, a curtain-raiser to the main event

Right from the start of the 20-lap race, Clark got down to the job of making up for a fluffed start. Ninth first time round, he led by lap 4. He opened a cushion of 12.5 seconds by lap 8 over the second-place battle between Herrmann and von Trips, who had been trading blows since the start. In the other Ferrari, Hill was ninth and had just got past Surtees, who retired on lap 16 after a spin that left him unable to restart. At the end of lap 10,

➤ **Solitude Grand Prix.** Phil
Hill and Wolfgang von Trips
exchange points of view amid
attentive Ferrari personnel
during a wet practice session.
The rain helped to explain the
gap of 24 seconds between
their respective times, 4m
48.7s and 4m 24.1s.

➤ **Solitude Grand Prix.** Under
the watchful eyes of Luigi
Bazzi (far right), Wolfgang
von Trips prepares to set off
in the rear-engined Dino 156
with rain falling.

◄ **Solitude Grand Prix.** Bright sun drove away the clouds for the start of the race. In the middle of the front row, Wolfgang von Trips appears to dominate the scene. Among the other competitors arrayed across the track, we see Jim Clark's Lotus (#17) on the left and a fleet of Porsches driven by Dan Gurney (#22), Graham Hill (#6), Jo Bonnier (#4), John Surtees (#19) and Hans Herrmann (#5). Victory went to von Trips from Herrmann.

Clark had to make a pitstop to take on water, his engine ailing with a defective cylinder head gasket, and rejoined 10th, leaving Herrmann and von Trips to duel for the lead. The ferocity of their fight was illustrated by a sequence of lap records, Clark's first benchmark of 4m 8.0s was beaten in turns at 4m 7.5s (von Trips), 4m 7.0s (Herrmann), 4m 6.4s (von Trips) and 4m 6.0s (Herrmann) before von Trips dialled in a blinder of 4m 4.7s on lap 17 and took the lead in the process, reeling off the last three laps to beat Herrmann by nearly four seconds. Phil Hill was never in the hunt as his Dino was completely outclassed and he came home just seventh in front of the recovering Clark.

What counted as much as the result itself was the decisive manner in which Ferrari had achieved it against top-class opposition, with the fight for the remaining points-scoring places hard-fought and uncertain. Behind the duel for victory, just under one second separated the next three, all Porsches, with Bonnier third, Graham Hill fourth and Gurney fifth, the latter saying afterwards that he had never had to fight so hard for a fifth place. Ferrari's victory was also a source of personal satisfaction for von Trips, who proved for a second time how well he could perform in a car that prefigured the future with its rear-mounted 1.5-litre engine. He displayed this prowess again in the German Grand Prix run to Formula 2 regulations on the *Südschliefe* of the Nürburgring, where, driving a Porsche rather than a Ferrari, he finished a close second to Bonnier in typical Eifel rain and fog.

Enough to bring tears to your eyes

Portuguese Grand Prix, 14th August

Jack Brabham, 32 points; Bruce McLaren, 27 points; Stirling Moss and Innes Ireland, 11 points: with three Grands Prix to go, it was almost all over bar the shouting. It now seemed certain that Brabham would be World Champion for the second year running because, barring unforeseen circumstances, the possibility of his faithful right-hand man, McLaren, 11 years his junior, snatching the title looked extremely unlikely.

Two years earlier at this Boavista circuit in Porto, three Coopers in the hands of Brabham, Maurice Trintignant and Roy Salvadori had finished in the last three positions. The Surbiton-based constructor had made big strides since then but the track had not changed. With its rough surface punctuated by paving stones and tram lines, the 4.6-mile layout ran between telegraph poles, concrete barriers and buildings with straw bales providing only scant protection. 'It was so bumpy it made your eyes blur,' recalled Phil Hill.

Ferrari entered Hill and von Trips in front-engined Dino 246s that looked no different from the cars seen at Silverstone and it came as a surprise that at the end of the first practice session their times were on a par with those of the quickest British single-seaters. Dan Gurney was fastest in his BRM at 2m 27.81s, confirming that he was back at the top of his game, shading Moss's Lotus (2m 28.32s) and Brabham's Cooper (2m 28.43s). Next day, however, the improvements of the times of all but one of the works Lotuses, Coopers and BRMs relegated the Dinos to the middle of the pack even if they too were faster than on the previous day. The third and last session gave the Italians little

‣ **Portuguese Grand Prix.** Dealing with cobbles and tram lines, Hill held second place behind John Surtees's Lotus for eight laps until steering and clutch problems put paid to his efforts.

⌄ **Portuguese Grand Prix.** Von Trips, who came round in last place on the first lap after contact with another car, roars down the asphalt alongside the Atlantic Ocean on his way to fourth place just behind Jim Clark.

PORTUGUESE GRAND PRIX

Porto, 14th August 1960, 55 laps (4.602 miles/7.407km), 253.137 miles/407.385km • Starters 15, finishers 7

RACE				PRACTICE	
1st	Jack Brabham	Cooper T53 Climax S4	2h 19m 0.03s	3rd	2m 26.05s
2nd	Bruce McLaren	Cooper T53 Climax S4	+57.97s	6th	2m 27.44s
3rd	Jim Clark	Lotus 18 Climax S4	+1m 53.23s	8th	2m 28.36s
4th	**Wolfgang von Trips**	**Ferrari Dino 246 V6**	**+1m 58.81s**	**9th**	**2m 28.40s**
5th	Tony Brooks	Cooper T51 Climax S4	49 laps	12th	2m 32.12s
6th	Innes Ireland	Lotus 18 Climax S4	48 laps	7th	2m 27.52s
DNF	Phil Hill	Ferrari Dino 246 V6	30 laps (accident)	10th	2m 28.42s

Pole position: John Surtees (Lotus 18 Climax S4), 2m 25.56s, 113.829mph/183.190kph **Fastest race lap:** Surtees, 2m 27.53s, 112.309mph/180.744kph **Winner's average speed:** 109.268mph/175.849kph **Drivers' championship:** 1st Brabham 40, 2nd McLaren 33, 3rd Ireland 12, 6th von Trips 8, 9th Phil Hill 7, 11th Allison 6, 19th Ginther 2 **Constructors' championship:** 1st Cooper-Climax 48, 2nd Lotus-Climax 28, 3rd Ferrari 19

cause for joy. If seeing Brabham (2m 26.05s) on the front row with Gurney (2m 25.63s) was no surprise, John Surtees's pole position in 2m 25.56s stunned everybody. After missing the previous day's session due to transmission failure, the motorcycle ace had spent several laps tucked behind Gurney's BRM both to learn the circuit and to take advantage of his slipstream before beating him. Considering that the BRM was equipped with a 'bacon-slicer' single rear brake in an unprotected central position next to the gearbox, this was a potentially dangerous exercise, especially on a circuit that did not forgive the slightest mistake. Henry Taylor and Jim Clark found this out to their cost, the former because he had to withdraw with an injured arm, the latter because his mechanics had to burn midnight oil rebuilding his Lotus.

On Sunday, the flag fell in front of a first row in disarray as Graham Hill came through from the second row to slot in between Brabham and Gurney. The first lap was pretty tumultuous as Gurney, who had slightly jumped the start, slammed the door on Brabham, prompting an error by the championship leader that saw him fall back to eighth place, while Moss and Surtees followed with the two Hills now in their wake, Graham ahead of Phil. The other Ferrari, meanwhile, was last, half a lap behind with its nose bearing traces of an incursion into the straw bales. Even though von Trips's mistake blighted hopes of an upturn in Ferrari's fortunes, the horizon soon began to brighten. By lap 10, Phil Hill, wrestling with his car, was in fourth place behind Gurney, Surtees and Moss, then moved up after Gurney fell back with engine problems and Moss pitted due to plug trouble.

But second place was as good as it got for the American driver. As well as having niggles with his clutch and brakes, Hill had to deal with constant harassment from Brabham, who remained

as rough and tough as he had been in his early midget car days. Finally, Phil missed a gearchange and hit a pavement and straw bales on lap 29, retiring soon afterwards. Von Trips, who had carved his way up from the back, was now sixth and gained two more places when Tony Brooks (Cooper) pitted with a gearbox problem and Surtees retired due to a pierced radiator. Clark was now in von Trips's sights but a final push by the Lotus man deprived him of a place on the podium, where Brabham and McLaren duly occupied the first two steps, and the Australian confirmed his second world title with his fifth consecutive Grand Prix win.

Did Maranello see in this unexpectedly favourable result proof that there was still life left in the Dino, that perhaps the front-mounted engine was not yet consigned to the past? Phil Hill for one did not follow this line of thinking and when asked to do a succession of tests in the quest to improve the Dino's road-holding, he tried to play down progress. Ferrari was also determined to extract every ounce of power from the Dino in order not to be dominated by the English single-seaters in the forthcoming Italian Grand Prix at Monza.

Maranello's fears of humiliation on home ground turned out to be groundless. While the Italian organisers insisted that the banked oval would be used, the British constructors made it clear that they would only participate if the race was confined to the road course. Both sides stuck to their guns, so BRM, Cooper and Lotus withdrew, while also forbidding their drivers from taking part independently. Was their decision an implicit admission of the fragility of their cars on a rough-surfaced oval they judged to be dangerous or a wish to avoid a pointless trip as the world titles were already decided? Their reasoning was ambiguous.

American history repeats itself

Italian Grand Prix, 4th September

The first day's practice saw nine Formula 1 and seven Formula 2 cars roar out onto to the famous Italian circuit, the 'second-division' cars called in to boost the sparse field. Ferrari was present with four cars and also provided the engines in two Coopers entered by Eugenio Castellotti. The Ferraris, incidentally, were entered by SEFAC, acronym for *Società Esercizio Fabbriche Automobili e Corse*, the new legal entity under which Enzo Ferrari now fielded his cars. There was a smattering of other 2.5-litre machinery with Climax or Maserati power, while three Porsches looked like the most promising of the 1.5-litre runners. There was no particular selection criteria, just the need to cobble together a half-decent field.

The next day saw three Ferrari Dino 246s monopolise the front row. A very quick, determined Phil Hill, who seemed to have retreated into his shell, claimed pole position with a time of 2m 41.4s, almost two seconds faster than Richie Ginther (2m 43.3s) and over three seconds better than Willy Mairesse (2m 43.9s). Using and even abusing the slipstream of these cars, Wolfgang von Trips (2m 51.9s) in a 156 emerged as fastest of the Formula 2

▲ **Italian Grand Prix.** The Dino 156 was again entrusted to Wolfgang von Trips and he used it to set the fastest time in the race's Formula 2 category. The only significant modifications that distinguished it from the car seen at Solitude were various new and repositioned air intakes.

▼ **Italian Grand Prix.** The Formula 2 Ferrari was almost a carbon copy of the future Formula 1 model, with three twin-choke Weber carburettors, unequal-length double-wishbone rear suspension, co-axial springs and telescopic shock absorbers, inboard rear disc brakes, a multi-disc dry clutch and a five-speed gearbox.

brigade, earning a place on the third row. In comparison, Giulio Cabianca (Cooper-Ferrari) and Hans Herrmann (Porsche), respectively the best of the other F1s (2m 49.3s) and F2s (2m 58.3s), seemed condemned to play the role of also-rans.

As the Scuderia had no serious rivals, it looked like the race would be a dull one, although the prospect seemed to make no difference to the usual fervour surrounding the Italian Grand Prix, with a large crowd flocking to the circuit. For those in the main grandstands, every lap brought the chance to see the cars twice, once when setting off round the road course and again when heading out on the banked sections.

On the first lap, Ginther led both times the field went down the main straight, with Hill hot on his heels. Behind them, Mairesse let von Trips use his slipstream in keeping with a pre-agreed strategy, although this assistance for the 1.5-litre car became unavailable when Mairesse had to stop for fresh tyres. The outcome between the leading duo was not decided until half distance, when Hill finally got the better of his stubborn fellow American and pulled away to win by nearly two and a half minutes, with Mairesse completing a 1–2–3 for the big Ferraris. There would probably have been a Ferrari in fourth place as well

▲ Italian Grand Prix. Romolo Tavoni gives Enzo Ferrari his comments on the times set by his drivers. They looked good as the Ferraris were up against only second-rate opposition thanks to the defection of the English constructors and three Dino 246s filled the front row of the grid.

➤ Italian Grand Prix. Phil Hill presses on towards his maiden Grand Prix victory, and the first for an American driver for 39 years.

ITALIAN GRAND PRIX

Monza, 4th September 1960, 50 laps (6.214 miles/10.000km), 310.686 miles/500.000km • Starters 16, finishers 10

RACE				PRACTICE	
1st	Phil Hill	Ferrari Dino 246 V6	2h 21m 9.2s	1st	2m 41.4s
2nd	Richie Ginther	Ferrari Dino 246 V6	+2m 27.6s	2nd	2m 43.3s
3rd	Willy Mairesse	Ferrari Dino 246 V6	49 laps	3rd	2m 43.9s
4th	Giulio Cabianca	Cooper T51 Castelotti S4	48 laps	4th	2m 49.3s
5th	Wolfgang von Trips	Ferrari Dino 156 V6 1.5	48 laps	6th	2m 51.9s
6th	Hans Herrmann	Porsche 718 F4 1.5	47 laps	10th	2m 58.3s

Pole position: Phil Hill, 2m 41.4s, 138.596mph/223.048kph **Fastest race lap:** Phil Hill, 2m 43.6s, 138.596mph/220.048kph; von Trips, 2m 51.7s, 130.282mph/209.668kph **Winner's average speed:** 132.063mph/212.534kph **Drivers' championship:** 1st Brabham 40, 2nd McLaren 33, 3rd Phil Hill 15, 6th von Trips 10, 8th Ginther 8, 12th Allison 6, 15th Mairesse 4 **Constructors' championship:** 1st Cooper-Climax 48, 2nd Lotus-Climax 28, 3rd Ferrari 26

had von Trips not had to stop on lap 39 of the 50 to have his rear tyres checked, allowing Cabianca to get ahead. Nonetheless, the little Ferrari won the Formula 2 contest by a whole lap from two closely matched Porsches, Hans Herrmann snatching sixth place on the line from team-mate Edgar Barth.

Unexciting though it was, the race provided a rich seam of information. Important factors from the perspective of the following season were that the Porsches, unlike the 1.5-litre Ferrari, had not only had to refuel but Herrmann and Barth had

also never been in a position to rattle von Trips, notwithstanding the help he received from the slipstreams of his sister cars. Was this a sign that Ferrari had already honed its weapons to perfection for future battles?

The result had a particularly agreeable taste for Phil Hill. Not only had he achieved his first Grand Prix victory but it was also the first for an American driver since Jimmy Murphy's success in his Duesenberg in the 1921 Grand Prix de l'ACF at Le Mans. That day another American, Ralph de Palma in a Ballot, had followed

◄ **Italian Grand Prix.** In keeping with a pre-arranged race strategy to gain the upper hand in the battle with the Formula 2 Porsches, Wolfgang von Trips took advantage of the slipstream from Willy Mairesse's Dino 246. It paid off as the German emerged victorious in the category with fifth place overall.

Formula 1 World Championship (Drivers) *Top three plus Ferrari drivers*

	1st Jack Brabham	2nd Bruce McLaren	3rd Stirling Moss	5th Phil Hill	6th Wolfgang von Trips	8th Richie Ginther	12th Cliff Allison	15th Willy Mairesse
Argentine GP	0	8	0	0	2	–	6	–
Monaco GP	0	6	8	4	0	1	0	–
Dutch GP	8	0	3	0	2	1	–	–
Belgian GP	8	6	0	3	0	–	–	0
GP de l'ACF (France)	8	4	–	0	0	0	–	0
British GP	8	–3	–	0	1	–	–	–
Portuguese GP	8	6	0	0	3	–	–	–
Italian GP	–	–	–	8	2	6	–	4
United States GP	3	4	8	1	–	–	–	–
Total	**43**	**34**	**19**	**16**	**10**	**8**	**6**	**4**

Murphy home, and 39 years later this little historical detail was neatly repeated at Monza with Ginther's second place. Of rather less importance, considering that the drivers' title had already been decided, the fact that Hill was (temporarily) in the top three in the championship ranking was of little interest.

Four weeks after the success at Monza, the Formula 2 Modena Grand Prix left Ferrari dissatisfied, its two entries vanquished by Jo Bonnier's Porsche. Run over 100 laps of the 1.45-mile circuit just down the road from Maranello, the race saw Richie Ginther finish second in the front-engined 1.5-litre Dino from Syracuse, while Wolfgang von Trips, who had looked to be on course for victory in the rear-engined Dino 156 he had used at Monza, finished third after a delay to deal with a hydraulic leak in the master cylinder.

Still, it was obvious that Ferrari was ready for the new 1.5-litre Formula 1 even if one aspect of the regulations, the weight limit, had not been finalised. However, when the CSI ruled shortly afterwards, on 11th October, that the Formula 1 World Championship would be run to a maximum weight of 450kg, the future could not have looked any rosier for Maranello. Enzo Ferrari had finally given in: 'The rear engine has won the day!'

On 16th October, Phil Hill was at Riverside for a 200-mile race in which he finished seventh in the Le Mans-winning 250 TR 59/60 entered by Eleanor von Neumann.

Five weeks later, on 20th November, Hill was back at the same track for the United States Grand Prix at the wheel of a Cooper-Climax run by Yeoman Credit, Ferrari having refused to take part in a race with nothing at stake. So, the fact that he came home sixth and finally finished fifth in the World Championship standings was of minor significance. Proving

Formula 1 World Championship (Constructors)

	1st Cooper-Climax	2nd Lotus-Climax	3rd Ferrari
Argentine GP	8	–1	6
Monaco GP	–6	8	4
Dutch GP	8	6	2
Belgian GP	8	2	3
GP de l'ACF (France)	8	–2	0
British GP	8	6	–1
Portuguese GP	8	4	3
Italian GP	0	–	8
United States GP	–4	8	–
Total	**48**	**34**	**26**

World Sports Car Championship

	1st Ferrari	2nd Porsche	3rd Maserati
Buenos Aires 1,000Km	8	–4	3
Sebring 12 Hours	–4	8	0
Targa Florio	6	8	0
Nürburgring 1,000Km	–4	6	8
Le Mans 24 Hours	8	0	0
Total	**22**	**22**	**11**

that he was more than just 'the best American road-race driver of recent years', as Denis Jenkinson had written after the Italian Grand Prix, brought another implication. The future would give him the opportunity to prove it, but before seeing how, we will stay in the United States where it all began.

El Batallador
A portrait of Phil Hill

Philip Toll Hill Jr, born in Miami on 20th April 1927, was the first son of Philip Toll Hill Sr and Lela Long Hill. The youngster led a peripatetic life that took him to New York, Hollywood and Pasadena while the Hill family grew larger with the arrival of another boy and a girl. In 1931, they finally settled on the Pacific coast in Santa Monica, where Hill found his investigations under the bonnet of his mother's Marmon Speedster more interesting that his piano lessons. His Aunt Helen gave his interest in cars a decisive push, first by allowing the boy free rein behind the wheel of her Packard, then by giving him the Ford Model T he so badly wanted when he was just 12 years old.

Pushed by Hill Sr, he continued his reluctant studies while in his free time he pursued his automotive passion by working in local garages. After graduating in business administration from the University of Southern California in June 1947, he broke away from the family yoke and became full-time assistant to a mechanic looking after the midget car of a local star. He was delighted: 'I was just a mechanic's helper, but I had an identity, I had a real label which I could hang onto at last.'

As his passion for automobiles intensified, he bought an MG TC with his aunt's help. While it was far from being his first car, it was the one in which he competed in his first races and he scored an inaugural victory in July 1949 at an evening meeting in Gardena. At the time he was working in Beverly Hills as a car salesman (not his strong point) at International Motors, a car dealership belonging to Roger Barlow and Louis van Dyle. They sold a wide range of automobiles including Simcas, MGs, Jaguars, Rolls-Royces and Mercedes-Benz to a very select clientele that included Gary Cooper, Clark Gable and Humphrey Bogart.

Gaining self-esteem

Two encounters were to guide his course in life. The first was with Californian mechanic Richie Ginther, a small man of slight build with a freckled face. The two met in 1946 at a party thrown by Ginther's brother and found they not only shared intense enthusiasm for cars but also lived in the same part of Santa Monica. Working together at International Motors cemented their friendship, which remained undiminished when Ginther moved on in 1950 to work at the Douglas aviation company and later served in the Korean War. The second encounter was with Frenchman Bernard Cahier, who had arrived in Los Angeles without a job and joined them at International Motors as a salesman. An enthusiastic and go-getting spirit, Cahier went racing in his free time with his MG TD and wielded his camera with great skill to immortalise on film the early exploits of someone who was to become a great buddy.

Hill continued his racing apprenticeship. He bought a Jaguar XK120 in Britain with financial help from International Motors, then traded up to an Alfa Romeo 8C-2900B before getting his hands on another XK120 entered for him by Jaguar's West Coast distributor. As the successes accumulated, his self-esteem increased in proportion. Despite some difficulties adapting to the stresses and strains of motor racing, he was now sure that this was the life for him. An important moment came on 20th July 1952 when he scored his first victory in a Ferrari, at Torrey Pines driving a 212 Export Barchetta that he had been able to acquire from Luigi Chinetti for $6,000, half the model's cost in Europe, thanks to Chinetti's growing interest in nurturing the careers of future champions.

Another major milestone came in November 1952 when Hill, partnered by Arnold Stubbs, finished sixth in the Carrera Panamericana at the wheel of a Ferrari 212 Vignale coupé belonging to Allen Guiberson. It was a real feat as he suffered from sinusitis and stomach problems that made the five-day marathon a nightmare for him. This race marked Hill's international début and underlined his penchant for long-distance events, something that also became a hurdle when he later tried to move up to single-seaters.

In March 1953 he took part in his first 12 Hours of Sebring when Bill Spear, an experienced driver who had finished fourth at Le Mans the previous year in a Cunningham C4-R

shared with its constructor, invited him to co-drive his Ferrari 225 S spyder. It did not end well. Forty-five minutes after taking over from the owner, Hill suffered brake failure and the car destroyed itself against a disused military barracks. Luckily, he escaped unhurt.

He had already visited Le Mans in 1952 as a spectator and returned in June 1953 to team up with Fred Wacker in an OSCA MT4. Their race lasted eight hours and Tom Cole's fatal accident at Maison Blanche, announced at dawn, left a very deep impression that would change Hill's perception of motor racing for ever: 'I was beginning to be very much aware of the risks connected with fast driving at that time.' But his passion for racing was not affected in the least.

In July, he shared a Ferrari 340 Mexico Vignale with Chinetti for his first 12 Hours of Reims until the brakes gave up after four hours. While the outcome did nothing to boost his reputation, his maiden experience of the Champagne plain is worth mentioning as this was the circuit at which he would make his début in Formula 1 in the Grand Prix de l'ACF five years later.

▲ Phil Hill scored his first noteworthy victory at Torrey Pines in a Ferrari 212 Barchetta in 1952, beating the second-placed finisher by two laps.

At the end of the year Hill tackled the Carrera Panamericana again with another Ferrari provided by Guiberson, this time a 340 Mexico Vignale coupé with Ginther as co-driver. On the third leg between Puebla and Mexico, in a downhill section following a steep rise, the Ferrari arrived at a hairpin and could not stop in time, shooting off the road backwards and bouncing twice against rocks before coming to rest. Unscathed, Hill and Ginther quickly leapt out, aware that the previous day Antonio Stagnoli had perished when fire engulfed his crashed Ferrari 375 MM, his co-driver, Giuseppe Scotuzzi, having already been killed in the accident. When the two Americans got back on the road, they understood the reason for their shunt: spectators had removed the road sign indicating the corner.

'I look for the fighter'

On 23rd November 1954, Hill and Ginther were back for another Carrera Panamericana, this time at the wheel of a Ferrari 375 MM Vignale courtesy of Guiberson. Without underestimating other serious Ferrari rivals such as Luigi Chinetti (375 MM) and Alfonso de Portago (750 Monza), the driver they most feared was Umberto Maglioli — a true long-distance specialist — competing solo in a 375 Plus. Driving a Lancia Aurelia, Maglioli had finished second in the 1951 Mille Miglia and fourth in the 1952 Panamericana, and had looked on course for victory in the 1953 Panamericana when his 375 MM lost a wheel at high speed, following which he swapped over to the similar car of Mario Ricci/Forese Salviati, which lay eighth at the time, and won three stages to help it reach sixth place at the finish. His 1954 season brought a triumphant début in the 1,000Km of Buenos Aires, winning with Giuseppe Farina in a 375 MM.

After accidents on the Giro di Sicilia and the Mille Miglia, Maglioli was determined to win the Panamericana in a 375 Plus provided for him by Erwin Goldschmidt. Hill was equally keen to succeed, despite his 375 MM, a well-used car that had first raced 18 months earlier, showing its age and having a top speed a good 20mph slower than Maglioli's car. The anticipated battle unfolded over eight stages. As Hill's Ferrari was more agile, he gained time in the mountains only to lose it on the plains. At the finish, after 1,907 arduous miles, Maglioli was 24 minutes 24 seconds ahead of the driver nicknamed 'El Batallador' by the local press.

'I look for fighters,' Chinetti was used to saying and he had found one. When news of Hill's performance reached Maranello, Enzo Ferrari took notice as well. At *Il Commendatore*'s request, Hill, who had already met Mr Ferrari a year earlier, went to Maranello in the spring of 1955, accompanied by Ginther. In *Automobile Quarterly*, Hill spoke at length about the visit, which marked the start of a long relationship between the two men.

He grew tired of waiting in one of 'those gloomy offices' before Mr Ferrari condescended to see him and felt himself gradually invaded by feelings of insignificance as the time dragged on. When Ferrari, patronising and full of himself as usual, finally received him, Hill was, he admitted, 'at the peak of my discomfort', a feeling that was just as strong when he was offered a drive at the forthcoming Le Mans. As he had received a proposal from Cunningham and was in discussion with Guiberson about more races, Hill did not blurt out the eager 'yes' that Ferrari felt entitled to hear. It was obvious that his hesitant affirmation disappointed *Il Commendatore*. But even though Hill admitted that he felt a certain admiration for the 'Lord' of Maranello, he was not ready to sacrifice himself.

Hill said about the years that followed: 'I learned that Ferrari was satisfied with no less than one hundred percent enthusiasm from his drivers all the time, no matter what the circumstances.'

'What do you think of our great protagonist?' Ferrari asked him, speaking of Maglioli and his performance in the recent Panamericana. Hill said he was 'just fine'. It was the answer Ferrari had been waiting to hear and he offered him the role of Maglioli's co-driver at Le Mans. Phil accepted: 'Oh… Oh that would be great. That would be fine. I look forward to it.' With the deal sealed, Enzo gave him a tour of the factory, where he was invited to see 'the great cars you will be driving'.

When they were visiting the test bed, an enthusiastic Ferrari wanted Hill to share his admiration for an in-line six-cylinder four-cam engine. Hill, who was well used to Jaguar's straight-six, thought this nothing to make a song and dance about and, after a long period of reflection, his answer of 'very good' seemed to be far from satisfactory, judging by the way Ferrari, almost swooning in front of his creation, reacted to the comment. That was all it took to impose a misunderstanding between them that lasted throughout the eight years they worked together. At that time, in 1955, the two men did not have the same reference points. Ferrari never travelled far from Maranello and all he really knew about the North American scene had come from drivers he respected who had raced there, such as Alberto Ascari, who had competed in the Panamericana and the Indy 500, and Piero Taruffi, winner of the 1951 Panamericana with Chinetti. The only event that Hill could even vaguely compare to Le Mans was the 12 Hours of Sebring, which had also been a round of the World Sports Cars Championship since its inception two years earlier. This ignorance also extended to American drivers other than those whom Chinetti promoted in Maranello. It was true, of course, that in Europe Enzo Ferrari had a pool of talent from which he could pick and choose as the fancy took him.

His first official Ferrari experience

At Le Mans in 1955, Hill and Maglioli were lying fourth when the tragic accident occurred, then moved up to third

Luigi Chinetti is seen at the start of the 1953 Carrera Panamericana in which he shared a Ferrari 375 MM Vignale with Alfonso de Portago. The three-time Le Mans winner, NART founder and US Ferrari importer played a crucial role in the early days of Phil Hill's career.

In 1955, Umberto Maglioli is all smiles but Phil Hill looks a little glum prior to Le Mans, where they shared a Ferrari 121 LM. They were in fourth place at the time of the tragedy and retired during the evening when third.

◄ Having just won the 1956 Swedish Grand Prix at the wheel of a Ferrari 290 MM, Phil Hill and Maurice Trintignant share their joy. The Frenchman, victorious at Le Mans in 1954 and in the Monaco Grand Prix in 1955, was always quick while keeping something in reserve, so he was a good example to follow.

▼ After winning the 1958 Buenos Aires 1,000Km, Phil Hill and Peter Collins raced together once more at Sebring, where they are pictured, and again tasted victory at the wheel of a 250 TR. Collins's career was tragically cut short in its prime at the Nürburgring later in the year.

before clutch failure brought their race to a halt after five hours. The American's first official outing did nothing to boost his reputation in Maranello even though at the beginning of the season in the 12 Hours of Sebring he and Carroll Shelby had finished second in their 750 Monza behind the winning D-type Jaguar of Mike Hawthorn/Phil Walters after protests following a confused finish. However, this subdued start mattered little because by 1956 Hill was among a very large — even excessive — number of Ferrari works drivers: besides Juan Manuel Fangio, whom Hill revered as a god, he could measure himself against some ten team-mates over the season, including Italians Eugenio Castellotti and Luigi Musso, Germans Wolfgang von Trips and Hans Herrmann, Spaniard Alfonso de Portago, Frenchmen Maurice Trintignant, André Simon and Robert Manzon, Englishman Peter Collins and Belgian Olivier Gendebien. Among this 'foreign legion' managed by Eraldo Sculati, certain links began to be forged.

Quite soon, Gendebien and Trintignant began to stand out and it was with them that Hill started to build a very solid set of results in endurance races in 1956, taking second place in the Buenos Aires 1,000Km with Gendebien and victory in the Swedish Grand Prix with Trintignant. In 1957, which saw Fangio depart to his first love, Maserati, and Hawthorn arrive, as well bringing the tragic deaths of Castellotti and de Portago, Hill started to develop a good partnership with Collins, the pair finishing second in the Swedish Grand Prix and then winning the Venezuelan Grand Prix. Driving the new 250 Testa Rossa, they got off to a scintillating start in 1958 with two major early-season victories in quick succession in the Buenos Aires 1,000Km and the 12 Hours of Sebring.

In Formula 1, Collins was not quite as fast as Hawthorn but he was more consistent and had become a benchmark. When he arrived at Ferrari in 1956, his first four Grands Prix brought two wins (Spa and Reims) and two shared second places (Monaco and Silverstone), a splendid sequence of results that might have helped him to become World Champion had he not done as requested at Monza and handed over his car to Fangio. The following year there was little he could do in Formula 1 with an uncompetitive car but endurance racing enabled him to avoid a winless season and begin 1958 in style.

The reliable benchmark

Collins was overshadowed by his 'ami mate' and accomplice Hawthorn from the start of the 1958 season and was also occasionally slower than Musso, but for Hill in endurance racing Collins was the reliable benchmark against whom he could measure himself. In practice for that year's Buenos Aires 1,000Km, the American got round in 3m 27.5s compared with 3m 32.0s for Collins and in the closing stages of the race he set a new lap record at 3m 25.9s. Of course, this was not the same as achieving such superiority in a single-seater but it was always better to be quicker than one's team-mate.

Whether or not it was a consequence, Hill was allowed to test a Dino 246 in practice for the following weekend's non-championship Buenos Aires Grand Prix, which was to be run in two heats with von Trips competing in the first and Hill the second. On Friday he was surprised by the nimbleness of a car with which he was still getting to grips: 'After you handle a GP machine, a sports car seems rather clumsy and sluggish,' he told William F. Nolan. On Saturday he equalled von Trips's performance. But that was as far as it went. The German crashed in the first heat and had to retire, so Hill never got to race. It was not the first time his hopes of participating in a Grand Prix had been dashed as he had made a brief appearance in practice at Reims the previous year before being called in.

Hill felt all the more frustrated because he reckoned he had been fully up to the task of driving a Formula 1 car for at least two seasons and felt that Enzo Ferrari, who always liked playing the field with his drivers, had not been honouring his oft-repeated promises to give him the opportunity he wanted so badly and was certainly warranted by his successes in endurance events. This was highlighted in particular at Le Mans a few months later when Hill won in extreme conditions created by, in the words of Christian Moity, 'the most insane downpour on a track that had had more than its fair share of showers and tornados', playing his part flawlessly alongside team-mate Gendebien. But even this brilliant success seemed to change nothing.

Knowing that it would attract the ire of *Il Commendatore*, Hill jumped at Jo Bonnier's offer to drive one of his Maserati 250Fs in the upcoming Grand Prix de l'ACF. Ferrari team manager Romolo Tavoni went ballistic when he found out and threatened to throw the American out of the Scuderia if he raced against his own team. But Hill held firm: his intention was not to pose a threat to Ferrari but to show what he was capable of doing. A well-deserved seventh place in the two-year-old car rewarded his audacity. As Musso's death in the race left a seat vacant, Hill was given a Formula 2 Dino in the German Grand Prix at the Nürburgring, where another Ferrari fatality, that of Collins, led to Hill's elevation to become a permanent member of the Formula 1 driver line-up.

He took part in the last two Grands Prix of the year, in Italy and Morocco, when the outcome of the World Championship assumed maximum importance because Ferrari's Hawthorn and Vanwall's Moss were battling for the title. At the finale in Casablanca, he played the role of supportive team-mate by ceding his second place to Hawthorn so that the blond Englishman could be crowned champion.

Making his mark

The Scuderia was badly hit by the deaths of Musso and Collins while Hawthorn's decision to retire was another blow. In terms of his results, Hill looked the obvious choice to spearhead the Italian team's attack in 1959. If he was dreaming about this, he was soon brought back to earth. Tony Brooks, who had been somewhat overshadowed by Moss at Vanwall, became available after the British team's withdrawal and arrived at Maranello with fellow Englishman Cliff Allison, Belgian Olivier Gendebien, Frenchman Jean Behra and American Dan Gurney. They were joined when the time was right by German Wolfgang von Trips plus Italians Giulio Cabianca, Giorgio Scarlatti and Ludovico Scarfiotti.

Right from the start Hill lived up to his growing reputation by winning the 12 Hours of Sebring for the second time in a row. It was a collective victory as he shared it with Gendebien, Gurney and Chuck Daigh, but a fully deserved one after a brilliant display at the height of a storm redolent of Le

Mans. It turned out to be his only endurance success of the season as his car then let him down four times, notably at Le Mans when leading with Gendebien, allied to Ferrari's inability to counter the ambitions of other manufacturers, particularly Aston Martin, which won three World Sports Car Championship races out of five, but also Porsche.

In Formula 1, he made an indifferent start to the season while finding his feet, finishing fourth in Monaco after three spins and sixth in the Netherlands, but he found renewed form at Reims. On a high-speed circuit where the Ferraris were in their element, he followed Brooks home to give the Scuderia a decisive 1–2 in a race run in such roasting heat that he had to be helped from his cockpit afterwards, while third-placed Jack Brabham suffered even more severely and collapsed after climbing out of his Cooper. Doubts about his ability to be a real Grand Prix driver had assailed Hill after Monaco but this fine result in France quelled them. And even if a few worries still lurked, his third and second places in Germany and Italy were enough to banish them for good. In contrast, the first United States Grand Prix held at Sebring — truly a home race for him — was a source of frustration as his three team-mates, including von Trips making a return from Porsche, out-qualified him and his race ended early with clutch failure. Still, his season overall, after producing both consolation and disappointment, yielded fourth place in the World Championship, behind champion Brabham and third-placed Moss in their rear-engined Coopers, and team-mate Brooks in second place after two victories.

➤ When finally allowed to make his Formula 1 début with the Scuderia, Hill did so with panache, at the wheel of a Dino 246 at the 1958 Italian Grand Prix. Pictured venturing out for practice, he qualified seventh, dramatically snatched the lead at the start, set the fastest lap of the race and came home third.

➤ Hard at work at Reims accelerating out of *Thillois* in his ill-handling Dino 246, Hill finished second in the 1959 Grand Prix de l'ACF behind Ferrari team-mate Tony Brooks.

The frontal appearance of the Ferrari 156 earned it the 'Sharknose' nickname. Here at the Dutch Grand Prix, Phil Hill finished second in #1 just behind team-mate Wolfgang von Trips.

1961
TRIUMPH AND TRAGEDY

During his press conference on Monday 13th February 1961, Enzo Ferrari provided more proof that the rear-mounted engine had finally conquered his doubts. But before discovering which doubts, it would be useful to immerse oneself in the ambience of that time. What follows, written by Gérard Crombac in *Sport Auto* a year later, gives great insight into the cult status that Ferrari enjoyed: 'The star of the day was the *Commendatore* himself. Enzo, immaculately dressed in a green loden overcoat, walked — strutted almost — among the journalists and behind his glasses his keen eyes didn't miss a thing. He went from group to group registering the reactions on the faces, dispensing paternal greetings here and there. A small court buzzed around him soliciting a statement, an attitude to be photographed, a friendly gesture. Occasionally, he stopped and people crowded around him as, in a loud voice, he gave his opinion on a technical point, a race rule or an item of sporting policy. While he has often been criticised, it should be acknowledged that only a character as strong and as single-minded as his could be the driving force behind an organisation as go-ahead as it is productive.'

The 'Sharknose'

The Formula 1 chassis was redesigned and lightened compared with the Formula 2 version that had won the Solitude Grand Prix in 1960 and its coil-spring suspension was inspired by that

of its rivals, Lotus and Cooper. In addition, to ensure victory everywhere, the team could rely on two types of V6 engine that were mainly the work of chief engineer Carlo Chiti. The first was the previous year's version with a 65-degree vee angle and two valves per cylinder, and with power output announced as 180bhp. Its flexibility made it the right weapon for low/medium-speed circuits such as Monaco, Zandvoort and the Nürburgring. The second, with a 120-degree vee angle, was completely new. Its lowered centre of gravity and extra 10bhp meant that it was ideal for high-speed tracks like Spa, Reims and Monza.

Compared with its rivals, Ferrari thus had an abundance of resources at its disposal, enhanced by a power advantage — with either engine — because Cooper and Lotus, using Coventry Climax engines, had to make do with the 1960 four-cylinder Formula 2 unit while awaiting the V8 expected mid-season. BRM was in the same boat as its in-house V8 was still in the development phase. And Porsche also had to embark on the season with its four-cylinder boxer engine while its engineers readied an eight-cylinder version.

Another important aspect of the new Formula 1 Ferrari was that it had a non-synchromesh five-speed gearbox that was, in the words of Phil Hill, 'astoundingly easy to shift'.

Was the Ferrari's very streamlined nose with its two distinct air intakes the result of a search for efficacy or just for aesthetic reasons? In any case, the design earned the 156 the nickname 'Sharknose'. Just a reminder: historically speaking there was nothing new about this configuration as the ephemeral Sacha-

◄ Ferrari 156s raced in 1961 with two versions of the 1.5-litre V6 engine, the newer unit with 120-degree vee angle providing more power than the older 65-degree type. This car, as driven to victory by Giancarlo Baghetti in the 1961 Syracuse Grand Prix, has the 65-degree engine.

➤ The cut-off Kamm tail, named after German aerodynamicist Wunibald Kamm, was used by Ferrari to good effect. The rear of the 250 TRI 61 in which Olivier Gendebien/Phil Hill won the 1961 Le Mans 24 Hours is a perfect illustration of its application.

Gordine and a version of the Maserati 250F had both used comparable designs. Another sign that Maranello had not completely broken with its past was that the cars were still fitted with Borrani wire wheels.

Faithful to Kamm's theories

In the presentation of new sports cars, the about-turn in Ferrari's thinking was even more pronounced. As with the single-seater's 1.5-litre V6, the 2.4-litre version was installed in the mid-engined position in a tubular chassis with bodywork by Fantuzzi. While the twin-nostril front end was obviously inspired by the Formula 1 car, the design of the rear remained faithful to Kamm's theories as it was cut off and topped with a lateral spoiler. However, according to Ferrari the expected benefits of a reduction in aerodynamic drag calculated in the wind tunnel had not yet been translated onto the track. But without anticipating the future, what really underlined the novelty for Ferrari was the aluminium strip (later known as a spoiler) mounted on the top edge of the engine cover. According to in-house test driver Richie Ginther, who had come over from California for the press launch, it was the only tweak that Chiti and Fantuzzi could find to prevent the rear of the 246 SP from going light and wandering all over the road in corners.

But the revolution was still a partial one as Maranello persevered with the front-engined Testa Rossa (250 TRI 61). The power of its 3-litre V12 (300bhp at 7,500rpm against 266bhp at 8,000rpm for the Dino 246) could make a big difference depending on the nature of the circuit — Le Mans for example. It turned out to be the right decision.

And what about Ferrari's rivals? Maserati did not commit to a works entry and relied on private teams to fight on with the *Tipo 60s* and *Tipo 61s* and, above all, two mid-engined *Tipo 63s* with, for the moment, the four-cylinder motor bored out to 3 litres until the in-house V12 was ready. And finally, Porsche announced the imminent arrival of new 718 RS coupés and spyders powered by a 2-litre flat-eight engine.

So, the Scuderia looked to have all the necessary firepower for the World Sports Car Championship, which was dying on its feet because, for subsequent years, only Grand Touring cars would be eligible to compete for the ultimate prize. This decision delighted Ferrari and led to uproar elsewhere because it was basically an unbidden gift to the Italian manufacturer, whose GTs were dominant. Ferrari's only likely rivals would be Aston Martin, which was counting on Italian coachbuilder Zagato to lighten and beef up the underpowered DB4 GT, and Jaguar, whose new E-type, launched early in 1961, immediately showed promise even if the company hesitated about becoming involved on a works basis.

As for drivers, Enzo Ferrari put his confidence in Phil Hill, Wolfgang von Trips and Richie Ginther for the single-seaters, and Olivier Gendebien and Willy Mairesse — whose skills as a test driver were much valued — for endurance events.

'As per usual'

Sebring 12 Hours, 25th March

'As per usual' wrote Christian Moity about Phil Hill and his sidekick Olivier Gendebien's victory in the 12 Hours of Sebring, the first World Sports Car Championship event of the season. It was the pair's second victory together in Florida and Hill's third. But while Maranello was again able to count on the speed and long-distance racing intelligence of a duo who usually waited for rivals to fall by the wayside, this time they clinched victory after a white-knuckle gamble in their works 250 TRI 61.

There were two other works Ferraris at Sebring, the Giancarlo Baghetti/Willy Mairesse 250 TRI 60 and the Richie Ginther/ Wolfgang von Trips 246 SP, backed up by an armada of privateer entries. They faced strong opposition from Maserati, including two cars entered by Camoradi for Stirling Moss/Graham Hill (*Tipo* 61) and Masten Gregory/ 'Lucky' Casner (*Tipo* 63). Porsche, although not a likely contender for outright victory, was represented by two works 718 RS 61s entrusted to Hans Herrmann/Edgar Barth and Jo Bonnier/Dan Gurney, plus the usual posse of spyders run by privateers.

The impetuous, fiery, talented Gregory in his *Tipo* 63 hit the front right from the start while Moss fluffed his getaway as his battery failed. After three laps, Gregory gave way to pressure from Pedro Rodríguez in his NART-entered 250 TR 59/60. Phil Hill, remaining faithful to his usual strategy of not upping the pace until half distance, moved over to let Ginther's 246 SP through into third place. Richie was hell-bent on catching Rodríguez, who was unable to fend off the little Californian's incisive attacks, and at midday, two hours into the race, the 246 SP was in front with the Rodríguez car, now driven by younger brother Ricardo, hot on its tail.

By half distance, the Mexican brothers had built up a two-lap lead over Hill/Gendebien, who began to ask themselves if their wait-and-see strategy was the right one. Then their #61 fell even further behind due to a calamitous refuelling stop. Several victory contenders had already quit: Graham Hill's *Tipo* 61 Maserati joined the dead car park after a blown exhaust while Moss, called on to back up Gregory/Casner in the *Tipo* 63, had been forced to retire with suspension failure. In the Ferrari camp, von Trips had crashed out due to broken steering, damaging the 246 SP beyond immediate repair. Team manager Romolo Tavoni, always a dab hand when it came to reshuffling driver line-ups, assigned von Trips and Ginther to lend a hand to Baghetti and Mairesse. While at that moment not all the Maseratis had dropped out, it was only a matter of time before all but one of them did, the exception being the *Tipo* 60 of Briggs Cunningham/Bill Kimberly/Walt Hansgen that

SEBRING 12 HOURS

Sebring, 25th March 1961, 210 laps (5.200 miles/8.369km), 1,081.600 miles/1,740.666km • Starters 65, classified finishers 35

1st	Phil Hill/Olivier Gendebien	**Ferrari 250 TRI 61 (0792 TR)**	**12h 02m 11.01s**
2nd	Giancarlo Baghetti/Willy Mairesse/Richie Ginther/Wolfgang von Trips	**Ferrari 250 TRI 60 (0780 TR)**	**208 laps**
3rd	Pedro Rodríguez/Ricardo Rodríguez	Ferrari 250 TR 59/60 (0746 TR)	207 laps
4th	Hap Sharp/Ronnie Hissom	Ferrari 250 TR 59 (0766 TR)	203 laps
5th	Bob Holbert/Roger Penske	Porsche 718 RS 61	199 laps
6th	Jim Hall/George Constantine	Ferrari Dino 246 S (0778)	199 laps
8th	George Reed/Bill Sturgis	Ferrari 250 TR 59/60 (0770 TR)	196 laps
10th	Denise McCluggage/Allen Eager	Ferrari 250 GT SWB (1931 GT)	183 laps
12th	Gaston Andrey/Allen Newman/Robert Publicker	Ferrari 250 GT California	180 laps
18th	William Helburn/Skip Hudson/John Fulp	Ferrari Dino 196 S (0776)	173 laps
DNF	Ed Hugus/Alan Connell	Ferrari Dino 246 S (0784)	– (transmission)
DNF	Fernand Tavano/George Arents	Ferrari 250 GT SWB (2455 GT)	– (differential)
DNF	**Richie Ginther/Wolfgang von Trips**	**Ferrari 246 SP (0790)**	**– (steering arm)**
DNF	Pete Lovely/Jack Nethercutt	Ferrari 250 TR 59 (0768 TR)	– (oil pump)

Fastest race lap: Stirling Moss (Maserati Tipo 61), 3m 13.2s, 96.894mph/155.936kph **Winner's average speed:** 89.860mph/144.617kph
FIA World Sports Car Championship:[1] 1st Ferrari 8, 2nd Porsche 2

[1] Scoring system for the top six places was 8–6–4–3–2–1; only the manufacturer's highest-placed car scored points

➤ **Sebring 12 Hours.** Phil Hill and Olivier Gendebien got the 1961 season off to a fine start at Sebring by leading home a works Ferrari 1–2 in their 250 TRI 61, now with revised bodywork, including front grille, that gave it a very similar look to the new 246 SP.

▼ **Sebring 12 Hours.** The 250 TR 59/60 driven by the Rodríguez brothers dated from 1958 and had already accumulated its fair share of miles. It was a thorn in the side of the works cars, taking the lead on a few occasions. Despite problems with the electrics and probably brake issues as well, it finished third. Here, Ricardo is at the wheel, having just lapped a Lola Mk1 driven by Charles Kurtz/Millard Ripley.

came home in 19th place. Neither of the works Porsches saw the chequered flag.

Wisdom rewarded? Lucky intervention from the hand of fate? Whatever. Just before 7pm the NART Ferrari pitted with no electrics and fading brakes: the 20-minute stop seemed interminable. Phil Hill seized his chance and went for it. Setting the second-fastest lap of the race in 3m 13.8s (rather slower than Moss's best of 3m 12.2s), he installed himself in the lead. At 10pm, Hill and Gendebien clinched their second Sebring win in front of the sister works car of Baghetti/Mairesse/Ginther/von Trips. But it was third-placed Pedro and Ricardo Rodríguez, a lap behind, who captured the hearts of the public.

A spat between friends

Targa Florio, 30th April

A month after the Florida walkover, Ferrari tackled the Targa Florio in a very relaxed state of mind. Having pushed back the first Porsche at Sebring to fifth place, Ferrari already enjoyed a big lead over the German manufacturer in the World Sports Car Championship. So, in the light of past results the Sicilian event did not look as if it would overly shake up the existing hierarchy.

After 10 laps of the *Piccolo Circuito delle Madonie*, victory for the Wolfgang von Trips/Olivier Gendebien 246 SP added a further eight points to Maranello's tally. But it had not been an easy task as a quick look at the list of retirements showed: they included the works Ferraris of Phil Hill/Richie Ginther (246 SP) and Ricardo Rodríguez/Willy Mairesse (250 TRI 61).

The Porsche RS 61s were known to be quick and reliable in the Sicilian twists and turns, an environment that did not suit the Maserati *Tipo* 63s, and the podium was duly completed by two German cars driven by Jo Bonnier/Dan Gurney and Hans Herrmann/Edgar Barth. Two Maseratis followed in the hands of Nino Vaccarella/Maurice Trintignant and Umberto Maglioli/Giorgio Scarlatti, with another Porsche, the 356 B Carrera Abarth of Paul Ernst Strähle/Antonio Pucci, sixth.

The classification would have had a very different look if Stirling Moss, superbly supported by Graham Hill, had not been let down by his Porsche's transmission a few miles from the finish, while he was repelling the assaults of von Trips in maximum attack mode. Even more so if Gendebien, Hill's teammate, had not decided at the start to race with von Trips rather than with his usual partner at the wheel of their new 246 SP. Hill was not at all happy with this sudden change even though it was based on the strategy decided before the start: namely, that in case of a breakdown in the early stages of the race, the Florida

◀ **Targa Florio.** The master and one of racing's most gifted youngsters — Stirling Moss and Ricardo Rodríguez — crossed swords in Sicily. Rodríguez retired his Ferrari because of a punctured radiator while broken transmission ended Moss's race in his Porsche.

⌃ **Targa Florio.** Olivier Gendebien at the wheel of the 246 SP in which he won with Wolfgang von Trips. It was his second victory in the Sicilian classic, his first having come in 1958 with Luigi Musso.

➤ **Targa Florio.** With cars started at intervals, the 'hares' often stumbled over the 'tortoises', as seen here with Wolfgang von Trips's #162 246 SP and Ricardo Rodríguez's 250 TRI 61 sandwiching the Fiat 8V Zagato of Sergio Mantia/ Giovanni Napoli.

⌃ Targa Florio. Wolfgang von Trips's Ferrari scorecard in the Sicilian classic read as follows: third in 1958 (in a 250 TR with Mike Hawthorn), second in 1960 (in a Dino 246 S with Phil Hill), first in 1961.

⌃ Targa Florio. Just after the finish, a delighted Olivier Gendebien hops into the winning Ferrari to join Wolfgang von Trips.

TARGA FLORIO

Piccolo Madonie, 30th April 1961, 10 laps (44.7 miles/72.0km), 447.4 miles/720.0km • Starters 54, classified finishers 19

1st	Wolfgang von Trips/Olivier Gendebien	Ferrari 246 SP (0790)	6h 57m 39.4s
2nd	Jo Bonnier/Dan Gurney	Porsche 718 RS 61	7h 02m 03.2s
3rd	Hans Herrmann/Edgar Barth	Porsche 718 RS 61	7h 14m 14.0s
4th	Nino Vaccarella/Maurice Trintignant	Maserati Tipo 63	7h 28m 49.6s
5th	Umberto Maglioli/Giorgio Scarlatti	Maserati Tipo 63	7h 40m 04.2s
6th	Paul Ernst Strähle/Antonio Pucci	Porsche 356R Carrera Abarth GTL	7h 48m 25.8s
NC	Pietro Ferraro/Armando Zampiero	Ferrari 250 GT SWB (1813 GT)	10 laps
NC	Giuseppe Gasso/Giovanni Giordano	Ferrari 250 GT LWB	10 laps
DNF	Ricardo Rodríguez/Willy Mairesse	Ferrari 250 TRI 61 (0780 TR)	3 laps (fuel tank)
DNF	Phil Hill/Richie Ginther	Ferrari 246 SP (0796)	0 laps (accident)

Fastest race lap: von Trips, 40m 03.4s, 67.013mph/107.847kph **Winner's average speed:** 64.270mph/103.433kph

FIA World Sports Car Championship: 1st Ferrari 16, 2nd Porsche 8, 3rd Maserati 3

winners could fall back on the 246 SP of Ginther and von Trips. This was a risk that Gendebien, who was supposed to do the first stint, was not prepared to take.

With cars starting in numerical order at intervals, a visibly edgy Hill (#164) roared off in pursuit of von Trips (#162) and Rodríguez (#160). He caught von Trips near Bivio Polizzi and tried to muscle his way past, rightly judging that he was being held up. The result was contact and a spin that ended with Hill's car pointing the wrong way. Helped by a handful of spectators, Hill was soon turned around and shot off after von Trips, whom he sliced past without difficulty before setting off after Rodríguez. He overtook the Mexican near Collesano after some 35 miles of pedal-to-metal motoring. But that was as far as he got. In the downhill section leading towards Campofelice, Hill came into a corner far too quickly, shot off the road and slammed into a wall, inflicting terminal damage on his 246 SP. It was a rare — very rare — accident in his career, but it occurred just as von Trips was stunning everybody with his own performance.

Did this episode leave a grudge between the two men for the rest of the season? Obviously, it is easy to speculate when one knows what happened afterwards. Even so, it is worthwhile posing the question in the light of what was to follow.

On the last lap, von Trips set a new record in 40m 3.25s, a time that he himself did not think he was capable of achieving. Asked before the start by Raymond Miomandre from *L'Automobile* about the kind of times he was hoping to set, he had declared: 'It's impossible to lap in under 41 minutes. As for getting near the 40-minute barrier, only one of us can do it — Stirling Moss!'

One against three

Monaco Grand Prix, 14th May

Two weeks later the glittering Principality of Monaco was the theatre for the first World Championship Grand Prix of 1961. A major shake-up in the sporting regulations awaited the teams as the organisers this year fixed the number of starters at 16, wishing to minimise risk on this short and tightly confined circuit. The 16 would comprise 12 invited drivers plus four selected from the other 12 on the entry list according to their practice times. Ferrari's abundance of resources meant that it could afford to mix its options, so Richie Ginther — one of those who had to qualify — had a 120-degree V6 while Phil Hill and Wolfgang von Trips used 65-degree versions.

Stirling Moss in his Lotus 18 with four-cylinder Coventry Climax power was in scintillating form and set the pace in the three practice sessions, taking pole position with a time of 1m 39.1s. Of course, practice and the race were very different challenges, but on Saturday evening the grid line-up gave cause for reflection: would Jim Clark, quickest in the first session before wrecking his car, thereby eliminating himself from the second and third sessions, have knocked Moss off pole if he had had the chance? As it was, Clark's time (1m 39.6s) placed him third, with Ginther (1m 39.3s) between the Lotuses on the front row, the Ferrari's engine advantage not having made the expected difference. Better things had also been hoped for from Phil Hill and Wolfgang von Trips, who set the same time (1m 39.8s) to take up fifth and sixth positions on the grid after Graham Hill's BRM.

◄ Monaco Grand Prix. Jim Clark is captured having his first look at Ferrari's challenger for the new 1.5-litre Formula 1 era. The #36 car is Richie Ginther's while behind it Wolfgang von Trips is seated in his #40. Among the bystanders is Ferrari chief engineer Carlo Chiti (white shirt and tie), lost in conversation.

► Monaco Grand Prix. In 1960, Richie Ginther created a major surprise in the Principality when he drove the first rear-engined single-seater Ferrari. For the 1961 race, he was the first to be given a 120-degree V6 in his Ferrari 156, which he manhandles round the *Gazomètre* hairpin during practice.

► Monaco Grand Prix. Phil Hill (#38) and Richie Ginther (#36) occupy second and third places behind Stirling Moss's winning Lotus. They ran like this between laps 41 to 59 before switching positions. Jo Bonnier's Porsche follows.

▲ **Monaco Grand Prix.** Wolfgang von Trips started from the third row of the grid and was never really in the hunt due to a sluggish 65-degree engine. Seen at the *Gazomètre* hairpin during practice, he finished fourth, two laps behind the winner.

◄ **Monaco Grand Prix.** Richie Ginther started the race on the front row and led for the first 13 laps. Here, visibly exhausted, he has just finished a heroic drive to second place behind the uncatchable Stirling Moss.

MONACO GRAND PRIX

Monaco, 14th May 1961, 100 laps (1.954 miles/3.145km), 195.4 miles/314.5km • Starters 16, finishers 13

RACE				PRACTICE	
1st	Stirling Moss	Lotus 18 Climax S4	2h 45m 50.1s	1st	1m 39.1s
2nd	**Richie Ginther**	**Ferrari 156 V6 120°**	**+03.6s**	**2nd**	**1m 39.3s**
3rd	**Phil Hill**	**Ferrari 156 V6 65°**	**+41.3s**	**5th**	**1m 39.8s**
4th	**Wolfgang von Trips**	**Ferrari 156 V6 65°**	**98 laps**	**6th**	**1m 39.8s**
5th	Dan Gurney	Porsche 718 F4	98 laps	10th	1m 40.6s
6th	Bruce McLaren	Cooper T55 Climax S4	95 laps	7th	1m 39.8s

Pole position: Moss, 1m 39.1s, 70.990mph/114.248kph **Fastest race lap:** Ginther & Moss, 1m 36.3s, 73.055mph/117.570kph
Winner's average speed: 70.704mph/113.787kph **Drivers' championship:**[1] 1st Moss 9, 2nd Ginther 6, 3rd Phil Hill 4, 4th von Trips 3
Constructors' championship:[2] 1st Lotus-Climax 8, 2nd Ferrari 6, 3rd Porsche 2

[1] Scoring system for the top six places was 9–6–4–3–2–1 [2] Scoring system for the top six places was 8–6–4–3–2–1; only the manufacturer's highest-placed car scored points

Ginther led the pack into the *Gazomètre* hairpin and managed to fend off Moss until lap 14, when the Englishman took the lead despite his engine having a power deficit of around 20bhp. He would stay in front until the chequered flag. Was it a breeze? No way. He had to spend the next 86 laps repelling attacks from different drivers glued to his gearbox, starting with Jo Bonnier (Porsche), who got past Ginther at the same time as Moss. Phil Hill then displaced Bonnier on lap 26, having climbed from seventh place on lap 1 and getting the better of Ginther on lap 24. Determined to close the gap to the dark blue Lotus with its white noseband, Hill's deficit was 10 seconds by lap 40, with Ginther fourth behind the Porsche after a brief skirmish with von Trips in fifth place. A lap later, Ginther got past Bonnier and now the two Ferraris homed in on Moss together with the Porsche in their wake.

By lap 45, this trio of pursuers was eight seconds behind the Lotus, then seven seconds at lap 50 (half distance), then five seconds at lap 60, with Moss having to draw upon all of his talent. Suddenly Bonnier was seen walking back to his pit as his Porsche's carburation had gone on the blink, leaving the two Ferraris on their own to challenge Moss. The next 10 laps were a mirror image of the previous ones except that Hill was now under pressure from Ginther and beginning to tire as he strove to keep the gap to Moss from widening again. 'I was starting to have carburation problems,' stated Hill, and his Ferrari was also running out of brakes. When the gap started to stretch, from five to six-and-a-half seconds, he signalled that he no longer felt able to influence the outcome of the race and let Ginther past on lap 65 for his turn to have a go.

Ginther gave it his all in a final desperate charge in the last quarter of the race to get within overtaking distance of Moss.

Not enough superlatives exist to describe Stirling's ease and talent behind the wheel that day as he put in a drive that would go down in the annals. On lap 80, the Lotus's advantage was still much the same, six seconds, but Ginther kept at it and set his fastest lap of the race so far on lap 84 in 1m 36.3s. On the following lap, Moss equalled his time; Richie's pugnacity was matched by Stirling's steely determination. By lap 96, with just four laps to go, they were separated by four-and-a-half seconds, and by the finish the gap was just 3.6 seconds. Suddenly time and history stood still! Moss and Ginther had both driven the races of their lives. The other two Ferraris came home next, Hill in third place and von Trips, who had been handicapped by throttle problems, a very distant fourth, two laps down.

In 'Monogasque Murmurs' (*sic*), Denis Jenkinson's short tailpiece to his race report in *Motor Sport*, he posed the question: 'Who is Paul Ritchie Ginther?' His answer took up four lines: 'He rode as passenger to Phil Hill in a 4.1-litre Ferrari in the Mexican road race when they chased Maglioli in the works 4.9-litre Ferrari in 1954, and has been test driving for the Scuderia Ferrari for 12 months.'

Crushing domination

Dutch Grand Prix, 22nd May

Less than a week later, the Zandvoort sand dunes replaced the winding Monaco streets for the first practice session of the Dutch Grand Prix, which was scheduled to be held on Monday. If the late arrival of the transporter from Maranello meant that Ferrari's rivals had the track to themselves early on, their respite

 **▲ Dutch Grand Prix.** Wolfgang von Trips leads Phil Hill. Apart from Jim Clark occasionally poking his nose in between them, the German driver's advantage was always slender and he won by less than a second.

➤ Dutch Grand Prix. Richie Ginther started on the front row and spent more than half the race sandwiched between Jim Clark and Stirling Moss, but the latter slipped past on the very last lap to relegate the Ferrari driver to fifth place.

◄ **Nürburgring 1,000Km.** Marie-Claire Gendebien checks a time she has just clocked under the watchful eye of her husband; Romolo Tavoni makes notes, his paperwork resting on the tail of the #4 246 SP; Ricardo Rodríguez and Richie Ginther look on, frozen to the bone.

◄ **Nürburgring 1,000Km.** The echelon start, with the cars lined up in the order of practice times, shows the main protagonists in the hours to come: #4 Richie Ginther/ Olivier Gendebien Ferrari 246 SP; #20 Stirling Moss/Graham Hill Porsche RS 61; #3 Phil Hill/ Wolfgang von Trips Ferrari 246 SP; #21 Jo Bonnier/Dan Gurney Porsche RS 61; #1 Masten Gregory/'Lucky' Casner Maserati Tipo 61; #23 Hans Herrmann/ Edgar Barth Porsche RS 61; #60 Willy Mairesse/Giancarlo Baghetti Ferrari 250 GT SWB; #11 Jim Clark/Bruce McLaren Aston Martin DBR1-300; and #5 Pedro Rodríguez/Ricardo Rodríguez Ferrari 250 TRI 61.

➤ **Nürburgring 1,000Km.**
Richie Ginther drives towards third place in the 246 SP he shared with Olivier Gendebien; Wolfgang von Trips gave them a helping hand after his car's retirement.

➤ **Nürburgring 1,000Km.**
Legends in racing are forged on results and derring-do. While the careers of the Rodríguez brothers were cruelly and prematurely cut short, especially in Ricardo's case, both certainly made their mark. Right at the end of the Nürburgring race, Pedro's 250 TRI 61 broke a front wheel halfway round the circuit, but he still got the car back to the pits despite its sorry state before resuming to confirm second place.

with an ever-brisker sequence of laps that ran 9m 25.9s (lap 5), 9m 22.2s (lap 6), 9m 18.4s (lap 7) and 9m 15.8s (lap 8), all of which were far quicker than Moss's sports car record of 9m 33.7s from the previous year. So great was his advantage by lap 10, when he pitted for refuelling and handover to von Trips, that the German was able to resume without losing the lead. By the time the pattern of the race had settled down after all the pitstops, the Ginther/Gendebien car was second, followed by Casner's Maserati, Graham Hill's Porsche, the Rodríguez Ferrari, Maglioli's Maserati and McLaren's Aston Martin.

On lap 16, rain began to fall and quickly turned to sleet and snow, but von Trips took to the dreadful wintry conditions like the proverbial duck to water. When Graham Hill pitted early in the Porsche, on lap 18, to hand back to Moss, second-placed Gendebien began to come under threat and had to yield his place within just two more laps due to a spin and also because the combination of the cold air and soaking conditions was causing the 246 SP's carburettors to ice up. At the end of that lap, Gendebien made his pitstop, during which a mechanic wielded a hammer to flatten the cooling louvres on the car's expansive rear bodywork. By the time Ginther could resume, his Ferrari had dropped to fifth place. When von Trips made his own stop a lap later, the air intakes on the tail section were closed up in similar fashion before Hill took over again. The net effect was that the Ferrari's lead over Moss's Porsche was slashed from 4m 34s before the stop to only 1m 35s after it,

and the Italian car's engine was popping and banging with the continuing problem of carburettor icing. Was Stirling going to be able to challenge for the lead? That question was never answered because the Porsche's four-cylinder engine cried enough on lap 22.

Soon the rain stopped and the temperature began to edge upwards, and with that Hill's Ferrari returned to full song, now with Casner's Maserati second and the Rodríguez Ferrari third. But then, on lap 25, the leading Ferrari hit a stream of water at high speed, spun wildly and bounced off the banks before coming to rest, with Hill thankfully unhurt. After a flamboyant start, the race in which he had wanted to redeem himself had ended as disconsolately as the Targa Florio — on foot. To cap it all, von Trips was transferred to the sister 246 SP in the closing stages and went on to finish third with Ginther and Gendebien behind the winning Maserati of Gregory/Casner and the Rodríguez brothers in second place.

With the finish in sight, Pedro Rodríguez, who was on the same lap as the leaders, added to the drama. On the penultimate lap at the *Karussell*, his NART Ferrari suffered broken spokes in its front-right wheel and he had to drive the best part of half a lap at restrained speed to reach the pits, with the wheel falling apart as he did so and eventually leaving him hobbling along on the brake disc. After a wheel change and a few other repairs, he rejoined to massive applause and without losing position, one lap down and two-and-a-half minutes behind von Trips at the chequered flag.

NÜRBURGRING 1,000KM

Nürburgring, 28th May 1961, 44 laps (14.173 miles/22.810km), 623.633 miles/1,003.640km • Starters 63, classified finishers 37

1st	Masten Gregory/Lloyd 'Lucky' Casner	Maserati Tipo 61	7h 51m 39.2s
2nd	Pedro Rodríguez/Ricardo Rodríguez	Ferrari 250 TRI 60 (0780 TR)	43 laps
3rd	**Richie Ginther/Olivier Gendebien/Wolfgang von Trips**	**Ferrari 246 SP (0790)**	**43 laps**
4th	Carlo Mario Abate/Colin Davis	Ferrari 250 GT SWB (2163 GT)	43 laps
5th	Willy Mairesse/Giancarlo Baghetti	Ferrari 250 GT SWB (2417 GT)	43 laps
6th	Fritz Hahnl/Helmut Zick	Porsche Carrera Abarth	43 laps
12th	Helmut Felder/Peter Nöcker	Ferrari 250 GT SWB (1917 GT)	41 laps
15th	Sepp Liebl/Jo Siffert	Ferrari 250 500 TRC (MDTR)	40 laps
16th	Georges Berger/'Beurlys' (Jean Blaton)	Ferrari 250 GT SWB (1965 GT)	40 laps
DNF	**Phil Hill/Wolfgang von Trips**	**Ferrari 246 SP (0796)**	**– (accident)**
DNF	Denise McCluggage/Allen Eager	Ferrari 250 GT SWB (1931 GT)	– (accident)
DNF	Antonio Gentil de Herédia/Antonio Herédia de Bandeira	Ferrari 500 TR	– (unknown)
DNF	Georges Gachnang/Maurice Caillet	Ferrari 250 TR	– (engine)

Fastest race lap: Phil Hill, 9m 15.8s, 91.803mph/147.744kph **Winner's average speed:** 79.334mph/127.675kph
FIA World Sports Car Championship: 1st Ferrari 22, 2nd Maserati 11, 3rd Porsche 9

Los Hermanos Rodríguez
Pedro and Ricardo

Although Luigi Chinetti was a reputed talent spotter, the remarkable thing about the Rodríguez brothers, Pedro and Ricardo, was just how skilled they were at such a young age in an era when 'training grounds' in motor racing were still in their infancy.

The brothers, of course, were helped by their wealthy father, a former champion motorcyclist, and their reputation was so precocious that some doubted the veracity of their early exploits in Mexico. When they spread their wings outside their home country, however, those who crossed swords with them, including Richie Ginther, recalled duels in which the professionals did not always come out top, starting in 1957.

In December that year, the brothers both exploded onto the scene at the Bahamas Speed Week, where they mixed it with some of the world's best, 15-year-old Ricardo in a Porsche 550 RS and 17-year-old Pedro in a NART-run Ferrari 500 TR. The following year their father put them forward for the Le Mans 24 Hours in the same NART Ferrari, but the organisers refused to let Ricardo take part because of his age. Pedro instead raced with José Behra and performed well until overheating problems brought retirement. In 1959, Chinetti persuaded the brothers, not without difficulty, to compete in their first Le Mans together in an OSCA, saying that if they did not accept his offer, it would be difficult for him to give them anything better the following year. As Chinetti remembered, 'They listened to me and they were in the lead in their category when engine failure eliminated them in the late evening.' What happened afterwards is the stuff of legend.

▼ Luigi Chinetti was well-known for keeping a look-out for feisty drivers and these remarkable brothers certainly gave him double satisfaction. Here he is with Pedro (left) and Ricardo at Le Mans.

An unmitigated triumph

Le Mans 24 Hours, 10th–11th June

And so Le Mans rolled round and old hands Olivier Gendebien and Phil Hill were faced with a dilemma: should they race at their own pace despite knowing that the Rodríguez brothers would be going all out from the beginning in their identical Ferrari 250 TRI 61 in NART colours? Even if it was somewhat exaggerated to present the race in this stark way, everyone expected that it would boil down to a duel between, in the words of Christian Moity, 'two talented adolescents apparently not yet tempered for an event of such proportions' and two seasoned winners at the top of their game.

To broaden the picture, the battle in the sports car category involved three works Ferraris, the other two being the Willy Mairesse/Michael Parkes 250 TRI 61 and the Richie Ginther/Wolfgang von Trips 246 SP. Maserati opposition comprised three cars run by Briggs Cunningham (a *Tipo* 60 and two *Tipo* 63s) and one by the Scuderia Serenissima (a *Tipo* 63). Two Aston Martin DBR1s driven by Jim Clark/Ron Flockhart and Roy Salvadori/Tony Maggs rounded off the list of potential outright winners.

While determined to put on a dominant performance, Maranello was also looking to prepare for the future and entered an experimental *Berlinetta* that combined a 250 GT chassis with a V12 Testa Rossa engine and Superfast II bodywork. This car, the forerunner of the famous GTO, was driven by Fernand Tavano (winner in the previous year's GT category) and Giancarlo Baghetti (a comparative unknown who had just achieved two successive non-championship F1 victories). In the meantime, Ferrari was betting on a raft of 250 GT SWBs, including a NART entry for Stirling Moss/Graham Hill, to fight off three Aston Martin DB4 GTs developed by Italian coachbuilder Zagato.

'When right from the start the #17 Ferrari driven by Pedro Rodríguez set off in hot pursuit of the leaders,' wrote Christian Moity, 'the crowd was seized with amazement tinged with joy! This soon turned into a state bordering on delirium when shortly afterwards the young Mexican managed to hustle past #10 with Gendebien at the wheel to take the lead.' And that was only on lap 6! The first hour was all about the Rodríguez Ferrari. By the end of the second hour, Ginther briefly held the lead but then fell back slightly, leaving it up to Gendebien to either speed up or play a waiting game. Pedro, though, saw things differently: he just continued to race hard until it was time to hand over to his younger brother. Gendebien/Hill, Pedro/Ricardo — the

race swapped leaders but the pace never slackened. And then it began to rain. The drivers of the leading cars did their utmost not to give the other the slightest advantage. By late evening, a mere 10 seconds separated Ricardo from Phil. As night began to shroud the circuit and the rain stopped, the gap between the two Ferraris, incredibly, was never more than five seconds.

Midnight. Gendebien/Hill were in the lead with the Rodríguez brothers in hot pursuit. They had covered 110 laps, some 920 miles, which was close to a record distance at this stage of the race. It was all so thrilling for the spectators that the grandstands remained as tightly packed at this time of night as they had been at the start of the race. But this was when nerves among Ferrari personnel began to jangle.

'The pit kept telling Gendebien to slow down and of course this was the proper way to win Le Mans,' recalled Hill, 'but we simply couldn't afford to leave the Rodríguez boys any kind of sizeable lead.' The American even went out to the signalling pits at *Mulsanne*, away from the rest of Ferrari's people, to urge his team-mate to keep up his pace. 'This was a calculated risk but one which I felt was justified,' Hill added. Still the two Testa Rossas remained separated by no more than a few seconds. And behind them there were four more Ferraris in the first eight places.

For the rest of the night, the battle raged at the same frenetic pace. As dawn broke, it reached fever pitch. The factory decided that the time had come to deal with the insolent young Mexicans who had become such a thorn in its side. With Ricardo in the lead and Gendebien still close behind, third-placed Parkes, although three laps down, joined up with his works colleague to go for the kill. Far from giving in, Ricardo, who was quicker than his elder brother, increased his lead to 12 seconds. When Parkes fell back, struggling with the intensity of the battle, Gendebien really went for it and finally took the lead, although Ricardo hit back with a string of fast laps. Then he stopped to hand over to his older brother at 7.05am. When Pedro restarted the #17 Ferrari, its engine coughed into life and then misfired so badly around his first lap that he pitted again and stopped short in the pitlane. It was as if an icy hand had suddenly seized the collective heart of the NART pit in its grasp. The mechanics rushed to the stricken car. Gendebien passed by once, then twice, while the American crew tried to pinpoint the problem. Spectators in the grandstands kept their eyes on the troubled pit. A faulty condenser was eventually found to be the cause of the engine's ills. Changing it took only two minutes but the car had been stopped for more than 20 minutes.

When Pedro rejoined, the three works Ferraris were in

◀ **Le Mans 24 Hours.** A Ferrari squadron races past the signalling pits at *Mulsanne*, their pronounced Kamm tails making the two front-engined Testa Rossas (#10 and #17) and the rear-engined 246 SP (#23) look remarkably similar from the rear. The cars were crewed by Olivier Gendebien/Phil Hill (#10), Ricardo Rodríguez/Pedro Rodríguez (#17) and Richie Ginther/Wolfgang von Trips (#23).

▶ **Le Mans 24 Hours.** Olivier Gendebien leads Richie Ginther during the prolonged duel that ended shortly after 8am on Sunday when the Dino 246 S (#23) retired after running out of fuel.

⌃ **Le Mans 24 Hours.** Ricardo Rodríguez at the wheel of the NART-entered 250 TRI 61 shortly before its retirement in the pits with engine failure just two hours from the finish. The rear corner bears the scars of intense combat that had not let up since the start of the race.

◄ **Le Mans 24 Hours.** After the demise of the Rodríguez car, Olivier Gendebien could afford to relax a little and glimpse victory, his third. Second-placed works team-mates Michael Parkes and Willy Mairesse would not pose a threat.

command, the Gendebien/Hill Testa Rossa leading the Ginther/ von Trips 246 SP and the Mairesse/Parkes Testa Rossa, with the NART car now six laps behind. But Maranello's men did not have time to gloat as von Trips's Ferrari, which was scheduled to come in and refuel, ran out of petrol just before *Mulsanne*. The fatigue caused by looking after four cars had overcome Romolo Tavoni's vigilance. This elevated Pedro, who was still lapping quickly, to third place, with the second Testa Rossa in his sights. This was like a red rag to a bull. Once again he hit the loud pedal and set the fastest lap of the race with a time of 3m 59.9s, an average speed of 125.51mph. At 10.50am, continuing his brilliant display, he shot past Mairesse just after *Arnage*. Soon he pulled back one lap on the leading Ferrari, then another on the stroke of midday. The brothers had regained four laps in as many hours.

There was no way Maranello would be satisfied with victory going to a non-works Ferrari should the leader encounter trouble. So Willy Mairesse, whose fiery temperament rather than his undoubted skill has too often been emphasised, was entrusted with the job of delivering the final blow, having been briefed until then to hold back. Shortly after 2pm Pedro pitted and the stop seemed to go on forever. The damage had been done: the relentless high-speed running, further encouraged by Mairesse's turn of speed, had finally proved too much for the NART Ferrari's engine, which had blown a piston. The car was pushed away behind the pits under the watchful eyes of Laura Ferrari, Enzo's wife, seated in one of Ferrari's support cars. Ten minutes later the Rodríguez family, mother and father included, left the circuit.

In the eyes of much of the public, the Mexican prodigies were the moral winners of the race. The twin facts that Gendebien and Hill had scored another victory together and that Ferrari had clinched the World Sports Car Championship title were of secondary importance.

Maranello was also amply compensated in the 2,501–3,000cc GT category as the Pierre Noblet/Jean Guichet and Bob Grossman/André Pilette 250 GTs achieved a 1–2 finish. The experimental works entry driven by Tavano/Baghetti expired in the 13th hour with an overheating engine after a below-par performance. Among the other Ferraris, Moss's 250 GT SWB retired, victim of a sliced hose pipe, on his last appearance in the race, which he had led on so many occasions but never won.

As for Ferrari's rivals, Maserati had some cause for satisfaction because the Cunningham-entered *Tipo* 63 came home fourth driven by Augie Pabst/Dick Thompson, but the American team's other entries did not survive the rigours of the race. The Aston Martins were in the hunt for a while but their overall performance failed to live up to expectations. In the sports car category, Clark's exciting display in the opening hours of the race, hot on Moss's heels, came to a halt during the night due to clutch failure. The Salvadori/Maggs DBR1 went out with a split fuel tank shortly after 10am on Sunday when in fourth place. None of the Zagato coupés saw the chequered flag.

LE MANS 24 HOURS

Le Mans, 10th–11th June 1961, 332 laps (8.364 miles/13.461km), 2,781.618 miles/4,476.580km • Starters 55, classified finishers 22

1st	**Olivier Gendebien/Phil Hill**	**Ferrari 250 TRI 61 (0794 TR)**	**332 laps**
2nd	**Willy Mairesse/Michael Parkes**	**Ferrari 250 TRI 61 (0780 TR)**	**329 laps**
3rd	Pierre Noblet/Jean Guichet	Ferrari 250 GT SWB (2689 GT)	316 laps
4th	Augie Pabst/Dick Thompson	Maserati Tipo 63	310 laps
5th	Masten Gregory/Bob Holbert	Porsche 718 RS 61 Spyder	308 laps
6th	Bob Grossman/André Pilette	Ferrari 250 GT SWB (2731 GT)	308 laps
DNF	Pedro Rodríguez/Ricardo Rodríguez	Ferrari 250 TRI 60 (0792 TR)	305 laps (engine)
DNF	**Richie Ginther/Wolfgang von Trips**	**Ferrari 246 SP (0790)**	**231 laps (out of fuel)**
DNF	**Fernand Tavano/Giancarlo Baghetti**	**Ferrari 250 GT SWB EXP (2643 GT)**	**163 laps (engine)**
DNF	Carlo Mario Abate/Maurice Trintignant	Ferrari 250 GT SWB (2733 GT)	162 laps (differential)
DNF	Stirling Moss/Graham Hill	Ferrari 250 GT SWB (2735 GT)	121 laps (water leak)
DNF	George Arents/George Reed	Ferrari 250 GT SWB (2725 GT)	76 laps (short circuit)
DNF	Georges Berger/Lucien Bianchi	Ferrari 250 GT SWB (2129 GT)	60 laps (clutch)

Fastest practice lap: Ginther, 4m 02.8s, 124.017mph/199.586kph **Fastest race lap:** Ricardo Rodríguez, 3m 59.9s, 125.516mph/201.999kph
Winner's average speed: 115.901mph/186.524kph **FIA World Sports Car Championship:** 1st Ferrari 30, 2nd Maserati 14, 3rd Porsche 11

A stroll in the park

Belgian Grand Prix, 18th June

Having won the World Sports Car Championship, Ferrari now threw all its resources into the Formula 1 campaign. On paper, it looked a fairly straightforward task because three of the six remaining Grands Prix — Belgian (Spa), ACF (Reims) and Italian (Monza) — would take place on circuits that favoured power.

There was also the delicate role played by the human element. In *Yankee Champion*, Phil Hill told William F. Nolan about his feelings, particularly about Wolfgang von Trips, whom he feared the most. And with good reason. The title? 'Trips wanted it very much, and so did I. And despite the fact that we were members of the same team, we each knew that we'd have to fight with everything we had to win the title. Therefore, the tension continued to build from race to race.' There was also tension between various factions of the Scuderia, as he explained in an article he wrote in *Automobile Quarterly* called 'A championship season and other memories'. He argued that most of the stresses within the team throughout the season could have been avoided if Enzo Ferrari had designated 'a

no. 1 driver and no. 2 driver etc, as was the custom in other teams'. But which one? Himself or von Trips? The answer was obvious to Hill, but it was now a fratricidal struggle because von Trips, whose numerous accidents had earned him the nickname 'Count von Crash', had become just as quick a driver by knowing how to control his nerves when Hill was on the slippery slope of losing his.

Following Le Mans, the Belgian Grand Prix at Spa provided further proof that Ferrari was by far the dominant force. The Scuderia entered three works cars powered by 120-degree V6s plus a car with the 65-degree version run by Equipe Nationale Belge for Olivier Gendebien as a reward for his performance in the Sarthe. Friday's practice was cut short following a serious accident when Cliff Allison, formerly a Ferrari driver, lost control of his Lotus and was thrown out when it crashed, receiving serious leg and pelvic injuries that caused him to give up racing. Saturday saw Maranello demolish its rivals. Hill banged in a lap in 3m 59.3s to clinch pole ahead of von Trips (4m 0.1s) and Gendebien (4m 3.0s), with John Surtees in a Cooper (4m 6.0s) the only driver to disrupt the Ferrari domination by lapping fractionally quicker than Ginther (4m 6.1s). Behind the Ferraris, the other leading drivers in their BRMs, Lotuses and Coopers were in some disarray trying to make their presence felt while

◄ **Belgian Grand Prix.** Two Americans meet up as Richie Ginther says 'Hi' to Augie Pabst, who was making an off-duty visit to Spa after finishing fourth at Le Mans with Dick Thompson in a Maserati *Tipo* 63.

⌃ Belgian Grand Prix. Carlo Chiti and Phil Hill have a chinwag before practice begins. Despite appearances, everything turned out well for the American driver, who started on pole and went on to win on one of his favourite circuits.

➤ Belgian Grand Prix. For his home race, Olivier Gendebien was entered by Equipe Nationale Belge in a 156 presented in Belgium's racing colour but the three-time Le Mans winner's hopes of glory did not last beyond lap 7. Here he leads Phil Hill and Wolfgang von Trips through *Eau Rouge*.

◄ **Belgian Grand Prix.** Phil Hill leads Wolfgang von Trips in their no-holds-barred battle that started on lap 8 and lasted until lap 25, when the American took the lead and went on to win by a short head.

► **Grand Prix de l'ACF.** Led by Richie Ginther, the Ferraris locked out the front row at Reims ahead of Stirling Moss (Lotus) and Graham Hill (BRM). The fourth Ferrari driver in the race, Giancarlo Baghetti, is in the centre towards the back of the grid.

awaiting the promised Coventry Climax V8. Among them, of course, was Stirling Moss at the wheel of a finely tuned Lotus that simply was not quick enough.

Come the race, Phil Hill's red Ferrari roared past the pits in the lead at the end of lap 1 but next time round it was Gendebien's yellow one in front. Over the next six laps, the Le Mans winners sparred with each other, putting on a show as they both knew

that the American would come out on top, Gendebien fully aware that he could not keep up this pace without risking damage to his car's inferior engine. Von Trips lagged just a little behind: was he just waiting to see how things would play out? Then the German driver decided to up his pace and on lap 9 he got past Hill to take the lead. Gendebien, running third, was now having problems fighting off Ginther, who was getting to grips with the

BELGIAN GRAND PRIX

Spa-Francorchamps, 18th June 1961, 30 laps (8.761 miles/14.100km), 262.840 miles/423.000km • Starters 21, finishers 13

RACE				PRACTICE	
1st	Phil Hill	Ferrari 156 V6 120°	2h 03m 03.8s	1st	3m 59.3s
2nd	Wolfgang von Trips	Ferrari 156 V6 120°	+00.7s	2nd	4m 00.1s
3rd	Richie Ginther	Ferrari 156 V6 120°	+19.5s	5th	4m 06.1s
4th	Olivier Gendebien	Ferrari 156 V6 65°	+45.6s	3rd	4m 03.0s
5th	John Surtees	Cooper T53 Climax S4	+1m 26.8s	4th	4m 06.0s
6th	Dan Gurney	Porsche 718 F4	+1m 31.0s	10th	4m 08.4s

Pole position: Phil Hill, 3m 59.3s, 131.805mph/212.119kph **Fastest race lap:** Ginther, 3m 59.8s, 131.529mph/211.676kph
Winner's average speed: 128.148mph/206.235kph **Drivers' championship:** 1st Phil Hill 19, 2nd von Trips 18, 3rd= Moss & Ginther 12, 6th Gendebien 3 **Constructors' championship:** 1st Ferrari 22, 2nd Lotus-Climax 12, 3rd Cooper-Climax 4

circuit on his first visit. By lap 12, the little Californian was third and he continued to push.

At half distance, 15 laps, Hill and von Trips were at each other's throats, exchanging the lead several times, with Ginther 13 seconds behind. Over the next five laps, Richie got a little closer, proving that his speed was down to his skills by setting a new lap record of 3m 59.8s on lap 20, and leaving Gendebien far behind. But that was as far as it went because Ginther was then reminded by a pit signal stating 'GINT 3RD' that he had to curb his élan and respect team orders. Up front, Hill, handicapped by a piece of gravel that had got under his visor, continued to fight off von Trips, and did so successfully because he led all but one of the final 10 laps to win by 0.7sec and head an extraordinary team result, with four Ferraris filling the first four places. It was enough to send Maranello into a state of ecstasy.

Behind the Ferraris, all their rivals were reduced to walk-on roles, gradually running out of puff while trying to follow. Surtees's Cooper was the first non-Italian car in fifth place in front of the Porsches of Dan Gurney and Jo Bonnier, followed by eighth-placed Moss. In the championship, Hill now led with 19 points with von Trips second on 18, and Moss and Ginther tied for third with 12 apiece. And Reims was the next stop…

The other race of the century

Grand Prix de l'ACF, 2nd July

After Spa, it looked like a similar scenario would unfold in the French Champagne region. But egos clashed from the outset in the searing heat of the weekend at Reims, especially when Wolfgang von Trips announced towards the end of the first practice session that he wanted to try Phil Hill's car, because his best time (2m 26.4s) was rather slower than Hill's (2m 24.9s). Team manager Romolo Tavoni gave the green light despite the drivers having agreed at the beginning of the season not to do this, but it mattered not because Hill was still quicker after the exchange. The next two sessions confirmed the anticipated hierarchy: the Ferraris occupied the front row of the grid with Hill on pole position, von Trips next to him and Richie Ginther (2m 26.8s) completing the line-up. Behind, Stirling Moss (2m 27.6s) and Jim Clark (2m 29.0s) in their Lotuses clung to the vain hope that they could play a role in disrupting the expected course of a race that already looked over before it had begun.

There was a fourth Ferrari in the field that looked unlikely to play anything other than a minor role. The 156 provided by Maranello to the *Federazione Italiana Scuderie Automobilistiche* (FISA) only had a 65-degree V6 and its driver, Giancarlo Baghetti, was not experienced, even if he arrived in France on the back of two impressive victories in Italian non-championship Formula 1 races at Syracuse and Naples. Although these successes had been achieved in a car that was obviously a cut above the rest, Baghetti had still beaten drivers of the calibre of Stirling Moss, Jack Brabham, Jo Bonnier and Dan Gurney. In fact, he was no dilettante, with plenty of talent and sufficient eagerness to learn that he had spent time pounding round the Modena circuit coached by Piero Taruffi. During Friday's practice, he ran for around 10 laps behind Hill and von Trips to learn the best lines at Reims. All the same, he qualified only 12th.

Phil Hill took the lead at the start of the 52-lap race on an afternoon of such intense heat that a newly resurfaced section of track at *Thillois* was already beginning to break up. Von Trips glued his car to the tail of Hill's from the beginning and on lap 13 Hill let him pass, either through team orders or wisdom. At this point, Ginther ran third, although he had surrendered the position to Moss for three laps after a quick spin, but next time round the Englishman was hit by the first of a long series of problems that dropped him down the field. After a display of skilful driving had brought him up the field, Baghetti was now involved in a tough battle for fourth place with the works Lotuses of Jim Clark and Innes Ireland, and within two more laps he had got past both Scots to put Ferraris in the first four places. The walkover looked to be materialising as forecast.

Suddenly the race was turned on its head. Von Trips crawled into the pitlane and stopped. Ferrari had put extra stone protection in front of the radiator on each of its cars but a large stone had pierced this barrier on von Trips's car and damaged the radiator, causing terminal overheating. Hill was back in front. No longer under pressure from his German team-mate, he controlled the race with Ginther in second place, 14 seconds behind, while Baghetti was just managing to hold off Clark and Ireland, who in turn were being pressured by the Porsches of Dan Gurney and Jo Bonnier. On lap 25, just when the Porsche attacks on the Lotuses looked likely to pay off, Ginther spun wildly at *Thillois* and fell 21 seconds behind the leader. In the pits, Tavoni, scratching his head, sensed that it was all starting to go wrong and told his drivers to lift off.

Although Ginther respected the instruction, he seemed more incisive than Hill and closed the gap. By lap 38, the American

◄ **Grand Prix de l'ACF.** After Richie Ginther's retirement on lap 41, Giancarlo Baghetti in the sole-surviving Ferrari, its nose lowered as he brakes for *Thillois*, leads the Porsches of Jo Bonnier and Dan Gurney.

➤ **Grand Prix de l'ACF.** Dan Gurney, the only man left to battle it out with Giancarlo Baghetti after Jo Bonnier fell back, leads the Ferrari at *Thillois* as the race nears its conclusion. In the heat that day, Gurney clenched a handkerchief between his teeth to try to keep himself a little cooler.

➤ **Grand Prix de l'ACF.** Giancarlo Baghetti, who had remained tucked in behind Dan Gurney's Porsche on the last lap, has just made his winning move in front of a huge crowd. Raymond Roche, the man waving the chequered flag, had never seen anything like it.

GRAND PRIX DE L'ACF

Reims-Gueux, 2nd July 1961, 52 laps (5.158 miles/8.301km), 268.248 miles/431.704km • Starters 26, finishers 15

RACE				PRACTICE	
1st	Giancarlo Baghetti	Ferrari 156 V6 65°	2h 14m 17.5s	12th	2m 30.5s
2nd	Dan Gurney	Porsche 718 F4	+00.1s	9th	2m 29.6s
3rd	Jim Clark	Lotus 21 Climax S4	+1m 01.1s	5th	2m 29.0s
4th	Innes Ireland	Lotus 21 Climax S4	+1m 10.3s	10th	2m 29.8s
5th	Bruce McLaren	Cooper T55 Climax S4	+1m 41.8s	8th	2m 29.4s
6th	Graham Hill	BRM P48/57 Climax S4	+1m 41.9s	6th	2m 29.1s
9th	**Phil Hill**	Ferrari 156 V6 120°	50 laps	1st	2m 24.9s
DNF	**Richie Ginther**	Ferrari 156 V6 120°	41 laps (oil pressure)	3rd	2m 26.8s
DNF	**Wolfgang von Trips**	Ferrari 156 V6 120°	18 laps (engine)	2nd	2m 26.4s

Pole position: Phil Hill, 2m 24.9s, 128.160mph/206.254kph **Fastest race lap:** Phil Hill, 2m 27.1s, 126.243mph/203.169kph
Winner's average speed: 119.846mph/192.874kph **Drivers' championship:** 1st Phil Hill 19, 2nd von Trips 18, 3rd= Moss & Ginther 12,
5th Baghetti 9, 8th Gendebien 3 **Constructors' championship:** 1st Ferrari 30, 2nd Lotus-Climax 16, 3rd Porsche 9

drivers were only nine seconds apart and now Hill was being harried by Moss, who kept nipping away at the Ferrari's heels even though he was a lap behind. Then Hill spun at *Thillois* and the two cars collided. Stirling rejoined but Phil stalled his engine, his foot having slipped off the accelerator because of the impact. As Hill recalled: 'This spin was horrible. It should have been a simple 360-degree turn, costing me no more than a few seconds at most. Richie had just spun in *Thillois* with no serious results.' But this time it was different. A dead alternator meant no charge for the battery, so the starter motor would not operate. Hill got out of the car and used all his strength to try to push-start it. Ginther flew past and still Hill pushed. When the V6 finally burst into song, Hill, on the verge of collapsing from exhaustion, had dropped to tenth place.

Ginther, now in the lead, was beginning to dream of his first Grand Prix victory until he made a brief and pointless pitstop just one lap later. His engine was losing oil pressure and he thought a top-up of oil would be a good idea, overlooking the fact that the rules did not allow this, so Tavoni just had to wave him away. This put Ginther in range of Baghetti and the two Porsches that continued to tail the newcomer's Ferrari. A lap later, on lap 40, the gap was much closer, with only 100 metres separating the leading Ferrari from the pursuing trio. Next time round, Baghetti screamed past in the lead followed by Bonnier and Gurney. A sudden drop in oil pressure at *Muizon* had put paid to Ginther's hopes.

Thereafter, everything changed at a frantic pace, with twist after twist. Back in 1953, the Fangio/Hawthorn duel in the Grand Prix de l'ACF had captivated spectators at Reims and when the English driver took the chequered flag in first place the crowd had gone wild. *Autosport* called it 'The race of the century'. Maybe, but what happened eight years later at the same circuit was just as thrilling. On lap 49, with three laps to go, Gurney and Baghetti tore down the Soissons road side-by-side with Bonnier just a couple of car lengths behind. The American snatched the lead at *Thillois* but the Italian repassed him on the pits straight.

As they began the last lap, with Bonnier now out of the picture with an ailing engine, Gurney was ahead. He was still in front at *Muizon*, at the top of *La Garenne* on the way to *Thillois*, and then on the exit from this final corner. This time the American, biting even harder on the handkerchief that had been clenched between his teeth since the start, began to contemplate the win that was his for the taking. But Reims, with its long pits straight, had its own peculiarity: namely, he who came out of *Thillois* leading a pack often lost his advantage by the finish line. During practice two days earlier, Baghetti had learned the skills of slipstreaming in the wake of his more experienced team-mates. Now he put a little bit of that know-how into practice. Tucked in behind the Porsche, he suddenly jinked out to the left, drew level with the American, overtook him, and crossed the finishing line to win by 0.1sec.

Raymond 'Toto' Roche, the well-known Reims character with the chequered flag in his hands who had seen it all before, was flabbergasted.

Italy was gripped by a wave of ecstasy, thinking it had found its new Tazio Nuvolari, Achille Varzi or Alberto Ascari.

And Phil Hill still led the World Championship — by just a single point.

At breakneck speed

British Grand Prix, 15th July

In complete contrast to the heat wave at Reims, the fifth round of the Formula 1 World Championship at Aintree took place under gloomy skies from the moment practice kicked off. The Ferraris again proved their superiority over their rivals on this flat artificial circuit a couple of miles from Liverpool. In the second practice session on Thursday, held by some miracle on a dry track, Phil Hill clinched pole position as the first to lap in 1m 58.8s, a time that was then uncannily emulated by the sister Ferraris of Richie Ginther and Wolfgang von Trips as well as by Jo Bonnier's Porsche. The two Friday sessions in pouring rain were harbingers of the conditions that would reign in a race that looked promising for the Scuderia. Phil Hill (2m 5.8s) again bettered von Trips (2m 6.2s) and Ginther (2m 6.4s), with Stirling Moss (Lotus) now ready to pounce. Giancarlo Baghetti was given another chance and this time was completely out of his depth, winding up 19th on the grid.

As anticipated, it was raining for Saturday's race. Just before the start of the 75-lap contest, Moss, who was obviously delighted to be competing at home in the wet, gave a series of jubilatory waves. He relished these conditions, which levelled the playing field and were tailor-made for his talent. As things turned out, however, the race was all about Ferrari. Phil Hill led until lap 7, when he swerved to avoid Keith Greene's spinning Gilby-Climax, letting von Trips into the lead. Moss, initially fourth, then third after passing Ginther on lap 6, put on the best show he could, thrilling the partisan crowd, and raised a huge cheer when he overtook Hill's Ferrari to take second place on lap 10. Then Stirling set about von Trips and was right on his tail from lap 14, matching the German's every move as they threaded their way through backmarkers. On lap 24, he momentarily lost his Lotus's back end on a sheet of water, performed a neat 360-degree spin in the Grandstand corner, and carried on as if nothing had happened, thanks to his singular skills in such conditions, although now he was 10 seconds behind the leader. When the rain had stopped as half distance approached, Moss's challenge faded, along with his brakes, and his retirement on lap 44 put the Ferraris back into their 1–2–3, von Trips from Hill and Ginther.

So Ferrari came away from the home of the famous Grand National with a triple. The only shortcoming for the Scuderia was Baghetti's below-par performance, the new Italian star never showing any sign of fulfilling the promise glimpsed at

Reims. After getting himself up to 10th place, he went wide in Waterway Corner and his race ended against some railings on lap 27.

Phil Hill had one of the scariest moments of his life when he aquaplaned off the track at Melling Crossing. He saw his whole career about to flip as he felt his gripless car, with all four wheels locked, career towards a telephone pole. 'Finally my wheels cut down through the water enough to get a grip and I missed the post by a hair. That ruined my concentration,' he wrote in *Automobile Quarterly*. The incident left its mark on him for the rest of the season.

▼ **British Grand Prix.** Victorious at Syracuse and Naples, and then at Reims, Giancarlo Baghetti had come to be regarded by the *Tifosi* as their new racing hero. Everything that followed proved to be a much tougher challenge and he never did fulfil their hopes.

◄ **British Grand Prix.** Only 19th on the grid at Aintree, Giancarlo Baghetti learned the hard way that Grands Prix could unfold very differently. Jack Fairman's four-wheel-drive Ferguson P99 sits alongside with Wolfgang Seidel's Lotus 18 behind.

▼ **British Grand Prix.** At the foot of the grandstands also used for the famous Aintree racecourse, Phil Hill (#2), Richie Ginther (#6) and Jo Bonnier (#8) occupy the front row with Wolfgang von Trips (#4) and Stirling Moss (#28) behind. Hill made the best getaway.

⋀ British Grand Prix. Phil Hill led the race until lap 7, when he was baulked by a tailender and had to relinquish the lead to Wolfgang von Trips. He went on to finish second to von Trips despite scaring himself when his Ferrari aquaplaned at Melling Crossing.

➤ British Grand Prix. Phil Hill leads Richie Ginther during the closing stages, with a dry line beginning to appear. Ginther refrained from battling with Hill throughout the race.

BRITISH GRAND PRIX

Aintree, 15th July 1961, 75 laps (3.000 miles/4.828km), 225.000 miles/362.100km • Starters 30, finishers 17

RACE				PRACTICE	
1st	Wolfgang von Trips	Ferrari 156 V6 120°	2h 40m 53.6s	4th	1m 58.8s
2nd	Phil Hill	Ferrari 156 V6 120°	+46.0s	1st	1m 58.8s
3rd	Richie Ginther	Ferrari 156 V6 120°	+46.8s	2nd	1m 58.8s
4th	Jack Brabham	Cooper T55 Climax S4	+1m 08.6s	9th	1m 59.4s
5th	Jo Bonnier	Porsche 718 F4	+1m 16.2s	3rd	1m 58.8s
6th	Roy Salvadori	Cooper T53 Climax S4	+1m 26.2s	13th	2m 00.8s
DNF	Giancarlo Baghetti	Ferrari 156 V6 65°	29 laps (accident)	19th	2m 02.0s

Pole position: Phil Hill, 1m 58.8s, 90.908mph/146.303kph **Fastest race lap:** Tony Brooks (BRM P48/57 Climax S4), 1m 57.8s, 91.680mph/147.545kph **Winner's average speed:** 83.906mph/135.034kph **Drivers' championship:** 1st von Trips 27, 2nd Phil Hill 25, 3rd Ginther 16, 4th Moss 12, 5th Baghetti 9, 9th Gendebien 3 **Constructors' championship:** 1st Ferrari 38, 2nd Lotus-Climax 16, 3rd Porsche 11

What aggravated Hill even more was Enzo Ferrari's continuing unwillingness to designate a number one driver. Hill had long been a witness to the internal quarrels that corroded the atmosphere within the Scuderia. Mr Ferrari seemed to take almost Machiavellian pleasure in stirring things up, with the battles between egos that tore apart engineers and drivers providing fertile ground for his nefarious games. This time, though, Hill was in the running for the World Championship title with every possibility of success, and now no further proof was needed that von Trips's sheer speed was forcing the American driver to take risks that seemed foolhardy to him. Furthermore, von Trips, who never provided much technical input, was benefiting from the excellence of a car on which Hill had done most of the core development, together with Ginther.

A heaven-sent ally

German Grand Prix, 6th August

Three weeks later, the German Grand Prix was bathed in a wave of emotion because Wolfgang von Trips was racing on home ground, close to his family domain, the castle at Burg Hemmersbach, just 60 miles from the Nürburgring. Ferrari again entered four cars but this time the man in the extra one, with a 65-degree V6 as usual, was Willy Mairesse.

On Friday morning, the Ferraris were unable to show their true pace as their shock absorbers bottomed out in places and gave rise to erratic roadholding. Jo Bonnier's Porsche was initially untouchable when he set a time of 9m 6.6s, against which the Ferraris did not measure up too well, with Hill unable to better 9m 10.2s, von Trips on just 9m 23.5s with his engine playing up, and Ginther at 9m 23.8s. Mairesse, getting to grips with both the car and the track, was even further back. In the afternoon, while the German driver had to wait while his engine was changed, Hill wrestled his unstable car around in 9m 3.0s, 'getting round some corners more by luck than judgment' if *Motor Sport*'s Denis Jenkinson is to be believed. But when Hill, with his intimate

knowledge of the *Nordschliefe* combined with consummate skill, finally got it all together in a well-set-up car, he really went for it and astonished everybody with a time of 8m 55.2s. Having pulled a magical lap out of the bag, almost a gift from the gods, he had no need to push things any further.

The looming threat to Ferrari of the new Coventry Climax V8 engine finally materialised, for the exclusive use on this occasion of the reigning World Champion, Jack Brabham, in the back of his Cooper. The engine's début, however, was so hurried that its installation even looked unfinished, with the exhaust pipes, which were notably more voluminous than those of the four-cylinder version, extending beyond the rear of the basically unchanged Cooper chassis. However, the V8 soon showed during Friday's practice that its claimed 174bhp was indeed on tap as Brabham produced a promising lap of 9m 15.6s compared with the 9m 10.6s he achieved in his four-cylinder car. Even better, on Saturday morning, once some of the inevitable teething troubles had been overcome, one being that the front of the engine scraped the track over bumps, Brabham improved to 9m 1.4s, just beating Stirling Moss's 9m 1.7s in his Lotus 18/21, now with new, smoother bodywork. Brabham and Moss duly joined Phil Hill on the four-abreast front row with Bonnier, who had improved to 9m 4.8s.

◄ **British Grand Prix**. Laura Ferrari, Enzo's wife, was an unexpected visitor to the podium, seeking to sharing the limelight with victorious Wolfgang von Trips and second-placed Phil Hill.

➤ **German Grand Prix.** The jostling pack crowds into the *Südkehre* just after the start with barely a Ferrari in sight other than Phil Hill's pole-winning but slow-starting #4 car. Jack Brabham (Cooper) leads, hounded by Stirling Moss (Lotus) and the three bulky-looking Porsches of Jo Bonnier (#8), Dan Gurney (#9) and Hans Herrmann (#10). Brabham went off during this first lap, leaving Moss to vanquish the Ferraris.

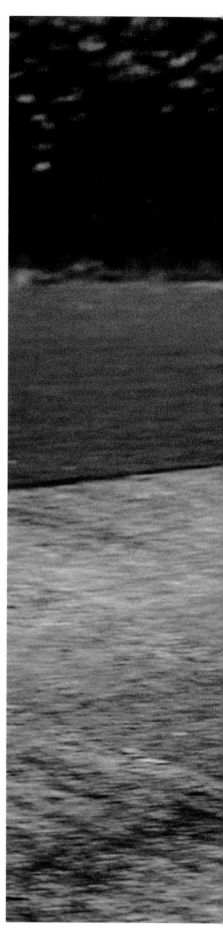

When von Trips finally had his replacement engine installed for Saturday's practice, he put in a 9m 5.5s that assured him of a start on the second row alongside Graham Hill's BRM (9m 6.4s) and Dan Gurney's Porsche (9m 6.6s). The other two red cars were way back, Mairesse 13th (9m 15.9s) and Ginther 14th (9m 16.6s). Collectively, this was Ferrari's worst qualifying position of the year, but at least, with Hill on pole, Maranello could heave a sigh of relief, mixed with some worry as rain was expected for the race.

The forecast turned out to be correct and on Sunday morning it began to pour 30 minutes before the start. And then the rain stopped with 10 minutes to go, leaving everybody scratching their heads about tyre choice in the face of threatening skies. Ferrari heeded the advice of Dunlop's Vic Barlow and, like most, opted for normal rubber despite expressing a preference for wet-weather tyres. On the other hand, Moss went against Barlow's guidance and started the race on 'green spot' D12s (so called

⌃ German Grand Prix. Willy Mairesse got as high as sixth at the wheel of the only 65-degree V6 Ferrari in the race but crashed on the 14th lap.

➤ German Grand Prix. Wolfgang von Trips rounds the *Karussell*. He was third behind Phil Hill in the first half of the race and mostly in front of him in the second. He owed his second place in the results to a daring move in sight of the finish.

because of the green stickers that identified them). Although these were wet-weather tyres, they were pretty effective in dry conditions too, as Innes Ireland had demonstrated in his Lotus two weeks earlier by overcoming stormy conditions to win the Solitude Grand Prix, a race that Ferrari had skipped.

While Moss's choice at the Nürburgring was a daring one, it was carefully calculated. Like a gambler hiding his cards, he had the green stickers on the tyre sidewalls concealed by black paint. To illustrate his guile in tyre matters, it is worth diverting just briefly to previous occasions when he outfoxed his rivals. In 1958 in Argentina, he had won with tyres literally worn down to the canvas to save a pitstop against the more powerful Ferraris that had eaten up their rubber more quickly. He had done the same thing in 1959 at Monza, where he had bet on a non-stop race and preserved his tyres while losing none of his speed to vanquish Ferrari in a less powerful but lighter car.

This Nürburgring race proved him right. On the first lap, Brabham led initially but lost control of his V8 Cooper in a corner that was still wet and ended up in a hedge, luckily without injury. On the second lap, Graham Hill's race also ended abruptly after a collision with Gurney, who was able to continue. Two of the potential winners were out already.

Meanwhile, Moss had established himself at the front. First time past the pits he had a two-second lead over Hill's Ferrari while von Trips was only sixth after a poor start. Despite the track still being damp and with his Lotus on full tanks, Moss drew away from the pursuing Ferrari and covered his second lap in just 9m 13.8s. Soon it was von Trips who became the man to watch. By lap 5, the German driver was gaining strongly on his team-mate and had closed the deficit to five seconds. 'Taffy' was in scintillating form, getting the most out of a car that was becoming lighter as its fuel load lessened and the track dried. On lap 6, he set a new outright record at 9m 8.1s, and over the next two laps he reduced it twice more, in turn to 9m 4.3s and 9m 1.6s, and on the second of those laps he managed to get past Hill, who was briefly hindered by a sticky gearbox.

With von Trips now Moss's immediate threat, the intensity moved up another notch and Stirling's advantage began to shrink. Cheered on by his home crowd, the German driver produced two more record laps, stopping the clock at 9m 1.1s (lap 9) and 8m 59.9s (lap 10), to put himself nine seconds behind Moss. But the spectators barely had time to rejoice as third-placed

◄ **German Grand Prix.** Stirling Moss has just scored his 17th and last Grand Prix victory in magnificent style. Wolfgang von Trips would never again see a chequered flag.

GERMAN GRAND PRIX

Nürburgring, 6th August 1961, 15 laps (14.173 miles/22.810km), 212.602 miles/342.150km • Starters 26, finishers 17

RACE				PRACTICE	
1st	Stirling Moss	Lotus 18/21 Climax S4	2h 18m 12.4s	3rd	9m 01.7s
2nd	Wolfgang von Trips	Ferrari 156 V6 120°	+21.4s	5th	9m 05.5s
3rd	Phil Hill	Ferrari 156 V6 120°	+22.5s	1st	8m 55.2s
4th	Jim Clark	Lotus 21 Climax S4	+1m 17.1s	8th	9m 08.1s
5th	John Surtees	Cooper T53 Climax S4	+1m 53.1s	10th	9m 11.2s
6th	Bruce McLaren	Cooper T55 Climax S4	+2m 41.4s	12th	9m 13.0s
8th	Richie Ginther	Ferrari 156 V6 120°	+5m 23.1s	14th	9m 16.6s
DNF	Willy Mairesse	Ferrari 156 V6 65°	13 laps (accident)	13th	9m 15.9s

Pole position: Phil Hill, 8m 55.2s, 95.337mph/153.430kph Fastest race lap: Phil Hill, 8m 57.8s, 94.883mph/152.700kph
Winner's average speed: 92.336mph/148.600kph Drivers' championship: 1st von Trips 33, 2nd Phil Hill 29, 3rd Moss 21, 4th Ginther 16,
6th Baghetti 9, 11th Gendebien 3 Constructors' championship: 1st Ferrari 44, 2nd Lotus-Climax 24, 3rd Porsche 11

Hill, hanging on closely to his team-mate, covered the same lap in 8m 57.8s, reminding everyone that in his determination not to be outshone by von Trips, he too was a *Ringmeister*!

For von Trips, catching Moss was one thing but overtaking him was quite another, especially with renewed rain about to become the Englishman's ally. Two laps later it began to fall. Stirling, given an advantage again on his D12s, which had shown remarkable durability, opened up a comfortable cushion and put himself out of reach of the two Ferraris, which were now locked in their own combat behind. On the 14th and penultimate lap, Hill passed von Trips. On the last lap, the American was still in front at the *Karussell* and there was no change as the two cars tackled the crest at the *Antoniusbuche* bridge, only a couple of miles from the finish. Hill told the story of what happened next in *Automobile Quarterly*: 'I was ahead on the long straight to the finish when we ran into this wall of water from a sudden rainstorm typical of the Eifel Mountains and both of us nearly crashed. Trips got straightened out first and scrambled across the line ahead of me.'

Thanks to this risky passing move, von Trips retook the championship lead with four points in hand over Hill, 12 over Moss and 17 over Ginther, who finished eighth. The fourth Scuderia driver, Mairesse, had put on a brilliant display until he went off on lap 14, also caught out by the rain. So it looked likely that the title would be decided at Monza, a circuit all the more favourable to Ferrari as the Italian Grand Prix would be run on the combined road and banked track. The previous year, the British entrants had judged the fast, bumpy banked sections too dangerous and had refused to race on them, but now they had had a change of heart.

The revelation!

Pescara Four Hours, 15th August

Since 1924, the year of the first race at Pescara — won incidentally by Enzo Ferrari at the wheel of an Alfa Romeo — aces like Tazio Nuvolari, Achille Varzi, Rudolf Caracciola and Juan Manuel Fangio had all competed on this long circuit, an experience they never forgot. The route, on public roads, was shaped almost like an equilateral triangle consisting of two relentless straights linked by a twisty, mountainous section that became the graveyard of many hopes. In 1957, Stirling Moss in his Vanwall won the only Formula 1 Grand Prix held at Pescara, adding his name to the illustrious list of winners. Now, four years later, this majestic circuit rediscovered its former glory for four hours.

There was a plethora of Ferraris entered but really only two contenders, the Richie Ginther/Giancarlo Baghetti 246 SP and the Scuderia Centro-Sud 250 TR for Giorgio Scarlatti/Lorenzo Bandini. Opposition came from two Maserati *Tipo* 63s for Jo Bonnier and Nino Vaccarella, 'Lucky' Casner's *Tipo* 61 and a pair of *Tipo* 60s in the hands of Mennato Boffa and Raffaello Rosati, all of whom opted to drive single-handed despite the scorching hot weather that was forecast for race day. Three Porsche RS 61 spyders completed the list of strong contenders, but the *Tifosi* present in their thousands saw the 246 SP as the likely winner because it was the only car to break the 10-minute barrier in practice with a time of 9m 49.4s.

Initially, that expectation looked correct, for Ginther, despite

PESCARA FOUR HOURS

Pescara, 15th August 1961, 23 laps (15.894 miles/25.579km), 355.970 miles/572.878km • Starters 47, classified finishers 28

1st	Lorenzo Bandini/Giorgio Scarlatti	Ferrari 250 TRI 61 (0780 TR)	23 laps
2nd	Karl Orthuber/Edgar Barth	Porsche 718 RS 61	22 laps
3rd	Mennato Boffa	Maserati Tipo 60	22 laps
4th	George Arents/Sterling Hamill	Ferrari 250 GT SWB (2725 GT)	22 laps
5th	Colin Davis	OSCA 1600 S	21 laps
6th	Sergio Bettoja/'Kim'	Ferrari 250 GT SWB (2767 GT)	21 laps
7th	Alberico Cacciari/Luigi Bertocco	Ferrari 250 GT SWB (2095 GT)	21 laps
DNF	Carlo Mario Abate	Ferrari 250 GT SWB (2733 GT)	22 laps (out of fuel)
DNF	**Richie Ginther/Giancarlo Baghetti**	**Ferrari 246 SP (0790)**	**10 laps (steering)**
DNF	Willy Mairesse/Pierre Dumay	Ferrari 250 GT SWB (2729 GT)	2 laps (accident)

Fastest race lap: Ginther, 9m 55.5s, 96.085mph/154.634kph **Winner's average speed:** 88.993mph/143.220kph

FIA World Sports Car Championship:[1] 1st Ferrari 24 (34)[2], 2nd Maserati 14 (16)[2], 3rd Porsche 11 (14)[2]

[1] Half points were awarded for this race owing to its shorter duration (less than the FIA's minimum of six hours or 1,000km)

[2] Figure in brackets indicates all points scored; only the best three results counted towards the championship

---

having to stop to check flexing rear suspension at the start of the race, held off Vaccarella and battled for the lead with Casner. But both Maserati and Ferrari soon suffered setbacks. Bonnier retired his *Tipo* 63 on the first lap with engine trouble while Bandini's 250 TR lost three minutes having an oil leak detected and plugged, and dropped to 37th place. To this duel between Maranello and Modena was added the one between fans of Baghetti, boosted by his lucky but well-deserved Formula 1 victory in the Grand Prix de l'ACF six weeks earlier, and those of Bandini who, at the time, was just a young hopeful dreaming of becoming a champion. At Pescara, Bandini became the fans' favourite.

After his early stop, Bandini needed only two laps to claw back 20 places. He made more progress with Vaccarella's retirement on lap 8 followed by Baghetti's two laps later, just after taking over from Ginther. When Bandini handed over to Scarlatti, just before half distance, the Ferrari lay second, five minutes behind Casner's Maserati. However, Scarlatti soon proved unable to close the gap, so Guglielmo 'Mimmo' Dei, boss of Scuderia Centro-Sud, put Bandini back in the car to show what he could do.

Bandini drove like a man possessed and ate into the gap until Casner crashed on lap 14 of the 23. Was this a consequence of Bandini's challenge or a blunder by a tailender when being lapped? Whatever, Bandini now led the race while Casner headed for hospital. The Italian newcomer held on to claim victory after a masterly performance on the day of the Festival of the Virgin.

A title from tragedy

Italian Grand Prix, 10th September

What was at stake in Italy was beginning to prey on Phil Hill's nerves. And practice did nothing to calm the situation for him. On Friday, while he was quicker than Wolfgang von Trips (2m 48.9s against 2m 50.3s), he was two seconds slower than Richie Ginther (2m 46.8s), whose 156 was equipped with a more powerful version of the 120-degree V6. And now in the mix came Ricardo Rodríguez, the 19-year-old Mexican prodigy making his F1 début for Ferrari with breathtaking ease by recording 2m 49.6s on his first day of practice with only a 65-degree V6.

On Saturday, the American remained in an unsettled state. The previous day he had complained about his V6's inability to rev properly and had asked for the gearbox to be examined, which caused a fuss. His suspicions about the gearbox were confirmed when it was discovered that it contained two second gears, so naturally he demanded that this be rectified. However, the engine continued to worry him, something he raised with all the senior Maranello men present, including Enzo Ferrari himself.

'All you have to do is stop complaining and just drive the car,' was *Il Commendatore*'s scathing comment. Hill had become rather used to Mr Ferrari's barbs. During a test session at Monza in his presence, the American had made the mistake of complaining

▲ **Italian Grand Prix.** Ferrari brought out the heavy artillery for its home race with no fewer than five red 156s. The one in the foreground, without Ferrari's emblematic shield, is Giancarlo Baghetti's Scuderia Sant'Ambroeus entry.

➤ **Italian Grand Prix.** Wolfgang von Trips was outshone by his team-mates during the first practice session. Here he gets ready to tackle the second session, which saw him claim pole position from the remarkable Ricardo Rodríguez.

in carefully chosen words about his car's windscreen, which was generating such violent turbulence at helmet level that his vision was blurred. Overhearing this remark, Mr Ferrari had turned towards him and spat out: 'Put your foot down and forget your head.'

Although Hill went faster on Saturday, lapping in 2m 47.2s, he ended up only fourth on the grid, sharing the second row with Ginther. He persuaded Ferrari to change his engine for the race and when the suspect unit was dismantled the mechanics discovered that Hill's concerns had been entirely valid because an inlet valve spring had broken. Meanwhile, it was von Trips and Rodríguez who went head-to-head for pole position, with the German driver just managing to pip the precocious youngster — and now Ferrari's new blue-eyed boy — by 0.1sec with a lap in 2m 46.3s. Ricardo's performance was as sensational as it was unexpected.

Behind the works Ferrari drivers, Giancarlo Baghetti, now in a Scuderia Sant'Ambroeus Ferrari with a 120-degree V6, shared the third row with Graham Hill, who was quickest of the British entrants thanks to his BRM now being powered by a new in-house V8, although for the race he opted for the reliability of the usual four-cylinder Coventry Climax. Another driver trying a V8 for the first time was Stirling Moss, but it was so troublesome that he could qualify only 11th and ended up racing a four-cylinder works Lotus 21 after gentlemanly Innes Ireland suggested a car swap.

On the starting grid, von Trips gave interviews with obvious relish, but Hill wanted to keep focused on the job in hand. Without being overly worried, he knew how important it would be to make a good start and avoid tackling the banked section for the first time amidst the pack. Once the cars had been unleashed, his fears were allayed because he found himself second at the entry to the *Curva Grande*, slotted in behind Rodríguez and followed by Ginther and Jack Brabham's fast-starting Cooper, with von Trips a little further back after a sluggish getaway, then Graham Hill's BRM and Jim Clark's Lotus close behind. By the end of lap 1, Phil was in the lead, from Ginther, Rodríguez, Clark, Brabham, von Trips and Baghetti.

On the second lap, all hell broke loose under braking for the *Parabolica*, the fast 180-degree bend leading back onto the main straight. Behind the top four, von Trips pulled towards the left for the best racing line into the turn and caught the front of Clark's Lotus. Both cars shot up the earth bank, the Ferrari whirling wildly round and round with horrific force and throwing out its driver. Spectators tightly packed against the fencing were mown down by the car as it scythed past them and 14 were killed, with many more injured, before the wrecked

machine rolled back down the bank and came to a halt in the middle of the track, close to where von Trips's inert body lay on the grass verge. He had been killed instantly. Clark had escaped serious harm and, badly shaken, parked his Lotus at the trackside.

When Hill, still under pressure from Ginther, passed the scene next time round, he knew it was serious — but not how serious. 'People had been crashing all season and there had been no fatal accidents,' he told William F. Nolan in *Yankee Champion*. 'This looked bad, but no worse than many others.'

The race continued. On lap 9, while Hill and Ginther were still battling hard up front, followed by Rodríguez and Baghetti, Brabham retired with an overheating engine. Thanks to his disappearance, Gurney, who had been under pressure from Moss since the start, was now fifth, 20 seconds behind the leaders. At the end of lap 13, there was a reshuffle in the order as the four Ferraris tackled the *Parabolica* in line astern, but only the two leaders finished the lap. Rodríguez and Baghetti, both let down by their engines at almost the very same moment, crawled into the pits at a snail's pace and played no further part. Moss and Gurney, who were virtually inseparable, inherited third and fourth places, and then battled over the second spot on the podium after Ginther quit on lap 24 with yet another Ferrari engine failure.

'Thus, I was the only Ferrari left… and for myself,' Hill recounted in *Inside track*, adding that he was less worried about the title than about his engine. A retirement here and also in the final round at Watkins Glen would cost him the title, leaving it either with von Trips posthumously or with Moss, should the Englishman be able to overcome his points deficit by taking a win and a second place in both of these races with Hill not scoring. Moss's title prospects were in suspense until lap 31, when Gurney got past him, and then shattered entirely on lap 37 when he had to bring his Lotus into the pits with a broken left-front wheel bearing. This time, as so often before, the tightly stretched thread that linked him to the world title had finally snapped. Nothing, though, was yet decided for Hill, who had to win to put himself beyond von Trips's score because of the rule that only the best five results from eight races could be counted.

Hill was finally able to release himself from his anxieties when, after 43 laps, he crossed the finishing line in first place and became the new World Champion. He had no idea about the gravity of the drama that had been played out on the second lap and asked Chiti for news about von Trips. The Italian engineer mumbled a reply. Given his haggard look, Hill suspected the worst. When he learned the truth after the usual ceremonies

➤ **Italian Grand Prix.** Three Ferraris on the banking: Richie Ginther leads Phil Hill, who has Jim Clark's Lotus to his left, with Wolfgang von Trips trailing.

➤ **Italian Grand Prix.** Straight after his victory, Phil Hill and chief engineer Carlo Chiti are in deep discussion, most probably about the accident that had happened on the second lap of the race. At this moment, Hill remains unaware of the true scale of the tragedy that had taken the lives of Wolfgang von Trips and 14 spectators.

Wolfgang von Trips
A true sporting spirit

Wolfgang Graf Berghe von Trips was one of those drivers who flirted with death the most. When he made his single-seater début in 1956 during practice for the Italian Grand Prix at Monza, he wrecked his Lancia-Ferrari in a violent crash in the *Curva Grande* from which he emerged almost completely unscathed. Luigi Musso was the victim of a similar accident in the race and a metallurgical analysis revealed that in both cases the cause was a fractured steering arm. In 1958, again at Monza for the Italian Grand Prix and this time at the wheel of a Dino 246, von Trips ended up in hospital for several months after tangling with Harry Schell's BRM just after the start.

His career owed more to his talent and his tenacity than to the fact that, as the only son of a family without financial worries, he had money, although not as much as some people made out. In hill-climbing, a branch of motor sport that required real courage bordering on rashness and exceptional skills to tackle the challenge posed by the proximity of precipices, he won the 1958 European

⌄ On Saturday 1st September 1956, Wolfgang von Trips is all smiles as he gets ready to take part in the second practice session for the Italian Grand Prix at the wheel of a Lancia-Ferrari D50. A few laps later a broken steering arm in the *Curva Grande* cut short his début in Formula 1, fortunately without harm to him.

Championship driving a Porsche RSK. 'He made no bones about it when it came to seeking his limits but just went for it,' stated Richard von Frankenberg, 'and if he exceeded them, he had such reflexes that he was able to regain control of his car with absolute mastery.'

What Enzo Ferrari and Gino Rancati wrote about Von Trips's second place behind 51-year-old Piero Taruffi in the Mille Miglia of 1957 best describes the driver and the man he was.

When the competitors arrived in Bologna during the final stages of the race, Ferraris occupied the top three places, with Peter Collins in the lead, Taruffi second and von Trips third. Taruffi was an eclectic driver who had racked up impressive results, but he admitted to Enzo Ferrari, who was waiting in Bologna, that he was exhausted and additionally troubled by a rear axle that was on the verge of breaking. A personal element was also added to this stressful situation: he had promised his wife that he would retire if he won the race, and had been extremely hopeful of doing so, but now that was in doubt. In his memoir *Le Mie Gioie Terribili*, Enzo Ferrari described what happened next. 'I explained to

him in a few short words that although Collins was firmly ensconced in the lead, he was also having problems with his rear axle (the Englishman retired near Parma). The only other driver who posed a threat to him was von Trips. But I said to him that von Trips, who had a remarkable sense of team spirit, would obey my orders and, even when he saw Taruffi and caught his Ferrari, he refused to become involved in a scrap with him.'

Von Trips himself, as recounted by Gino Rancati in the book *Ferrari, Lui*, described the episode differently. At the end of the race, the German driver 'had tried to pass Taruffi, but his more experienced team-mate fended off his attacks on each occasion'. Was this down to respect for the team orders given to him or perhaps just his chivalrous spirit coming into play? Everybody is free to judge, but what is known is that von Trips finished the race just one second behind Taruffi on the road.

▾ A greeting from Wolfgang von Trips to Bernard Cahier, whom he has just recognised in the group of photographers immortalising his joy at winning the British Grand Prix at Aintree.

ITALIAN GRAND PRIX

Monza, 10th September 1961, 43 laps (6.214 miles/10.000km), 267.190 miles/430.000km • Starters 32, finishers 12

RACE				PRACTICE	
1st	Phil Hill	Ferrari 156 V6 120°	2h 03m 13.0s	4th	2m 47.2s
2nd	Dan Gurney	Porsche 718 F4	+31.2s	12th	2m 52.0s
3rd	Bruce McLaren	Cooper T55 Climax S4	+2m 28.4s	14th	2m 53.4s
4th	Jackie Lewis	Cooper T53 Climax S4	+2m 40.4s	16th	2m 54.0s
5th	Tony Brooks	BRM P48/57 Climax S4	+2m 40.5s	13th	2m 52.2s
6th	Roy Salvadori	Cooper T53 Climax S4	42 laps	18th	2m 55.2s
DNF	Richie Ginther	Ferrari 156 V6 120°	23 laps (engine)	3rd	2m 46.8s
DNF	Giancarlo Baghetti	Ferrari 156 V6 120°	13 laps (engine)	6th	2m 49.0s
DNF	Ricardo Rodríguez	Ferrari 156 V6 65°	13 laps (fuel pump)	2nd	2m 46.4s
DNF	Wolfgang von Trips	Ferrari 156 V6 120°	1 lap (accident)	1st	2m 46.3s

Pole position: von Trips, 2m 46.3s, 134.512mph/216.476kph **Fastest race lap:** Baghetti, 2m 48.4s, 132.835mph/213.777kph
Winner's average speed: 130.076mph/209.337kph **Drivers' championship:** 1st Phil Hill 34 (38)1, 2nd von Trips 33, 3rd Moss 21,
4th Ginther 16, 7th Baghetti 9, 11th Gendebien 3 **Constructors' championship:** 1st Ferrari 40 (52)1, 2nd Lotus-Climax 24, 3rd Porsche 17

[1] *Figure in brackets indicates all points scored; only the best five results counted towards the championship*

for the winner, he was completely dumbfounded and deeply shocked. But he did not cry or weep, contrary to some press reporting. He had freely accepted the risks taken to reach this point in time just as von Trips had done, but with the difference that the German driver had seemed more detached from the dangers involved. Was this perhaps a consequence of coming from a noble German background where emotions were repressed and true feelings hidden?

The season concludes

After his funeral in Burg Hemmersbach, Wolfgang von Trips's coffin was placed upon his Ferrari cabriolet to the sound of Chopin's funeral march and taken to be laid to rest in the family chapel in Kerpen. Phil Hill and Richie Ginther were among the pallbearers. The rain that had poured down since the start of the ceremony made climbing up the slope to the chapel difficult. 'We clambered up, eight of us, slipping in the mud, bearing the heavy casket,' Hill remembered. 'I never experienced anything so profoundly mournful as that day.' Laura Ferrari represented her husband but Romolo Tavoni was absent. He told Anthony Pritchard in the article 'Year of the Shark', published in *Motor Sport* in November 2011, that he had been prevented from taking part in the proceedings by Enzo Ferrari, although he had spent several days with von Trips's family according to Graham Gauld in *Modena Racing Memories*.

Shortly afterwards, Hill, who stayed on in Maranello at Tavoni's request, was having a coffee in the hotel opposite the factory when Enzo Ferrari came over to his table. Visibly exhausted, his eyes were hollow and grey stubble covered his cheeks because he had missed his usual daily visit to the barber's. The reason for his despondency was that he was under attack again from the fickle Italian press. As with the Mille Miglia tragedy in 1957 and Luigi Musso's death in 1958, newspapers were vilifying him. Motor racing was judged to be immoral; fingers were pointed at a manufacturer accused of sacrificing robustness for lightness in order to win. Maybe so, but in a sport in which weight was the enemy, Enzo Ferrari had never gambled with it to the extent of putting the lives of his drivers in danger, and mechanical failure on a Ferrari had rarely been the cause of a fatal accident.

This renewed attack from the newspapers came only a few weeks after the burden of the prolonged trial concerning the Mille Miglia tragedy of 1957 had finally been lifted from his shoulders. After the works Ferrari crash in which Alfonso de Portago, co-driver Ed Nelson and nine spectators had been killed, *Il Commendatore* had been charged with responsibility for the deaths and the case had dragged on for the best part of four years. During the latter stages of the trial in Mantua, he had sowed seeds of doubt about his willingness to continue in motor racing, pursuing 'an activity whose only reward was to be considered an assassin', but his ordeal had finally ended in acquittal by the judge on 26th July. Now, von Trips's accident at

Monza had put him back in the torture chamber, metaphorically speaking, although this time the pain did not have time to fester in quite the same way because storm clouds were gathering in Maranello.

However, while waiting to see what the future held, Ferrari's season ended in a blaze of glory with a fifth Formula 1 World Championship drivers' title, a first Formula 1 Constructors' Cup and a seventh World Sports Car Championship crown.

For Phil Hill, however, there was the significant disappointment that Mr Ferrari prevented him from taking part in the final race of the season, the United States Grand Prix, his home event, on the pretext of saving money. Nonetheless, the new World Champion did attend but it left a bitter memory, as he told Chris Nixon in *Motor Sport* in September 2001: 'I went to Watkins Glen, of course, but I was just driven round on a lap of honour on the back of a convertible. I was really sick about that, for that day should have been the crowning glory of my career, the biggest day of my life.'

Storms ahead

The crisis that exploded at the end of October had been brewing for a long time. It was already perceptible in 1959, but really began to unfold at the beginning of 1960 when Laura Ferrari started to stick her nose into all aspects of the Ferrari team's activities, sowing disarray everywhere. At the circuits, she dictated to drivers and mechanics, and cut back on travel expenses. In Maranello, she argued with people in the offices and workshops, reprimanded managers in front of their juniors without paying heed to their seniority and admonished them without knowing the facts, as when she accused Carlo Chiti of not paying rent for his apartment even though his contract guaranteed that it was rent-free. Besides stirring up trouble behind the scenes, she had also begun to display erratic behaviour in public. In *Modena Racing Memories*, Graham Gauld described a scene during the British Grand Prix at Aintree when, for no apparent reason, she sprayed Tavoni with Coca-Cola in the Liverpool hotel where the team was staying.

The issues went deeper still. According to Tavoni, Laura Ferrari had always meddled in the company's commercial activities, to the point of asking her husband to speed up sales if she thought she had insufficient money to meet her needs and those of his family. Family — or families? By October 1961, a rumour was circulating that Mr Ferrari was on the point of 'legitimising an unknown male' whom he would put in charge

of his business. The truth was that he had an illegitimate son who was not permitted by Laura to have the Ferrari name. There had been Alfredino 'Dino' Ferrari, the only son whom she had lost in 1956 when he was aged only 24. There would never be a Piero Ferrari — and as long as she lived she never gave in. Another rumour feeding all the acrimony swirling around Maranello was the one that Ferrari had already divorced his wife and was preparing to gift her his fortune in cash estimated at more than a billion *Lire* as well as several of his properties.

Things came to a head that October. It was common knowledge that Mrs Ferrari had stormed into the office of Girolamo Gardini, the sales manager, and slapped him at the end of a vicious diatribe in which she accused him of being a

▼ Enzo Ferrari's wife, Laura, seen here at Le Mans in 1961, poked her nose here, there and everywhere. For some she was her husband's ear; for others she was an unsettling presence. Her interference both at the circuits and in Maranello triggered a protest from important management figures at the company.

thief, like all the others. The accusation was all the more serious because Gardini was an exceedingly loyal lieutenant to Mr Ferrari, having joined him in 1942 when aged only 21, and was judged to be good at his job at a time the company's road cars were selling in growing numbers. Was this incident the start of the breakaway by a group of senior Ferrari staff? The straw that broke the camel's back? Sources diverge.

It was true that the rebels could no longer put up with Laura Ferrari's interference and they wanted to let Enzo Ferrari know that it had to stop. Verbally? They had already mentioned the problems on various occasions, but he had always replied that his wife's behaviour was none of their business and that he gave them enough authority to do their job without recourse to him. By letter? Although Tavoni, their spokesman, favoured speaking to Mr Ferrari about their position, the others preferred a written approach. Apart from Gardini, these others were Carlo Chiti (engineer), Giotto Bizzarrini (engineer), Ermanno Della Casa (administrative manager), Federico Giberti (factory manager), Enzo Selmi (chief personnel officer) and Fausto Galassi (foundry

manager). Despite Tavoni's reticence, a letter was written by the lawyer chosen to represent them.

Mr Ferrari did not respond. He just fired the 'troublemakers', even though they formed the backbone of his company. Was this a decision to affirm his authority? Maybe an outburst of anger after a setback in love (it was common knowledge in Maranello that he had been courting Luigi Musso's ex-girlfriend Fiamma Breschi)? After a private *tête-à-tête* with each of the dismissed employees, Ferrari relented with Gardini, Giberti and Galassi, and took them back. But not his former secretary, Romolo Tavoni, one of his most faithful servants who had become team manager, but was now shown the door after 11 years' service.

Although the Ferrari company was shaken to its foundations, the unrelenting urgency of motor racing waited for no man. The following year, Grand Touring cars were to replace sports cars and prototypes in the World Sports Car Championship, while in Formula 1 there were signs all around that the British teams were sure to raise their game after their hesitant start to the 1.5-litre era. So, for Mr Ferrari, it was time to reshuffle his cards to meet

◄ Carlo Chiti joined Ferrari in 1952 and was shown the door in 1961 on Enzo Ferrari's whim. He was responsible for the development of the 1958 Formula 1 Dino 246, the Formula 2 and Formula 1 156s of 1960 and 1961, and the 246 SP. Here he reassures Phil Hill during practice for the 1961 Italian Grand Prix.

Formula 1 World Championship (Drivers) *Top three plus other Ferrari drivers*

	1st Phil Hill	2nd Wolfgang von Trips	3rd Stirling Moss	4th Dan Gurney	5th Richie Ginther	9th Giancarlo Baghetti	14th Olivier Gendebien
Monaco GP	4	3	9	2	6	–	–
Dutch GP	6	9	3	0	2	–	–
Belgian GP	9	6	0	1	4	–	3
GP de l'ACF (France)	0	0	0	6	0	9	–
British GP	6	9	0	0	4	0	–
German GP	–4	6	9	0	0	–	–
Italian GP	9	0	0	6	0	0	–
United States GP	–	–	0	6	–	–	0
Total	**34**	**33**	**21**	**21**	**16**	**9**	**3**

the new challenges. Above all, he needed someone to take charge of the technical side of his racing team. He found himself faced with making a delicate choice between searching for the right skills and rewarding loyalty. And, of course, betting on youth.

His choice was 26-year-old Mauro Forghieri. Mauro's father, Reclus, had joined Scuderia Ferrari in 1937 as a machinist and after the war-time hiatus had returned to his old employer in Maranello and stayed until retirement in 1973. So, the loyal father was ideally placed to help his son join Ferrari in 1957 as a trainee before becoming a full-time employee in January 1960 after graduating from Bologna University, even if Mauro's dream had in fact been to work in the world of aeronautics.

What Mr Ferrari told the young Forghieri on 30th October left him open-mouthed in astonishment, as he recalled in *Forghieri on Ferrari*: 'From now on you're responsible for all sporting activities and testing!' More than a little taken aback, Forghieri protested that he lacked experience. To his stuttering hesitation, Ferrari's answer brooked no reply: 'Do your job as a technician and I'll do the rest!'

The reorganisation continued. To replace Tavoni, Ferrari brought in Eugenio Dragoni, who had made his fortune in cosmetics and the pharmaceutical industry. Passionate about racing, Dragoni had been behind the founding of Scuderia Sant'Ambroeus in 1951 with the main aim of bringing on young Italian drivers and enabling the best of them to reach Formula 1, as happened with Giancarlo Baghetti.

'It was only after I signed the contract that everything blew up,' said Phil Hill of the 'palace revolution' at Ferrari. With the departure of Chiti and Tavoni, he no longer had his best footholds in Maranello. He had matured with them and his victories were as much theirs as his. In particular, he owed a lot to Chiti, the father of the 156, including his world title. Chiti was

Formula 1 World Championship (Constructors)

	1st Ferrari	2nd Lotus-Climax	3rd Porsche
Monaco GP	–6	8	2
Dutch GP	8	4	0
Belgian GP	8	0	–1
GP de l'ACF (France)	8	4	6
British GP	8	0	2
German GP	–6	8	0
Italian GP	8	0	6
United States GP	0	8	6
Total	**40**	**32**	**22**

World Sports Car Championship

	1st Ferrari	2nd Maserati	3rd Porsche
Sebring 12 Hours	8	0	–2
Targa Florio	8	3	6
Nürburgring 1,000Km	–6	8	–1
Le Mans 24 Hours	8	3	2
Pescara Four Hours	–4	–2	3
Total	**24**	**14**	**11**

an artist with a methodical mind in a barrel-like body. Although he was prone to outbursts of childish anger when he did not get immediate satisfaction, he was a competent and ingenious workaholic. Hill would also miss Richie Ginther, who had left for BRM.

The coming season already had a bitter taste for Phil Hill. And with good reason.

The date is 24th February 1962 and the
Maranello courtyard is hosting a display of
shiny red Ferraris. In the photo are three of the
four spyders that were on show plus a 156, one that
would never race in the configuration revealed that day.

1962
DOUBT CREEPS IN

M aranello, Saturday 24th February. 'What are your thoughts on the new Le Mans regulations?' Giovanni Canestrini asked Enzo Ferrari. Facing *Il Commendatore* at the annual press conference flanked by master coachbuilder Pinin Farina were 120 journalists from all over the world. Ferrari's answer was a bombshell: 'I won't race at Le Mans because my cars don't comply with Appendix A. I was warned about the requirements of this appendix too late.' Four days later the entry list for the Sarthe event was closed. On it were four works Ferraris and two from NART entered in the 'experimental' category with engine sizes between 2,000cc and 3,000cc. Olivier Gendebien/Phil Hill, Willy Mairesse/Michael Parkes, Giancarlo Baghetti/Lorenzo Bandini and Pedro Rodríguez/Ricardo Rodríguez were announced as works drivers (for the time being) as the American team had not yet named its line-ups. Ferrari was a realist and also a cunning calculator who often took offence and used these earth-shattering announcements in which threats combined with bluster to best serve his own ends. It was impossible to believe that the subject had not been raised during the visit to Maranello of Jacques Finance, president of the Sporting Commission of the Automobile Club de l'Ouest (ACO), organisers of Le Mans, prior to this 'mediafest'.

'Mobile gas guzzlers'

So what was all the hoo-ha about? The origin of the dispute went back to 1st December 1961 when the regulations for Le Mans had been unveiled to the press. While it was clear that the event would be part of the World Sports Car Championship, which included the International Championship for GT Manufacturers open to GTs with a cubic capacity of over 1,000cc (we will come back to that later), the ACO took a different stance from that of the FIA's *Commission Sportive International* (CSI). Without breaking away from the international body, Le Mans and a number of other organisers — those for Sebring, the Targa Florio and the Nürburgring — were determined to have their own way and promote a category of cars called prototypes or experimental vehicles as close as possible to what a grand touring car should be. In other words, the Le Mans lawmakers wanted to get rid of the monsters or 'mobile gas guzzlers' as they saw it.

But a question mark hung over this type of Le Mans car, which, although watered down, raised doubts about its validity when the mechanical aspects had no restrictions. By increasing the capacity limit to 4 litres, the ACO was clearly aiming to attract American manufacturers. Was it not another incitement to an arms race in terms of power? In addition, the ACO now required a passenger compartment 'free of mechanical elements' and a windscreen with a base measuring at least 90cm (35.5 inches) across and 20cm (7.8 inches) high. The result was that the sports cars made by Ferrari in compliance with CSI regulations were effectively excluded from Le Mans — so only Ferrari's GT cars would go to Le Mans. Setting a deadline was also a way of applying pressure, so Ferrari would wait before entering while a fresh wind was starting to blow from the west.

Diversity, multiplication and shared laurels

In the meantime, there were four sports cars, Dinos in all but name, although they would not be given this moniker until later. For the moment, Maranello continued to use the in-house designation in which the first two figures indicated the cubic capacity and the third the number of cylinders. Externally, nothing distinguished them from one another. The key measurements were length 406cm (178.0 inches), width 148cm (62.6 inches), height 97cm (41.3 inches), wheelbase 232cm (94.5 inches) and front and rear tracks 120cm (56 inches). They all had tubular chassis, independent suspension and five-speed gearboxes. The only differences between them were their engines and thus their weight and tyres.

The 196 SP's target was the European Hillclimb Championship and twisty circuits so it had a 2-litre 60-degree V6 with a single overhead camshaft and its power output had been increased to 210bhp at 7,500rpm. The 246 SP, winner of the previous year's Targa Florio, continued its career under the new bodywork imposed by the regulations so the driver could use the rear-view mirror — at last. While the engine was unchanged, the angle of the V6 was now 65 degrees and it delivered around 270bhp at 7,500rpm. A 248 SP and a 268 SP completed the line-up. Strictly speaking, the V8 engine in these models was not a novelty at Ferrari but it owed nothing to the preceding Lancia design by Vittorio Jano because it was the work of Carlo Chiti, who had designed it before his departure. It was a 90-degree V8 with a single overhead camshaft. The respective cubic capacities of the cars were 2,458cc (3.03 x 2.59 inches) and 2,645cc (3.03 x 2.79 inches) with power outputs of 250bhp and 265bhp.

The new 1962 competition Berlinetta, chassis 3223 GT, was supposed to be delivered to Scuderia Serenissima (also known

➤ Only a trained eye could identify the distinction of this 156, which was shorter than the previous version, with a more inclined windscreen. Just visible at the far end of the display is the future GTO, which was yet to be homologated. This is chassis 3223 GT, the first of the famous line.

➤ Enzo Ferrari's annual press conference was the moment for journalists to talk to the Scuderia's current drivers in addition to seeing its latest racing cars. In the foreground, a grinning Willy Mairesse is having a chat with a couple of interested onlookers.

as Scuderia SSS Repubblica di Venezia) and raced at Sebring by Carlo Mario Abate/Nino Vaccarella. It differed from the 250 GT SWB to such an extent that it was basically a new car but was homologated as a derivative. Designed by Giotto Bizzarrini with bodywork penned by Sergio Scaglietti, it stood out visually from the prototype tested by Stirling Moss at Monza the previous September by its cut-off tail. Its plunging front with its smaller grille and ventilation air intakes closed by moveable shutters remained unchanged, as did the front suspension consisting of double wishbones with coil springs and dampers. At the live-axle rear, however, to improve a twitchy drivetrain 'helper' coil springs supplemented the semi-elliptic leaf springs, the replacement of which by regular coil springs would have required a chassis modification that would have invalidated the homologation. The 3-litre V12 engine that had powered the previous Berlinetta and the Monza prototype was installed, but with a dry sump and a power output of around 300bhp at 7,400rpm.

And so to Formula 1. The 156 that held pride of place at the head of this dazzling scarlet parade was shorter and lower than the previous model and had lost some of its finesse, while a more steeply angled windscreen and a rectangular side-mounted air intake further distinguished it from the 1961 car. The example on display was an experimental one, with four overhead camshafts and a gearbox mounted in front of the rear axle, and never raced in this form, but for normal use the V6 remained in twin-cam configuration and put out about 188bhp at 9,600rpm for the 65-degree version and about 195bhp at 10,000rpm for the 120-degree version. Suspension-wise, the front still had the double-wishbone and anti-roll bar set-up, while at the rear there was a reinforcing link connecting the stub axles to the chassis in an attempt to improve the car's erratic roadholding.

While awaiting on-track evidence of the usefulness of the modifications, which, in Phil Hill's opinion, were nothing more than a facelift, two races in Florida became the focal point of Enzo Ferrari's attention. For the first time, the GTs would be battling for the manufacturers' titles, with one awarded for each of three divisions defined by engine capacity. In Ferrari's case, this was Division III, over 2,000cc, for cars complying with the CSI's definition of 'production-based' and requiring 100 examples to have been built. Resigned, *Il Commendatore* quipped: 'If everything works out, henceforth we'll now have to be content with a third of the glory and a third of the laurels!' Consolation for Ferrari, however, came in the form of the *Challenge Mondial de Vitesse et Endurance* (World Speed and Endurance Challenge), which was open to sports cars and created by the organisers of the four blue-riband events on the calendar: the Sebring 12 Hours, the Targa Florio, the Nürburgring 1,000Km and the Le Mans 24 Hours. For this contest, a single title was awarded — no sharing!

No point in racing

Daytona Three Hours, 11th February

Obviously, the Daytona Three Hours, the opening round of the International Championship for GT Manufacturers, bore no comparison to the far more arduous 12 Hours of Sebring. And there was no 250 GTO (Omologato) even though it was now homologated to take on an armada of Chevrolet Corvettes and Pontiac Tempests plus a pair of Jaguar E-types in Division III. There were, however, four 250 GT SWBs plus the 250 Sperimentale (2643 GT) entrusted to Stirling Moss, so the result looked a foregone conclusion. Sure enough, three hours later the Englishman, who was delighted to have buried the hatchet with Enzo Ferrari and exhilarated at the prospect of driving his cars, gave Maranello the nine points that went with victory in the Division III GT category at the end of a race in which he finished fourth overall.

Moss described it as 'an easy race' and wrote that his only memory was of an 'amusing start'. He was not averse to hogging the limelight and when standing in his starting circle he gave an interview while getting ready to sprint across the track. Then the flag dropped to remind him that he had a race to win. But for Phil Hill, teamed with Ricardo Rodríguez in a 246 SP entered by NART, it was a very different story. He was in the lead when he had to stop to have an imprudent seagull removed from his radiator, gifting first place to Dan Gurney, who was driving solo in a Lotus 19 Monte Carlo. On lap 44, the loss of the fuel filler cap obliged Hill to pit again before a trip up the escape road in Turn 1 ended his charge to close the gap to his fellow countryman. Behind, Jim Hall in his Chaparral was breathing down his neck. This turned the closing laps into a real cliff-hanger.

With two laps to go, Gurney had a two-minute lead over Rodríguez and reckoned that he had the race won. Suddenly, the Climax engine in the Lotus cut out in the banked corner and he freewheeled towards the finishing line, making sure he did not cross it. He parked his car beside the wall, got out, gave the engine a brief once-over without much hope and went to ask the clerk of the course how much time was left until the end of the race. He then jumped back into the cockpit. Rodríguez and Hall were on their last lap. The end of the story caused controversy

DAYTONA THREE HOURS

Daytona, 11th February 1962, 82 laps (3.810 miles/6.132km), 312.440 miles/502.824km • Starters 50, classified finishers 31

1st	Dan Gurney	Lotus 19 Climax	3h 00m 04.0s
2nd	Phil Hill/Ricardo Rodríguez	Ferrari 246 SP (0796)	82 laps
3rd	Jim Hall	Chaparral 1	82 laps
4th	Stirling Moss	Ferrari 250 GT EXP (2643 GT) (1st GT+2.0)	80 laps
5th	George Constantine	Ferrari 250 TR 59/60	79 laps
6th	Dick Rathmann	Chaparral 1	79 laps
8th	John Fulp/Skip Hudson	Ferrari Dino 246 S (0784)	78 laps
12th	'Fireball' Roberts	Ferrari 250 GT SWB (2725 GT)	77 laps
15th	Ricardo Rodríguez/Pete Ryan	Ferrari TRI 61 (0794 TR)	76 laps
16th	Olivier Gendebien	Ferrari 250 GT SWB (2845 GT)	75 laps
18th	Doug Thiem	Ferrari 250 GT SWB	75 laps
DNF	Innes Ireland	Ferrari 250 GT SWB (2735 GT)	59 laps (brakes)

Fastest race lap: Rodríguez (Ferrari 246 SP), 2m 0.6s, 108.857mph/175.188kph **Winner's average speed:** 104.101mph/167.534kph **FIA International Championship for GT Manufacturers (GT Division III, over 2,000cc):**[1] 1st Ferrari 9, 2nd Chevrolet 4, 3rd Jaguar 2

[1] Scoring system for the top six places was 9–6–4–3–2–1; only the manufacturer's highest-placed car scored points

for a long time. Did Gurney use the Lotus's electric starter when the flag fell to cover the handful of yards separating him from the finishing line to win the race? Or did he take advantage of the slope to do so as he claimed for a long time? In the end, film and photos confirmed the first hypothesis.

The foregoing was of only passing interest in Maranello, where the future occupied everybody's thoughts. Remember that Moss, after his brief gallop at Monza in the prototype of the future GTO, had found that it showed promise but was difficult to drive because of a lack of rigidity in the rear axle. For young Mauro Forghieri, who was tasked with finding a solution, it was the start of long bouts of testing. During one exercise on a section of the *Autostrada del Sole* linking Bologna to Florence, Willy Mairesse was at the wheel when a gust of wind at the exit from a tunnel sent the prototype careering into a barrier, luckily without serious consequences for either car or driver. Testing involved chassis 3223 GT, which Enzo Ferrari had decided not to sell to Scuderia Serenissima after all, because he did not want to be overshadowed by the team's owner, Count Giovanni Volpi, and 3387 GT. It was the latter that was destined to make the GTO's race début in the Sebring 12 Hours and with only two weeks to go, on 10th March, it was at Monza for evaluation by Lorenzo Bandini. The mood among the Ferrari personnel present that day, including Enzo himself, was somewhat strained, but when Bandini lapped quicker than Moss had managed the previous September, everybody was all smiles again. The future looked rosy — and so it would be — but without Bizzarrini.

Mission accomplished

Sebring 12 Hours, 24th March

A month after Daytona, Phil Hill and Olivier Gendebien were back at Sebring. Given their past performances here, it would be no exaggeration to say that the place, the ambience and the race suited them down to the ground. While Hill was not from the same bourgeois background as Gendebien, they had in common the fact that they both spoke French, did not throw their weight around and were scrupulously honest. They were brilliant long-distance drivers, each as quick as the other. The bond between them arose not just from teamwork during races, in which they displayed complementary talents, but also because they liked each other. But this time they had team orders. Their priority was to win Division III at the wheel of 3387 GT, the GTO entrusted to them by Maranello and entered under the NART banner.

Were their ambitions greater than they seemed on paper as their chances in the overall classification looked slim? Among the favourites in Luigi Chinetti's camp were Stirling Moss and Innes Ireland, who preferred to race the team's 250 TRI 61 after finding that the alternative 248 SP was too slow, leaving it to be raced by John 'Buck' Fulp/Pete Ryan. Logically, Moss/Ireland would be quicker than Hill/Gendebien, without even mentioning the Rodríguez brothers at the wheel of an aging but

▲ **Sebring 12 Hours.** Could the NART 250 TRI 61 that Innes Ireland (pictured) shared with Stirling Moss have won the race? Early refuelling carried out at 11.37am, but declared illegal shortly after half distance, left the question unanswered and allowed the similar car of Jo Bonnier/ Lucien Bianchi to take victory.

◄ **Sebring 12 Hours.** The second GTO built, 3387 GT, was entrusted to Phil Hill and Olivier Gendebien, who were told to finish in the points. They did that in style by finishing second overall and winning the GT Division III category after a flawless race.

> ➤ **Sebring 12 Hours.** Despite appearances, Jo Bonnier (left) and Lucien Bianchi (second from left) were the winners, but Phil Hill (right) and Olivier Gendebien could rightly be very happy because their second place was a priceless success for Ferrari in immediately putting the 250 GTO on the map.

still very fast 246 SP, plus Bob Grossman/Alan Connell in a 246 S and Jo Bonnier/Lucien Bianchi in a Scuderia SSS Repubblica di Venezia 250 TRI 61, the car in which Hill/Gendebien had won the previous year's race.

In terms of outright victory, the most serious threats to the 11 Ferraris, eight of which were entered by NART, came down to three Maseratis and two Chaparrals. The cars from Modena included two *Tipo* 64s, one entered by Briggs Cunningham for Walt Hansgen/Dick Thompson, the other by Scuderia SSS Repubblica di Venezia for Carlo Mario Abate/Nino Vaccarella. Maserati was very much focused on the development of the future *Tipo* 151 coupés destined for Le Mans so the *Tipo* 64s were evolutions of the *Tipo* 63 seen in the Pescara Four Hours in August 1961. While the car was still powered by the same rear-mounted 3-litre V12, its stand-out feature was rear suspension combining the theoretical advantages of an independent configuration with those of the de Dion axle by means of a truss. Another potential threat from Modena came in the form of a Cooper Monaco powered by a four-cylinder Maserati engine

in the hands of Bruce McLaren/Roger Penske, as proved by its fourth-fastest time in practice.

Negligence on the part of NART? Intransigence by the organisers who were completely overwhelmed by events? Many years later, Moss continued to fume about the disqualification of the 250 TRI 61 he shared with Ireland, all the more so as this event turned out to be the last endurance race of his career. Let us gloss over the fact that Ireland shot into the lead right from the start and duelled with the elder Rodríguez for 11 laps. Instead, let us jump forward to the key moment 37 minutes into the race. The Ferrari pitted not to refuel, which could not be done until lap 20 in compliance with the regulations, but to have fresh brake pads fitted. Nobody knew how many laps had been covered, NART included, so a marshal broke the seal on the filler cap on his own initiative and a mechanic interpreted this as a signal to fill up the car. Moss then roared off in pursuit of the Rodríguez brothers, who were now providing the excitement in a race in which the Maserati challenge had already expired, although they

SEBRING 12 HOURS

Sebring, 24th March 1962, 206 laps (5.200 miles/8.369km), 1,071.253 miles/1,724.014km • Starters 55, classified finishers 18

1st	Jo Bonnier/Lucien Bianchi	Ferrari TRI 61 (0792 TR)	12h 01m 53.4s
2nd	**Phil Hill/Olivier Gendebien**	**Ferrari 250 GTO (3387 GT) (1st GT+2.0)**	**196 laps**
3rd	Bill Wuesthoff/Bruce Jennings/Frank Rand	Porsche 718 RS 60	195 laps
4th	Fabrizio Serena di Lapigio/Sterling Hamill	Ferrari 250 GT SWB (2725 GT)	190 laps
5th	Bruce McLaren/Roger Penske	Cooper Monaco T57	190 laps
6th	Hap Sharp/Jim Hall/Ronnie Hissom/Chuck Daigh	Chaparral 1	189 laps
8th	Ed Hugus/George Reed	Ferrari 250 GT EXP (2643 GT)	187 laps
13th	Pete Ryan/John Fulp	Ferrari 248 SP (0806)	176 laps
34th	Charlie Hayes/Carl Haas/Chuck Dietrich	Ferrari 250 GT SWB (3327 GT)	147 laps
DNF	Bob Grossman/Alan Connell/Pedro Rodríguez	Ferrari 246 S (0784)	97 laps (oil pressure)
DNF	Fernand Tavano/Colin Davis	Ferrari 250 GT SWB (2945 GT)	– (engine)
DNF	Pedro Rodríguez/Ricardo Rodríguez	Ferrari 246 SP (0790)	– (engine)
DNF	George Constantine/Gaston Andrey	Ferrari 250 TR 59/60 (0746 TR)	– (rear axle)
DSQ	Innes Ireland/Stirling Moss	Ferrari TRI 61 (0794 TR)	– (illegal refuelling)

Fastest race lap: Ricardo Rodríguez (Ferrari 246 SP), 3m 12.4s, 97.297mph/156.584kph **Winner's average speed:** 89.028mph/143.265kph
FIA International Championship for GT Manufacturers (GT Division III, over 2,000cc):[1] 1st Ferrari 18, 2nd Chevrolet 6, 3rd Jaguar 5

[1] This race was also the first round of the World Speed and Endurance Challenge

themselves went out at about half distance when their engine gave up the ghost.

Well into the second half of the race, with 128 laps completed, the outcome of the Sebring 12 Hours was decided. The British duo looked to have the race sewn up as they were in the lead with two laps in hand over the Bonnier/Bianchi Ferrari, which had clutch problems. But discussions had been going on among the race officials. After initially planning to penalise Moss/Ireland 15 seconds for refuelling too soon, they instead chose to disqualify them. Forty laps later, Pedro Rodríguez, now installed in the Grossman/Connell Dino 246 S after the retirement of his own car, went out with clutch failure, leaving Bonnier/Bianchi to win from Hill/Gendebien, who had done everything asked of them.

A real victory!

Brussels Grand Prix, 1st April

A week later, the Brussels Grand Prix followed Sebring. Replacing the balmy Florida weather were typical cold April temperatures accompanied by wind and rain to welcome the cars and drivers competing in the first Formula 1 race of the European season. It was a non-championship event run over three 22-lap heats on the 2.8-mile Heysel circuit. Before Mauro Forghieri left for the Belgian capital, Enzo Ferrari said to him: 'Don't even think about touching the chassis set-ups; you don't change a winning car. And don't forget that the person who chose you knows more than you do.' This was enlightening when we learn what happened later.

Unfortunately for Ferrari, Willy Mairesse won overall in Brussels on 1st April, a very appropriate date in the light of what followed. Even if his victory — aggregated from third place in the first heat and wins in the second and third heats — looked reassuring at first glance, the result, achieved with the 65-degree V6, was misleading because the top contenders fell by the wayside. Jim Clark, on pole in his V8 Climax-engined Lotus 24, suffered premature valve failure; Graham Hill (BRM), winner of the first heat, was disqualified at the start of the second because he was unable to fire up his V8; and Stirling Moss, who finished second in the first heat thanks to a stunning comeback after going down an escape road on the first lap, retired while leading the second heat due to a broken camshaft in his Climax V8. So the result showed that while the jury was still out regarding the reliability of the British V8s, they certainly had ample power, the BRM's 185bhp at 10,300rpm and the Climax's 190bhp at 9,600rpm sowing consternation in Maranello. Another concerning aspect was roadholding, for Mairesse spun many times during the proceedings.

➤ **Brussels Grand Prix.** This non-championship Formula 1 race, which attracted a top-class field, saw Willy Mairesse not only score his maiden single-seater victory but also claim a rare success for the revised 156. He was as feisty and focused as ever — and full of confidence.

▼ **Brussels Grand Prix.** Mairesse has every reason to be delighted. Third in the first heat after starting behind a V8-powered front row comprising Jim Clark and Stirling Moss in their Lotuses and Graham Hill's BRM, he won the other two heats to claim a significant confidence-boosting victory for himself but one that led Ferrari down the garden path.

End of reign

Pau Grand Prix, 23rd April

Things seemed to look up in Pau although Pedro Rodríguez's second place in a 120-degree V6 Ferrari behind the uncatchable Maurice Trintignant's Lotus gave false hope. The works Coopers and Porsches were absent and the Mexican, who made a stunning start, owed his place on the podium to the retirements of Jim Clark's Lotus and Jo Bonnier's Porsche. A very focused Lorenzo Bandini, driving the Ferrari used in Brussels, just about put on the performance that team manager Eugenio Dragoni expected of him by finishing fifth behind the privately entered V8 BRMs of Jackie Lewis and Tony Marsh.

But this Easter Monday left an indelible mark on the world of motor racing for a very different reason. On the day Trintignant triumphed in Pau, Moss was racing in the Glover Trophy at Goodwood in a Lotus 18/21 in UDT-Laystall colours and seemed to come into the St Mary's right-hander too quickly. Why was he too far out to the left? Why, after finding himself on the grass, did he just plough straight on into the bank against which the Lotus destroyed itself? All he could remember was the fact that he held the hand of a nurse, Anne Strudwick, during the 40 minutes it took the emergency team to extricate him from the twisted tubes of the chassis that had folded back around him. For Enzo Ferrari, who had never hidden his enormous respect for the English driver, the shock was all the greater, especially as Moss was soon to have been seen driving Ferraris regularly.

Moss's conditions, including that his entrant must continue to be Rob Walker, had been accepted in Maranello and his first Formula 1 outing in a 156 was scheduled for 12th May at Silverstone in the non-championship International Trophy. In addition, UDT-Laystall had ordered a GTO for him and after running at the Le Mans test weekend on 6th–7th April it had been at Goodwood ready for him to race later that fateful day. The spats of the past had certainly been forgotten. Back in 1952, Moss had been promised a Ferrari 500 Formula 2 car in the Bari Grand Prix and had travelled specially from London to drive it, but the car was instead given to Piero Taruffi and Stirling only learned about this on the spot. It had taken him 10 years to forgive that slight.

In the meantime, the Aintree International 200 on 28th April gave a foretaste of how the Formula 1 World Championship was going to unfold. While there were no Porsches and the Coopers were still powered by the four-cylinder Climax engine, Phil Hill and Giancarlo Baghetti in their 120-degree V6 Ferraris found themselves up against the latest iterations of the Lotus (Jim Clark), Lola (John Surtees) and BRM (Graham Hill and Richie Ginther) powered by V8 engines. The Ferrari men finished third and fourth, Hill from Baghetti, the latter having put on such a polished performance that he looked able to get the better of his team-mate. Despite the decent finishing positions, the result was a worrying one for Ferrari. As well as being beaten by Clark, who led from the third lap, the Italian cars were outclassed by Bruce McLaren's second-placed Cooper and also by the quickest of the BRMs (Hill) and Lolas (Surtees) before their retirement. There were mitigating factors, however, as Phil Hill was suffering from a severe cold and had no second gear for 15 laps, while the 156's roadholding was still as erratic as ever.

The *Tifosi's* choice

Targa Florio, 6th May

At the beginning of May there was still hope that Stirling Moss, despite being in a coma in the Atkinson Morley hospital in London, would be able to race again, but the prospect of a short convalescence was becoming increasingly remote and the 46th Targa Florio took place without him.

The number of Ferraris on the entry list, 14, did not seem excessive when compared to the quantity of Alfa Romeos, and the most serious of them would be the three Dinos driven by Phil Hill/Olivier Gendebien (268 SP), Willy Mairesse/Ricardo Rodríguez (246 SP) and Giancarlo Baghetti/Lorenzo Bandini (196 SP). Once again, the race looked like being a duel with Porsche and there were strong entries for Nino Vaccarella/Graham Hill (718 GTR) and Dan Gurney/Jo Bonnier (718 WSR) in Scuderia SSS Repubblica di Venezia colours. This team widened its potential podium contenders by entrusting the Maserati *Tipo* 64 seen at Sebring to Carlo Mario Abate/Colin Davis. The race was also the third round of the International Championship for GT Manufacturers, Divisions II and III, in which a Ferrari 250 GTO (Giorgio Scarlatti/Pietro Ferraro) and two Porsche 356 B Carrera Abarth GTLs (Hans Herrmann/Herbert Linge and Antonio Pucci/Edgar Barth) had the best chances of victory for their respective marques.

As was often the case on the Piccolo Circuito delle Madonie, practice dashed the hopes of the most experienced contenders. Phil Hill in his 268 SP was the victim of a throttle problem as

▲ **Targa Florio.** A brain-storming session at Ferrari where it was all looking rosy before Phil Hill took over the 268 SP in which Olivier Gendebien is seen at the wheel. Mauro Forghieri (right) and Lorenzo Bandini (upper left) listen attentively to the Belgian driver's comments.

➤ **Targa Florio.** More comments, but this time those made by Ricardo Rodríguez with emphatic gestures for his seated fellow drivers, Giancarlo Baghetti (left) and Willy Mairesse; that is probably Mauro Forghieri with his back to us.

◄ **Targa Florio.** This is the 246 SP of winners Willy Mairesse and Ricardo Rodríguez backed up by Olivier Gendebien, who had been left without a drive following Phil Hill's terminal 'off' in the 268 SP. The car's regular drivers put in scintillating performances before Gendebien added the finishing touches to a dominant victory.

▼ **Targa Florio.** Proof that the 196 SP looks like a 246 SP is supplied by this photo of Lorenzo Bandini with its hand-written dedication to Bernard Cahier, the man who took it. The damaged tail section with its rather haphazard fixing was the result of Giancarlo Baghetti's third-lap spin.

he tackled a corner and with all four wheels locked his car plunged down a slope beside a farm building. Thankfully he was unhurt but the Dino was destroyed. Team manager Eugenio Dragoni, though, attributed the crash to human error rather than mechanical failure and chose to sideline Hill and favour Gendebien by assigning him to be the third driver of the Mairesse/Rodríguez car. It was common knowledge that Dragoni and Hill could not stand each other. The authoritarian team manager, who was Milanese more than Italian, was very nationalistic and had little sympathy with any driver who overshadowed home-grown talent. Baghetti, despite his skills, owed his rise to fame to Dragoni, while Bandini, a mechanic from the age of 15 working in a garage in Milan, was a protégé.

Come the race, Mairesse allowed his fiery temperament full rein and covered the first of the 10 laps in 40m 43.3s. In the 246 SP's wake, drivers either followed or disappeared, second-placed Gurney becoming one of the latter when he crashed out second time around due to brake trouble. Gurney's demise elevated Baghetti's 196 SP but the Italian ruined it by spinning on the third lap, returning to the pits with his car's tail section flapping, which at least gave co-driver Bandini an opportunity to show what he could do by getting back among the front-runners and giving the *Tifosi* good reason to shout themselves hoarse. At the end of his first lap, Bandini was sixth, then after one more lap — half distance — he was fifth having got past the Herrmann/Linge Porsche. Meanwhile, Ludovico Scarfiotti's 2-litre OSCA had inherited second place with the Dino's

delay but only lasted another lap before quitting with engine failure, leaving Scarlatti's GTO in the top three in front of the Vaccarella/Hill Porsche coupé in which Bonnier had now been installed following Gurney's exit. Another notable retirement on lap 4 was the *Tipo* 64, Abate/Davis having reached sixth at one point.

Into the second half of the race, Rodríguez took over from Mairesse and continued to extend the Dino's lead while Bandini was still going hell for leather. At the end of lap 6, which he covered in just 41m 2s, Bandini handed back to Baghetti. A lap later Rodríguez, now almost 20 minutes ahead of his pursuers, pitted. Was he a little peeved at having to hand over to Gendebien? Or had he forgotten team orders? Whichever, he arrived a lap later than he should have done, leaving Gendebien waiting for a whole lap with his helmet on before taking over for his stint and powering onwards to victory. None of this was any problem for the *Tifosi* of Sicily, for they had waited a long time for such a fine Ferrari performance. Baghetti made it a 1–2 by matching the flawless Bandini's performance in his last stint and finishing ahead of Bonnier at the wheel of a practically brakeless Porsche.

Scarlatti was a lucky fourth in the GTO after a minor knock on the last lap that forced him to change the right-hand front wheel with the on-board jack. Even so it was a well-deserved result as he had spent nine of the 10 laps behind the wheel, as Ferraro, the car's owner, had been rather sluggish during his single lap. The GTO also won the GT category, which was what mattered most to Maranello.

TARGA FLORIO

Piccolo Madonie, 6th May 1962, 10 laps (44.7 miles/72.0km), 447.4 miles/720.0km • Starters 46, classified finishers 21

1st	Willy Mairesse/Ricardo Rodríguez/Olivier Gendebien	Ferrari 246 SP (0796)	7h 02m 56.3s
2nd	Giancarlo Baghetti/Lorenzo Bandini	Ferrari 196 SP (0804)	7h 14m 24.0s
3rd	Nino Vaccarella/Jo Bonnier	Porsche 718 GTR	7h 17m 20.0s
4th	Giorgio Scarlatti/Pietro Ferraro	Ferrari 250 GTO (3451 GT) (1st GT+2.0)	7h 22m 08.1s
5th	Roger de Lageneste/Jean Rolland	Ferrari 250 GT SWB (2807 GT)	7h 44m 33.0s
6th	Hans Herrmann/Herbert Linge	Porsche 356B Carrera Abarth GTL	7h 45m 26.0s
19th	Umberto de Bonis/Roberto Fusina	Ferrari 250 GT	–
NC	Giuseppe Crespi/Alberto Federici	Ferrari 250 GT SWB (1813 GT)	–
DNF	André Simon/Fernand Tavano	Ferrari 250 GT SWB (2973 GT)	–
DNS	**Phil Hill/Olivier Gendebien**	**Ferrari 268 SP (0802)**	**– (practice accident)**
DNS	**Phil Hill**	**Ferrari 250 GTO (3413 GT)**	**–**

Fastest race lap: Mairesse, 40m 0.3s, 66.979mph/107.793kph **Winner's average speed:** 63.468mph/102.142kph **FIA International Championship for GT Manufacturers (GT Division III, over 2,000cc):**[1] 1st Ferrari 27, 2nd Chevrolet 6, 3rd Jaguar 5

[1] This race was also the second round of the World Speed and Endurance Challenge

Hoping for a rosier future

Dutch Grand Prix, 20th May

While awaiting the Nürburgring 1,000Km where, in the event of victory, Ferrari's domination in sports and GT cars would be confirmed, the opening round of the Formula 1 World Championship took place at Zandvoort. As it is never over until the fat lady sings, nothing prevented Ferrari from hoping for a good result in the Dutch Grand Prix. But even before the first practice sessions, things were looking bleak and more was needed than just hope.

Mauro Forghieri had been in England a few weeks earlier to talk to UDT-Laystall representatives and had seen for himself that competitiveness was sorely lacking in the Prancing Horse camp. On 12th May, the International Trophy at Silverstone was the first full-scale dress rehearsal for the coming season. Up against the best English cars, Innes Ireland at the wheel of the Ferrari 156 that Stirling Moss should have driven finished fourth, a lap behind Graham Hill's BRM, winner by a hair's breadth from Jim Clark's Lotus and John Surtees's Lola. In fact, Clark had been leading but was given erroneous information and lifted off, thinking that his victory was assured, only for Hill to pass him at Woodcote, the last corner before the finishing line. Questioned by Forghieri, Ireland, who knew the Lotuses and Coopers like the back of his hand, was critical of the Ferrari, judging that it lagged behind its rivals apart from its exceptional gearbox.

Just a week later at Zandvoort, the gap was huge. While there were surprises from the new Cooper T60 (with Climax V8 engine coupled to a six-speed Knight gearbox) and Porsche 804 (with eight-cylinder air-cooled engine and disc brakes) because of their slimness compared to the previous models, the new Lotus 25 amazed everybody. Its monocoque structure, made from riveted aluminium panels incorporating the fuel cells in two box sections, was ground-breaking. The car was much more rigid than its multi-tubular predecessor, the Lotus 24, and just over 24lb lighter, although its narrow monocoque was so low that it obliged Clark, around whom Colin Chapman had designed the car, to adopt a semi-reclined driving position that he took a little time to get used to.

During the Friday morning practice session, Clark got among the front-runners with a time of 1m 36.1s compared with 1m 36.5s for Phil Hill and 1m 33.3s for Graham Hill; the Scot then amazed everybody in the afternoon with a lap in 1m 33.6s. Ferrari's

fightback was but a pale shadow in comparison. Hill went a bit quicker in 1m 35.0s and Baghetti improved his morning time by three seconds (1m 36.3s against 1m 39.3s) putting him just behind Ricardo Rodríguez (1m 36.1s). Despite new rear suspension and a wider track, the reigning World Champion was wrestling with his car round the circuit, while the BRMs looked as if they were on rails. At the end of the first day's practice, Graham Hill was a full second quicker than Clark while BRM team-mate Richie Ginther set the fourth-best time in 1m 34.5s, putting him in front of his former colleagues at the Scuderia. The next day, what was more worrying under threatening skies was that while the Ferraris were unable to improve on the times set on Friday, Surtees stunned everybody by clinching pole at the wheel of a Lola powered by the Climax V8 for the first time.

Surtees's time was 1m 32.5s. Gérard 'Jabby' Crombac, the noted French journalist, said it was a time-keeping error. But perhaps it also exemplified perfect symbiosis between the skills of a prolific designer, Eric Broadley, and Surtees's talent as a test driver? Probably both! While an improvement in practice of 4.5 seconds gave food for thought, Surtees had no time to confirm whether or not it was a flash in the pan because the Lola was eliminated shortly after the start of the race, on lap 9, in an accident caused by front suspension failure. The five years Surtees had spent at Vincent-HRD, the motorcycle manufacturer, had enabled him to acquire mechanical knowhow on a par with that of an engineer and it was in his nature to impose his choices or modify an approach during car development. Observing that Lola had beaten Lotus in sports car racing, Surtees, when driving a Cooper T53 run by the Yeoman Credit Racing Team, had asked Broadley the previous year to build a Formula 1 car. This Lola Mk4 had been entered at Brussels by the Bowmaker-Yeoman Credit team, as it was now called, but Surtees retired in the second heat due to engine failure after finishing fifth in the first, even though he was up against more powerful cars.

After making a scintillating start, Clark pitted on lap 12 due to transmission problems and left Graham Hill to take command. Behind, Phil Hill emerged on top from a brief scrap with Ireland and found himself behind Bruce McLaren's Cooper in third place, which became second on lap 21 after the New Zealander's retirement with gearbox failure. That put two Hills at the head of the field, with Trevor Taylor's third-placed Lotus closing the gap as his Climax V8, a freshly overhauled one, bedded itself in. When this engine had failed during the first practice session, Chapman had put it in his private plane and flown it to Coventry Climax's workshops in England before returning with it on Saturday evening so that it could be installed in Taylor's car in the nick of time for the race.

➤ **Dutch Grand Prix.** As Mauro Forghieri talks to Phil Hill, Porsche's Jo Bonnier listens in. The Maranello men are probably discussing the 156's erratic roadholding, which left the reigning World Champion struggling everywhere in the Dutch dunes.

▼ **Dutch Grand Prix.** Whether or not it was the result of what was being said in the accompanying photo, widening the rear track of Phil Hill's 156 did not provide the hoped-for improvements.

◄ **Dutch Grand Prix.** Ricardo Rodríguez (left) and Giancarlo Baghetti look puzzled. The 156s had dominated the previous year's race at Zandvoort but now their cars, without the widened rear track, were in trouble. The Italian, a calmer character than his Mexican team-mate, finished just shy of the podium.

▼ **Dutch Grand Prix.** Ricardo Rodríguez is seen in practice at the wheel of Giancarlo Baghetti's 156. The Mexican's race finished six laps from the chequered flag after a drive in which his combative spirit saw him alternate the best (fifth place after falling to the bottom of the timesheets) and the worst (two off-course excursions).

DUTCH GRAND PRIX

Zandvoort, 20th May 1962, 80 laps (2.605 miles/4.193km), 208.433 miles/335.440km • Starters 20, finishers 9

RACE				PRACTICE	
1st	Graham Hill	BRM P57 BRM V8	2h 11m 2.1s	2nd	1m 32.6s
2nd	Trevor Taylor	Lotus 24 Climax V8	+27.2s	10th	1m 35.4s
3rd	**Phil Hill**	**Ferrari 156 V6 120°**	**+1m 21.1s**	**9th**	**1m 35.0s**
4th	**Giancarlo Baghetti**	**Ferrari 156 V6 120°**	**79 laps**	**12th**	**1m 36.3s**
5th	Tony Maggs	Cooper T55 Climax S4	78 laps	15th	1m 37.5s
6th	Carel Godin de Beaufort	Porsche 718 F4	76 laps	14th	1m 37.4s
DNF	**Ricardo Rodríguez**	**Ferrari 156 V6 120°**	**74 laps (accident)**	**11th**	**1m 36.1s**

Pole position: John Surtees (Lola Mk4 Climax V8), 1m 32.5s, 101.399mph/163.187kph **Fastest race lap:** Bruce McLaren (Cooper T60 Climax V8), 1m 34.4s, 99.358mph/159.902kph **Winner's average speed:** 95.439mph/153.595kph **Drivers' championship:**[1] 1st Graham Hill 9, 2nd Taylor 6, 3rd Phil Hill 4, 4th Baghetti 3 **Constructors' championship:**[2] 1st BRM 9, 2nd Lotus-Climax 6, 3rd Ferrari 4

[1] Scoring system for the top six places was 9–6–4–3–2–1 [2] Scoring system for the top six places was 9–6–4–3–2–1; only the manufacturer's highest-placed car scored points

The race order remained unchanged until the 62nd lap, when Taylor dislodged the Ferrari, now hindered by an oil leak, from second place, but the American driver soldiered on and was lucky to finish on the podium. Baghetti drove a calculated race, rewarded by getting among the points scorers as early as lap 12 and finally crossing the line in fourth place, a lap behind his team leader. In contrast, Rodríguez's race was a succession of highs and lows. He spun on the fourth lap and collected Jack Brabham's Lotus 24, leaving the Australian, who was now racing under his own colours, to limp round to the pits to retire. The Mexican, meanwhile, took two laps to extricate his car from trackside sand before resuming at the back of the field. He then put in a stunning comeback drive and fought his way up to sixth place in Baghetti's wake before trying to pull off a rash overtaking move on his team-mate and going off with just six laps to go.

If the result was better than expected for Ferrari, it did not fool anyone, any more than the 1–2 scored the same day in the Naples Grand Prix by Willy Mairesse and Lorenzo Bandini in what was a walkover because of weak opposition. Compared with the 156, the V8-powered English cars were quicker, braked better and had superior roadholding and acceleration. Furthermore, it would soon become clear that minor tweaks here and there would not be enough to enable Maranello to remain competitive let alone contemplate beating its rivals. The situation was made even more difficult by Eugenio Dragoni's overbearing and unnecessary criticism of Phil Hill, who now wanted to concentrate fully on his driving rather than testing. Had Wolfgang von Trips's death blunted Hill's speed? Dragoni claimed that it had but Hill denied it. He had been no more affected by the German's fatal accident than by those that had

taken Peter Collins, Alfonso de Portago, Luigi Musso, Jean Behra and Mike Hawthorn, although he had been more affected by Hawthorn's loss because that had happened in a road accident rather than in a race. And Hill's subdued performance at Aintree had owed nothing to a passing dip in form but to a 156 that had been quite simply slower than its rivals. That said, the American had suffered from a stubborn case of flu that affected him until the Targa Florio. In addition, Ferrari's hasty search for solutions seemed to be fruitless, as was apparent at Zandvoort, where the use of a wider rear track helped to improve roadholding but at the expense of top speed due to increased drag.

On top of all that, Ferrari was overstretched. The sheer effort required for the Scuderia's multiple commitments with single-seaters, sports cars and GTs was intense, especially when the calendar became crowded, as it did at this stage of the season. Following the simultaneous Dutch and Naples Grands Prix, the Nürburgring 1,000Km followed one week later and then came the Monaco Grand Prix just one more week after that.

Setting the record straight

Nürburgring 1,000Km, 27th May

Phil Hill wanted to set the record straight and arrived in the Eifel full of determination as he felt very much at home at the Nürburgring. In addition, he was due to partner Olivier Gendebien in the 246 SP with which his co-driver had finished

▲ **Nürburgring 1,000Km.** In the starting line-up, Giancarlo Baghetti poses beside the 196 SP that he shared with Lorenzo Bandini and in which he set the tenth-quickest time in practice. Beyond the unexpected interloper, the MG Midget of Jed Noble/Derrick Astle, are the 250 TRI 61 of Carlo Mario Abate/ Nino Vaccarella and the 250 GTO driven by Umberto Maglioli/ Gotfrid Köchert. None of these cars saw the chequered flag.

◄ **Nürburgring 1,000Km.** Phil Hill and Mauro Forghieri engage in a lively discussion seconds before the start while Olivier Gendebien (left) and Eugenio Dragoni listen at either side. The two other helmeted drivers in this scene are Pedro Rodríguez (walking towards his 268 SP) and Dan Gurney (at rear left with Porsche team manager Huschke von Hanstein).

third in the previous year's race. The Rodríguez brothers were also present at the wheel of a sister model that had run as a 246 SP at Sebring but had now become a 268 SP powered by a 2.6-litre version of the V8, while Lorenzo Bandini/Giancarlo Baghetti drove the 196 S that they had raced in the Targa Florio. A novelty from Maranello was an experimental Berlinetta, a GTO chassis into which a 4-litre V12 had been shoehorned, entrusted to Ferrari's two test drivers, Willy Mairesse and Michael Parkes, and entered not as a GT but in the over-4-litre sports car category. In addition to this works foursome, seven other Ferraris took part, including the ageing but well-prepared 250 TRI 61 driven by Carlo Mario Abate/Nino Vaccarella in Scuderia SSS Repubblica di Venezia colours, and two GTOs in the hands of Umberto Maglioli/Gotfrid Köchert and Giorgio Scarlatti/Pietro Ferraro. Without belittling the opposition, only the Porsches of Dan Gurney/Jo Bonnier (718 GTR) and Graham Hill/Hans Herrmann (718 WRS) were a match for the powerful Italian cars, although they were uncertain challengers because the development of their in-house disc brakes had been a source of ongoing problems for Stuttgart since the start of the season.

During practice to determine the starting order of the Le Mans-type line-up, Phil Hill laid down a marker with a lap in 9m 25.5s followed by Mairesse (9m 34.8s), Gurney (9m 36.4s), Pedro Rodríguez (9m 40.5s) and Graham Hill (9m 42s). Next up was Bruce McLaren (9m 43.1s) in the previous year's Aston Martin while Jim Clark (9m 48.9s) created a sensation in his little Lotus 23 with just 100bhp. And that was only the beginning because on Sunday this tiny Lotus and its driver were dazzling.

The Nürburgring was an arena in which ambitions were often shattered and legends born. It took Clark only 11 laps to write his name indelibly in the track's annals in tricky conditions that saw it rain on some parts of the circuit but not others. When the field crossed the finishing line after the first lap, Clark was an

▼ **Nürburgring 1,000Km.** From left, this line-up comprises the Dan Gurney/Jo Bonnier Porsche 718 GTR (#110), the Pedro Rodríguez/Ricardo Rodríguez Ferrari 268 SP (#93), the Graham Hill/Hans Herrmann Porsche 718 WRS (#111), the Bruce McLaren/Tony Maggs Aston Martin DBR1 (#96), the Jim Clark/Trevor Taylor Lotus 23 (#84), the Pietro Ferraro/Giorgio Scarlatti Ferrari 250 GTO (#54), the Hans Walter/Herbert Müller Porsche RS 61 (#70) and the Lorenzo Bandini/Giancarlo Baghetti Ferrari 196 SP (#72) having its last-minute tyre change.

incredible 27 seconds in front of Gurney, with Mairesse third, Graham Hill fourth and Phil Hill fifth. Second time round, Clark's margin over Gurney had stretched to 47 seconds, then 73 seconds on lap 3, and so it continued as Clark romped away relentlessly, the track now drying.

Meanwhile, the first works Ferrari fell by the wayside. At the start, Pedro Rodríguez's engine had refused to fire and he had set off late but soon fought his way up the order, reaching fifth place after passing Phil Hill, only for a touch of red mist to descend and cause him to put the 268 SP in a ditch on the fifth lap. Scarlatti, who was much less comfortable on the 'Ring than in Sicily, emulated that a lap later by going off in Ferraro's GTO.

With the sun breaking through, Clark covered his seventh lap in 9m 46.3s, better than his practice best, while Gurney remained second in front of Mairesse, with Abate now fourth and the Hills fifth and sixth, Graham still ahead of Phil. By now the gap between the Lotus and the Porsche was 100 seconds but it would not increase any further, for track conditions were now beginning to favour the more powerful cars and the leader's car, losing ground, was also jumping out of gear and suffering from deteriorating brakes. Now Phil Hill decided that it was time to start pushing, setting a time of 9m 31.9s on lap 8 and displacing both his English namesake and Abate in quick succession, after which Abate almost immediately slammed into the rear of Marcello de Luca's Alfa Romeo Zagato and retired.

Everyone was zeroing in on Clark, with Mairesse now leading the chase after getting past Gurney. On lap 10, Clark's lead dropped to 55 seconds, then 42 seconds next time round. His advantage was melting away but at the same time he was starting to struggle in the cockpit because a leak from the Climax engine's exhaust manifold was causing poisonous gas to accumulate in the cockpit. With his concentration failing, Clark missed a gearchange and shot off the track on lap 12, thankfully without harm, but his race was run.

Pitstops quickly followed and by the time the race had settled down again, on lap 14, the Hill/Gendebien 246 SP led the Mairesse/Parkes 4-litre Berlinetta by 24 seconds, with the Bonnier/Gurney Porsche a somewhat distant third. Soon it seemed to be all over bar the shouting as the two Ferraris became ever more firmly ensconced in the first two places. The

> **Nürburgring 1,000Km.** Olivier Gendebien stops on lap 31 to hand over to Phil Hill with rain pouring down. Eleven laps earlier, under a threatening sky, they had made a good call in stopping for rain tyres, a decision that allowed them to shrug off the danger of Willy Mairesse/ Michael Parkes in their GTO-like experimental Berlinetta claiming victory. Hill reeled off the remaining 13 laps without incident.

NÜRBURGRING 1,000KM

Nürburgring, 27th May 1962, 44 laps (14.173 miles/22.810km), 623.633 miles/1,003.640km • Starters 67, classified finishers 27

1st	**Phil Hill/Olivier Gendebien**	**Ferrari 246 SP (0790)**	**7h 33m 27.7s**
2nd	**Willy Mairesse/Michael Parkes**	**Ferrari Berlinetta EXP (3673 SA)**	**7h 35m 49.2s**
3rd	Graham Hill/Hans Herrmann	Porsche 718 WRS	7h 42m 24.6s
4th	Bruce McLaren/Tony Maggs	Aston Martin DBR1/300	42 laps
5th	Peter Nöcker/Wolfgang Seidel	Ferrari 250 GT SWB (1917 GT) *(1st GT+2.0)*	41 laps
6th	Edgar Barth/Herbert Linge	Porsche 356B Carrera Abarth GTL	41 laps
7th	Jean Guichet/Pierre Noblet	Ferrari 250 GT SWB (2689 GT)	40 laps
10th	Henri Oreiller/Roger de Lageneste	Ferrari 250 GT SWB (2787 GT)	40 laps
17th	Georges Gachnang/Edouard Grob	Ferrari 250 TR (0742 TR)	38 laps
DNF	Umberto Maglioli/Gotfrid Köchert	Ferrari 250 GTO (3527 GT)	14 laps (ignition)
DNF	**Lorenzo Bandini/Giancarlo Baghetti**	**Ferrari 196 SP (0804)**	**13 laps (oil leak)**
DNF	Georges Berger/'Elde' (Léon Dernier)	Ferrari 250 GT SWB Drogo	11 laps (accident)
DNF	Carlo Mario Abate/Nino Vaccarella	Ferrari 250 TRI 61 (0792 TR)	7 laps (accident)
DNF	Giorgio Scarlatti/Pietro Ferraro	Ferrari 250 GTO (3451 GT)	5 laps (accident)
DNF	**Pedro Rodríguez/Ricardo Rodríguez**	**Ferrari 268 SP (0806)**	**5 laps (spun off)**

Fastest practice lap: Phil Hill, 9m 25.5s, 90.229mph/145.210kph **Fastest race lap:** Phil Hill, 9m 31.9s, 89.220mph/143.585kph **Winner's average speed:** 82.516mph/132.797kph **FIA International Championship for GT Manufacturers (GT Division III, over 2,000cc):**1 1st Ferrari 36, 2nd Chevrolet 6, 3rd Jaguar 5

1 *This race was also the third round of the World Speed and Endurance Challenge*

Berlinetta was less fuel-efficient than the 246 SP and required longer refuelling stops, while the open car lost a little time when Gendebien, under threatening skies, pitted for a tyre change that turned out to be unnecessary. If there was any suspense, it came from Bonnier's Porsche in the closing stages. Although Phil Hill's lead remained comfortable as he drove his final stint, second-placed Parkes found himself under pressure when the Swede decided to go for broke. With eight laps to go, Bonnier was 32 seconds behind Parkes but chiselled away at the gap until it was just 13 seconds with two laps remaining, at which point his charge was cruelly terminated by gearbox failure. That gifted third place to the Hill/Herrmann Porsche spyder, which had been a model of consistency if not ultimately on the pace.

With three victories in three races, the overall result was a positive one for Ferrari even if there were a few niggles to be sorted out. Once again, the 268 SP did not last long enough to prove that the V8 option was the right one. Bandini, who set off in last place because his 196 SP was still midway through a last-minute tyre change when the drivers sprinted across the track at the start, retired after 13 laps due to an oil leak before Baghetti had a chance to get behind the wheel. Maglioli's GTO went out with ignition problems but all was not lost in the GT category as the Peter Nöcker/Wolfgang Seidel 250 GT SWB won the class, adding nine points to Maranello's championship tally.

Bandini learns the ropes

Monaco Grand Prix, 3rd June

The first of the three practice sessions for the Monaco Grand Prix took place four days later and the organisers continued to ignore common sense in their method of selecting entries. Ten drivers, two from five works teams, were given automatic invitations, leaving the 11 or 12 privateers to fight it out for the remaining six places on the grid. It was a questionable system when former winners like Maurice Trintignant and Jack Brabham were among those who had to battle for a place, along with John Surtees and Roy Salvadori at Lola and Innes Ireland at the UDT-Laystall team. Ferrari, meanwhile, had nominated Phil Hill as one of its official entries but not specified the other name, so Willy Mairesse, Lorenzo Bandini and Ricardo Rodríguez also had to earn a place in the race.

Thursday's session helped to clarify things. Graham Hill (BRM), Jim Clark (Lotus) and Surtees laid down markers by being the only drivers to lap in under 1m 38s. Phil Hill was closest to them at 1m 38.0s, but his team-mates were considerably slower, Rodríguez by two seconds, Bandini by four seconds and Mairesse by a staggering 10 seconds. However, there was a

⌃ Monaco Grand Prix. Willy Mairesse started from the second row in his usual push-on style but was only 11th first time round. His seventh-place finish was due as much to retirements as to an engine that lost power towards the end of the race.

➤ Monaco Grand Prix. Jo Bonnier keeps his Porsche on an outside line so that Lorenzo Bandini can nip past during his fine drive to third place, with John Surtees's Lola immediately behind. Bearing down on the group are the leader, Graham Hill (BRM), and second-placed Jim Clark (Lotus).

◄ **Monaco Grand Prix.** The cars have passed the halfway mark and this photo prefigures the jousts in subsequent years between Lorenzo Bandini and John Surtees when team-mates at Ferrari. They went at it hammer and tongs, swapping places for most of the race.

➤ **Monaco Grand Prix.** Phil Hill accelerates out of *Tabac* corner in his vain attempt to snatch victory from Bruce McLaren. He set his fastest time of the race on the last lap.

▼ **Monaco Grand Prix.** Alone! Lorenzo Bandini enjoys a moment of solitude on his way to third place. Like Willy Mairesse's car, his had a windscreen extension.

surprise on Friday morning on a wet track when Mairesse joined Graham Hill as the only two drivers to get below the two-minute mark. Phil Hill spent his time running in a 156 with its gearbox installed between the engine and the rear axle, while Bandini and Rodríguez just racked up laps. Next day, the sun returned and Mairesse again stood out from the pool of Scuderia drivers into which Eugenio Dragoni dipped as the mood took him. Without posing a direct threat to duellists Clark and Graham Hill, Mairesse's 1m 36.4s equalled the times of Bruce McLaren (Cooper) and Dan Gurney (Porsche), but the New Zealander achieved his time first and denied 'Wild Willy' a place on the front row. Phil Hill and Bandini ended up two rows behind their team-mate, while Rodríguez was unable to qualify despite being quicker than invitees Jo Bonnier (Porsche) and Trevor Taylor (Lotus).

Taking advantage of Louis Chiron's slight hesitation when he dropped the flag, Mairesse, his natural impetuosity getting the better of him, shot through from the second row and muscled his way past Clark and Graham Hill to take the lead in the *Gazomètre* hairpin in a slide that forced McLaren to go wide. Behind, the accelerator on Richie Ginther's BRM jammed open and the American skittled his way through several other cars, eliminating not only himself but also Gurney's Porsche and Trintignant's Lotus, as well as delaying Innes Ireland's Lotus.

By the end of the lap, Phil Hill was briefly third and Bandini, who had been clever enough to avoid the chaos at the start by squeezing close against the balustrade, was fifth, but Mairesse was now only 11th, having been quickly overtaken by McLaren before spinning in the Station hairpin. The Belgian never got back among the front-runners because he was hindered by gearbox trouble and later a loss of oil pressure that brought about his retirement near the end of the race.

Graham Hill shot past McLaren on the seventh lap to take the lead. Clark, now third, was all over the New Zealander in his attempts to snatch second, which he managed to do on lap 28, by which time Brabham had relegated Phil Hill to fifth with Bandini right behind him. The Italian buckled down to following his team leader and learning the ropes while fending off Surtees, a harbinger of their duels to come, but on lap 45 the Englishman got ahead. After the retirements of Clark (lap 55) and Brabham (lap 77), Phil Hill was third with Surtees fourth and Bandini fifth, but on lap 87 Surtees decided to let the young Italian back in front and the Ferrari pulled away.

With just ten laps to go, Graham Hill's BRM still led from McLaren but now his V8 was losing its edge and the gap was gradually shrinking, from 45 seconds to 26. Meanwhile, the Ferrari pit kept Phil Hill informed about the situation and

MONACO GRAND PRIX

Monaco, 3rd June 1962, 100 laps (1.954 miles/3.145km), 195.4 miles/314.5km • Starters 16, finishers 6

RACE					PRACTICE	
1st	Bruce McLaren	Cooper T60 Climax V8	2h 46m 29.7s		3rd	1m 36.4s
2nd	**Phil Hill**	Ferrari 156 V6 120°	+1.3s		9th	1m 37.1s
3rd	**Lorenzo Bandini**	Ferrari 156 V6 120°	+1m 24.1s		10th	1m 37.2s
4th	John Surtees	Lola Mk4 Climax V8	99 laps		11th	1m 37.9s
5th	Jo Bonnier	Porsche 718 F4	93 laps		15th	1m 42.4s
6th	Graham Hill	BRM P57 BRM V8	92 laps		2nd	1m 35.8s
7th	**Willy Mairesse**	Ferrari 156 V6 120°	90 laps (engine)		4th	1m 36.4s
DNS	**Ricardo Rodríguez**	Ferrari 156 V6 65°	–		–	1m 40.1s

Pole position: Jim Clark (Lotus 25 Climax V8), 1m 35.4s, 73.744mph/118.679kph **Fastest race lap:** Clark, 1m 35.5s, 73.666mph/118.554kph
Winner's average speed: 70.461mph/113.396kph **Drivers' championship:** 1st= Graham Hill & Phil Hill 10, 3rd McLaren 9, 5th Bandini 4,
6th Baghetti 3 **Constructors' championship:** 1st Cooper-Climax 11, 2nd= BRM & Ferrari 10

gave him free rein, by means of a 'flat out' signal, to eat into the gap separating him from McLaren, and he did just that with redoubled determination when the BRM driver's retirement on lap 93 turned his quest into an attempt to win the race. On lap 95, with five laps to go, the Ferrari was 12 seconds behind McLaren's Cooper, then 11, eight and a half, seven, five — and at the finish only 1.3 seconds separated the dark green car from the red one.

Although he did not win, Phil Hill drove one of the best races of his career that day, while Bandini came home third after a circumspect performance. With the two Hills now level at the top of the championship rankings, Maranello must have felt some satisfaction, but it would have been short-lived because the deficiencies of the 156 would very likely be rather more exposed at the next round, at high-speed Spa-Francorchamps.

At daggers drawn

Belgian Grand Prix, 17th June

Four Ferrari 156s at Spa! Taking everything into account, this was a bravura show of strength. After returning from Monaco, the team had had to launch simultaneous preparation exercises for the Belgian Grand Prix and Le Mans while looking ahead to future battles, so turning up at Spa with four cars, three of which had modified front suspension, was a real feat. Whether or not this pressure was a factor, practice revealed a lack of effective development compared with rivals who could be more focused on the task at hand.

Phil Hill ended the first practice session in second place on

the timesheets with a lap in 3m 59.8s, beaten only by Trevor Taylor with 3m 59.3s in his Lotus 24. In the second session, the Ferrari driver improved slightly to 3m 59.6s and put himself on the second row of the grid alongside Innes Ireland in his Lotus. After a low-key performance in the opening practice sessions, Willy Mairesse proved that he wanted his moment in the sun in front of his home crowd by securing a place on the third row with a lap in 3m 59.8s alongside Ricardo Rodríguez on 4m 1.0s. Giancarlo Baghetti was back on the sixth row on only 4m 8.0s because his practice had been cut short when he crashed in the first session after losing his car's engine cover on the climb from *Eau Rouge*, emerging unhurt although repairs to his badly damaged car were only completed in the nick of time for the race. While the British V8 engines helped BRM, Cooper and Lotus to monopolise the front row after lapping up to 10 seconds quicker than in 1961, Ferrari set much the same times as the previous year, the wider rear track of the 156s significantly penalising straight-line speed on this fast circuit.

Jim Clark's performance in his new Lotus 25 was outstanding. He started from the middle of the fifth row because of engine difficulties during practice but made startling progress. He was fifth on lap 5, then reached second place within three more laps after gobbling up Graham Hill's BRM, Bruce McLaren's Cooper and Mairesse's Ferrari despite being hindered briefly by problems with his visor that had somehow become twisted. He ate into the gap separating him from team-mate Taylor, whom he passed for the lead on the next lap and remained there for the rest of the race, winning by three-quarters of a minute and leaving the lap record at 3m 55.6s. It was perhaps not a typical Clark victory but it was his first in a World Championship Grand Prix. 'A fine

▲ **Belgian Grand Prix.** Pictured during practice, Willy Mairesse enjoyed his moment of glory as the hero of a whole nation when he briefly led his home race but unfortunately his efforts brought no reward as he went out of the race after a collision with Trevor Taylor's Lotus that left him injured and facing a spell on the sidelines.

➤ **Belgian Grand Prix.** Ferrari's Eugenio Dragoni criticised third-placed Phil Hill after the race for supposedly making insufficient effort despite driving on the limit for 32 laps. Even so, his fastest lap (3m 59.0s) was two seconds slower than Mairesse's best (3m 57.0s).

◀ **Belgian Grand Prix.** Ricardo Rodríguez and Phil Hill went head-to-head throughout the race. The gap between the two Ferraris was so small that no other car could slot in between them.

▾ **Belgian Grand Prix.** Ricardo Rodríguez drove a stunning race and showed that he had nothing to envy Phil Hill, holding off the American until the last corner of the last lap. This practice shot of the younger Rodríguez brother gives a good view of the rear-end design of his 156.

win for Lotus,' was the sober title above Denis Jenkinson's report in *Motor Sport*. 'Clark wins at last,' was fervent Lotus admirer Gérard 'Jabby' Crombac's headline in *Sport Auto*. It was the beginning of the legend of the young farmer from the Highlands. In comparison, his rivals were just simply human beings.

The other distinctive feature of the race was the ding-dong battle between Mairesse and Taylor. The Belgian went into attack mode from flag-fall. Fifth at the end of the first lap, he came round in the lead ahead of Taylor on lap 4, and the pair then swapped positions, with Mairesse briefly holding the lap record at 3m 57.4s, until Clark hauled them in. Still their battle continued, now with Taylor trying to hang on to his team leader, while Graham Hill and McLaren ran fourth and fifth, followed by Phil Hill and Rodríguez slipstreaming each other and changing places, just as they had done since the start.

If Mairesse was waiting for Taylor to make a mistake and get ahead again, it nearly came on lap 17, just after half distance, when the Belgian had slipped a little further behind. The Englishman came slithering into *La Source* too quickly, missed his braking point and locked up a rear wheel, but just about kept control although he lost three seconds and contact with Clark in the process. Cheered on by his home crowd, Mairesse put pedal to metal. Although he did not close the gap in dramatic fashion, he gradually inched closer. On lap 20, when McLaren retired with a blown engine, Mairesse caught Taylor and they renewed their duel with even more intensity, passing and repassing up to three times per lap, and raising their pace so that the rate at which Clark continued to pull away fell from two seconds a lap to one. Mairesse was in front on laps 21 and 22 but on the next three it was Taylor's turn. However, neither was destined to go

beyond lap 26. In the *Blanchimont* left-hand curve just before the Club House and *La Source* hairpin, Taylor lost control of his Lotus. Mairesse tried to go through on the inside to avoid him but in vain. The two cars collided and the Lotus shot off the track, cut down a telephone pole and destroyed itself in a ditch. The Ferrari turned over and caught fire. Taylor was unhurt despite being thrown out while Mairesse, who had to be extricated from his burning 156, suffered an injury to his face and minor burns.

The incident elevated Graham Hill to second place and left the two surviving Ferrari drivers — Baghetti had retired with engine problems after only four laps — battling for third place, with Rodríguez holding the advantage. It stayed like that for the last seven laps until the last corner of the last lap, when Phil Hill forced his way past his Mexican team-mate at *La Source* and crossed the finishing line inches ahead to inherit a place on the podium that had seemed out of reach seven laps earlier. Still, it did nothing to change Eugenio Dragoni's opinion of his performance. Objectively speaking, Hill's showing had not equalled that of Mairesse, who had driven a brilliant, daring race until the accident. The animosity between the two men was exacerbated when Hill overheard the report that Dragoni gave Ferrari of the race: '*Commendatore*? Yes, yes, but your great champion did nothing, nothing,' the American remembered him saying. It was obvious that he was deeply hurt and the fact that he felt he was being made the scapegoat could not be ignored. However, the truth was that Hill was on the edge of a slope that was made all the more slippery as he was in competition with his team-mates — and the social unrest that was about to hit Italy did not spare Ferrari.

BELGIAN GRAND PRIX

Spa-Francorchamps, 17th June 1962, 32 laps (8.761 miles/14.100km), 280.363 miles/451.200km • Starters 19, finishers 11

RACE					PRACTICE	
1st	Jim Clark	Lotus 25 Climax V8	2h 7m 32.5s		12th	4m 04.9s
2nd	Graham Hill	BRM P57 BRM V8	+44.1s		1st	3m 57.0s
3rd	Phil Hill	Ferrari 156 V6 120°	+2m 06.5s		4th	3m 59.6s
4th	Ricardo Rodríguez	Ferrari 156 V6 120°	+2m 06.6s		7th	4m 01.0s
5th	John Surtees	Lola Mk4 Climax V8	31 laps		11th	4m 04.4s
6th	Jack Brabham	Lotus 24 Climax V8	30 laps		15th	4m 08.2s
DNF	Willy Mairesse	Ferrari 156 V6 120°	26 laps (accident)		6th	3m 59.8s
DNF	Giancarlo Baghetti	Ferrari 156 V6 120°	4 laps (ignition)		14th	4m 08.0s

Pole position: Graham Hill, 3m 57.0s, 131.805mph/212.119kph **Fastest race lap:** Clark, 3m 55.6s, 133.874mph/215.449kph **Winner's average speed:** 131.895mph/212.265kph **Drivers' championship:** 1st Graham Hill 16, 2nd Phil Hill 14, 3rd= McLaren & Clark 9, 7th Bandini 4, 8th= Baghetti & Rodríguez 3 **Constructors' championship:** 1st BRM 16, 2nd Cooper-Climax 15, 3rd Ferrari 14

Same faces in the victory circle

Le Mans 24 Hours, 23rd–24th June

Necessity is the mother of invention, and as a victory at Le Mans was as good as a world title, Enzo Ferrari unsurprisingly stopped sulking and accepted the capricious demands of the Le Mans organisers. The four experimental cars that had been lined up in the factory yard at the beginning of June arrived at scrutineering. Two were Dinos, one the 246 SP seen at Daytona and in Sicily but this time allocated to the Rodríguez brothers, the other a 268 SP for Giancarlo Baghetti/Ludovico Scarfiotti that had only seen action at the Le Mans test weekend and now looked slightly different, with its panoramic glass section inserted in the windscreen now running from one wing to the other. Backing them up and spearheading Ferrari's attack were two 330s powered by 4-litre V12 engines. One, earmarked for Michael Parkes/Lorenzo Bandini, was another experimental model with GTO bodywork, replacing the similar car seen at the Nürburgring after that had been badly damaged by Mairesse during a test on the open road. The other big-engined car, entrusted to Olivier Gendebien/Phil Hill, was a 330 TRI LM with 390bhp and a dry weight of 820kg, making it a slightly more civilised version of the monster cars that supposedly had been eliminated by the Le Mans organisers.

Winning Le Mans often depends on combining forces and, should the works cars fail, Maranello could rely on two other official representatives in the form of valiant 250 TRI 61s entered by Scuderia SSS Repubblica di Venezia (Jo Bonnier/Dan Gurney) and NART (John Fulp/Pete Ryan). Extra support was provided by the GTs, with no fewer than six 250 GTOs and an array of 250 GT SWBs, including the famous 'Bread Van' for Carlo Mario Abate/Colin Davis with redesigned bodywork by Drogo. In all, 15 Ferraris took part.

◄ **Le Mans 24 Hours.** A tightly packed gaggle of cars in the Esses just after the start includes the #17 Bob Grossman/'Fireball' Roberts Ferrari 250 GTO, the #9 Peter Sargent/Peter Lumsden Jaguar E-type, the #24 John Whitmore/Bob Olthoff Austin-Healey, #18 John Fulp/Pete Ryan 250 TRI 61, the #15 Jo Bonnier/Dan Gurney 250 TRI 61, the #21 George Reed/Ed Hugus Ferrari 250 GT SWB Exp and, bringing up the rear, the #16 Carlo Mario Abate/Colin Davis 250 GT SWB Drogo.

◄ Le Mans 24 Hours. The Rodríguez brothers had exploded on the scene at Le Mans the previous year. Once again, they injected a huge dose of excitement into the 1962 race before being eliminated by a defective gearbox bearing. When this photo was taken on Saturday evening, Ricardo was in the lead after three hours of flat-out driving at the wheel of the 246 SP.

▼ Le Mans 24 Hours. A fast, reliable, front-mounted 4-litre V12 with classic independent rear suspension was the choice of Olivier Gendebien and Phil Hill in their quest for their third joint victory at Le Mans. On Saturday evening the Belgian in the 330 TRI LM got down to laying the foundations of what would be his fourth win in the Sarthe classic.

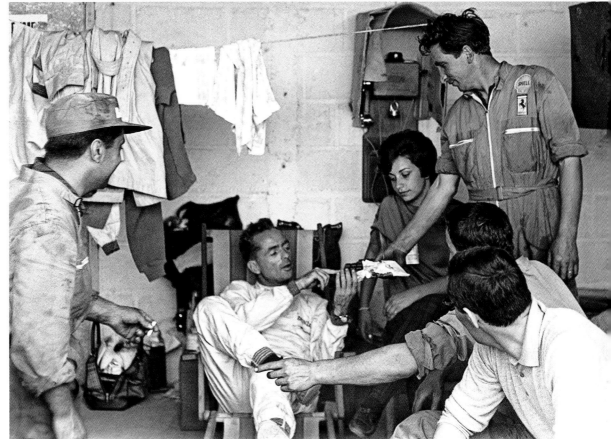

▲ **Le Mans 24 Hours.** Entered by the Scuderia SSS Repubblica di Venezia, the Jo Bonnier/Dan Gurney 250 TRI 61 had new bodywork compared with that seen at Sebring. Its 15th place after an hour's racing was as good as it got, for the car retired just after 7pm with broken transmission.

➤ **Le Mans 24 Hours.** Phil Hill, fatigued just after handing over to co-driver Olivier Gendebien, wonders which piece of chocolate to choose. Gendebien leads comfortably and all is well apart from a potential problem with the clutch.

What could the opposition do in the face of this onslaught? At scrutineering it was fairly obvious that Maranello's rivals seemed ill-prepared to take the fight to Ferrari with cars seemingly built to satisfy the demands of the importers rather than the aims of the manufacturers. Thus, the Aston Martin DP212 owed much to the requests made by Marcel Blondeau and Claude Leguezec, the make's representatives in France. It had a six-cylinder engine inherited from the DB4 GT with a cubic capacity increase to 4 litres, a platform chassis with steel box section members reinforced by a tubular structure, a five-speed gearbox and light-alloy bodywork. Driven by Graham Hill and Richie Ginther, it was an enticing cocktail, but did have a big drawback as the team had very little knowledge of Le Mans, their running time on the circuit limited to the April test weekend with the engine installed in the DB4 GT Zagato entered by Frenchmen Jean Kerguen/'Franc' (Jacques Dewes). This Zagato, now with its original straight-six reinstalled, was also at the start plus another one driven by Mike Salmon/Ian Baillie. None of the Astons saw the chequered flag.

The Maserati *Tipo* 151, a project initiated by Briggs Cunningham and Colonel John Simone, the French Maserati importer with Jean Thépenier, seemed a more competitive proposition. Would it be too far-fetched to suggest that it was the heir to the extravagant 1957 450 S coupé? It had basically the same double-overhead-camshaft aluminium V8 engine but with capacity reduced from 4.5 to 4 litres and the same five-speed gearbox/axle combination clothed in audacious closed bodywork with tiny doors. When the ACO's Jacques Finance visited Modena to view the car, he said, jokingly, to its designer, Giampaolo Dallara: 'I want to be able to get into this car, and do be careful, I am not a contortionist.' When the car arrived for scrutineering, it had only been tested on the Modena and Monza circuits with a few runs on the *Autostrada del Sol* in addition. Even so, there were three *Tipo* 151s on the grid: Cunningham entered two for Bruce McLaren/Walt Hansgen and Bill Kimberly/Dick Thompson and Maserati France supplied a third for Maurice Trintignant/Lucien Bianchi.

Jaguar's presence with three E-types was subdued almost to the point of anonymity. This was not helped by the fact that the Coventry manufacturer itself refused to enter what were strictly series production cars against the racing GTs, leaving it up to its customers to try to bring back the halcyon days of the pre-1957 era. Thus, Cunningham entered one E-type for himself and Roy Salvadori, with Peter Sargent/Peter Lumsden driving Sargent's example, and Maurice Charles sharing his car with John Coundley.

At 4.45am on Sunday, the #28 Ferrari 268 SP driven by

Ricardo and Pedro Rodríguez stopped for good with a terminal gearbox problem. Some experienced observers judged this to be the consequence of their reckless speed, conveniently forgetting that without the ferocity of the Mexican pair's attack the race would have just been a battle of wear and tear between Ferraris. Apart from the Aston Martin DP212 leading the first lap and briefly getting in front again at a refuelling stop during the second hour, the Gendebien/Hill 330 TRI LM had immediately taken charge of the race, lapping in under four minutes in the early stages, and nobody except the Mexican brothers was ever in a position to knock them off their pedestal — and Pedro and Ricardo did it with all the brashness of youth. They took the lead in the early evening of Saturday thanks to the thirst of the big Ferrari, which consumed fuel at the prodigious rate of around 5.65mpg, and proceeded to thrill the spectators as they tried to open up a gap. Hill hit back immediately by retaking the lead and setting a new lap record at 3m 57.3s (126.891mph), finally beating the 3m 58.7s established by Mike Hawthorn in a Ferrari five years earlier. In the hours that followed, the two Ferraris were never separated by more than a lap until the 268 SP succumbed to a broken gearbox bearing.

That left Gendebien/Hill with a three-lap lead over the Baghetti/Scarfiotti 268 SP and the Jean Guichet/Pierre Noblet GTO, and an eight-lap advantage over other GTOs driven by Bob Grossman/'Fireball' Roberts and Fernand Tavano/André Simon, with yet another GTO, the 'Elde'/'Beurlys' car, rounding out the top six. The first intruders to break up this Italian armada, although well behind, were the Sargent/Lumsden and Cunningham/Salvadori E-types, racing in tandem and betting on more casualties among the front-runners.

Until then luck had been on their side. The 250 TRI 61 and the 250 GT Drogo run by Scuderia SSS Repubblica di Venezia retired late on the first afternoon due to broken transmissions. At 9pm the first of the *Tipo* 151s went out when the Kimberly/Thompson car slid into the barrier at *Tertre Rouge*. Shortly before midnight, the works 330 LM, which had lost a lot of time after Parkes put it into the *Mulsanne* sand trap on the first lap, retired with a punctured radiator. Not long afterwards, DP212 joined the dead car park after dynamo trouble and then a blown cylinder head gasket. At 1am, John Simone, who feared for the safety of his drivers, called in the Trintignant/Bianchi *Tipo* 151 after it had been eating up tyres at the rate of a set every 10 laps. The McLaren/Hansgen *Tipo* 151 had started well, lying second behind the Rodríguez brothers in the third hour, before also displaying an excessive appetite for tyres, dropping back and recovering to fifth place by the time it went out with piston failure soon after 5am.

Would Lady Luck continue her mischief making? The

▲ **Le Mans 24 Hours.** Late on Sunday morning, the 250 GTO of Bob Grossman/'Fireball' Roberts lies in third place as it passes the 250 TR 61 that Pete Ryan marooned in the sand bank at *Mulsanne* at 4am. In the background is the Jack Fairman/Tom Dickson Tojeiro, victim of gearbox gremlins soon after midnight.

➤ **Le Mans 24 Hours.** It is almost over provided that the clutch does not give up the ghost. The Rodríguez brothers had never given Phil Hill/Olivier Gendebien (and by extension Mauro Forghieri) a moment's respite until they retired in the early morning.

LE MANS 24 HOURS

Le Mans, 23rd–24th June 1962, 331 laps (8.364 miles/13.461km), 2,768.367 miles/4,455.255km • Starters 55, classified finishers 18

1st	Olivier Gendebien/Phil Hill	Ferrari 330 TRI LM (0780/0808 TR)	331 laps
2nd	Jean Guichet/Pierre Noblet	Ferrari 250 GTO (3705 GT) (1st GT+2.0)	325 laps
3rd	'Elde' (Léon Dernier)/'Beurlys' (Jean Blaton)	Ferrari 250 GTO (3757 GT)	313 laps
4th	Briggs Cunningham/Roy Salvadori	Jaguar E-type Lightweight	309 laps
5th	Peter Sargent/Peter Lumsden	Jaguar E-type Lightweight	309 laps
6th	Bob Grossman/'Fireball' Roberts	Ferrari 250 GTO (3387 GT)	296 laps
9th	Ed Hugus/George Reed	Ferrari 250 GT SWB EXP (2643 GT)	280 laps
DNF	Giancarlo Baghetti/Ludovico Scarfiotti	Ferrari 268 SP (0798)	230 laps (gearbox)
DNF	Fernand Tavano/André Simon	Ferrari 250 GTO (3769 GT)	202 laps (differential)
DNF	Pedro Rodríguez/Ricardo Rodríguez	Ferrari 246 SP (0796)	174 laps (gearbox)
DNF	Nino Vaccarella/Giorgio Scarlatti	Ferrari 250 GTO (3445 GT)	172 laps (engine)
DNF	Innes Ireland/Masten Gregory	Ferrari 250 GTO (3505 GT)	165 laps (starter/battery)
DNF	John Fulp/Pete Ryan	Ferrari 250 TRI 61 (0794 TR)	150 laps (accident)
DNF	Michael Parkes/Lorenzo Bandini	Ferrari 330 LM (3765 LM)	56 laps (radiator)
DNF	Georges Berger/Robert Darville	Ferrari 250 GT SWB (2445 GT)	35 laps (accident)
DNF	Dan Gurney/Jo Bonnier	Ferrari 250 TRI 61 (0792 TR)	30 laps (differential)
DNF	Carlo Mario Abate/Colin Davis	Ferrari 250 GT Drogo (2819 GT)	30 laps (gearbox)

Fastest practice lap: Hill, 3m 55.1s, 128.079mph/206.123kph **Fastest race lap:** Hill, 3m 57.3s, 126.885mph/204.202kph

Winner's average speed: 115.245mph/185.469kph **FIA International Championship for GT Manufacturers (GT Division III, over 2,000cc):**[1] 1st Ferrari 45, 2nd Jaguar 9, 3rd Chevrolet 6

[1] This race was also the fourth and final round of the World Speed and Endurance Challenge, which finished as: 1st Ferrari 40, 2nd Porsche 23, 3rd Alfa Romeo 7

◄ **Le Mans 24 Hours.** As was said at the time, could Pierre Noblet and Jean Guichet have won had they had upped the pressure to try to break the fragile transmission of the 330 TRI LM driven by the Scuderia's number-one team? After third place the previous year in a 250 GT SWB, the pair drove a flawless race in Guichet's own GTO and moved up another step on the podium.

► **Grand Prix de l'ACF.** There were no Ferraris at Rouen so Bernard Cahier was able to share a smile with his friends Dan Gurney (the winner) and Phil Hill, who, as he did not have a drive, was able to give full rein to his passion for photography.

retirements at just after 9am of the Tavano/Simon GTO and the Baghetti/Scarfiotti 268 SP, the latter another victim of gearbox gremlins, helped the Jaguars move up two places, leaving the GTOs of Grossman/Roberts and 'Elde'/'Beurlys' in an increasingly vulnerable position, even if the best of the GTOs, the Guichet/Noblet car, looked fairly secure in second place. At 11am, after 19 hours of racing, Englishmen Sargent/Lumsden were only a lap behind Belgians 'Elde'/'Beurlys' and two adrift of Americans Grossman/Roberts. An hour later, the Jaguar drivers were hammering along on the same lap as the Equipe Nationale Belge GTO when suddenly fate intervened while the American GTO was in the pits for a routine stop. When its driver tried to restart the engine, nothing happened: the starter motor had become contaminated by an oil leak and the mechanics had to remove it, dismantle it and clean it with petrol. The Belgians passed before the Americans could rejoin, now under real threat from the E-types running in fifth and sixth places.

Meanwhile, the 330 TRI LM continued to lead handsomely despite its clutch having begun to act up since mid-morning, causing its drivers to slacken their pace to between 4m 15s and 4m 20s per lap. At 2pm, the podium looked settled with Gendebien/Hill first, Guichet/Noblet second and 'Elde'/'Beurlys' third. Behind, the Jaguars were still running line astern in front of Grossman, who was now in a lonely sixth place. And in the last

10 minutes of the race the American-entered Jaguar snatched fourth place from its English rival, which limped across the finishing line, a victim of transmission problems.

When Phil Hill clinched his third victory in the Sarthe classic, little did he know that he had just scored his last major success at the wheel of a Ferrari, while Gendebien, victorious for a record fourth time, was about to announce his retirement from racing.

The omens at this time were dispiriting, the circumstances outside anyone's control. Italian industry was about to be shaken by a wave of metalworkers' strikes and Maranello, dependent on its suppliers, was not spared. This was why no Ferraris were entered for the Grand Prix de l'ACF at Rouen on 8th July, just at the peak of social unrest in Italy that culminated in three days of clashes over that same weekend between police and demonstrators in Turin, the headquarters of Fiat. The only consolation for Phil Hill was that Graham Hill and Jim Clark retired at Rouen, allowing the American to hold on to his second place in the World Championship.

In addition, the arrival of Ferrari's promised four-valve V6 kept being postponed, while the new chassis on which Mauro Forghieri had been working was no more than a modified version of the previous one. It had undergone considerable revision,

particularly at the rear with a beefed-up engine compartment, a consequence of the gearbox being mounted at the very back of the chassis, and new suspension arms. The driving position was more reclined and the car had shed 88lb in weight, but the gap to its English rivals was so big that this partial revamp was not enough. The Formula 1 races that followed, therefore, were all the more painful for Maranello.

Shared laurels and a world title

The calendar for the 1962 International Championship for GT Manufacturers was a packed one that stretched relentlessly forward to the Paris 1,000Km at Montlhéry in October. Having won the World Speed and Endurance Challenge after its victory at Le Mans, Ferrari tackled the Trophées d'Auvergne meeting at the Charade road circuit near Clermont-Ferrand with all the more determination as success in this volcanic region of France would add a second world title to its 1962 laurels. Enzo Ferrari kept his promise made at the beginning of the season not to enter a works car against his customers (with the exception of Sebring), letting them represent him with four 250 GT SWBs and

two GTOs, plus the Scuderia SSS Repubblica di Venezia 250 TRI 61 in the experimental category.

The presence of three Lotus 23s and the hilly character of the circuit promised hope of an open race but it failed to materialise. While pole-sitter Paul Hawkins was soon let down by his transmission and was forced to continue with only two gears, and Bernard Consten finished only ninth, Alan Rees brought his Lotus home in second place, with ample time over 38 laps to appreciate Carlo Mario Abate's consummate skills at the wheel of the winning Scuderia SSS Repubblica di Venezia GTO. Overall, it was a fairly monotonous race in which Abate, ninth on the first lap because he possessed somewhat limited peripheral vision that made Le Mans-type starts difficult for him, went on to take the lead four laps later. Behind, his rivals had no choice but to resign themselves to playing follow my leader, with two exceptions: Jean Guichet was pushing hard when he went over kerbing in his GTO, allowing André Simon in a 250 GT SWB to snatch his place on the podium, and Tony Maggs's determination to match the pace of the Ferraris was rewarded with seventh place in a DB4 GT Zagato, the only Aston Martin in the race.

Thanks to this fifth consecutive class victory, Ferrari already had the International Championship for GT Manufacturers title sewn up in Division III (over 2,000cc). In fact, the Italian cars were never really up against rivals who could pose any threat,

TROPHÉES D'AUVERGNE

Charade, 15th July 1962, 38 laps (5.005 miles/8.055km), 190.196 miles/306.090km • Starters 33, classified finishers 22

1st	Carlo Mario Abate	Ferrari 250 GTO (3445 GT) (1st GT+2.0)	2h 35m 25.0s
2nd	Alan Rees	Lotus 23	+1m 38.1s
3rd	André Simon	Ferrari 250 GT SWB (2972 GT)	+2m 30.1s
4th	Jean Guichet	Ferrari 250 GTO (3705 GT)	+2m 41.4s
5th	Henri Oreiller	Ferrari 250 GT SWB (2787 GT)	+3m 46.8s
6th	Pierre Noblet	Ferrari 250 GT SWB (2689 GT)	37 laps
8th	Roger de Lageneste	Ferrari 250 GT SWB (2807 GT)	36 laps
11th	Nino Vaccarella	Ferrari 250 TRI 61 (0792 TR)	36 laps

Fastest practice lap: Paul Hawkins (Lotus 23), 3m 54.7s, 76.903mph/123.764kph Fastest race lap: Vaccarella, 3m 57.1s, 75.995mph/122.302kph
Winner's average speed: 73.426mph/118.168kph FIA International Championship for GT Manufacturers (GT Division III, over 2,000cc): 1st Ferrari 54, 2nd Jaguar 9, 3rd Chevrolet 6

TOURIST TROPHY

Goodwood, 18th August 1962, 100 laps (2.400 miles/3.862km), 240.000 miles/386.200km • Starters 33, classified finishers 19

1st	Innes Ireland	Ferrari 250 GTO (3505 GT) (1st GT+2.0)	2h 33m 06.8s
2nd	Graham Hill	Ferrari 250 GTO (3729 GT)	+3.4s
3rd	Michael Parkes	Ferrari 250 GTO (3589 GT)	+54.2s
4th	Roy Salvadori	Jaguar E-type Lightweight	99 laps
5th	David Piper	Ferrari 250 GTO (3767 GT)	98 laps
6th	Dick Protheroe	Jaguar E-type	93 laps
DNF	Chris Kerrison	Ferrari 250 GT SWB (2735 GT)	91 laps (accident)
DNF	John Surtees	Ferrari 250 GTO (3647 GT)	61 laps (accident)

Fastest practice lap: Ireland, 1m 28.4s, 97.738mph/157.294kph Fastest race lap: Surtees, 1m 28.6s, 97.499mph/156.910kph Winner's average speed:
94.026mph/151.320kph FIA International Championship for GT Manufacturers (GT Division III, over 2,000cc): 1st Ferrari 63, 2nd Jaguar 12, 3rd Chevrolet 6

BRIDGEHAMPTON 400KM

Bridgehampton, 16th September 1962, 87 laps (2.860 miles/4.603km), 248.835 miles/400.461km • Starters 20, classified finishers 12

1st	Pedro Rodríguez	Ferrari 330 TRI LM (0780/0808 TR)	2h 47m 48.0s
2nd	Bob Grossman	Ferrari 250 GTO (3387 GT) (1st GT+2.0)	85 laps
3rd	Charlie Hayes/Ed Hugus	Ferrari 250 GTO (3223 GT)	84 laps
4th	Millard Ripley/Charles Kurtz	Porsche 718 RS 61	84 laps
5th	David Schiff/William Wonder	Porsche 718 RS 60	83 laps
6th	Walt Hansgen	Jaguar E-type	82 laps
8th	Chris Kerrison	Ferrari 250 GT SWB (1931 GT)	81 laps
11th	Chuck Dietrich/John Baxter	Ferrari 250 GT SWB (3327 GT)	72 laps
12th	Harry Theodoracopulos/Filippo Theodoli/Freddie Barrette	Ferrari 250 GT SWB (1461 GT)	72 laps
DNF	Doug Thiem	Ferrari 250 GT SWB (3005 GT)	6 laps (universal joint)

Fastest practice lap: Rodríguez, 1m 49.6s, 93.942mph/151.185kph Fastest race lap: Rodríguez, 1m 50.2s, 93.430mph/150.361kph Winner's average speed:
88.970/143.183kph FIA International Championship for GT Manufacturers (GT Division III, over 2,000cc): 1st Ferrari 72, 2nd Jaguar 16, 3rd Chevrolet 9

like Jaguar and Aston Martin, especially as the latter competed in the over 3,000cc category.

The remaining races on the calendar changed nothing. The Tourist Trophy at Goodwood on 18th August went to Innes Ireland in the UDT-Laystall GTO after a stirring drive, giving the Prancing Horse another nine points. It was a similar story in the Bridgehampton 400Km on 16th September, when Pedro Rodríguez in the Le Mans-winning 330 TRI LM beat the GTOs of Bob Grossman and Charlie Hayes/Ed Hugus. However, the Paris 1,000Km at Montlhéry a month later would leave a deeper impression, as we shall see.

End of the road

British Grand Prix, 21st July

Due to continuing industrial and social upheaval in Italy, only one Ferrari arrived at Aintree for the British Grand Prix, for Phil Hill to drive on a track he did not particularly like. His weekend was something of a nightmare. Equipped with the 156 seen in practice in Monaco, with the final drive mounted behind the gearbox, he had a dismal time throughout practice. After using the first session on Thursday to find his feet, his best lap of 1m 57.8s that day left him more than three seconds behind Jim Clark's Lotus. While the next day's first session gave him a brief glimmer of hope with a time of 1m 56.6s, he ended up way down the order in the second session, earning a place on the fifth row between Roy Salvadori (Lola) and Tony Maggs (Cooper) with a lap in 1m 56.2s. By comparison, Clark clinched pole with 1m 53.6s while John Surtees's Lola (1m 54.2s) and Innes Ireland's Lotus (1m 54.4s) completed the front row.

Hill had the reputation of being a driver who did not know the meaning of the word 'quit', especially as he was the reigning World Champion and as such a benchmark, but if ever there was a race in which he hit rock bottom, then this was it. While Clark romped away at the head of the field pursued by Surtees, Bruce McLaren (Cooper), Graham Hill (BRM) and Jack Brabham (Lotus), an order that did not change from lap 29 until the end of the 75-lap contest, the lone Ferrari driver occupied the midfield. Initially 11th behind Richie Ginther (BRM), he moved up to 10th after Salvadori retired 35th time round. This became ninth when Ginther had a long pitstop due to a detached wire on his BRM's fuel pump. And that was how it stayed until lap 47, when the American pitted due to ignition failure and bowed out. When it came to totting up the points afterwards, the situation

◄ **British Grand Prix.** This 156, with its final drive behind the gearbox, had last been seen in Monaco during practice. The configuration offered better weight distribution and therefore improved roadholding.

➤ **British Grand Prix.** Phil Hill's despair and powerlessness are written on his face as he makes a futile and exhausting attempt to find some speed. He ended practice only 12th on the grid.

⌄ **British Grand Prix.** Phil Hill has no need to look in his rear-view mirrors to measure his solitude at an Aintree circuit that he found dull and on which he seems completely alone, which was indeed the case for most of the race until his retirement on lap 47.

BRITISH GRAND PRIX

Aintree, 21st July 1962, 75 laps (3.000 miles/4.828km), 225.000 miles/362.100km • Starters 21, finishers 16

RACE				PRACTICE	
1st	Jim Clark	Lotus 25 Climax V8	2h 26m 20.8s	1st	1m 53.6s
2nd	John Surtees	Lola Mk4 Climax V8	+49.2s	2nd	1m 54.2s
3rd	Bruce McLaren	Cooper T60 Climax V8	1m +44.8s	4th	1m 54.6s
4th	Graham Hill	BRM P57 BRM V8	1m +56.8s	5th	1m 54.6s
5th	Jack Brabham	Lotus 24 Climax V8	74 laps	9th	1m 55.4s
6th	Tony Maggs	Cooper T60 Climax V8	74 laps	13th	1m 57.0s
DNF	Phil Hill	Ferrari 156 V6 120°	47 laps (distributor)	12th	1m 56.2s

Pole position: Clark, 1m 53.6s, 95.070mph/153.000kph Fastest race lap: Clark, 1m 55.0s, 93.914mph/151.140kph Winner's average speed: 92.255mph/148.470kph Drivers' championship: 1st Graham Hill 19, 2nd Clark 18, 3rd McLaren 16, 4th Phil Hill 14, 9th Bandini 4, 11th= Baghetti & Rodríguez 3 Constructors' championship: 1st Lotus-Climax 24, 2nd BRM 23, 3rd Cooper-Climax 21, 4th Ferrari 14

was far from rosy as he had dropped from second to fourth in the standings.

The Scuderia was caught in a downward spiral from which it would only emerge with great difficulty. Hill, who had been in the doghouse since the start of the season, was left to carry the can. This was also the case at the next race, at the Nürburgring, where Eugenio Dragoni and Mauro Forghieri seemed to pay more attention to the efforts of Surtees than to those of their own number-one driver.

A desperate situation

German Grand Prix, 5th August

Seasons and races follow one another but can be very different. In 1961, Stirling Moss scored one of the greatest victories of his glittering career at the Nürburgring, beating two Ferraris at the top of their game. A year later, the champion without a crown had been forced to retire through injury and the performance of the Ferraris was so bad from the beginning of practice that it almost seemed as if the cards had been rigged.

In the second session on Friday, Phil Hill took 9m 33s to lap the 14-mile circuit compared with 8m 55.2s the previous year, improving to 9m 24.7s the next day in typical Eifel drizzle. Only one of his team-mates, Ricardo Rodríguez in an old car with just a 65-degree V6, did better by lapping at 9m 14.2s, while Giancarlo Baghetti and Lorenzo Bandini (in Mauro Forghieri's revamped car) were in even worse shape at 9m 28.1s and 9m 39.7s respectively, hopeless times that were in the same bracket as those set by 1.5-litre Formula 2 cars competing in the German

Grand Prix five years earlier. The comparison was all the more galling when their four quickest rivals, all driving for different marques, set their best times the same day, in the order Dan Gurney's Porsche (8m 47.2s), Graham Hill's BRM (8m 50.2s) Jim Clark's Lotus (8m 51.2s) and John Surtees's Lola (8m 57.5s).

Graham Hill had benefited from a new BRM until its destruction in the first practice session. A camera had been mounted on Dutch driver Carel Godin de Beaufort's Porsche but fell off when the World Championship leader was close behind. The BRM hit the camera and went out of control, wrecking itself in a series of rolls, luckily without harm to its driver. Tony Maggs arrived at the scene almost immediately in his V8-powered Cooper and, given no warning of oil on the track, crashed and destroyed his car as well, so had to fall back on a four-cylinder version for the race.

Phil Hill's lightning start, a pretty rash one as he used most of the pitlane, saw him in third place at the end of the first lap behind Gurney and the other Hill. But it was a flash in the pan as it lasted for only two laps. What followed, including a stop fifth time round to swap his goggles for a visor, was an inexorable slide down the order until his retirement on lap 9 with completely worn-out rear shock absorbers when in tenth place. As proof of his powerlessness, both McLaren and Surtees got past him, as did Clark after starting last due to his blunder in forgetting to switch on his Lotus's fuel pumps. Rodríguez also bested Phil as he dealt with a track that was shrouded in mist or soaking wet from sudden showers, perhaps enjoying extra luck endowed by the four-leaf clover in gold and diamonds given to him by his father. Ricardo finished sixth, far ahead of tenth-placed Baghetti after a very slow but consistent race. At least Baghetti performed better than Bandini, who came in to

⌃ German Grand Prix. Without being revolutionary, Mauro Forghieri's take on the 156 resulted in a cleaner-looking, lighter car with a narrower chassis. Here it is given the once-over in the Nürburgring paddock by some curious onlookers, including journalist Denis Jenkinson at far right.

➤ German Grand Prix. Together with a very attentive Phil Hill, Mauro Forghieri gives Lorenzo Bandini his final recommendations concerning the revamped 156 he is about to drive. Bandini was a good test driver and soon got the upper hand over Giancarlo Baghetti.

◄ **German Grand Prix.** Watched by Mauro Forghieri and Phil Hill at far left, Lorenzo Bandini sets off in the revised 156, making its competition début. The use of a conventional air intake instead of 'nostrils' is obvious but note too the very prominent front anti-roll bar. The car was slow in practice and crashed out on lap 4 of the race after an unconvincing performance.

▼ **German Grand Prix.** With its modified rear shock absorbers, Phil Hill's 156 gave him the opportunity to shine briefly for two laps at the Nürburgring. A pitstop to change his visor was a prelude to his retirement on lap 9 with broken rear suspension.

GERMAN GRAND PRIX

Nürburgring, 5th August 1962, 15 laps (14.173 miles/22.810km), 212.602 miles/342.150km • Starters 26, finishers 16

RACE					PRACTICE	
1st	Graham Hill	BRM P57 BRM V8	2h 38m 45.3s		2nd	8m 50.2s
2nd	John Surtees	Lola Mk4 Climax V8	+2.5s		4th	8m 57.5s
3rd	Dan Gurney	Porsche 804 F8	+4.4s		1st	8m 47.2s
4th	Jim Clark	Lotus 25 Climax V8	+42.1s		3rd	8m 51.2s
5th	Bruce McLaren	Cooper T60 Climax V8	+1m 19.6s		5th	9m 00.7s
6th	**Ricardo Rodríguez**	**Ferrari 156 V6 65°**	**+1m 23.8s**		10th	9m 14.2s
10th	**Giancarlo Baghetti**	**Ferrari 156 V6 120°**	**+8m 14.7s**		13th	9m 28.1s
DNF	**Phil Hill**	**Ferrari 156 V6 120°**	9 laps (suspension)		12th	9m 24.7s
DNF	**Lorenzo Bandini**	**Ferrari 156 V6 120°**	4 laps (accident)		18th	9m 39.7s

Pole position: Gurney, 8m 47.2s, 96.784mph/155.759kph **Fastest race lap:** Graham Hill, 10m 12.2s, 83.326mph/134.100kph
Winner's average speed: 80.281mph/129.200kph **Drivers' championship:** 1st Graham Hill 28, 2nd Clark 21, 3rd Surtees 19, 5th Phil Hill 14, 9th= Bandini & Rodríguez 4, 12th Baghetti 3 **Constructors' championship:** 1st BRM 31, 2nd Lotus-Climax 27, 3rd Cooper-Climax 23, 4th Ferrari 15

retire at the end of lap 4 after stoving in his radiator when he left the track at the *Karussell*. The best adjective to describe Ferrari's situation was probably 'desperate'.

Up front, it was a close contest as Graham Hill, lacking his new BRM, beat Surtees by just 2.5 seconds. Hill never put a foot wrong even though his Lola-mounted rival kept the BRM in his sights but in the end decided to apply constant pressure rather than try to win the race at all costs. Was this new-style wisdom and maturity displayed by Surtees enough to comfort Enzo Ferrari in his decision to hire the former motorcycle racing champion? In fact, *Il Commendatore* had first approached the Englishman a year earlier before asking him a second time if he would join the Scuderia. First time round, Surtees had turned down the offer because he did not want to become mixed up in the politics of a team with five drivers, including two Italians, a decision guided by the painful memory left by Colin Chapman's proposal to him for the 1962 season. Chapman had wanted Surtees to be Lotus's number-one driver and had asked him to choose between Jim Clark and Innes Ireland as his team-mate. When Surtees opted for Clark, Ireland, who had been contractually the team leader, felt that he had been pushed out. Exasperated by the political row triggered by his choice, Surtees instead went to Lola, leaving Clark as team leader and Trevor Taylor the number two.

Did Enzo Ferrari contact Surtees again after the German Grand Prix? Whether or not he did does not really matter as the Englishman had never been closer to joining Maranello. Ferrari had always thought that any champion motorcycle rider had the potential to become a champion on four wheels, and way back in 1932 had created the Scuderia Ferrari Motociclismo with this in mind. So it was that he had always followed the careers of the finest motorcycle racers very closely, particularly when British riders raced for Italian teams such Moto Guzzi, Gilera and MV Agusta.

Bitter dregs

Italian Grand Prix, 16th September

After the previous year's tragedy, Monza had undergone a considerable revamp and safety precautions had been overhauled. Apart from the start/finish straight and the *Lesmo* curve, spectators were only allowed to watch from infield areas of the track. Each corner was now bordered by steel guardrails and tall fences were installed in front of spectator areas. Another change was that the distance of the race, now run just on the road circuit, was increased to 307.3 miles.

Even though the World Championship chase had boiled down to a scrap between Graham Hill and Jim Clark, the Scuderia turned up with no fewer than five 156s: the new one seen in Germany was now entrusted to Willy Mairesse (back after his Spa accident), there were regular cars with the centrally mounted gearbox for Phil Hill, Ricardo Rodríguez and Giancarlo Baghetti, and this time Lorenzo Bandini had to make do with the old model with its 65-degree engine. Even though the team did its damnedest, it was not enough. Perhaps 'pathetic' might be a better adjective to describe the Ferraris' performances as they seemed to reel from their rivals' onslaught like punch-drunk boxers.

◀ **Italian Grand Prix.** Proof of the effort made by Ferrari for Monza was the fact that Willy Mairesse, making his return to racing after his Spa injuries, drove a rebodied version of the 156 seen at the Nürburgring in Lorenzo Bandini's hands. The Belgian damaged the car's radiator grille by hitting Masten Gregory's UDT-Laystall Lotus in practice.

▼ **Italian Grand Prix.** The tail section of Willy Mairesse's revised 156 is not hiding the eagerly awaited four-valve V6 but a regular 120-degree version. He probably regretted the fact that he was not at the wheel of the very latest iteration with a completely redesigned rear end, especially as he had spent the preceding week at Monza testing it.

> **Italian Grand Prix.** Giancarlo Baghetti (foreground) and Lorenzo Bandini are ready to go out in one of the two practice sessions at Monza. Their results were sobering to say the least, with only 17th and 18th places respectively on the grid. Ricardo Rodríguez in #4 did better and started 11th.

▼ **Italian Grand Prix.** These three 156s travelled in convoy for some of the race. Giancarlo Baghetti (#2) drove strongly after a disastrous practice session to finish fifth, Ricardo Rodríguez (#4) dropped out with an ignition problem on the 64th lap, and fourth-placed Willy Mairesse (#8) just missed out on a podium finish.

ITALIAN GRAND PRIX

Monza, 16th September 1962, 86 laps (3.573 miles/5.750km), 307.268 miles/494.500km • Starters 21, finishers 12

RACE				PRACTICE	
1st	Graham Hill	BRM P57 BRM V8	2h 29m 08.4s	2nd	1m 40.38s
2nd	Richie Ginther	BRM P57 BRM V8	+29.8s	3rd	1m 41.80s
3rd	Bruce McLaren	Cooper T60 Climax V8	+57.8s	4th	1m 41.80s
4th	**Willy Mairesse**	**Ferrari 156 V6 120°**	**+58.2s**	**10th**	**1m 42.80s**
5th	**Giancarlo Baghetti**	**Ferrari 156 V6 120°**	**+1m 31.3s**	**18th**	**1m 44.40s**
6th	Jo Bonnier	Porsche 804 F8	85 laps	9th	1m 42.60s
8th	**Lorenzo Bandini**	**Ferrari 156 V6 65°**	**84 laps**	**17th**	**1m 44.30s**
11th	**Phil Hill**	**Ferrari 156 V6 120°**	**81 laps (suspension)**	**15th**	**1m 43.40s**
14th	**Ricardo Rodríguez**	**Ferrari 156 V6 120°**	**64 laps (engine)**	**11th**	**1m 43.10s**

Pole position: Jim Clark (Lotus 25 Climax V8), 1m 40.35s, 128.175mph/206.278kph **Fastest race lap:** Graham Hill, 1m 42.30s, 125.732mph/202.346kph **Winner's average speed:** 123.616mph/198.940kph **Drivers' championship:** 1st Graham Hill 36, 2nd McLaren 22, 3rd Clark 21, 5th Phil Hill 14, 10th Baghetti 5, 11th= Bandini & Rodríguez 4, 13th= Mairesse 3 **Constructors' championship:** 1st BRM 37, 2nd= Lotus-Climax & Cooper-Climax 27, 5th Ferrari 18

At the end of Friday's session, Graham Hill, the only driver to break into the 1m 40s bracket with a lap in 1m 40.7s, putting nearly a second between his BRM and Jim Clark's Lotus (1m 41.5s), dashed any hopes that Mairesse (1m 42.9s) might have entertained of playing a leading role. Phil Hill (1m 43.4s) also knew that his chances of a good result were severely compromised and in addition his mechanics were baffled by the fact that his engine would not pull maximum revs. The next day, while Clark (1m 40.35s) and Graham Hill (1m 40.38s) were duking it out for the 100,000 *Lire* offered by the organisers for the quickest lap in practice, the Ferraris were suffering from chronic oversteer. Mairesse went a tenth of a second quicker thanks to a combination of daring and sheer determination and clinched a place on the fifth row, while Rodríguez (1m 43.1s) sat on the sixth row. Hill, unable to improve, languished on the eighth row, with Bandini (1m 44.3s) and Baghetti (1m 44.4s) sharing the row behind.

Mairesse never had that little bit of luck that makes an exceptional driver a champion. In terms of speed, courage (which often bordered on recklessness) and talent (particularly as a test driver) he was never found wanting, but his anxiety and bullish desire to do well meant that he walked on a tightrope from which he often fell either because of error or bad luck. At Spa there had been the incident with Trevor Taylor. Now, here at Monza, his carburettor flooded, leaving him stuck on the grid while the entire field roared past before he finally set off in last place. The fact that Clark made the best start before falling back and retiring on lap 13 with a gearbox failure, and

that Graham Hill took up the lead followed by BRM team-mate Richie Ginther, was of little interest to the spectators because in Italy they always have eyes only for their own. Mairesse's efforts gave them heart. He was 15th second time round and 12th on the third lap. By the time of Clark's demise, he was the highest of the Ferrari drivers, ninth with Rodríguez and Baghetti on his gearbox, Phil Hill further back and Bandini but a distant speck on the horizon.

John Surtees in his Lola had put second-placed Ginther under some pressure but by lap 43, precisely half distance, he was forced to throw in the towel because of a blown piston. Now Dan Gurney (Porsche) and Bruce McLaren (Cooper) led the pursuit, followed by Tony Maggs (Cooper) and Jo Bonnier (Porsche), with the Ferrari trio of Mairesse, Baghetti and Rodríguez next in close formation, until the Mexican's engine let him down. It was time for the other two Ferraris, Baghetti now ahead of Mairesse, to stage a final charge and they made up ground impressively. Maggs, who had to come in to refuel, was Baghetti's first victim. McLaren, whose Cooper was equipped with bigger fuel tanks than those in Maggs's car, fell back. When Baghetti also got past both Porsches, Bonnier first, then Gurney, the crowd went wild because the driver from Milan was now third. On the next lap, though, there was hush again, for he had spun in the *Parabolica* and fallen back to seventh. Mairesse then pulled out all the stops. After running sixth when Baghetti looked set for a place on the podium, the Belgian was now fifth with McLaren and Gurney ahead of him. The American slowed just before his final drive let him down after 66 laps, so 'Wild Willy' moved up to third, then on lap 84 he passed the New Zealander amid a roar of excitement. Over the next five laps, Bruce calmly waited for his chance and kept his Cooper tucked in behind the Ferrari. If Mairesse had forgotten that streamlining often played a crucial role at Monza, as at Reims, McLaren soon reminded him. Just when Graham Hill and Ginther tackled their final lap, and Phil Hill, five laps down, saw the end in sight for his drive from hell, the Cooper shot past the Ferrari in the *Curva Grande* to snatch third place on the line. So Mairesse finished fourth and Baghetti fifth.

The farce is over

In the World Championship standings, Graham Hill's second successive victory put him comfortably at the top of the table after Monza. With Phil Hill getting ever closer to conceding his title, Ferrari, still under pressure from the strikes that were paralysing Italian industry, decided soon after Monza that it would not take part in the last two rounds, in the United States and South Africa. Although Lorenzo Bandini and Giancarlo Baghetti were told by letter that they were free to drive elsewhere, it was too late for them to find other seats. Ricardo Rodríguez found himself in the same position but his father's money enabled him to get a drive in the non-championship Mexican Grand Prix. Mairesse, whose development work was much appreciated by Mauro Forghieri, escaped this clear-out, prefiguring a realignment of the Scuderia's thinking that Enzo Ferrari would clarify in December.

Phil Hill, however, had not waited for any authorisation to look for a drive with another team. Fed up with Ferrari's Machiavellian methods and despondent after a string of setbacks, he added substance to the rumours floating round the Monza paddock by embarking on discussions with Carlo Chiti about driving for Automobili Turismo e Sport (ATS). The former chief engineer at Ferrari had designed a new Formula 1 car in five months around a V8 of his own creation working alongside ex-Ferrari colleagues Romolo Tavoni and Girolamo Gardini with funding from Giorgio Billi, Count Giovanni Volpi and Jaime Ortiz-Patiño. Had Phil Hill decided to leave Ferrari or had he been given the boot? The simple answer is that we do not know. 'The farce is over,' he wrote in conclusion of his long collaboration with Enzo Ferrari. Helped by time and reflection, he acknowledged that his ego had prevented him from appreciating the depths of the man. However, unlike the names of Mairesse, Bandini and Baghetti, his was not on the list of entries made for the United States Grand Prix before Ferrari's decision not to attend. The American was initially entered in a works Porsche alongside Gurney and Bonnier, but after testing the car he decided against racing it and watched Clark's victory as an ordinary spectator.

A terrible tragedy

Ricardo Rodríguez intended to take full advantage of his new-found freedom. Winner with brother Pedro of the previous edition of the Paris 1,000Km, his participation in the 1962 race on 21st October was widely reported in the media. Since Le Mans in 1961, the Rodríguez brothers had enjoyed a privileged

▾ Ricardo Rodríguez, pictured at the Dutch Grand Prix, had a meteoric career that began when he was still an adolescent. Although he was only 20 when he lost his life during practice for the Mexican Grand Prix, he left an indelible mark on the sport.

relationship with the French public. Their youth and charisma seduced journalists from beyond the specialised press, one example being Olivier Merlin, a fine writer whose impassioned article in *Paris Match* shone a spotlight on these two young men who raced against death.

While the world title in the over 2-litre GT category was already decided, the eight 250 GTOs that nonetheless turned up at Montlhéry included a new one for Pedro and Ricardo that had just been delivered to Luigi Chinetti's NART. That it had been specially prepared for the event was obvious in practice when Ricardo was able to lap even more quickly than the GTO driven by Lucien Bianchi/Willy Mairesse. The race was a walkover for the Mexican brothers, with Pedro taking an early lead and their car never being threatened thereafter. Along with Bianchi/Mairesse, another GTO driven by John Surtees/Michael Parkes, the 250 GT SWB of Ludovico Scarfiotti/Colin Davis and even the Aston Martin DB4 GT Zagato of Jim Clark/John Whitmore did their best to try to spoil the dazzling display, but in vain. At the finish, with their GTO wearing the appropriate #1, the brothers had a lap in hand over the Surtees/Parkes car.

On 1st November, Ricardo's death in the first practice session for the Mexican Grand Prix held in Mexico City, his birthplace,

◄ Bernard Cahier: 'We were approaching the end of the first practice session. Ricardo had set the fastest time when the loudspeakers suddenly announced that Surtees had gone quicker. The younger of the Rodríguez brothers immediately buckled his yellow helmet back on.'

PARIS 1,000KM

Montlhéry, 21st October 1962, 129 laps (4.837 miles/7.784km), 623.941 miles/1,004.136km • Starters 34, classified finishers 20

1st	Pedro Rodríguez/Ricardo Rodríguez	Ferrari 250 GTO (3987 GT) (*1st GT+2.0*)	6h 21m 58.7s
2nd	John Surtees/Michael Parkes	Ferrari 250 GTO (3647 GT)	128 laps
3rd	Ludovico Scarfiotti/Colin Davis	Ferrari 250 GT Drogo (2819 GT)	127 laps
4th	Jean Guichet/Pierre Noblet	Ferrari 250 GTO (3943 GT)	125 laps
5th	Willy Mairesse/Lucien Bianchi	Ferrari 250 GTO (3527 GT)	122 laps
6th	André Simon/Georges Berger	Ferrari 250 GT SWB (2973 GT)	121 laps
DSQ	'Beurlys' (Jean Blaton)/'Elde' (Léon Dernier)/'Remordu' (Guy Hancez)	Ferrari 250 GTO (3757 GT)	122 laps
DNF	Nino Vaccarella/Carlo Mario Abate	Ferrari 250 GTO (3445 GT)	50 laps
DNF	Edgar Berney/Jean Manuel Bordeu	Ferrari 250 GTO (3909 GT)	40 laps (engine)
DNF	Kalman von Csazy/Richard Hubert	Ferrari 250 GTO (3809 GT)	21 laps (accident)

Fastest practice lap: Pedro Rodríguez, 2m 51.4s **Fastest race lap:** Mairesse, 2m 52.3s, 101.058mph/162.637kph **Winner's average speed:** 98.007mph/157.727kph **FIA International Championship for GT Manufacturers (GT Division III, over 2,000cc):** 1st Ferrari 45 (81)[1], 2nd Jaguar 16, 3rd Chevrolet 9

1 *Figure in brackets indicates all points scored; only the best five results counted towards the championship*

Formula 1 World Championship (Drivers) *Top three plus Ferrari drivers*

	1st Graham Hill	2nd Jim Clark	3rd Bruce McLaren	6th Phil Hill	11th Giancarlo Baghetti	12th= Lorenzo Bandini	12th= Ricardo Rodríguez	14th Willy Mairesse
Dutch GP	9	0	0	4	3	–	0	–
Monaco GP	–1	0	9	6	–	4	0	0
Belgian GP	6	9	0	6	0	–	3	0
GP de l'ACF (France)	0	0	–3	–	–	–	–	–
British GP	–3	9	4	0	–	–	–	–
German GP	9	3	–2	0	0	0	1	–
Italian GP	9	0	4	0	2	0	0	3
United States GP	–6	9	4	–	–	–	–	–
South African GP	9	0	6	–	–	–	–	–
Total	42	30	27	14	5	4	4	3

touched people everywhere. As there was no Ferrari for him to drive, he was at the wheel of a Lotus 24 entered by Rob Walker. The young Mexican was on a charge to beat the fastest time that Surtees had just snatched from him when he came into the banked turn before the grandstands too quickly and ploughed into the barrier. He was thrown out of the car and died shortly after his transfer to hospital.

Had he been caught out by the Lotus's roadholding, which was known to be superior to that of the Ferrari but gave very little warning to the driver when he reached its limits, unlike the cars from Maranello? Very probably. He had been talking to Bernard Cahier a few minutes before the accident and had told him how 'exciting the Lotus was to drive compared with the Ferraris', a comment that adds weight to this hypothesis. Later, Ricardo's father, in the throes of grief, claimed that the accident had been caused by a broken bearing on the Lotus's right-rear wheel.

Not long afterwards, Surtees dumbfounded his doubters on early outings for Ferrari at Monza by setting lap records in what was apparently a 246 SP powered by a 3-litre V12. It was no big surprise to see him in Italy because he had gone ballistic at the United States Grand Prix about his Lola's shortcomings, including a steering breakage. Soon after this, Maranello hired another Englishman, Michael Parkes, as an engineering adviser, Mauro Forghieri having been much impressed by his performances at Brands Hatch on 6th August, when he won three of the day's four races, two of them in Ferraris.

Big changes were under way. Enzo Ferrari spoke about all this on 1st December when promoting his memoir *Le Mie Gioie Terribili*. It was an eagerly awaited press conference because from across the Atlantic a strong new wind was starting to blow.

Formula 1 World Championship (Constructors)

	1st BRM	2nd Lotus-Climax	3rd Cooper-Climax	6th Ferrari
Dutch GP	9	6	–2	4
Monaco GP	–1	0	9	6
Belgian GP	6	9	0	4
GP de l'ACF (France)	–4	0	6	–
British GP	–3	9	4	–
German GP	9	3	–2	1
Italian GP	9	0	4	3
United States GP	–6	9	–4	–
South African GP	9	–2	6	–
Total	42	36	29	18

International Championship for GT Manufacturers

	1st Ferrari	2nd Jaguar	3rd Chevrolet
Daytona Three Hours	9	2	4
Sebring 12 Hours	9	3	2
Targa Florio	9	–	–
Nürburgring 1,000Km	9	–	–
Le Mans 24 Hours	9	4	0
Trophées d'Auvergne	–9	–	–
Tourist Trophy	–9	3	–
Bridgehampton 400Km	–9	4	3
Paris 1,000Km	–9	0	–
Total	45	16	9

German Grand Prix. Ferrari's new English star leads
Lotus's Scottish one: while Jim Clark dominated the
Formula 1 season with seven wins from ten starts,
John Surtees was only able to win once, but did so
in style here at the Nürburgring on a day when he
judged his performance as 'simply perfect'.

1963
THE MESSIAH ARRIVES

At his press conference on 1st December 1962, Enzo Ferrari, smiling and talkative, revived the past while simultaneously looking to the future — a tricky exercise. According to some of those present, *Il Commendatore* used all the tricks in his wide-ranging emotional repertoire to 'reward or blame', 'unveil or retract'. In short, he made it clear that Maranello, far from pulling out, would continue to race, but this time in a more measured and less costly manner after two very expensive seasons. With a competition staff of 94, the company's racing activities had swallowed up 400 million *Lire* in the 18-month period from 1st July 1960 to 31st December 1961 but had then increased so much that 397 million *Lire* — very nearly the same amount — had been spent in just 12 months.

Wait and see

The competition department was downsized, beginning with personnel, in particular drivers, who would now do all testing as had once been the case. To underline this change, Ferrari gave the names of former champions and 'faithful collaborators' such as Giuseppe Campari, Pietro Bordino, Carlo Salamano and Felice Nazzaro. For Phil Hill, this allusion was as demeaning as it was unfair because, having fulfilled his dream of becoming Formula 1 World Champion, he had decided to devote himself solely to his role at races.

For the new season, Ferrari's drivers would be Willy Mairesse, John Surtees and Michael Parkes, the latter entrusted with the development of prototypes. If other single-seater drivers were needed, they would be Italian. No names were announced but Ludovico Scarfiotti seemed likely to be among them. Eugenio Dragoni continued as team manager.

Mr Ferrari then went on to outline Ferrari's involvement in its different spheres of racing and confirmed that his cars would compete in all rounds of the Formula 1 World Championship. To this end, lighter and more rigid new chassis had been tested, for the moment with a V6 engine but with the possibility of moving on to a V8 or even a flat-12.

The 196 SP, the only survivor of a sports car formula that was now part of history, would be built if there was demand for it. In endurance, Maranello would continue to construct cars for the experimental prototype category whose maximum cubic capacity was still to be decided. In addition, the weight limits per category (15 in all) were still a mystery. Raising his voice, Ferrari underlined the fact by stating: 'We have to race at Sebring next March and we still don't know what kind of car to build!'

Clearly, he wanted to keep people guessing to protect himself from his rivals and perhaps he was right. On 30th November, the Automobile Club de l'Ouest (ACO), organiser of Le Mans, had announced its regulations for the following year's race. Overall, these were close to those of the Commission Sportive Internationale (CSI), which had been mainly inspired by the previous year's Appendix A. In other words, the International Trophy for Prototypes created in 1962 by the ACO was now officially rubber-stamped. For the moment the requirements, in particular the weight limitations, raised a few eyebrows, especially in Maranello, when they imposed a minimum weight for the prototypes that could not be more than five percent lower than that of the lightest car homologated in its category.

Concerning GTs, Maranello left its clients to defend the marque's interests in the 16 events on the calendar, which in addition to circuit races included hillclimbs, a rally and, for the first time, the Tour de France, described as a 'mixed competition'. All the events were given a coefficient according to their duration and renown, so points scores varied.

'All that weight at the rear'

In March, once the absurd weight scales had been sorted out, Ferrari presented two cars at Monza, a 250 P spyder and a 330 LM *Berlinetta*. Compared with the exuberant display of the previous year (five spyders and a GTO), the Prancing Horse's stall looked a little bare, but this time novelty counted more than quantity, if only to comply with the new regulations. One innovation was that the spyder's lines had been studied both on the track, at Modena using tufts of wool and spraying the bodywork with oil, and in the wind tunnel, using the full-scale facility at the University of Stuttgart, and consequently the car was free of appendages such as protruding air intakes. The design of the grille returned to its former rectangular shape while the roll-over bar acted as an integrated spoiler thanks to the way in which the panoramic windscreen channelled airflow. At the time this was a unique solution that Maranello kept closely guarded as an industrial secret.

The 3-litre V12 engine from the GTO was installed in the rear of the spyder's chassis, which was similar to that of the 248 SP but with the wheelbase lengthened by 3.1 inches. This choice of engine was intended to address the competition emerging from American rivals, even if it was a design solution that niggled

Enzo Ferrari, who, according to Mauro Forghieri, railed that the car could not possibly work 'with all that weight on the rear'. For the time being, the five-speed gearbox was mounted astern. The car weighed around 930kg.

Compared with the previous year's 330 LM, the 1963 version was bigger and had lost some of its elegance. Its power output was increased by around 10bhp thanks to a higher compression ratio of 9:1. The dimensions of the 4-litre V12 were the same (3.03 x 2.07 inches) and it was still fed by six twin-choke Weber carburettors. Its weight of 950kg remained unchanged.

Something new stirs in the west

The International Championship for GT Manufacturers had already begun at the Daytona Three Hours on 17th February, where Ford and General Motors no longer made any attempt to disguise their growing interest in racing, respectively via factory support for Shelby Cobras and Chevrolet Corvette Sting Rays. In particular, the Blue Oval had no fewer than four Cobras powered by Dearborn-supplied 4.2-litre V8 engines. However, the race ended with a Ferrari double, victory going to Pedro Rodríguez in a NART-entered GTO after a hard-fought duel with Skip Hudson's Cobra until its clutch failed, leaving Roger Penske's Mecom-entered GTO to claim second place. But the Ferrari win came in controversial circumstances because Mecom had lodged a protest during the race on the grounds that Rodríguez had illegally remained behind the wheel

rather than vacate the cockpit during his final refuelling stop. Disqualification loomed, but eventually Pedro was handed a 50-second penalty after the finish that simply reduced his winning margin over Penske.

Chronologically speaking, Ford's new involvement in motorsport went back to the participation of six Anglias in the 1962 Monte Carlo Rally. Henri Chemin and William Reiber of Ford France were behind this entry after receiving the green light from Henry Ford II. What had made it even easier for them to obtain his backing was that he had just taken full ownership of Ford of Britain and on his visits to Dagenham he had discovered a competition department that had achieved headlines with Ford-powered Formula Junior Lotuses but had made little impact in America. This activity convinced him of the importance of motorsport as an advertising tool. On returning to Dearborn, he broke the unofficial agreement made with the other American manufacturers and contacted Colin Chapman the day after the British Grand Prix. Less than six months later, Ford engines, sometimes with attention from Cosworth, were powering a range of cars including the Lotus Elan. Proof at the very beginning of 1963 that Ford intended to get into the winner's circle without delay was provided by various initiatives on both sides of the Atlantic. In Europe, three works Falcon Sprints competed in the Monte Carlo Rally and work was underway in Lotus's Cheshunt factory on a special version of the new Cortina. In America, Carroll Shelby was preparing his Cobras for the big sports car races in Florida and Eric Broadley was at the Racing Car Show in London unveiling his compact mid-engined Lola GT with the very same 4.2-litre Ford V8 engine. And all this was just the beginning…

DAYTONA THREE HOURS

Daytona, 17th February 1963, 81 laps (3.810 miles/6.132km), 308.630 miles/496.692km • Starters 42, classified finishers 26

1st	Pedro Rodríguez	Ferrari 250 GTO (4219 GT) *(1st GT+2.0)*	3h 0m 38.0s
2nd	Roger Penske	Ferrari 250 GTO (3987 GT)	+1m 12.0s
3rd	Dick Thompson	Chevrolet Corvette Sting Ray	78 laps
4th	Dave MacDonald	Shelby Cobra	77 laps
5th	Jo Bonnier	Porsche 356B Carrera Abarth	77 laps
6th	Johnny Allen	Chevrolet Corvette Sting Ray	76 laps
15th	'Fireball' Roberts/John Cannon	Ferrari 250 GTO (3223 GT)	65 laps
21st	David Piper	Ferrari 250 GTO (3767 GT)	58 laps
DNF	Innes Ireland	Ferrari 250 GTO (3589 GT)	4 laps (accident)

Winner's average speed: 102.074mph/164.272kph **FIA World Sports Car Championship (GT Division III, over 2,000cc):**[1] 1st Ferrari 9, 2nd Shelby 3, 3rd Jaguar 1

[1] *Scoring system for the top six places in this event was 9–6–4–3–2–1; only the manufacturer's highest-placed car scored points*

My mistake!

Sebring 12 Hours, 23rd March

The American presence at Sebring was so extensive in both the GT and prototype categories that it could almost be described as a tsunami. This onslaught consisted of seven Chevrolet Corvette Sting Rays, six Cobras (Shelby and AC) and two Chaparrals, and their drivers included names like Dan Gurney, Phil Hill and Ken Miles in the Shelby Cobras, and A.J. Foyt in one of the Corvettes. Ferrari, not wanting to be outdone in Division III of this second round of the International Championship for GT Manufacturers, and also the first event counting towards the World Speed and Endurance Challenge for prototypes, was represented by six GTOs entered by its clients to which were added, under the NART banner, a 330 TRI LM and a 268 SP for Pedro Rodríguez/Graham Hill and Harry Heuer/John 'Buck' Fulp respectively. Maranello's works entries comprised a 330 LM *Berlinetta* for Michael Parkes/Lorenzo Bandini and two 250 Ps for John Surtees/Ludovico Scarfiotti and Willy Mairesse/Nino Vaccarella.

This may have been Surtees's début for the Scuderia but his relationship with team manager Eugenio Dragoni was already strained. Interviewed in *Motor Sport* 53 years later, Surtees explained what happened at Sebring: 'Ludovico Scarfiotti was my co-driver, and we'd got the car set up as we wanted. The second, untested, car was for Nino Vaccarella and Willy Mairesse. But when we got to Sebring, Dragoni decided that our car should go to them and we got the other car. I was so upset I nearly walked out there and then. I was packing my bags when Scarfiotti persuaded me to stay.'

Twelve hours later, six Ferraris filled the first six places, with the works 250 Ps first and second, Surtees and Scarfiotti victorious. So what happened to the American attack? Phil Hill came round in first place on the first lap and the Cobras put on a show with Gurney just shy of a podium position for a while, before steering issues and his stubborn insistence on remaining behind the wheel for six hours resulted in him hitting a kerb, which led to a long pitstop. After Hill's early display of fireworks, he suffered brake problems before taking over Gurney's Cobra and handing his own to Miles. In the end, three out of the six 'snakes' at the start crossed the finishing line with Phil Hill/Ken Miles/Lew Spencer the best of them in 11th place and first of the over 4-litre GTs.

The two Chaparrals of Jim Hall/Hap Sharp and Bob Donner/Ronnie Hissom displayed mind-blowing acceleration and Hall

➤ **Sebring 12 Hours.** The #27 268 SP driven by Harry Heuer/ John 'Buck' Fulp is lined up alongside the #28 GTO of Jo Bonnier/John Cannon. The former suffered suspension problems after covering 160 laps and was classified 34th while the latter came home in 13th spot.

◄ **Sebring 12 Hours.** Standing behind their Ferrari 250 P, John Surtees (left) and Ludovico Scarfiotti pose for the camera, looking cheerful despite earlier rancour that had led the English driver to threaten to walk out. The driver in white overalls on the right is Ed Cantrell, who co-drove David Piper's #29 GTO.

➤ **Sebring 12 Hours.** Two of the American GTOs stood out by finishing fourth and sixth. The Mecom Racing #24 driven by Roger Penske/Augie Pabst came home in front of the Rosebud Racing Team's #25 in the hands of Richie Ginther/Innes Ireland.

◄ **Sebring 12 Hours.** Driven by Michael Parkes on one his rare off days, the works 330 LM finished its race against a tree on lap 72. The result was a punctured fuel tank that caused the Ferrari to be withdrawn, depriving Lorenzo Bandini of his stints behind the wheel.

▼ **Sebring 12 Hours.** Driving the 330 TRI LM that had won Le Mans in 1962, Pedro Rodríguez and Graham Hill were very soon handicapped by numerous problems, including an oil pump that went on the blink in corners, a broken rev counter, fumes leaking from the exhaust due to a split manifold and then, when night fell, defective lights. Despite all that, they still finished third.

▲ **Sebring 12 Hours.** After being deprived of a drive following Michael Parkes's blunder, Lorenzo Bandini lent Willy Mairesse and Nino Vaccarella a hand in the 250 P that Surtees and Scarfiotti had set up. On the evidence of an erroneous lap chart, Eugenio Dragoni believed them to be the winners until the organisers awarded victory to Surtees and Scarfiotti.

➤ **Sebring 12 Hours.** Despite the earlier spat, the #30 250 P's drivers achieved a happy outcome because they won the race, although exhaust fumes leaking into the cockpit caused Surtees to lose consciousness briefly after the finish.

SEBRING 12 HOURS

Sebring, 23rd March 1963, 209 laps (5.200 miles/8.369km), 1,086.853 miles/1,749.121km • Starters 65, classified finishers 42

1st	John Surtees/Ludovico Scarfiotti	Ferrari 250 P (0810)	12h 1m 15.6s
2nd	Willy Mairesse/Nino Vaccarella/Lorenzo Bandini	Ferrari 250 P (0812)	208 laps
3rd	Pedro Rodríguez/Graham Hill	Ferrari 330 TRI LM (0780/0808 TR)	207 laps
4th	Roger Penske/Augie Pabst	Ferrari 250 GTO (3987 GT) *(1st GT+2.0)*	203 laps
5th	Carlo Mario Abate/Juan Manuel Bordeu	Ferrari 250 GTO (3445 GT)	196 laps
6th	Richie Ginther/Innes Ireland	Ferrari 250 GTO (3589 GT)	196 laps
13th	Jo Bonnier/John Cannon	Ferrari 250 GTO (4219 GT)	186 laps
14th	Ed Cantrell/David Piper	Ferrari 250 GTO (3767 GT)	186 laps
18th	Charlie Hayes/Doug Thiem	Ferrari 250 GTO (3223 GT)	179 laps
34th	Harry Heuer/John Fulp	Ferrari 268 SP (0798)	160 laps (suspension)
DNF	Michael Parkes/Lorenzo Bandini	Ferrari 330 LM (4381 SA)	72 laps (spin, split fuel tank)

Fastest race lap: Surtees, 3m 11.4s, 97.806mph/157.404kph **Winner's average speed:** 90.408mph/145.498kph **FIA World Sports Car Championship (GT Division III, over 2,000cc):**[1] 1st Ferrari 36, 2nd Jaguar 10, 3rd Shelby 6

[1] *Scoring system for the top six places in this event was 27–18–12–9–6–3; this race was also the first round of the World Speed and Endurance Challenge (for sports cars)*

led briefly at the end of the first hour before the cars bowed out, respectively with a blown cylinder head gasket and transmission problems. The Corvette Sting Rays, all entered by privateers, were far too heavy to be competitive and were also hit with a variety of problems that meant none of them saw the chequered flag. Dick Thompson put on such a good performance at the wheel of the Sting Ray shared with Ed Lowther and Duncan Black that he was lying an impressive fifth, in front of the Roger Penske/Augie Pabst GTO, when eliminated by a blown head gasket in the tenth hour.

On Sunday evening, adding up the figures was child's play for Ferrari. Thanks to the additional nine points scored by the Penske/Pabst GTO, which finished fourth overall, Maranello tightened its grip on the International Championship for GT Manufacturers, and the points bagged by the winning 250 P in the World Speed and Endurance Challenge promised more successes to come.

In fact, there had been little doubt about the result from the second hour, when eight Ferraris lay in the top ten, headed by the NART car of Rodríguez/Hill that had led since the third lap. At half distance, four Ferraris filled the first four places with Rodríguez/Hill still in front tailed by Surtees/Scarfiotti, who were soon to take advantage of the leading car's problems and take command, followed by Mairesse/Vaccarella with Bandini now assisting after Parkes had spun the 330 LM off the track and into a tree. But Ferrari's 'six-out-of-six' result was not without further gnashing of teeth around Dragoni, who judged Mairesse/Vaccarella/Bandini to be the winners before finally

agreeing that the organisers' lap chart was correct in awarding victory to Surtees/Scarfiotti.

As for Ford, the poor performances of the Cobras at both Daytona and Sebring meant that the time had come to start taking some tough decisions in Dearborn.

No surprises

Le Mans test weekend, 6th–7th April

In the meantime, Maranello had other worries. Despite appearances, a hard winter had hindered the development programme of the prototypes and the new Formula 1 car, which was rumoured to be a break with the past. As in 1962, the calendar concentrated almost all the endurance races in the first half of the season before Formula 1 kicked off in Monaco. Almost nothing was said about the Le Mans test weekend, an occasion that remained as important as ever for Ferrari.

While Maranello's supporters at the circuit were almost swooning with admiration at the sight of their red goddesses, everyone was drawn by the sight and sound of the Rover-BRM gas turbine car as it whistled past. After the initial surprise had passed, people wondered if it might foreshadow the future. This 'wingless Boeing' driven by Graham Hill and Richie Ginther produced lap times close to those of Peter Lumsden's Lister-Jaguar, despite wriggling its inelegant bottom on the *Hunaudières* straight because its roadholding left much to be desired.

Bandini, Mairesse, Parkes, Scarfiotti and Surtees were on hand to test the 250 P and the 330 LM sent by Maranello. Throughout the weekend, which began in rain and finished in warm sunshine, the Ferraris had no serious rivals and achieved speeds never previously seen at the circuit. Each driver was determined to leave his mark with the 250 P. On Saturday, Mairesse set the ball rolling, becoming the first man to lap at over 205kph, equating to more than 127mph. Surtees then went quite a bit quicker, posting a lap at 130.9mph, before the Belgian hit back with 132.3mph. By the end of the day, another driver, Parkes, had beaten them both with an average of 132.9mph. And still there was more: next day Surtees concluded this battle of egos with a lap in 3m 45.7s, an average speed of 133.4mph. As for the 330 LM, Parkes emerged the fastest of its drivers and second fastest overall with a lap of 3m 51.4s; he also became the first to exceed 300kph on the *Hunaudières* straight with a speed of 304kph (188.8mph).

Slippery road

Targa Florio, 5th May

Enzo Ferrari always said that 2 litres were enough to win the Targa Florio, provided they came from Maranello, but Porsche had trumped this in 1960 by triumphing with the 1.6-litre RS

60. Now, three years later, Ferrari wanted to prove himself right after two wins with 2.4-litre V6s, but things had changed in Stuttgart. Although the 718 RS 63 models, similar to those of the previous year, had lost a few pounds with the help of aluminium and plastic materials, they had more power thanks to a 1,981cc eight-cylinder engine pushing out around 210bhp. Among other strong points were the car's Formula 1-derived front-wishbone suspension and Porsche's top-class driver line-up of Jo Bonnier/ Carlo Mario Abate in a coupé and Umberto Maglioli/Giancarlo Baghetti in a spyder. In the 2-litre GT category, Porsche beefed up its attack with a Carrera Abarth 2000 GS (Antonio Pucci/ Paul Ernst Strähle) and an original 2000 GS coupé (Edgar Barth/ Herbert Linge) with lines inspired by those of the eight-cylinder spyder, although it was powered by a 1,966cc four-cylinder engine developing around 160bhp.

To counter the German offensive, Maranello arrived with two 250 Ps and a 196 SP plus a 246 SP as a test mule. Michael Parkes/ John Surtees were down to drive the first of the red 3-litre cars with Nino Vaccarella/Willy Mairesse in the second. But was it a bad omen or just bureaucratic bloody-mindedness on the part of the local authorities that Vaccarella's driving licence had not been given back to him after a traffic accident? This forced Eugenio Dragoni to reshuffle his drivers, putting Ludovico Scarfiotti, who was Lorenzo Bandini's preferred team-mate in the 196 SP, with Mairesse. Ferrari's attack in the 2-litre sport

> **Targa Florio.** After practice, Willy Mairesse and Ferrari chief mechanic Giulio Borsari had plenty to be pleased about, but what lay ahead would wipe the smiles off their faces. Note that Mairesse's watch is an Omega Speedmaster.

category was completed by another 196 SP entered by Scuderia Sant'Ambroeus for Edoardo Lualdi/Umberto Bini. In addition, there were five privately entered GTOs.

Ferrari suffered a succession of misfortunes. Even before the official Friday practice session began, the 246 SP driven by Scarfiotti was destroyed by a fire caused by a fuel flashback. On Friday, Surtees had barely got under way when his 250 P's V12 failed. Andrew Hedges went off and damaged Kalman von Csazy's GTO, eliminating it from the race.

Maranello's bad luck continued in the race on Sunday. The engine in Lualdi's 196 P caught fire and he failed to complete the first lap, which saw Scarfiotti lead from Parkes, Bonnier, Bandini and Maglioli. By the end of the second lap, however, Scarfiotti was back in fifth place after a long stop to sort out carburettor trouble. On lap 4, Parkes stopped to hand over to Surtees with a 90-second lead over Abate while Mairesse, replacing Scarfiotti, slid down the order. Then everything seemed to conspire against the Scuderia. Not long after the start of lap 5, Surtees crashed out and 'Wild Willy' pitted for good. Thus, at half distance the Bonnier/Abate Porsche was 20 seconds in front of the works 196 SP in which Scarfiotti had now been installed, while the Maglioli/Baghetti Porsche was third.

Just in case anyone had forgotten that Scarfiotti was the reigning European hillclimb champion, he jogged their memory. Sixth time round, Scarfiotti, his 196 SP now with a dented right-hand front wing, was 1m 5s behind Abate, and then on the following lap he took advantage of the Porsche's stop to snatch the lead. Of course, Scarfiotti would have to stop as well, so he set about building up an advantage that reached 37 seconds by the time he handed over at the end of the lap to Mairesse, who was now preferred by Dragoni to Bandini for the final push for victory. It was 2pm. The threatening clouds that filled the sky grew darker, raising the possibility of local downpours. But that did not worry Mairesse. When it began to rain on lap 9, the Belgian passed the start/finish line 5m 12s after Bonnier, meaning that the Ferrari's lead was now 48 seconds.

Last lap! Another 850 corners later, Bonnier, pursued by the gathering storm, was greeted by the cannon blast that signalled the finish of each car. Officially, he and Abate had covered the 447.3 miles in 6h 55m 45.2s, giving a record average speed of 64.56mph. As the Porsche had started at 8.28am and the Ferrari at 8.34am, Mairesse had six minutes to secure victory. The hands of the stopwatch kept turning inexorably and the six minutes melted away: 40 seconds to go, then 30, then 20. Finally, the Ferrari limped into view, headlights blazing, with its rear bodywork scraping along the road behind it. Little more than

➤ **Targa Florio.** For the moment, Jo Bonnier and Carlo Mario Abate, winners of the race, were team-mates at Porsche, but they could hardly be called defectors from Ferrari because they came back to Maranello as clients and achieved success, particularly Abate.

▼ **Targa Florio.** With three laps completed, Surtees roars off in the 250 P that Parkes has just handed over to him in the lead. A lap later the motorcycle champion ruined their hopes of victory when he went off, inflicting terminal damage.

◀ **Targa Florio.** After being slowed early on by engine overheating and fuel-feed problems, it is now all over for the Scarfiotti/Mairesse 250 P, parked in front of the pits.

▼ **Targa Florio.** Lorenzo Bandini stops to hand over the 196 SP to Ludovico Scarfiotti. With both 250 Ps about to retire, it would soon be up to the Sebring winner to defend the Scuderia's colours.

▲ **Targa Florio.** Scarfiotti has just replaced Bandini in the 196 SP. He rejoined in second place behind the Bonnier/Abate Porsche and snatched the lead after a pedal-to-metal stint during which he damaged the Dino's right-hand front wing.

➤ **Targa Florio.** A sudden storm, a car out of control on a road transformed into a skating rink, a slow-speed rear-end impact — Mairesse, still wearing his helmet, explains to Scarfiotti the reasons that deprived them of victory.

TARGA FLORIO

Piccolo Madonie, 5th May 1963, 10 laps (44.7 miles/72.0km), 447.4 miles/720.0km • Starters 55, classified finishers 28

1st	Jo Bonnier/Carlo Mario Abate	Porsche 718 GTR	6h 55m 45.2s
2nd	**Lorenzo Bandini/Ludovico Scarfiotti/Willy Mairesse**	**Ferrari 196 SP (0802)**	**6h 55m 57.0s**
3rd	Edgar Barth/Herbert Linge	Porsche 356B Carrera 2000 GS	7h 26m 19.8s
4th	Maurizio Grana/Gianni Bulgari	Ferrari 250 GTO (3413 GT) *(1st GT+2.0)*	7h 26m 31.8s
5th	Antonio Pucci/Paul Ernst Strähle	Porsche 356B Carrera Abarth	7h 33m 37.4s
6th	Juan Manuel Bordeu/Giorgio Scarlatti	Ferrari 250 GTO (3445 GT)	7h 40m 16.4s
8th	Tommy Hitchcock/Zourab Tchkotoua	Ferrari 250 GTO (3647 GT)	10 laps
13th	Egidio Nicolosi/Luigi Taramazzo	Ferrari 250 GTO (3705 GT)	9 laps
DNF	**Michael Parkes/John Surtees**	**Ferrari 250 P (0810)**	**5 laps**
DNF	**Ludovico Scarfiotti/Willy Mairesse**	**Ferrari 250 P (0812)**	**5 laps**
DNF	Vito Coco/Salvatore Calascibetta	Ferrari 250 GT SWB (1791 GT)	1 lap
DNF	Edoardo Lualdi/Umberto Bini	Ferrari 196 SP (0790)	0 laps (fire)
DNS	Kalman von Csazy/Andrew Hedges	Ferrari 250 GTO (3809 GT)	– (practice accident)
DNS	**Willy Mairesse/Ludovico Scarfiotti**	**Ferrari 246 SP (0796)**	**– (fire in practice)**

Fastest race lap: Parkes, 40m 04.1s, 66.974mph/107.784kph **Winner's average speed:** 64.565mph/103.908kph
FIA World Sports Car Championship (GT Division III, over 2,000cc):[1] 1st Ferrari 54, 2nd Jaguar 10, 3rd Shelby 6

[1] Scoring system for the top six places in this event was 18–12–8–6–4–2; this race was also the second round of the World Speed and Endurance Challenge (for sports cars)

a mile from the finish, Mairesse had been caught out in heavy rain and had lost control of his car, going off at a mere 25mph and hitting a bollard. Although the impact had been quite light, it had been enough to tear off the retaining straps for the rear bodywork. When the cannon boomed as he passed the finish line, the Ferrari had lost the 47th Targa Florio by less than 12 seconds. As a measure of the ferocity of the battle between the top two, more than half an hour elapsed before the Barth/Linge Porsche arrived to claim third place and, to Stuttgart's delight, win the GT category by just 12 seconds from the fourth-placed GTO of Maurizio Grana/Gianni Bulgari. As *Il Commendatore* had said, 2 litres were enough to win in Sicily.

Aero

At Monza in May, Surtees tested a revised 156 that he had helped to develop. Its familiar 120-degree V6 engine was now equipped with Bosch direct fuel injection developed by Michael May, a Swiss engineer who had also raced in Formula Junior. Fuel injection was a major technological step forward for Ferrari as the British V8s were already equipped with a similar Lucas-developed system, but using indirect injection that was easier to fine-tune. Further helped by a lightened crankshaft, the engine could now exceed 10,000rpm and the power output was said

to be, perhaps a little optimistically, around 200bhp. Another important novelty was that the multi-tubular chassis no longer had curved tubes and was covered by riveted sheet aluminium to increase its rigidity. As this method was taken from the aviation industry, this version of the 156 acquired the 'Aero' name commonly employed today and used at the time by Maranello but not by the specialist press. There were also some suspension tweaks: at the front there was a lower wishbone with a much wider base and at the rear an inverted wishbone, an upper arm and twin radius arms. With wheelbase increased to 2,380mm (93.7 inches) and an overall length of 3,900mm (153.5 inches), the new iteration of the 156 distinguished itself from its British rivals by its longer, sleeker silhouette. Another improvement was the use of light-alloy wheels.

Eleven days after the Sicilian mishap, Surtees and Mairesse were back racing in Formula 1 in the International Trophy at Silverstone, the last of four 'pre-season' non-championship events run in England. It was an ideal playground for the British constructors to squabble among themselves and hone their weapons for the coming season. In the previous English events, Graham Hill, still loyal to BRM, had won the Lombank Trophy at Snetterton and the Aintree 200, while Innes Ireland had triumphed in the Glover Trophy at Goodwood in a BRM-powered Lotus. In between, Jim Clark had won for Lotus at Pau and Imola without having to stretch his talent.

➤ The Aero was much more than just an evolution of the 156. It was a turning point in Ferrari's history that justified the presence of Enzo Ferrari, Michael Parkes, Eugenio Dragoni and Lorenzo Bandini at Monza for its shakedown. Drivers John Surtees (at the wheel) and Willy Mairesse would prove the soundness of this technological realignment developed by Mauro Forghieri, who takes notes while his driver provides feedback. After persevering with wire wheels long after other manufacturers had abandoned them, Ferrari was finally using light alloy rims fixed with a central nut.

The arrival of the Ferraris at Silverstone was awaited all the more eagerly as their performance in testing at Monza had shown considerable promise, with Mairesse lapping in 1m 38.4s compared with 1m 40.35s for Clark, who had been pole sitter in his Lotus 25 at the previous year's Italian Grand Prix. The Italians, though, came back to earth at Silverstone with a resounding thump. Surtees's seventh-quickest time in 1m 36.2s put him on the second row, behind a front row that comprised a combination of the best the British had to offer with four different makes — Lotus, BRM, Cooper and Brabham — in the first four places. Mairesse's 1m 38.0s was only good enough for a place in the middle of the pack flanked by the BRM pair of Richie Ginther in a works car and Lorenzo Bandini racing for Scuderia Centro-Sud. Neither Ferrari saw the chequered flag, although at least Surtees had provided a glimmer of hope by matching the pace of the winner, Clark, before his retirement on lap 31 due to an oil leak. Mairesse fell victim to his usual impetuousness and crashed out at Stowe on lap 10.

SPA 500KM

Spa-Francorchamps, 12th May 1963, 36 laps (8.761 miles/14.100km), 315.408 miles/507.600km • Starters 32, classified finishers 23

1st	Willy Mairesse	Ferrari 250 GTO (4293 GT) *(1st GT+2.0)*	2h 38m 40.8s
2nd	Pierre Noblet	Ferrari 250 GTO (3943 GT)	+31.9s
3rd	Jo Siffert	Ferrari 250 GTO (3909 GT)	+2m 21.2s
4th	Gérald Langlois van Ophem	Ferrari 250 GT Drogo (2053 GT)	+3m 33.2s
5th	Chris Kerrison	Ferrari 250 GT Drogo (2735 GT)	34 laps
6th	Pat Fergusson	Lotus Elite	32 laps
18th	Hans-Georg Plaut	Ferrari 250 GT SWB (1917 GT)	29 laps
DNF	David Piper	Ferrari 250 GTO (3767 GT)	3 laps

Fastest race lap: Mairesse, 4m 07.4s, 127.489mph/205.174kph **Winner's average speed:** 119.261mph/191.932kph
FIA World Sports Car Championship (GT Division III, over 2,000cc):[1] 1st Ferrari 63, 2nd Jaguar 10, 3rd Shelby 6

[1] *Scoring system for the top six places in this event was 9–6–4–3–2–1*

It was well established that Mairesse, while pretty good in a single-seater, excelled in endurance sports car racing. He demonstrated this at Spa the day after his blunder at Silverstone and again a week later at the Nürburgring. At Spa on 12th May, he put on a stunning display at the wheel of a 250 GTO entered by Equipe Nationale Belge in the 500Km race, which counted for the International Championship for GT Manufacturers. He lost the lead on lap 20 due to a refuelling stop that was over a minute slower than that of Pierre Noblet in his own GTO, but despite this setback he only needed five laps to close the gap, retake the lead, fight off an attack from the Frenchman and cross the finishing line with a comfortable margin.

An uncontested victory

Nürburgring 1,000Km, 19th May

A week later at the Nürburgring, Willy Mairesse confirmed that his Spa victory was no fluke. The 250 P he shared with John Surtees set the fastest time in practice, eight seconds quicker than the Ferrari crewed by Ludovico Scarfiotti/Michael Parkes. As the Porsches driven by Edgar Barth/Herbert Linge and Jo

Bonnier/Phil Hill were way behind in third and fourth places, he was looking forward to a glorious morrow.

This was confirmed when Surtees moved in front at the end of the first lap and stayed there until he handed over to Mairesse after 14 laps. However, when the Belgian took over, the gap built up by Surtees over the sister Ferrari had been turned into a 10-second deficit thanks to a quicker driver swap from Scarfiotti to Parkes. Hill, who had replaced Bonnier on lap 12, was third, while Peter Lindner in his Jaguar E-type followed in fourth place trailed by Pierre Noblet in Jean Guichet's GTO.

Parkes did not enjoy his unexpected advantage for long. Shortly after finding his rhythm, he took too much of a risk lapping a backmarker and spun off into the parapet of the bridge spanning the *Aremberg* corner, wrenching off a rear wheel. Mairesse arrived at full speed and found himself confronted by a pile of debris with almost no room to pass but somehow managed to squeeze through, although the 250 P picked up a left-front puncture. At his pitstop for a fresh wheel, Mairesse then lost more time due to a recalcitrant jack and the fitting of an incorrectly sized wheel, so that by the time he could rejoin, with another replacement wheel, he had gone from being three minutes ahead of the Porsche to nearly seven minutes behind it, and also now behind the Noblet/Guichet GTO.

◄ **Nürburgring 1,000Km.** Pat Surtees was much more than a driver's wife. An essential pillar of her husband's career, she was an accomplished timekeeper and kept meticulous lap charts.

⌃ Nürburgring 1,000Km.
Surtees, backed up by Mairesse
in the 250 P that Dragoni had
prevented him from driving
at Sebring, forged a decisive
victory. For Mairesse, it was a
second consecutive win after his
success in the Spa 500Km the
previous Sunday.

⌄ Nürburgring 1,000Km. Jean
Guichet gets ready to relieve
Pierre Noblet at the wheel of the
250 GTO they shared.

The 250,000 spectators, kept updated by the loudspeakers, began to voice their fervour about the Porsche's performance, boosted by the prospect of more excitement because rain had begun to fall. On lap 20, Hill, continuing to extend his advantage, had his own calamity at *Aremberg* corner. Loss of grip on the wet track? Selecting the wrong gear? Whatever the reason, the rear wheels locked up and the Porsche skittered off the road into a ditch, leaving Mairesse the delighted recipient, for once, of an unexpected stroke of good fortune. On the same lap, the French-entered GTO let him past into the lead, so Maranello could breathe a little easier as half distance approached.

The fact that the German public were praying for another helping hand from the fickle goddess of fate to save Stuttgart

during the remaining 20 laps changed nothing. Surtees, who had to drive blind in torrential rain due to ineffective windscreen wipers, stayed in front, Noblet/Guichet remained on the same lap in second place, and Carlo Mario Abate/Umberto Maglioli in Scuderia Serenissima's bullet-proof 250 TRI 61 pushed the 2000 GS coupé of Hans Walter/Ben Pon, helped by relief driving from Barth and Linge, back to fourth place. But when it came to adding up the points, even though Ferrari had scooped the pool and could vaunt its success, it had suffered the loss of not one but two 250 Ps over the weekend, as Nino Vaccarella had destroyed his in practice and sent himself to hospital with a broken arm.

The following evening in Maranello, Enzo Ferrari's mind was occupied not by his successes in Germany or any juggling with figures. His future was at the nib of his pen. It was no longer a secret that Henry Ford II, in order to widen the scope of his motorsport plans, wanted to add endurance racing to his targets and go for victory in the Le Mans 24 Hours to give extra impetus to his commercial ambitions in the European car market.

▾ **Nürburgring 1,000Km.** Jean Guichet/Pierre Noblet finished second and won the GT category. This performance, along with many others they achieved together, helped them to attract the favours of Maranello for Le Mans — but with less success.

NÜRBURGRING 1,000KM

Nürburgring, 19th May 1963, 44 laps (14.173 miles/22.810km), 623.633 miles/1,003.640km • Starters 67, classified finishers 31

1st	John Surtees/Willy Mairesse	Ferrari 250 P (0812)	7h 32m 18.0s
2nd	Pierre Noblet/Jean Guichet	Ferrari 250 GTO (3943 GT) *(1st GT+2.0)*	+7m 45.0s
3rd	Carlo Mario Abate/Umberto Maglioli	Ferrari 250 TRI 61 (0792 TR)	43 laps
4th	Hans Walter/Ben Pon/Herbert Linge/Edgar Barth	Porsche 356B 2000 GS GT	43 laps
5th	'Elde' (Léon Dernier)/Gérald Langlois van Ophem	Ferrari 250 GT Drogo (2053 GT)	41 laps
6th	David Piper/Ed Cantrell	Ferrari 250 GTO (3767 GT)	41 laps
7th	Günther Lohsträter/Helmut Felder	Ferrari 250 GT SWB (1807 GT)	41 laps
8th	Chris Kerrison/Mike Salmon	Ferrari 250 GT Drogo (2735 GT)	41 laps
30th	Kalman von Csazy/Karl Foitek	Ferrari 250 GTO (3809 GT)	34 laps (accident)
DNF	Heini Walter/Herbert Müller	Ferrari 250 GTO (3909 GT)	9 laps (con rod)
DNF	Tommy Hitchcock/Zourab Tchkotoua	Ferrari 250 GTO (3647 GT)	– (accident)
DNF	**Ludovico Scarfiotti/Michael Parkes**	**Ferrari 250 P (0810)**	**– (accident)**

Fastest practice lap: Surtees, 9m 13.1s **Fastest race lap:** Surtees, 9m 16.0s, 91.771mph/147.691kph **Winner's average speed:** 82.911mph/133.433kph **FIA World Sports Car Championship (GT Division III, over 2,000cc):**[1] 1st Ferrari 81, 2nd Jaguar 14, 3rd Shelby 6

[1] *Scoring system for the top six places in this event was 18–12–8–6–4–2; this race was also the third round of the World Speed and Endurance Challenge (for sports cars)*

He reckoned it would be wiser to collaborate with Mr Ferrari than to waste time taking him on in battle. After an initial approach in April, *Il Commendatore* was getting ready to succumb to the 'Sirens from Dearborn' in the form of an industrial partnership based around two companies: Ferrari-Ford for the continuity of the current Scuderia Ferrari and Ford-Ferrari for the production of road cars. Enzo Ferrari as president of the first would hold 90 percent of the shares and enjoy complete autonomy in terms of decision making. He would be vice-president of the second with 10 percent of the shares and his role would be limited to that of technical production supervisor — a consultant in other words.

Thanks to books by Richard Williams and Luca Dal Monte, we now know that Mr Ferrari was on the point of signing the contract when he discovered a clause that curbed his absolute autonomy in managing the racing department. He was being asked to run the racing section with a fixed budget of 450 million *Lire* ($250,000 dollars) and would require Ford's agreement before that limit could be exceeded. 'It's completely unacceptable,' Ferrari roared. After 22 days of intense negotiations, it was all over. Henry Ford II went ballistic when he learned of this rebuff.

In contrast to Willy Mairesse, Lorenzo Bandini had to swallow a bitter pill at the start of his season. There was no Formula 1 seat for him at Ferrari and, with Enzo Ferrari's agreement, he returned to Scuderia Centro-Sud, Guglielmo 'Mimmo' Dei's team that he named in recognition of his role as Maserati agent for central and southern Italy. Bandini's career had got off to a promising start at the wheel of a Scuderia Centro-Sud Cooper-Maserati in 1961 with third places in Pau (behind Jim Clark and Jo Bonnier) and in Naples (behind Giancarlo Baghetti and Gerry Ashmore). He proved his all-round talent that same year with victory in the Pescara Four Hours sharing a Ferrari 250 TRI 61 with Giorgio Scarlatti.

Bandini continued to impress in 1963 with Scuderia Centro-Sud driving the ex-works BRM P57 that Graham Hill had raced in 1962. In the International Trophy at Silverstone on 11th May, he got the better of a duel with Mairesse but then pitted with an ignition problem; when the engine would not restart, his mechanics provided a helpful push that inevitably led to disqualification. Two weeks later the Italian had another setback in Monaco. As BRM's new car, the P61, was not ready for this race, the works team purloined Bandini's car, as allowed by its contract with Scuderia Centro-Sud. The way the race unfolded made this a doubly severe blow to the young Italian driver.

Down to the wire

Monaco Grand Prix, 26th May

Using the latest version of the Coventry Climax V8 in his Lotus 25, Jim Clark laid down his marker in Thursday's practice session with a lap in 1m 35.3s, which was much quicker than the BRMs of Graham Hill and Richie Ginther tied on 1m 37.0s.

Monaco Grand Prix. Willy Mairesse started in the middle of the field and got as high as sixth before a seized gearbox eliminated him. It was a big let-down after his successful start to the season in endurance racing.

Monaco Grand Prix. For a good part of the race John Surtees circulated right behind Graham Hill's second-placed BRM and eventually got past on lap 57, only to find that oil on his goggles after all that time following the BRM had affected his vision, forcing him to concede the place five laps later and briefly ease off while he put on his spare goggles.

▲ **Monaco Grand Prix.** After two-thirds distance, third-placed Surtees became concerned about his oil pressure and the men in fourth and fifth places, Richie Ginther (BRM) and Bruce McLaren (Cooper), closed in. Within the space of four laps, they were both able to pass the ailing Ferrari.

➤ **Monaco Grand Prix.** After Clark's retirement, Hill and Ginther gave BRM a double, while Surtees finished fourth behind McLaren. Here he appears to be fending off fifth-placed Tony Maggs's Cooper during the closing stages but in fact the South African was two laps behind.

MONACO GRAND PRIX

Monaco, 26th May 1963, 100 laps (1.954 miles/3.145km), 195.421 miles/314.500km • Starters 15, finishers 8

RACE				PRACTICE	
1st	Graham Hill	BRM P57 BRM V8	2h 41m 49.7s	2nd	1m 35.0s
2nd	Richie Ginther	BRM P57 BRM V8	+4.6s	4th	1m 35.2s
3rd	Bruce McLaren	Cooper T66 Climax V8	+12.8s	8th	1m 36.0s
4th	**John Surtees**	**Ferrari 156 V6 120°**	**+14.1s**	**3rd**	**1m 35.2s**
5th	Tony Maggs	Cooper T66 Climax V8	98 laps	10th	1m 37.9s
6th	Trevor Taylor	Lotus 25 Climax V8	98 laps	9th	1m 37.2s
DNF	**Willy Mairesse**	**Ferrari 156 V6 120°**	37 laps (gearbox)	**7th**	**1m 35.9s**

Pole position: Jim Clark (Lotus 25 Climax V8), 1m 34.3s, 74.604mph/120.064kph **Fastest race lap:** Surtees, 1m 34.5s, 74.446mph/119.809kph
Winner's average speed: 72.424mph/116.555kph **Drivers' championship:**[1] 1st Hill 9, 2nd Ginther 6, 3rd McLaren 4, 4th Surtees 3
Constructors' championship:[2] 1st BRM 9, 2nd Cooper-Climax 4, 3rd Ferrari 3

[1] Scoring system for the top six places was 9–6–4–3–2–1 [2] Scoring system for the top six places was 9–6–4–3–2–1; only the manufacturer's highest-placed car scored points

At Ferrari, Mairesse's 1m 37.6s was better than Surtees's 1m 38.7s but the next day the Englishman turned the tables after a final charge that put him third. Clark showed that the only battle he had to fight was with himself as he improved to 1m 34.3s to confirm pole position while Hill was second at 1m 35.0s. Surtees managed 1m 35.2s before his session was shortened by an 'off' in the chicane that damaged the 156's front suspension. Mairesse ended up eighth on 1m 35.9s. To avoid a repeat of the previous year's first-corner pile-up, the grid — now arranged two by two — formed up after the *Gazomètre* hairpin.

Lorenzo Bandini, deprived of his Scuderia Centro-Sud BRM, watched in a state of pent-up fury as the works BRMs raced home to a 1–2, Hill winning from Ginther. Driving for Ferrari the previous season, Bandini had finished a fine third behind Phil Hill, having protected his team leader from a hard-charging Surtees at the wheel of a Lola. Now, a year later, the Englishman was at Ferrari and the young Italian driver, who had been carrying the hopes of a whole nation, had not only been sidelined by Ferrari but had also been left as a spectator for this race, deprived of his car because BRM wanted it. Had Bandini been racing, he would have once again fought like a lion in his team leader's interests, this time by trying to fight off the attacks of Cooper's Bruce McLaren.

Clark led the 100-lap race from lap 18 to lap 79, when his gearbox jammed and left Graham Hill, trailing by 17 seconds in second place, with victory handed to him on a plate. That same lap, Surtees, concerned about fluctuating oil pressure, had had to allow McLaren to pass him. In the final laps, the Ferrari driver realised that his engine had every chance of surviving the race after all and put the hammer down to try to get back ahead of

McLaren, and by doing so claim a podium place. On the very last lap, Surtees set the fastest lap of the race at 1m 34.5s and got himself to within 1.3 seconds of the Cooper. In Monaco closing the gap to a rival is one thing but overtaking is another…

Bandini's feelings of frustration would have been intensified by Mairesse's mediocre performance. The Belgian ran seventh for a long time and briefly sixth before going out with a seized gearbox on lap 38.

Walking on water

Belgian Grand Prix, 9th June

On Friday, the day of the first practice session for the Belgian Grand Prix, spectators flocked to the circuit in large numbers because they thought they had found a new Messiah in local lad Willy Mairesse. Their hopes were fulfilled when 'Wild Willy' went faster than anyone else that day with a time of 3m 56.2s, followed by Jack Brabham in his eponymous car (3m 56.6s) and Surtees in the other Ferrari (3m 57.9s), the Englishman concerned about his car's oil temperature and its brakes. Normality returned the next day, however, with Graham Hill clinching pole position at 3m 54.1s, still driving his Monaco-winning BRM P57 because the new P61 continued to be delayed. Mairesse set the third-quickest time (3m 55.3s) for a place on the front row alongside Dan Gurney (3m 55.0s), who was thrilled to be behind the wheel of a Brabham that really suited him. Surtees lined up only tenth, plagued by endless gearbox problems, while Jim Clark was another whose performance was below par thanks to

➤ Belgian Grand Prix. Willy Mairesse, pictured with team manager Eugenio Dragoni, set the fastest time in the first practice session and ended the next one third quickest, giving him a place on the front row.

▼ Belgian Grand Prix. Mairesse was in his element in the early stages but ruined his chances by arriving at *La Source* far too quickly, jamming on his brakes and letting Jack Brabham and John Surtees past. A fuel-injection problem brought about his retirement soon after.

THE MESSIAH ARRIVES **199**

▲ **Belgian Grand Prix.** While Jim Clark's Lotus romped away at the head of the field, John Surtees was catching second-placed Graham Hill when he had to pit on lap 13 for attention to his engine's fuel injection. A blown piston brought about his retirement six laps later.

◄ **Belgian Grand Prix.** This race was supposed to be the stage for a Ferrari revival but it proved to be a fiasco. After the demise of both cars, John Surtees and Mauro Forghieri look understandably gloomy.

car vagaries. Trevor Taylor, Clark's team-mate, was very lucky to escape unscathed from a huge shunt at *Stavelot* when the lower wishbone on his Lotus 25's left-rear corner came adrift because a retaining bolt had not been fully tightened.

It could be argued that Clark ruined the race right from the start. Positioned on the right-hand side of the third row, he strayed into part of the pitlane during his lightning getaway to jump in front of all the front-row men and lead into *Eau Rouge*. He finished the opening lap with Graham Hill on his tail, the pair of them 15 seconds ahead of a group comprising Brabham, Gurney, Mairesse, McLaren and Surtees. By lap 5, Clark had driven home his advantage and Hill was eight seconds behind, with Surtees now running fourth in Brabham's wake. And so it continued, with Clark romping away to beat Bruce McLaren's Cooper by nearly five minutes after 32 laps of mastery in tough conditions. There had been a damp start to the race but then the sun had come out and for a while the track was dry, but rain returned at around half distance and grew heavier and heavier for the rest of the race, which the clerk of the course allowed to run to its full distance despite Lotus's Colin Chapman and BRM's Tony Rudd trying to insist that it should be stopped.

Clark's stunning performance was reminiscent of Fangio's in his Maserati 250F in the German Grand Prix six years earlier. At the Nürburgring in 1957, the Argentine driver had had to cope with a broken seat that tossed him around in the corners. At Spa, Clark found his car jumping out of fifth gear, requiring him to hold the gear lever in place on the straight downhill section to *Burnenville*, leaving him with only one hand on the steering wheel. Whether in Germany or in Belgium, both handicaps just added to the magnificence of these driving feats.

And what about the Ferraris? To say that their race was a disappointment would be an understatement. Mairesse ruined his chances of a good result on only the second lap by overshooting *La Source* hairpin while in third place trying to fend off Brabham and Surtees. He pitted on lap 5 for attention to his car's Bosch fuel-injection system and retired two laps later with engine failure. As for Surtees, from his fourth-row grid position he quickly picked off Gurney, Brabham and McLaren to install himself in third place. By lap 13, he was 27 seconds behind second-placed Hill when, like Mairesse before him, he pitted with fuel-injection trouble. After a long halt, he resumed for five more laps before throwing in the towel.

It was obvious that Ferrari would follow the trend towards engines with more cylinders. Maranello's V6 had reigned supreme over four-cylinder rivals only two seasons earlier but now the British teams all had V8s, supplied by Coventry Climax and BRM. Even ATS had arrived with a V8, débuting in Belgium with Giancarlo Baghetti and Phil Hill.

The Italian V6 had never stopped evolving under the guidance of first Carlo Chiti and then Mauro Forghieri, with two or four valves, single- or twin-plug ignition and carburettors or fuel injection, sometimes with developmental avenues progressing no further than the test bed. All the same, by 1962 the new V8s were matching the V6 for power, and by now the existing engine's 120-degree vee angle had also become a handicap in limiting how far the chassis could be slimmed down. This was one of several weak points that Maranello was hoping to fix with the design of its own V8 under Angelo Bellei, paying due attention to the earlier work of Vittorio Jano.

BELGIAN GRAND PRIX

Spa-Francorchamps, 9th June 1963, 32 laps (8.761 miles/14.100km), 280.363 miles/451.200km • Starters 20, finishers 6

RACE				PRACTICE	
1st	Jim Clark	Lotus 25 Climax V8	2h 27m 47.6s	8th	3m 57.1s
2nd	Bruce McLaren	Cooper T66 Climax V8	+4m 54.0s	5th	3m 56.2s
3rd	Dan Gurney	Brabham BT7 Climax V8	31 laps	2nd	3m 55.0s
4th	Richie Ginther	BRM P57 BRM V8	31 laps	9th	3m 57.6s
5th	Jo Bonnier	Cooper T60 Climax V8	30 laps	13th	4m 00.1s
6th	Carel Godin de Beaufort	Porsche 718 F4	30 laps	18th	4m 14.6s
DNF	**John Surtees**	**Ferrari 156 V6 120°**	19 laps (engine)	10th	3m 57.9s
DNF	**Willy Mairesse**	**Ferrari 156 V6 120°**	7 laps (engine)	3rd	3m 55.3s

Pole position: Graham Hill (BRM P57 BRM V8), 3m 54.1s, 134.732mph/216.830kph **Fastest race lap:** Clark, 3m 58.1s, 132.468mph/213.187kph **Winner's average speed:** 114.010mph/183.626kph **Drivers' championship:** 1st McLaren 10, 2nd= Hill, Ginther & Clark 9, 6th Surtees 3 **Constructors' championship:** 1st BRM 12, 2nd= Cooper-Climax & Lotus-Climax 10, 4th Ferrari 3

Victory promised, victory delivered!

Le Mans 24 Hours, 15th–16th June

Having won Le Mans four times in the past five starts, Ferrari arrived as favourites, especially as the test weekend in April had highlighted the excellence of its cars and the relative weakness of the opposition.

The Cobras seen at Sebring and elsewhere would have to overcome the handicap of coping with a 3.7-mile straight in roadster configuration with hard-tops that looked both inelegant and unsuitable. In the Aston Martin camp, in addition to the two DP214s entrusted to Bruce McLaren/Innes Ireland and Jo Schlesser/Bill Kimberly, John Wyer could also count on a DP215 driven by Phil Hill/Lucien Bianchi. Jaguar was still not prepared to enter cars on a works basis so Briggs Cunningham again flew the flag, sharing one of his three E-types — lightened cars equipped with Lucas fuel injection — with Bob Grossman and entrusting the other two to Walt Hansgen/Augie Pabst and Roy Salvadori/Paul Richards. Graham Hill had proved the effectiveness of the 'lightweight' E-type by beating Michael Parkes's GTO to win the Sussex Trophy at Goodwood two months earlier. A single Maserati from the previous year's trio of *Tipo* 151s owed its presence to Colonel John Simone's obstinacy and his hired drivers, André Simon and 'Lucky' Casner, were capable of upsetting the odds. The car had undergone a major revamp with better streamlined bodywork, a longer wheelbase and wider track front and rear, plus a V8 from Maserati's road-going 5000 GT complete with Lucas fuel injection.

An eye-catching newcomer was the Lola Mk6 GT, now with 4.7-litre V8 Ford power and with Richard Attwood and David Hobbs assigned as drivers. The fact that this car was even present at all was almost a victory in itself. The Lola arrived on Thursday morning, the day after scrutineering, but was given its official examination anyway because the scrutineers were obviously seduced by it. It contravened a regulation because its carburettor intake airbox blocked the driver's rearward vision, so Eric Broadley, the designer, had to discard the offending arrangement and instead fashion lateral air intakes before the car could be accepted and allowed to line up on the grid. Proof that the spirit of the regulations overcame the letter of the law, these tricky problems were discussed in an enclosure surrounded by a fence made of planks to keep them out of sight of bystanders and, above all, the prying eyes of the gentlemen of the press.

Just as Lola was about to claim racing fame, Ferrari intended to add to its own with 11 cars that made up almost a quarter of the field. For the first time in the history of the race, the positions in the echelon line-up were allocated according to practice times rather than engine capacity. Thanks to a lap in 3m 50.9s, Pedro Rodríguez/Roger Penske in their NART-entered 330 TRI claimed the first-ever pole position in front of the 250 Ps of Ludovico Scarfiotti/Lorenzo Bandini (3m 51.3s) and Michael Parkes/Umberto Maglioli (3m 51.6s), while the Hill/Bianchi Aston (3m 52s) and the Simon/Casner Maserati (3m 56.2s) pushed John Surtees/Willy Mairesse (3m 56.4s) in the third works 250 P back to sixth.

It was the same story in the categories for GTs and related prototypes, with the Ferrari 330 LMs of Dan Gurney/Jim Hall (NART), Jean Guichet/Pierre Noblet (entered by Noblet) and Jack Sears/Mike Salmon (Maranello Concessionaires) alternating with the two DP214s as far as 11th place in the order. The E-type driven by Hansgen/Pabst managed to split a bunch of four GTOs led by Fernand Tavano/Carlo Mario Abate but this did not ring any alarm bells because the Ferrari camp had learned the hard way that in the Sarthe the slightest mechanical glitch was enough to postpone hopes to the following year — and that was without taking into account human factors.

Just before 10.40am on Sunday, Surtees stopped to refuel and hand over to Mairesse. There was no rush; they had been in the lead since the fourth hour and Scarfiotti/Bandini were two laps behind, far ahead of the GTOs of Pierre Dumay/'Elde' and 'Beurlys'/Gérald Langlois van Ophem. Parkes/Maglioli were fifth after suffering fuel-feed difficulties early in the race, the Porsche of Edgar Barth/Herbert Linge was sixth and under threat from the Sears/Salmon 330 LM, an AC Cobra entered by *The Sunday Times* and driven by Ninian Sanderson/Peter Bolton was eighth, and the David Piper/Masten Gregory 330 LM was hot on its heels in ninth place, closing the list of Ferraris still in the hunt.

After a long battle with Gurney/Hall, Noblet/Guichet had been disqualified just after 11pm because they had not covered the distance imposed between stops to replenish oil, due to a mechanic failing to close the filler cap properly so that some oil had spilled out. Later that same hour, Abate had dashed Tavano's hopes of shining in front of his home crowd by slamming into the fencing at *Maison Blanche* while lying third. Shortly after midnight, Penske had been blinded by smoke from oil splashed on his Ferrari's exhaust pipes and went off at *Arnage* just after he had taken up third position. Gurney/Hall, victims of a broken driveshaft during the night, had ceded their provisional place on the podium to the Schlesser/Kimberly Aston Martin, the

▲ **Le Mans 24 Hours.** The first competitors to depart have already vanished out of shot, leaving this group in hot pursuit. These cars are headed by the #2 Maserati *Tipo* 151 driven by André Simon, who used his big V8's brute power to overtake various rivals on the *Hunaudières* straight and take the lead by the end of the lap. Prominent behind are the GTOs of Fernand Tavano/Carlo Mario Abate (#20) and 'Beurlys'/Gérald Langlois van Ophem (#24); the latter pairing finished the race in second place.

➤ **Le Mans 24 Hours.** Driving the 250 P with which they had won at the Nürburgring, John Surtees (at the wheel) and Willy Mairesse led from the fourth hour and looked on course for victory at mid-morning on Sunday. Then came disaster in the form of careless refuelling followed by a fire that literally reduced their hopes to ashes.

◀ **Le Mans 24 Hours.** The Jack Sears/Mike Salmon 330 LM sails through the Dunlop curve as the shadows lengthen on Saturday evening. Despite some impromptu contact with the barriers, it survived the race to finish fifth.

▼ **Le Mans 24 Hours.** The 250 P of Umberto Maglioli (at the wheel) and Michael Parkes led at the end of the third hour but then experienced a long delay with a fuel-pump problem that left little chance of victory. After dropping to 17th place, its drivers finished third, missing out on second place by little more than 100 yards.

➤ **Le Mans 24 Hours.** Lorenzo Bandini (left) gets ready to take over from Ludovico Scarfiotti for the last time in the 250 P, with victory in sight.

⌄ **Le Mans 24 Hours.** Bandini roars away for his final stint, 15 laps ahead of the 'Beurlys'/ Langlois van Ophem GTO in second place. At 4pm any remaining doubts were banished as he had the victory laurels plus a new distance record.

only one still racing but soon to join the list of retirements with a blown engine.

As expected and feared, interest in the race had waned after all of Maranello's rivals had fallen by the wayside. The Maserati had spent two hours in the lead and then disappeared in the third hour with a broken rear axle. The Ed Hugus/Peter Jopp AC Cobra had been disqualified for an illegal refuelling stop in the ninth hour having got as far as 11th place. Although the Lola had run into gear-selection trouble, it managed to get as high as eighth during the night and then crashed in the Esses in the early morning when Hobbs was unable to find the correct gear. The Aston Martins with the exception of the Schlesser/ Kimberly DP214 failed to make an impression: the Hill/Bianchi DP215 withdrew after three hours with gearbox problems, the McLaren/Ireland DP214 retired when its engine exploded going into the *Mulsanne* kink, and the DB4GT Zagato crewed by 'Franc'/Jean Kerguen, the marque's fourth entry, retired with a damaged rear axle after spinning on the oil spread by the McLaren/Ireland car.

And so at 10.40am Mairesse rejoined the race. But just after he applied the brakes for the first time, at the Esses, the right-hand flank of his Ferrari suddenly burst into flames. He tried to scrub off speed along the trackside fencing before bailing out of the car as the blaze took hold, damaging his right arm and aggravating the injuries he had incurred at Spa the previous year. The fire was the result of petrol spilled during a botched pitstop igniting after contact with the exhausts, although in the book *Forghieri on Ferrari* Daniele Buzzonetti claimed that fuel had seeped into the cockpit and caught light when Mairesse pressed the brake pedal for the first time, generating a spark when the pedal hit its stop. Despite his injuries, Mairesse returned to the Ferrari pits and expressed his displeasure to the Scuderia's chief mechanic before receiving attention to his injuries and heading for hospital.

Scarfiotti/Bandini inherited the lead and five hours later gave Ferrari its fourth consecutive Le Mans victory. Historically, it was the most important one for Italy, for an Italian car with Italian drivers had never won since the founding of the race in 1923. Alfa Romeo had been victorious for four years running, from 1931 to 1934, but never with an all-Italian crew: the 1931 winners, Tim Birkin and Earl Howe, were English, while in each of the following three years an Italian driver, Luigi Chinetti (1932 and 1934) and Tazio Nuvolari (1933), had shared the laurels with Frenchmen, namely Raymond Sommer (1932 and 1933) and Philippe Etancelin (1934).

And just to complete the festivities and mitigate the rancour of the *Tifosi* who had endured the Ford-Ferrari negotiations like a foreign takeover of their heritage, Scarfiotti/Bandini won the Index of Performance, improved the class 12 record (2,500–3,000cc) and broke the distance record held by Olivier Gendebien/Phil Hill since 1961. And to add to the Scuderia's joy, the 'Beurlys'/Langlois van Ophem GTO won the GT category, cementing Ferrari's lead in the International Championship for GT Manufacturers.

LE MANS 24 HOURS

Le Mans, 15th–16th June 1963, 338 laps (8.364 miles/13.461km), 2,834.515 miles/4,561.710km • Starters 49, classified finishers 12

1st	**Ludovico Scarfiotti/Lorenzo Bandini**	**Ferrari 250 P (0814)**	**338 laps**
2nd	'Beurlys' (Jean Blaton)/Gérald Langlois van Ophem	Ferrari 250 GTO (4293 GT) *(1st GT+2.0)*	322 laps
3rd	**Michael Parkes/Umberto Maglioli**	**Ferrari 250 P (0810)**	**322 laps**
4th	'Elde' (Léon Dernier)/Pierre Dumay	Ferrari 250 GTO (4153 GT)	321 laps
5th	Jack Sears/Mike Salmon	Ferrari 330 LM (4725 SA)	313 laps
6th	Masten Gregory/David Piper	Ferrari 250 GTO (4713 GT)	311 laps
DNF	**John Surtees/Willy Mairesse**	**Ferrari 250 P (0812)**	**252 laps (fire)**
DNF	Dan Gurney/Jim Hall	Ferrari 330 LM (4453 SA)	126 laps (gearbox)
DNF	Pedro Rodríguez/Roger Penske	Ferrari 330 TRI LM (0780/0808 TR)	113 laps (accident)
DNF	**Fernand Tavano/Carlo Mario Abate**	**Ferrari 250 GTO (4757 GT)**	**105 laps (accident)**
DNF	Jean Guichet/Pierre Noblet	Ferrari 330 LM (4381 SA)	75 laps (engine)

Fastest practice lap: Rodríguez, 3m 50.9s, 130.409mph/209.873kph **Fastest race lap:** Surtees, 3m 53.3s, 129.068mph/207.714kph **Winner's average speed:** 118.107mph/190.071kph **FIA World Sports Car Championship (GT Division III, over 2,000cc):**[1] 1st Ferrari 90, 2nd Jaguar 14, 3rd Shelby 6

[1] *Scoring system for the top six places in this event was 27–18–12–9–6–3; this race was also the fourth and last round of the World Speed and Endurance Challenge (for sports cars), which finished as: 1st Ferrari 72, 2nd Porsche 30, 3rd René Bonnet 19 (under 3,000cc category); 1st Ferrari 54 (over 3,000cc category)*

A glimmer of hope

Dutch Grand Prix, 23rd June

After the giddy exuberance engendered by their success in the Sarthe, all that Lorenzo Bandini and Ludovico Scarfiotti could really expect less than a week later at Zandvoort was to return to earth with a bump. On Friday morning, John Surtees topped the timesheets at 1m 33.7s, taking advantage of Jim Clark's absence because he was waiting for the delayed Team Lotus transporter to turn up, but in the afternoon the Scot dominated and turned in a time of 1m 33.0s. Graham Hill divided his time between his P57 and the new monocoque P61 before opting for the older car because the newer one's handling was erratic. Indirectly, Bandini was deprived of his Scuderia Centro-Sud entry once again and his frustration was intensified because the injured Willy Mairesse's seat had been given to Scarfiotti, whose single-seater experience was limited to a brief Formula Junior test and 10 laps of the Modena circuit in a Formula 1 car.

Scarfiotti, in fact, was no slouch and had racked up numerous victories since first making his mark with a class win in the 1956 Mille Miglia driving a Fiat 1100 TV. The following year he won an Italian GT championship and a hillclimb trophy at the wheel of a Fiat 8V Zagato, a model in which Bandini had also made his début before their careers went on to follow diverging paths, Formula Junior for Bandini and sports cars for Scarfiotti. The two men were also from very different backgrounds. Bandini, whose father had died when he was 15, worked as a mechanic in Milan before his first forays in racing. Scarfiotti came from an altogether more elevated background as his grandfather had been one of the founders of Fiat and his father had raced between 1927 and 1937. None of this really mattered as the *Tifosi* saw the pair as the heirs to Eugenio Castellotti and Luigi Musso at a time when Giancarlo Baghetti, who had never shown the same single-minded motivation, was squandering his talent as part of the disastrous ATS Formula 1 project.

While the Dutch circuit, with its curves and undulations through sand dunes, may not have been spectacular, it provided a useful performance yardstick and gave pointers about how the rest of the season might unfold. Specifically, since 1952 the winner of the Dutch Grand Prix had often gone on to become World Champion, the only exceptions being Stirling Moss (Vanwall, 1958), Jo Bonnier (BRM, 1959) and Wolfgang von Trips (Ferrari, 1961). The track was also a decent driving challenge but Scarfiotti's opportunity to learn his way round was compromised by an engine change on the first day of practice. The next day he could lap as much as he wanted but his best time (1m 35.6s) showed that a substantial gap separated him from Surtees (1m 33.0s). And, in turn, Surtees was quite some way adrift of a cross-section of English cars in the form of pole-sitter Jim Clark's Lotus (1m 31.6s), Graham Hill's BRM (1m 32.2s), Bruce McLaren's Cooper (1m 32.3s) and Jack Brabham's Brabham (1m 32.4s).

The 80-lap race could be summed up as a battle for the

> **Dutch Grand Prix.** Ludovico Scarfiotti made his Formula 1 début at Zandvoort when called up to replace the injured Willy Mairesse at short notice. He was the centre of attention, especially from Mauro Forghieri, but his track time during practice was cut short by a blown engine and he ended up on the fifth row of the grid.

Dutch Grand Prix. At the exit from *Tarzan* on the first lap, Clark is already in the lead and on course to cruise home to victory, while Surtees is seventh after a poor getaway. In order, the drivers between them are Bruce McLaren (Cooper), Graham Hill (BRM), Jack Brabham (Brabham), Tony Maggs (Cooper) and Richie Ginther (BRM).

Dutch Grand Prix. Learning the ropes, Ludovico Scarfiotti played himself in cautiously, moving up the order — thanks to retirements — to claim a début point for sixth place.

> **Dutch Grand Prix.** Surtees was second when he spun on lap 63, dropping him to fourth place behind Graham Hill (BRM) and Dan Gurney (Brabham), the latter having made fantastic progress from his 15th place on the first lap. When Hill retired, Surtees was elevated to third, albeit a lap behind winner Clark.

runner-up positions behind Clark, who led from start to finish and lapped the entire field. In the end, Dan Gurney, who had started last in his Brabham and also made a pitstop, took second place with Surtees third. After the late-race retirements of Brabham and Hill, who duelled for second place for a long time, there were signs that Clark might have gearbox problems but they never materialised. His victory put him top of the points standings.

Although Surtees claimed four points for his third place, what might he have achieved but for his car's wayward handling? When Hill pitted his BRM on lap 59 with its engine overheating, Surtees moved into second place but only stayed there for three laps. With Gurney closing in, the Englishman pushed the Ferrari as hard as it would go only to spin in the hairpin behind the pits. Still, Maranello had other reasons to be cheerful as Scarfiotti had driven the cautious and consistent race expected of somebody who was a virtual novice in single-seaters. From 11th on the grid, he was 10th by lap 20, then eighth at half distance and sixth at the finish, behind Innes Ireland (BRP) and Richie Ginther (BRM) in fourth and fifth places respectively. Although Scarfiotti gave himself a big scare when he spun 10 laps from the flag, he had done everything expected of him.

DUTCH GRAND PRIX

Zandvoort, 23rd June 1963, 80 laps (2.605 miles/4.193km), 208.433 miles/335.440km • Starters 19, finishers 11

RACE				PRACTICE	
1st	Jim Clark	Lotus 25 Climax V8	2h 8m 13.7s	1st	1m 31.6s
2nd	Dan Gurney	Brabham BT7 Climax V8	79 laps	14th	1m 36.2s
3rd	**John Surtees**	**Ferrari 156 V6 120°**	**79 laps**	**5th**	**1m 33.0s**
4th	Innes Ireland	BRP Mk1 BRM V8	79 laps	7th	1m 33.3s
5th	Richie Ginther	BRM P57 BRM V8	79 laps	6th	1m 33.3s
6th	**Ludovico Scarfiotti**	**Ferrari 156 V6 120°**	**78 laps**	**11th**	**1m 35.6s**

Pole position: Clark, 1m 31.6s, 102.396mph/164.790kph **Fastest race lap:** Clark, 1m 33.7s, 100.100mph/161.096kph **Winner's average speed:** 97.529mph/156.957kph **Drivers' championship:** 1st Clark 18, 2nd Ginther 11, 3rd= McLaren & Gurney 10, 6th Surtees 7, 10th Scarfiotti 1 **Constructors' championship:** 1st Lotus-Climax 19, 2nd BRM 14, 3rd= Brabham-Climax & Cooper-Climax 10, 5th Ferrari 7

Champagne Jimmy

Grand Prix de l'ACF, 30th June

Three days later, Reims-Gueux rocked to the roar of high-performance engines in the opening practice sessions for the Trophée Internationale de Vitesse for sports cars, prototypes and GTs, plus those for the Coupe Internationale de Vitesse des 'Juniors' and, of course, the 49th Grand Prix de l'ACF. Bad weather was forecast for the whole week and on Wednesday, the first day of this fiesta of speed that the Automobile Club de Champagne was accustomed to running in hot sunshine, it was raining. The Scuderia was involved on two fronts: for the Trophée it entrusted a 4-litre 250 P (in other words a 330 P) to Michael Parkes, while for the Grand Prix itself there was the usual pair of 156s. John Surtees's car stood out because of the addition of a wider air intake behind the roll-over bar to optimise air flow to the inlet trumpets. Ludovico Scarfiotti retained his seat thanks to the intervention of Enzo Ferrari, who persuaded Georges Filipinetti not to give the Italian driver his team's newly acquired Lotus-BRM.

Whether or not the Ferrari camp was experiencing an attack of the jitters or quite simply had too many commitments, Parkes was only ready to go out just when his Trophée Internationale de Vitesse session ended. Then it was the turn of the Formula 1 cars and Surtees spent time searching for the promised extra 14bhp only to discover that Scarfiotti's car was quicker, their respective times 2m 25.3s and 2m 24.4s, but both were nowhere near Jim Clark's 2m 21.0s. The others present — half of the field had not

yet arrived — encountered various difficulties, among them Graham Hill (3m 13.4s), who had decided to drive the monocoque P61 even though it remained somewhat under-developed.

Next day, the paddock was a sea of mud and those who risked venturing out on a track more suited to speedboats than racing cars had little hope of improving their times. Parkes (2m 31.2s) laid down a marker for the Trophée by lapping seven seconds faster than Jo Schlesser at the wheel of the Aston Martin DP215 seen at Le Mans. When the Formula 1 cars emerged, perhaps Surtees did not want to be overshadowed by his fellow countryman, for at the wheel of his usual 156 he showed he was just as brave but less incisive with a time of 2m 33.8s, almost three seconds better than Hill (2m 36.4s). At the end of the session Scarfiotti hit a tree in the very fast curve before the downhill section leading to *Thillois*, badly injuring his knee. Gear-selection problem? Aquaplaning? The crash happened at a remote part of the track, leaving the door open to all kinds of hypotheses, but its immediate effect was to make the injured Italian's seat available to other suitors.

One of them would obviously be Lorenzo Bandini, who was on a Grand Prix grid for the first time this year. Hill's decision to choose the P61 meant that the P57 earmarked for Scuderia Centro-Sud was at last available for Bandini, even if it was still considered to be the works team's spare. After missing two sessions, Bandini was in the pits when Friday's practice kicked off. An agonising wait began as he had to hang around until Clark in his Lotus 25 equalled the 2m 20.2s achieved by Parkes in the 330 P earlier in the afternoon, then watch Hill go hell for leather to clinch a place on the front row before getting into his car and managing to qualify by the skin of his teeth.

GRAND PRIX DE L'ACF

Reims-Gueux, 30th June 1963, 53 laps (5.158 miles/8.301km), 273.355 miles/439.922km • Starters 19, finishers 11

RACE				PRACTICE	
1st	Jim Clark	Lotus 25 Climax V8	2h 10m 54.3s	1st	2m 20.2s
2nd	Tony Maggs	Cooper T66 Climax V8	+1m 04.9s	8th	2m 24.2s
3rd	Graham Hill	BRM P61 BRM V8	+2m 13.9s	2nd	2m 20.9s
4th	Jack Brabham	Brabham BT7 Climax V8	+2m 15.2s	5th	2m 21.9s
5th	Dan Gurney	Brabham BT7 Climax V8	+2m 33.4s	3rd	2m 21.7s
6th	Jo Siffert	Lotus 24 BRM V8	52 laps	10th	2m 25.2s
DNF	**John Surtees**	**Ferrari 156 V6 120°**	12 laps (fuel pump)	4th	2m 21.8s
DNS	**Ludovico Scarfiotti**	**Ferrari 156 V6 120°**	– (practice accident)	–	2m 27.0s

Pole position: Clark, 2m 20.2s, 132.461mph/213.175kph **Fastest race lap:** Clark, 2m 21.6s, 131.147mph/211.061kph **Winner's average speed:** 125.311mph/201.669kph **Drivers' championship:** 1st Clark 27, 2nd Gurney 12, 3rd Ginther 11 7th Surtees 7, 11th Scarfiotti 1 **Constructors' championship:** 1st Lotus-Climax 28, 2nd Cooper-Climax 16, 3rd BRM 14, 5th Ferrari 7

➤ **Trophée Internationale de Vitesse.** This 250 TRI 61, which had already twice won the Sebring 12 Hours, was entered at Reims by Scuderia Serenissima for Carlo Mario Abate, who awaits the start. Given his practice times, he was an outsider, but he came through to win the 25-lap race after some of the more fancied runners dropped out.

▼ **Trophée Internationale de Vitesse.** Raymond Roche has just enough time to get out of the way as the Aston Martin DP215 (#4) of Jo Schlesser roars off with André Simon's Maserati *Tipo* 151 (#6) alongside. Michael Parkes in his 330 P (#10) is marooned, a victim of a cooked clutch.

▲ **Grand Prix de l'ACF.** While Dan Gurney's Brabham (#8) initially noses a little in front, Jim Clark's Lotus (#18) is about to take the lead, with Graham Hill's BRM (#2) between them. Straying into the pitlane deceleration zone are the Coopers of Bruce McLaren (#10) and Jo Bonnier (#44), the latter well beyond the demarcation line. In the middle, shrouded in haze, John Surtees has made a bad start in his Ferrari (#16), while on this side of the track Jack Brabham (#6) has Tony Maggs's Cooper (#12) tucked right behind.

The 25-lap Trophée Internationale de Vitesse, run on Sunday morning as a curtain-raiser to the Grand Prix, was a nightmare for Parkes and saw the elimination of all the favourites. While the English driver ruined his chances by cooking the clutch of his 330 P on the starting line, it took only ten laps for Schlesser, André Simon (Maserati *Tipo* 151), David Piper (Ferrari GTO) and Roy Salvadori (Cooper Monaco) to screw up theirs as well, either through incidents or breakdowns. Once Parkes managed to get to his pit after covering most of the first lap at a snail's pace and then getting out and pushing his car from *Thillois*, he was finally able to join the race. Meanwhile, Carlo Mario Abate moved into the lead at half distance in Scuderia Serenissima's elderly but bullet-proof 250 TRI 61 and stayed there to claim a victory that

was quite a bitter pill for those in Maranello who had had high hopes for the 330 P.

If the Trophée race was one disappointment for the Scuderia, the Grand Prix served up another. In 1958, Mike Hawthorn had completely dominated the race, leading from start to finish and only lifting off towards the end because he did not want to lap Fangio. Nicholas Watts christened the painting he dedicated to this victory *Champagne Mike*. So what can be said about Jim Clark's lonely race?

In keeping with his usual style, the Scot shot away from his rivals right from the start. Taxing the Laws of Physics to the limit in the *Gueux* curve, then in *Muizon* and *Thillois*, braking as late as possible and accelerating as soon as he could, he pulled away from the pack to lead by two seconds at the end of the first lap and fifteen by the tenth. Behind him, a pack squabbled over second place, the cars changing position frequently, with Surtees among them. Eventually the Ferrari driver took charge of this group, only to coast into the pits on lap 11 with his fuel pump inoperative; he did rejoin, right out of the running, but his car expired out on the circuit two laps later. After half distance, some loss of engine performance slowed the flying Lotus and Brabham was able to gain some ground, but then the rain returned and mitigated Clark's engine handicap, allowing him to go on to win

➤ **Grand Prix de l'ACF.** On lap 10, second-placed John Surtees is hotly pursued by Jack Brabham (Brabham), Trevor Taylor (Lotus) and Bruce McLaren (Cooper). Next time round the Ferrari stopped at its pit with a malfunctioning fuel pump, which simply needed a new fuse. The car retired two laps later.

▼ **Grand Prix de l'ACF.** Lorenzo Bandini's BRM (#46), Chris Amon's Lola (#30) and Maurice Trintignant's Lotus (#28) brake hard for *Thillois.*

TROPHÉES D'AUVERGNE

Charade, 7th July 1963, three hours (5.005 miles/8.055km), 226.468 miles/364.465km • Starters 31, classified finishers 27

1st	Lorenzo Bandini	Ferrari 250 TRI 61 (0792 TR)	46 laps
2nd	Tony Hegbourne	Lotus 23B Ford	46 laps
3rd	Carlo Mario Abate	Ferrari 250 GTO (4757 GT) (1st GT+2.0)	45 laps
4th	Herbert Müller	Porsche 718 RS 61	45 laps
5th	Mike Beckwith	Lotus 23B Ford	44 laps
6th	Edgar Barth	Porsche 356B 2000 GS GT	44 laps
9th	David Piper	Ferrari 250 GTO (4491 GT)	43 laps
11th	Daniel Siebenmann	Ferrari 250 GT	37 laps

Fastest practice lap: Hegbourne, 3m 49.7s **Fastest race lap:** Bandini & Hegbourne, 3m 50.1s, 78.307mph/126.023kph **Winner's average speed:** 75.484mph/121.480kph **FIA World Sports Car Championship (GT Division III, over 2,000cc):**[1] 1st Ferrari 126, 2nd Jaguar 20, 3rd Shelby 15

[1] Scoring system for the top six places in this event was 9–6–4–3–2–1

his third consecutive Grand Prix, while Tony Maggs (Cooper) was a surprise runner-up and Hill brought his new BRM home third, his position unaffected by the one-minute penalty received for a push-start on the grid. *Champagne Jimmy* indeed!

What about Bandini? While Clark was soon so far ahead that he could not even see his closest pursuer, the Italian had all the leisure in the world to recognise his. From the tenth lap onwards, he began to cross swords with Maurice Trintignant's Lotus and the Lola driven by New Zealander Chris Amon, who was about to celebrate his 20th birthday. 'A quarrel between the old and the new,' was how this hotly contested scrap was described. It lasted until lap 37 when problems blunted their speed although all three finished. It was almost an internecine Ferrari fight between a former team member (Trintignant), a current one (Bandini) and a future star (Amon). More anon!

Scotland the Brave

British Grand Prix, 20th July

Could Clark secure his fourth Grand Prix win in a row? As he had already visited Silverstone earlier in the year for the International Trophy and won, the answer had to be a resounding 'yes'. If Thursday morning's session still left a smidgen of doubt, his 1m 34.4s set in the afternoon was enough to give him pole position and dampen the hopes of his rivals. Jack Brabham, well aware that nine points added to the 27 already scored by Clark would almost certainly make him World Champion, discarded his usual methodical approach and went hell for leather straight away, setting a 1m 36.0s in the

morning that team-mate Dan Gurney narrowly beat with 1m 35.8s. It was a similar story at BRM, where Graham Hill, back in a P57, quickly went about setting a time, his 1m 35.4s a second slower than Clark.

Lorenzo Bandini was reunited with his BRM for the afternoon session. It was painted red to distinguish it from the works P57s and that made it look rather like a Ferrari 156. With Maranello making just a single entry, John Surtees had two 156s at his disposal and chose the better one to get round in a time of 1m 35.8s during the afternoon. There was a lot of chatter in the paddock with people asking what else Bandini — Italy's best driver — had to do to convince Ferrari to give him a seat, seeing as Willy Mairesse was still convalescing after his Le Mans crash and Ludovico Scarfiotti was deliberating about his future in racing following his Reims accident.

Bandini had proved his merit yet again two weeks earlier by winning the Trophées d'Auvergne at Charade at the wheel of the Scuderia Serenissima 250 TRI 61 that had won at Reims. He had been up against a field that contained several front-runners from the Reims race, including the GTOs driven by Carlo Mario Abate and David Piper, plus four Lotuses led by Tony Hegbourne. While Abate spoiled his race and that of several other drivers by stalling on the grid, Bandini showed his talent with a flawless three-hour drive, playing a waiting game to defeat Hegbourne by pulling back on the track the time lost at each refuelling stop, setting a new lap record in the process.

At Silverstone, Bandini provided additional confirmation that his star was on the rise. He was slower than Richie Ginther in an identical BRM on the Thursday but then matched the American's pace on the Friday. This performance gave Bandini a place on the third row behind Surtees, who was knocked off

➤ **British Grand Prix.** Eugenio Dragoni and Pat Surtees had little to smile about as neither of the two 156s available to their driver was quick enough to put him on the front row — a handicap on a circuit wide enough to enable cars to start four abreast.

▼ **British Grand Prix.** Although Dan Gurney, Jack Brabham and Bruce McLaren have got the jump on pole-sitter Jim Clark, who is just nosing ahead of John Surtees's Ferrari, the Scot soon made amends for his poor start and took the lead on lap 4.

◄ **British Grand Prix.** The duel between John Surtees and Graham Hill began on lap 2 and continued throughout the race. Initially they fought over fifth place but retirements up ahead elevated them both to podium positions by three-quarter distance.

➤ **British Grand Prix.** Luck or judgement? When Hill's BRM ran out of fuel on the last lap, Surtees capitalised, his Ferrari having no trouble in lasting the distance thanks to a subsidiary fuel tank installed specially for the race.

the front row by Gurney, Brabham and Hill, all of whom went quicker in Friday morning's final practice session.

Would the race see another solo demonstration by the Scot? At first the answer looked like it might be 'no'. When the start was given, in beautiful sunny weather, Brabham, Gurney, McLaren and Hill all got away in front of Clark, leaving him fifth at the end of the first lap. Three laps later, however, the lap chart had a familiar look to it, with the green-and-yellow Lotus in the lead while its pursuers fought among themselves. Soon Surtees came into the picture, setting the fastest lap of the race third time round and putting Hill under pressure, showing that the 156's performance was on a par with that of the BRM. Hill and Surtees remained head-to-head for most of the race, gaining places with the retirements of McLaren (lap 6), Brabham (lap 28) and Gurney (lap 60) while Clark vanished into the distance.

To find much excitement, it was necessary to look further down the order, in particular at the battle during the first third of the race between Bandini, Ginther and Jo Bonnier (Cooper), who were all evenly matched, with Innes Ireland (BRP) and Chris Amon (Lola) behind them. It was obvious that the Italian was on good form but he was having to cope with a breakage in the supporting structure for the gear lever and on lap 42 missed

a downward gearchange when braking for Stowe, sending him into a spin that caused no damage but lost him a few seconds. He was as quick as Ginther and when Bonnier retired on lap 66 he moved up to fifth place in a race that had now turned into a procession behind Clark — before the improbable occurred.

Clark knew that as the end of the race approached fuel consumption could make the difference and he began to lift off. When Gurney retired, his lead over Hill and Surtees, who were still almost joined at the hip, was nearly 50 seconds, but this now dwindled, but only by a perfectly harmless second per lap. Surtees had also been concerned about fuel thirst, his mechanics having warned him that consumption was very high at Silverstone, and he had worked with them for most of the night to make an additional tank. On the other hand, in the BRM camp an engine change on Hill's car the day before the race had upset the team's fuel-consumption calculations. Was it a foreseeable consequence or simply bad luck? Just as Clark claimed yet another victory, the BRM coughed and spluttered halfway round the last lap. Surtees gladly accepted the gift to snatch second place while Hill coasted over the line with a dead engine.

The Scottish farmer took great delight in reminding everyone

of his origins. True to a pre-prepared plan, his Lotus was installed on a tractor-drawn trailer and he set off for a lap of honour with Colin Chapman at his side accompanied by a piper playing *Scotland the Brave* instead of the traditional *God Save the Queen*.

So, Surtees finished second — but the Scuderia was torn between disappointment and satisfaction. Driving a 330 P, Michael Parkes had been expected to beat Roy Salvadori's Cooper Monaco in the supporting sports car race but instead there had been a fiasco for which he was entirely responsible. Doubtless noting that he had released the clutch too quickly on the grid at Reims, he did not give the throttle pedal enough of a push and stalled when the flag fell. He set off late, leaving chaos behind him, and never managed to close the gap to Salvadori before his fuel pump failed.

BRITISH GRAND PRIX

Silverstone, 20th July 1963, 82 laps (3.000 miles/4.711km), 240.037 miles/386.302km • Starters 23, finishers 13

RACE

1st	Jim Clark	Lotus 25 Climax V8	2h 14m 09.6s	
2nd	**John Surtees**	**Ferrari 156 V6 120°**	**+25.8s**	
3rd	Graham Hill	BRM P57 BRM V8	+37.6s	
4th	Richie Ginther	BRM P57 BRM V8	81 laps	
5th	Lorenzo Bandini	BRM P57 BRM V8	81 laps	
6th	Jim Hall	Lotus 24 BRM V8	80 laps	

PRACTICE

1st	1m 34.4s
5th	**1m 35.2s**
3rd	1m 34.8s
9th	1m 36.0s
8th	1m 36.0s
13th	1m 37.0s

Pole position: Clark, 1m 34.4s, 111.634mph/179.657kph **Fastest race lap:** Surtees, 1m 36.0s, 109.765mph/176.650kph **Winner's average speed:** 107.342mph/172.750kph **Drivers' championship:** 1st Clark 36, 2nd Ginther 14, 3rd= Hill & Surtees 13, 12th Scarfiotti 1 **Constructors' championship:** 1st Lotus-Climax 37, 2nd BRM 18, 3rd Cooper-Climax 16, 4th Ferrari 13

◄ **German Grand Prix.** Jim Clark (Lotus) made the best getaway at the Nürburgring to lead the field through the *Südkehre* followed by Richie Ginther (BRM), who briefly snatched the advantage later round the lap. The Coopers of Tony Maggs and Bruce McLaren are next in line with Surtees behind them, off to a bad start as usual.

▼ **German Grand Prix.** A lap later at the same spot, Surtees leads Clark and Ginther while McLaren holds off Hill. Hereafter, Surtees and Clark had a long-running duel before eventually the Ferrari driver pulled away to claim his first Grand Prix victory on four wheels.

A perfect race?

German Grand Prix, 4th August

Lorenzo Bandini tackled the German Grand Prix in a confident frame of mind after his fifth place at Silverstone, where he had also set the fourth-best lap of the race, quicker than either of the works BRMs that had finished ahead of him. Here at the Nürburgring, he was still flying Scuderia Centro-Sud colours and had confirmed that he was at the top of his game with a splendid performance in the Solitude Grand Prix a week earlier. In that German non-championship Formula 1 race, he had fallen back to tenth after losing two minutes due to a change of spark plugs, then recovered to fourth place on the heels of Innes Ireland's BRP after taking the lap record with a time that was superior to the best that Jim Clark had achieved in practice. Meanwhile, Willy Mairesse was now back for Ferrari after two months out of action, clearly facing a very demanding challenge on a circuit as tough as the Nürburgring.

On Friday morning under threatening skies, Mairesse set the sixth-best time in the first practice session while team leader John Surtees was utterly dominant with a time of 8m 46.7s.

Bandini, however, put the cat among the pigeons by being the only other driver to break the nine-minute barrier with a lap in 8m 59.3s, in front of Jim Clark (9m 2.0s) and Richie Ginther (9m 2.8s). Most drivers gave the afternoon session a miss due to showers and both Mairesse and Bandini preferred to wait for the sun promised for the weekend rather than sabotage their chances. Clark decided to brave the elements and got the measure of Surtees.

The weather forecast proved to be correct and the only session on Saturday was held in sunshine in which Clark snatched pole from Surtees with a lap at 8m 45.8s, the Ferrari driver using a fresh engine but proving unable to improve his stunning time from the previous day. Bandini dialled in a blinder in 8m 53.4s to keep himself on the front row between Surtees and Graham Hill (8m 57.2s), who tried his new P61 but opted for his trusty P57. It was an exceptional performance by Bandini as the BRM in question was the previous year's model, but it probably helped that his car was maintained by the factory under his close supervision; his spoken English may have been as rudimentary as the Bourne crew's grasp of his mother tongue but his mechanical competence and serious approach more than compensated. As Surtees observed, this was the moment when other teams began to see the young Italian driver in a new light.

> **German Grand Prix.** Runner-up Jim Clark smiles broadly as John Surtees receives justified acclaim after his first Formula 1 Grand Prix victory. Enjoying the moment with their driver are mechanics Ener Vecchi (left) and Giulio Borsari, the latter with an expression that conveys genuine admiration for the Scuderia's new winner.

Bruce McLaren (8m 57.3s) headed the second row with Ginther and Mairesse (9m 03.5s), the Belgian as feisty as ever in his 156 but unable to match his team leader's speed.

Bandini made a slow start and got hemmed in mid-pack, while Clark's brisk getaway seemed to promise his fifth win and another fairly soporific race, but that expectation was proved wrong despite the elimination in the early laps of some potential contenders. On only the first lap, Bandini tagged Innes Ireland shortly after the *Karussell*, losing a wheel in the process and forcing the Scot to retire his Lotus-BRM with damaged suspension. What happened to Mairesse on the next lap was much more serious. He was fighting his way up to the front-runners after a bad start when his Ferrari landed off-line after the *Flugplatz* hump, shot off sideways to the left, hit the bank,

bounced back onto the grass verge, demolished the protective fencing, veered off the track again, slid along and overturned, ejecting its driver and leaving a trackside first-aider dead after being hit by flying debris. Some eye-witnesses said that the crash had occurred because Mairesse's car had been disoriented by a gust of wind while airborne over the hump. He suffered breakages above both wrists plus fractures to a humerus, tibia and fibula, but the consequences of the accident left him with more than just physical scars.

Back at the front of the race, Ginther had made a blinder of a start that gave him a brief spell in the lead from Clark around the first lap, with Surtees soon joining them after a hesitant getaway. Second time round, Clark and Surtees pulled away on their own and began a long-running duel that saw the lead

GERMAN GRAND PRIX

Nürburgring, 4th August 1963, 15 laps (14.173 miles/22.810km), 212.602 miles/342.150km • Starters 22, finishers 9

RACE				PRACTICE	
1st	John Surtees	Ferrari 156 V6 120°	2h 13m 06.8s	2nd	8m 46.7s
2nd	Jim Clark	Lotus 25 Climax V8	+1m 17.5s	1st	8m 45.8s
3rd	Richie Ginther	BRM P57 BRM V8	+2m 44.9s	6th	9m 02.8s
4th	Gerhard Mitter	Porsche 718 F4	+8m 11.5s	15th	9m 20.9s
5th	Jim Hall	Lotus 24 BRM V8	14 laps	16th	9m 22.7s
6th	Jo Bonnier	Cooper T66 Climax V8	14 laps	12th	9m 16.0s
DNF	Willy Mairesse	Ferrari 156 V6 120°	1 lap (accident)	7th	9m 03.5s

Pole position: Clark, 8m 45.8s, 97.041mph/156.173kph **Fastest race lap:** Surtees, 8m 47.0s, 96.810mph/155.800kph **Winner's average speed:** 95.815mph/154.200kph **Drivers' championship:** 1st Clark 42, 2nd Surtees 22, 3rd Ginther 18, 14th Scarfiotti 1 **Constructors' championship:** 1st Lotus-Climax 43, 2nd= BRM & Ferrari 22

TOURIST TROPHY

Goodwood, 24th August 1963, 130 laps (2.400 miles/3.862km), 312.000 miles/502.115km • Starters 30, classified finishers 19

1st	Graham Hill	Ferrari 250 GTO (4399 GT) *(1st GT+2.0)*		3h 16m 45.6s
2nd	Michael Parkes	Ferrari 250 GTO (3729 GT)		+0.4s
3rd	Roy Salvadori	Jaguar E-type Lightweight		129 laps
4th	Jack Sears	Jaguar E-type Lightweight		129 laps
5th	David Piper	Ferrari 250 GTO (4491 GT)		128 laps
6th	Dick Protheroe	Jaguar E-type Lightweight		128 laps
8th	Roger Penske	Ferrari 250 GTO (4713 GT)		126 laps
10th	Chris Kerrison	Ferrari 250 GT SWB Drogo (2735 GT)		119 laps
DNF	Tommy Hitchcock	Ferrari 250 GTO (3647 GT)		15 laps (accident)

Fastest practice lap: Hill, 1m 27.0s, 99.310mph/159.824kph **Fastest race lap:** Hill, 1m 27.4s, 98.856mph/159.093kph **Winner's average speed:** 95.141mph/153.115kph **FIA World Sports Car Championship (GT Division III, over 2,000cc):**[1] 1st Ferrari 144, 2nd Jaguar 24, 3rd Shelby 15

[1] *Scoring system for the top six places in this event was 9–6–4–3–2–1*

change frequently, the Ferrari driver on top form and benefiting from the careful attention he had given to the set-up of his shock absorbers in practice to limit porpoising on the bumpy surface. Clark was struggling a little with the sound of his V8 seeming to indicate that the engine was lapsing onto seven cylinders from time to time before coming back on song, as if a spark plug was doing its job only intermittently.

By half distance, things were very much going Surtees's way as he had broken away from Clark and led by six seconds, with Ginther a minute and a half further back in third place, having to cope with a malfunctioning gear linkage that obliged him to steer his BRM with one hand. Two potential rivals from the sharp end of the grid had already fallen by the wayside, Hill on lap 2 with gearbox problems and McLaren on lap 4 when a suspension breakage sent his Cooper spinning off into the greenery, fortunately with little harm to the driver other than a few bruises.

Through the second half of the race, the gaps began to open up all the more quickly when 'Big John' covered the ninth lap in record time, at 8m 47s, while Clark decided to slacken his pace and focus on World Championship points. With two laps to go, 20 seconds separated the two drivers, then next time round it was 36.5 seconds, and at the finish, by which time something had detached itself in the Lotus's gearbox, the gap had stretched to 77 seconds.

Victory for Surtees! It was his first in the Formula 1 World Championship and the first for Ferrari in very nearly two years. He summed up his day by stating: 'I was quite simply perfect.' Was that just an inflated ego or objective assessment from a man known for that trait? Both probably. Would the outcome have been different if the two protagonists had been fighting with equal cars, if the Lotus's V8 Climax had not acted up? In the impromptu press briefing that Clark liked to give immediately after a race, he said that catching Surtees would not have been possible as the Ferrari driver was on top form that day, or, as the press release issued by the Automobil Club von Deutschland put it, '*Bombenform*' ('bombproof').

Another cold shower

Italian Grand Prix, 8th September

It was common knowledge that the British constructors were never keen on racing on the 'combined' Monza circuit using the high-speed banking. After the 1961 tragedy, the track's safety measures had been overhauled and the 1962 Italian

Grand Prix had been run on the road course only. Now, for this 1963 race, the Automobile Club of Milan decided that the banked oval would be used again, even though very little had been done to improve safety on the two high-speed 180-degree turns. This caused some misgivings about how the light, fragile cars would withstand the forces inflicted by the banked track, especially as the Nürburgring had revealed that the search for performance was often accompanied by structural fragility, as highlighted by the broken suspension arm on Bruce McLaren's Cooper.

Riding on the momentum of his German victory, Surtees had a slim chance of winning the title, mathematically speaking, so Ferrari's effort for its home race went up a gear. The new monocoque version of the 156 was now a reality and Surtees had done a lot of testing with it prior to the race. The basic structure consisted of four longerons in tubular steel incorporated into a fuselage with a double floor made from profiled small-diameter tubular elements covered in sheet aluminium tightly riveted together. As before, the engine was bolted to an additional bulkhead behind the seat. At the front, suspension loads were absorbed by a subframe that housed the steering, pedals, radiator and oil tank. In the centre, a second subframe accommodated the steering column and supported the dashboard. Surtees was pleased with the result. The monocoque was purposely designed to instil understeer so that if the rear wheels were to break away it would be down to driver error. Although the engine remained a V6 for now, its lack of torque would soon be a thing of the past because V8 and flat-12 alternatives were on the way and, according to rumours, would be officially unveiled a few months hence.

Would Surtees be able to beat Clark and postpone the Scot's crowning as World Champion? Many of the 100,000 spectators must have been asking themselves that question come race day but there were plenty who had eyes only for Lorenzo Bandini, who was back in a Formula 1 Ferrari at last. Watching from the sidelines, Ludovico Scarfiotti was ready, it was said, to go back on his earlier declaration that he would retire from racing after his Reims accident.

Friday's practice session got under way in fraught circumstances. After a particularly hard winter, the surface of the banked track had become even bumpier, such that cars bottomed out in several places, and the fear of breakages very quickly became a reality. McLaren's Cooper had been fitted with experimental rear hub carriers and soon one of the bearings broke up and caused the car to whirl like a Dervish. Then the left-rear stub axle sheared on Bob Anderson's Lola and flung the car into the guardrail at the top of the banking before it spun several times down the steep slope, leaving its driver shaken but unhurt. Jo Bonnier's response, on behalf of all the drivers, was to circulate a petition among the constructors to demand that the organisers confine the rest of the weekend's activity to the road circuit. Even before this initiative had time to achieve its aim, police stepped in and shut down the oval anyway, declaring it unsafe.

At this point, Surtees was quickest on the combined circuit with a time of 2m 39.8s followed by Graham Hill at 2m 40.0s in the BRM. When confined to the road course later in the day, the Ferrari driver, sticking with a spaceframe 156, managed to remain unbeaten, although only a tenth of a second separated his 1m 39.58s from Jim Clark's 1m 39.68s, the Lotus now equipped with a five-speed Hewland gearbox, with Hill close behind on 1m 39.75s. Bandini drove the 156 with which Surtees had won in Germany and acquitted himself well with a lap in 1m 40.1s.

The next day, the rain that upset the practice sessions for the GTs in the Coppa Inter-Europa gave way to bright sunshine. Surtees, this time at the wheel of the monocoque 156, laid down a marker after a few tweaks. His time of 1m 38.5s set a target for his adversaries, in particular Hill, who was next quickest at 1m 39.0s, also using his new monocoque car. Hill briefly came close with 1m 38.6s but Surtees then went quicker still at 1m 38.0s before twisting the knife on his final attempt with a 1m 37.3s, leaving Hill to start alongside him on the front row after the Londoner's best of 1m 38.5s pushed Clark (1m 39.0s) back to the second row alongside Richie Ginther (1m 39.2s), who was in the running for runner-up slot in the World Championship. Bandini ended up sharing the third row of the two-by-two grid with Dan Gurney's Brabham (1m 39.25s) as he was unable to improve upon his previous day's time.

While the Grand Prix was the focus of attention on race day, the Coppa Inter-Europa was well worth watching, at least in the over 2-litre category for GTs. This was the 20th round of the International Championship for GT Manufacturers and it gave Michael Parkes the opportunity to make amends for recent blunders. Two weeks earlier in the Tourist Trophy at Goodwood, Parkes had been a permanent thorn in the side of Graham Hill, both driving GTOs, Parkes in John Coombs's white car and Hill in the red-and-blue one run by Maranello Concessionaires. It had started badly for Hill when he collided with Innes Ireland's Aston Martin at the start and looked to have blown his chances of catching Parkes, but the reigning World Champion clawed back the time lost, took the lead at half distance and emerged victorious by less than half a second.

Now at Monza, Parkes had swapped cars and was in that Maranello Concessionaires GTO. He set the fastest time in Saturday morning's wet practice session to confirm his status as favourite, while Ulf Norinder and David Piper in their GTOs qualified next, ahead of works Aston Martin DP214s driven by Roy Salvadori and Lucien Bianchi. At the half-time refuelling stops, the Aston Martin mechanics were so efficient that Salvadori was able to leapfrog Parkes and take the lead, but the Ferrari driver wasted no time in going pedal to metal to reassert himself. This was the moment when the race was turned on its head. Salvadori, winner of Le Mans in 1959, had been keeping his engine below 6,000rpm, the traditional maximum for Aston Martin's big straight-six, until he realised that going up to 6,300rpm was enough to keep the GTO behind him. So that was just what he did, with all the more abandon as this race was officially the DP214's swansong. Thereafter, the two drivers swapped the lead every lap, the GTO losing on the straights what the DP214 conceded in the corners. They crossed the line almost neck and neck, Salvadori the narrow winner amid cheers from partisan spectators who briefly thought 'their' Ferrari had won. 'I was flat out all the time,' said Salvadori, reckoning that he drove the best race of his life that day. Parkes, beaten again, would have seen the outcome in a different light.

To the Grand Prix. Did Surtees have a problem with starts or was it just that Clark's swift departures gave that impression? At the Nürburgring, the Ferrari driver had been engulfed by cars behind while the Scot had made a perfect getaway. Now Jimmy's display rubbed salt in the wound. He shot through from the second row and took up station right behind Surtees, then jinked past the Ferrari at the *Curva Grande* to take the lead, no doubt believing that he had once again got the better of the field strung out behind him in Indian file. This time, though, the race unfolded differently. When the cars came round at the end of the first lap, Clark was back in third place, while Hill led Surtees. Second time round, Surtees briefly hit the front at *Lesmo* before ceding to Hill and crossing the line in the same order, but with Clark, Gurney and Bandini tight behind, each trying in vain to slipstream past the driver in front. Gradually, though, Surtees prevailed, with Clark locked to the Ferrari's tail, and after five laps the pair began to pull away.

Surtees was measuring himself against the championship leader, two years his junior. They had very different temperaments, Surtees a mercurial, strong-willed and plain-speaking individual, Clark a man whose placid demeanour belied a redoubtable fighting spirit. Over the first 16 laps they demonstrated this as Surtees deployed all the skills he had learned on motorcycles, zig-zagging from time to time to try to break the tow he was involuntarily providing, but to no

˄ Italian Grand Prix. Under the direction of Mauro Forghieri (left) and with Eugenio Dragoni (right) looking on, Surtees gets ready to give the 156 monocoque its shakedown at the Modena *aerautodromo*. Although a V6 is fitted here, the car was also tested with Maranello's new V8, which was not yet raceworthy. Notice that the fixing of the wheels with a central nut has been abandoned.

➤ Italian Grand Prix. The inspiration behind the 156's monocoque undoubtedly came from rival British cars, notably the Lotus 25, and even the Ferrari's rear suspension is similar with an upper connecting rod, inverted lower wishbone, radius rods, spring/damper combination and torsion bar.

◄ **Italian Grand Prix.** Another point in common with the English cars, in particular Lotus, is that the front suspension of the monocoque 156 rests on an upper arm that actuates a spring/damper combination within the chassis. Surtees started from pole but had to retire on lap 17 due to a valve failure.

▼ **Italian Grand Prix.** Although Surtees chose to race the monocoque car, Ferrari took two Aero models to Monza. While #4 remained unused, Lorenzo Bandini, back in a Formula 1 Ferrari at last, raced #2 until its retirement on lap 37 with gearbox failure.

avail. Behind this jousting pair, a hierarchy formed led by Hill scrapping with Gurney while Bandini pressured Ginther. The *tifosi* cheered on their Ferrari heroes until suddenly, at the end of lap 17, a blanket of silence enveloped the circuit. Clark came round alone in the lead. Shortly afterwards, Surtees stopped at his pit, his engine hobbled by a broken valve spring.

Now that Clark was no longer able to count on the Ferrari's tow, he became an easier target. Hill and Gurney upped the pressure on him, sowing doubts in his mind about whether he could hang on and win, while behind them Bandini went at it hammer and tongs with Ginther and Ireland for fourth place. Ferrari's remaining hopes, however, ended on lap 37 when Bandini, still running fourth, limped into his pit to retire with a broken gearbox. The disappointment was especially brutal considering that the Ferraris had been eliminated by breakages in an engine and a gearbox, the two components that never normally gave any trouble.

'An incomprehensible setback,' Surtees later told journalist Gordon Wilkins, referring to the mechanical failures, before adding that, contrary to what had been written in some reports, neither he nor Bandini had abused their engines, having never exceeded 10,000rpm even though the red line was set at 10,500rpm.

Now with five wins from seven races, Clark was confirmed as World Champion even though three rounds remained, while Lotus also clinched the constructors' championship.

ITALIAN GRAND PRIX

Monza, 8th September 1963, 86 laps (3.573 miles/5.750km), 307.268 miles/494.500km Starters 20, finishers 16

RACE				PRACTICE	
1st	Jim Clark	Lotus 25 Climax V8	2h 24m 19.6s	3rd	1m 39.00s
2nd	Richie Ginther	BRM P57 BRM V8	+1m 35.0s	4th	1m 39.19s
3rd	Bruce McLaren	Cooper T66 Climax V8	85 laps	8th	1m 40.50s
4th	Innes Ireland	BRP Mk1 BRM V8	84 laps	10th	1m 41.60s
5th	Jack Brabham	Brabham BT3 Climax V8	84 laps	7th	1m 40.40s
6th	Tony Maggs	Cooper T66 Climax V8	84 laps	13th	1m 42.20s
DNF	Lorenzo Bandini	Ferrari 156 V6 120°	37 laps (gearbox)	6th	1m 40.10s
DNF	John Surtees	Ferrari 156 V6 120°	16 laps (engine)	1st	1m 37.30s

Pole position: Surtees, 1m 37.30s, 132.193mph/212.744kph **Fastest race lap:** Clark, 1m 38.90s, 130.054mph/209.302kph **Winner's average speed:** 127.738mph/205.575kph **Drivers' championship:** 1st Clark 51, 2nd Ginther 24, 3rd Surtees 22, 14th Scarfiotti 1 **Constructors' championship:** 1st Lotus-Climax 51, 2nd BRM 28, 3rd Ferrari 22

COPPA INTER-EUROPA

Monza, 8th September 1963, three hours (3.573 miles/5.750km), 360.667 miles/580.437km • Starters 17, classified finishers 14

1st	Roy Salvadori	Aston Martin DP214 *(1st GT+2.0)*	101 laps
2nd	Michael Parkes	Ferrari 250 GTO (4399 GT) *(2nd GT+2.0)*	101 laps
3rd	Lucien Bianchi	Aston Martin DP214	98 laps
4th	David Piper	Ferrari 250 GTO (4491 GT)	98 laps
5th	Nando Pagliarini	Ferrari 250 GTO (3607 GT)	94 laps
6th	Egidio Nicolosi	Ferrari 250 GTO (3705 GT)	94 laps
7th	Ulf Norinder	Ferrari 250 GTO (3445 GT)	92 laps
8th	Gianni Roghi	Ferrari 250 GT SWB	82 laps
DNF	Vincenzo Zanini	Ferrari 250 GTO (3451 GT)	4 laps (accident)

Fastest practice lap: Parkes, 1m 49.4s **Fastest race lap:** Salvadori, 1m 43.5s, 124.274mph/200.000kph **Winner's average speed:** 120.222mph/193.479kph **FIA World Sports Car Championship (GT Division III, over 2,000cc):**[1] 1st Ferrari 159, 2nd Jaguar 25, 3rd Shelby 15

[1] *Scoring system for the top six places in this event was 9–6–4–3–2–1*

BRIDGEHAMPTON 500KM

Bridgehampton, 14th September 1963, 110 laps (2.860 miles/4.603km), 314.619 miles/506.330km • Starters 31, classified finishers 20

1st	Dan Gurney	Shelby Cobra *(1st GT+2.0)*	3h 26m 29.8s
2nd	Ken Miles	Shelby Cobra	+1m 26.2s
3rd	Walt Hansgen	Jaguar E-type Lightweight	109 laps
4th	Paul Richards	Jaguar E-type Lightweight	107 laps
5th	Allan Wylie	Chevrolet Corvette Sting Ray	101 laps
6th	Jack Moore	Chevrolet Corvette Sting Ray	101 laps
10th	Charlie Hayes/Bob Grossman	Ferrari 250 GTO (3223 GT)	100 laps
DNF	Ed Cantrell/Charlie Kolb	Ferrari 250 GTO (3767 GT)	–

Fastest practice lap: Miles, 1m 49.2s, 94.286mph/151.739kph **Fastest race lap:** Gurney, 1m 49.0s, 94.459mph/152.017kph **Winner's average speed:** 91.411mph/147.112kph **FIA World Sports Car Championship (GT Division III, over 2,000cc):**[1] 1st Ferrari 126 (186)[2], 2nd Jaguar 28 (29)[2], 3rd Shelby 24

[1] *Scoring system for the top six places in this event was 9–6–4–3–2–1*

[2] *Figure in brackets indicates all points scored; only the six best circuit results and the best hillclimb result counted towards the championship*

Respecting the chronology of events, it is time to turn to endurance events for a while. As both the Paris 1,000Km and the Avus Grand Prix had been cancelled, the Bridgehampton 500Km brought down the curtain on Divisions II and III of the International Championship for GT Manufacturers. Although Ferrari had already been crowned champions in Division III, the Bridgehampton race on 14th September was a significant one in richly rewarding Ford, with Shelby Cobras finishing 1–2. Among a mixed bag of 34 entries, three works Cobras were hot favourites against opposition that consisted of three E-type Jaguars entered by the Cunningham team and a couple of privateer 250 GTOs. However, more important than the victory itself was the fact that it was an all-American success. The outcome was decided just before half distance when Dan Gurney took advantage of the refuelling stops to snatch the lead from Walt Hansgen, the quickest of the Jaguar drivers, before going on to win with Ken Miles second in a sister Cobra. As for the GTOs, Charlie Hayes/Bob Grossman finished tenth while the Ed Cantrell/Charlie Kolb car retired soon after the start.

Was this Cobra victory a foretaste of what was to come? While it is always easier to see clues in hindsight, there is little doubt that the question was being asked in Maranello and elsewhere. In fact, in widening the scope of Ford's decision the previous year to take the plunge into motor racing, Dearborn had just added the development of its own GT coupé in collaboration with Lola — the GT40 — to the other projects already announced. Ford had bought two Lola GTs and used them to test various options at Goodwood and in Michigan during the summer. In addition, Lola's Eric Broadley had just moved into new premises in Slough in order to dedicate his efforts to this prestigious and lavishly funded endeavour. While Roy Lunn, creator of the Mustang, was in overall charge of the GT40 project, John Wyer was entrusted with the job of developing the cars in England prior to ensuring their success on the track. Or at least that was the plan.

With Maranello's compliments

Tour de France, 19–24 September

It would be an understatement to say that the history of the Tour de France Automobile has had its ups and downs. Created in 1899, the event went through a long period of oblivion before being reborn in 1951 thanks to the initiative of the Automobile Club de Nice and *L'Equipe*, France's daily sports newspaper. The 1955 Le Mans catastrophe nearly sounded its death knell but it survived and went on to provide a marvellous showcase for the cars from Maranello, with the help of Shell. Following the win in 1956 by Alfonso de Portago/Ed Nelson in a 250 GT, Ferrari had been unbeaten with three consecutive wins for Olivier Gendebien/Lucien Bianchi (1957–59), two more for Willy Mairesse/Georges Berger (1960–61) and one for André Simon/Maurice Dupeyron (1962), this last victory achieved in Simon's own 250 GT SWB against eight newer GTOs.

The 12th Tour de France Automobile counted for the International Championship for GT Manufacturers and was run in five legs between Strasbourg and Nice over a distance

▲ Tour de France. This is the Nürburgring *parc fermé*, with the Scuderia Serenissima GTO of Lorenzo Bandini/ Fernand Tavano in the foreground. Bandini knew the circuit well and had already won there so it was no surprise to see him come out on top in front of Lucien Bianchi/Carlo Mario Abate in the team's sister GTO. This car can be seen further along the row with the Jo Schlesser/Claude Leguezec #170 GTO parked beyond, its bodywork in the style of a 330 LM *Berlinetta*.

➤ Tour de France. Jo Schlesser started the event well, winning the opening hillclimb, finishing fourth here at the Nürburgring, winning again at Spa and taking third place at Reims, but after a long delay due to a broken valve he rashly missed checkpoints trying to make up time, a misdemeanour that inevitably brought disqualification.

Tour de France At Monaco for the final contest of the event, and with overall victory already sewn up, Jean Guichet rounds the *Gazomètre* hairpin on the tail of the Spinedi 250 GT SWB.

Tour de France. Lucien Bianchi (at the wheel) and Carlo Mario Abate were lying second at the end of the second stage and had every right to envisage a rosy outcome with their Scuderia Serenissima GTO. But in the Cognac region, Abate went off twice because of brake problems and the loaned Scuderia Filipinetti mechanics could only accomplish so many miracles in trying to repair the car. That was a pity, for the car dominated the Albi race and the three hillclimbs that followed. Despite the penalties incurred for not attempting to race their ravaged car at Monaco, they finished second overall.

of 3,645 miles, mainly on secondary roads, and included nine speed events on circuits and six hillclimbs. While 61 crews coveted outright victory plus success in the Index award, it was clear that with six GTOs and three 250 GT SWBs, including a Drogo-bodied version, Ferrari ought to triumph through sheer weight of numbers. Maranello was also represented by several top-line drivers, starting with the two Scuderia Serenissima crews (Lucien Bianchi/Carlo Mario Abate and Lorenzo Bandini/Fernand Tavano), one from NART (Jo Schlesser/Claude Leguezec) and privateers like Guido Fossati/Ariberto Francolini, Edgar Berney/Jean Gretener and, above all, Jean Guichet/José Behra. In particular, Guichet was out to prove a point after being eliminated from the previous year's race in a road accident on a liaison section.

After honours in the Turckheim–Trois Epis hillclimb went to Schlesser, the event moved to the Nürburgring, where Bandini, Bianchi and Guichet took the top three places. Schlesser emerged on top again at Spa after a hard-fought battle with Guichet, while Bianchi, his GTO now without its side windows after a crash, finished fourth behind Bandini. At the end of the first leg in Dinant, Schlesser led the GTOs, only one of which had dropped out, Berney's after Spa with broken transmission. In the 250 GT camp, the Chris Kerrison/Peter Raphael Drogo had been eliminated at the Nürburgring and the Heini Walter/Charly Müller SWB was outside the top five after finding problems in keeping the husband-and-wife Swiss crew of Gérard and Aghdass Spinedi at bay.

The second leg began the next day with a two-hour race at Reims. Schlesser and Guichet, at each other's throats right from the off, pulled away from their rivals, while Bandini and Bianchi became locked in a fierce battle behind them. The critical factor in both duels was to use the rival's slipstream to save fuel on a circuit where the GTOs might potentially struggle to reach the finish without a late 'splash and dash'. The wisdom of this fuel-saving tactic was proved by Guichet and Bianchi because they raced non-stop to finish first and second, in that order, whereas the other protagonists both needed a refuelling stop, Schlesser ending up ahead of Bandini. Thereafter, it all went horribly wrong for Schlesser because a halt of 1 hour 23 minutes for replacement of a broken valve spring in his GTO's engine led to disqualification, for he chose to miss two checkpoints in a vain attempt to make up time. Guichet then won at Rouen, the last contest before the cars ended the second leg in Caen, with Bianchi second and Bandini third.

At the start of the third leg, Guichet triumphed again, at Le Mans, where an increasingly fractious atmosphere developed within the Scuderia Serenissima team, specifically between co-drivers Bandini and Tavano. The difficulties had begun at Reims when there had been a shouting match after team-mates Bandini and Bianchi had indulged in an unnecessary intra-team skirmish and Bandini had lost out. In the Bandini/Tavano car at Le Mans, the tension boiled over when team manager Nello Ugolini made his choice about which of the co-drivers was going to take the wheel for the race. He chose Bandini, the recent winner of the Le Mans 24 Hours, but this did not go down well with Tavano, who had been born in Le Mans and wanted to shine in front of his home crowd. Was what happened next the consequence of that discord or simply because of fatigue after a difficult night on the road? Whatever, following the Aubisque and Tourmalet hillclimbs, Bandini crashed *en route* to Pau, damaging the Ferrari beyond repair and sending Tavano to hospital in Tarbes with a fractured arm and broken shoulder blade. Guichet drove cautiously in the Pyrenean passes before claiming another race win at Pau in the rain to end the third leg without any serious

TOUR DE FRANCE

France, 13th–23rd September 1963, five stages, total distance 3644.9 miles/5,866.0km • Starters 122, classified finishers 31

1st	Jean Guichet/José Behra	Ferrari 250 GTO (5111 GT) *(1st GT+2.0)*	1,430.687 miles/2,302.467km	
2nd	Lucien Bianchi/Carlo Mario Abate	Ferrari 250 GTO (5095 GT)	1,310.346 miles/2,108.798km	
4th	Gérard Spinedi/Aghdass Spinedi	Ferrari 250 GT SWB	1,252.837 miles/2,016.246km	
DNF	Edgar Berney/Jean Gretener	Ferrari 250 GTO (3909 GT)		Transmission
DNF	Jo Schlesser/Claude Leguezec	Ferrari 250 GTO (4713 GT)		Disqualification
DNF	Guido Fossati/Ariberto Francolini	Ferrari 250 GTO (4675 GT)		Accident
DNF	Lorenzo Bandini/Fernand Tavano	Ferrari 250 GTO (4757 GT)		Accident
DNF	Chris Kerrison/Peter Raphael	Ferrari 250 GT SWB Drogo (2735 GT)		Gearbox

FIA World Sports Car Championship (GT Division III, over 2,000cc):[1] 1st Ferrari 186, 2nd Jaguar 25, 3rd Shelby 15

[1] *Scoring system for the top six places in this event was 27–18–12–9–6–3*

rival other than the damaged Bianchi/Abate GTO, the front of which had been demolished by the Italian in an 'off' in the Cognac region.

Little changed during the last two legs. Although Bianchi/Abate won the race at Albi and the three hillclimbs that followed, Guichet remained firmly ensconced in the lead, winning the remaining races at Clermont-Ferrand and in Monaco to assure himself of victory in the overall classification as well as the GT category. Bianchi/Abate got their battered car to the finish in second place while Mr and Mrs Spinedi brought their 250 GT SWB home fourth, the only other Ferrari finisher.

'Guichet, imperious, disconcertingly at ease and devilishly talented, won this event in the true amateur spirit, but with the wisdom and science of a professional,' wrote Christian Moity. 'This double victory rewarded an intelligent driver who knew when to push,' stated *Sport Auto*. Was there a slightly chauvinistic slant to this praise? Perhaps, but it hailed the skills of a driver who was greatly appreciated in Maranello, as later events would confirm.

Hopes dashed

United States Grand Prix, 6th October

Even though the World Championship titles for drivers and constructors had been settled, the field for the United States Grand Prix was as strong as that seen at Monza apart from the noteworthy absence of Innes Ireland, who had been injured during practice for the sports car Washington Grand Prix in Seattle the previous weekend. Lotus entered a third car for Pedro Rodríguez, who, like Indycar driver Rodger Ward (Lotus-BRM), was making his first Grand Prix appearance. Phil Hill was also back at his home event but was really just fiddling

▼ **United States Grand Prix.** Surtees led almost three-quarters of the race at Watkins Glen with Graham Hill's BRM in close company, but then engine failure cruelled robbed him of victory.

UNITED STATES GRAND PRIX

Watkins Glen, 6th October 1963, 110 laps (2.300 miles/3.701km), 252.966 miles/407.110km Starters 21, finishers 9

RACE				PRACTICE	
1st	Graham Hill	BRM P57 BRM V8	2h 19m 22.1s	1st	1m 13.4s
2nd	Richie Ginther	BRM P57 BRM V8	+34.3s	4th	1m 14.0s
3rd	Jim Clark	Lotus 25 Climax V8	109 laps	2nd	1m 13.5s
4th	Jack Brabham	Brabham BT7 Climax V8	108 laps	5th	1m 14.2s
5th	**Lorenzo Bandini**	**Ferrari 156 V6 120°**	**106 laps**	**9th**	**1m 15.8s**
6th	Carel Godin de Beaufort	Porsche 718 F4	99 laps	19th	1m 22.3s
DNF	**John Surtees**	**Ferrari 156 V6 120°**	82 laps (engine)	3rd	1m 13.7s

Pole position: Hill, 1m 13.4s, 112.791mph/181.520kph **Fastest race lap:** Clark, 1m 14.5s, 111.137mph/178.858kph **Winner's average speed:** 109.908mph/176.879kph **Drivers' championship:** 1st Clark 51, 2nd Ginther 28, 3rd= Hill & Surtees 22, 10th Bandini 4, 15th Scarfiotti 1 **Constructors' championship:** 1st Lotus-Climax 51, 2nd BRM 35, 3rd Ferrari 24

around in the ATS adventure, having his fourth outing for the beleaguered team, 11th place at Monza his best result so far.

As John Surtees and Richie Ginther still had their sights set on the runner-up spot in the World Championship and were just a whisker apart on 22 and 24 points respectively, Ferrari and BRM sent reinforcements with this in mind. Bourne brought two P57s for Ginther while Maranello turned up with three 156s, including a monocoque, for Surtees. There was a minor surprise in the first practice session on Friday as Graham Hill topped the timesheets at 1m 13.4s, beating Clark (1m 13.5s) and Surtees (1m 13.6s), with Ginther (1m 14.0s) and Brabham (1m 14.3s) the only drivers to lap in the 1m 14s bracket. Bandini's time of 1m 15.8s represented an under-par performance in his Ferrari. The next day the only front-runners to improve were Gurney (1m 14.5s) and Brabham (1m 14.2s), so Friday's times broadly decided grid positions. Surtees, after an 'off' due to the breakage of a pin on a strut on the monocoque, was credited with a time of 1m 13.7s in the 156 Aero.

Clark began the race with a handicap as his fuel pump suffered a short circuit just when he was about to go out and take up position on the grid. He finally departed from the pits nearly a lap and a half behind the rest of the field and set about the task ahead of him. Cynics may have observed that this was perhaps the only way to prevent him from winning. Meanwhile, Graham Hill led away but Surtees got past on lap 7, although there was a question mark over whether or not his engine would allow him to fight off Hill's counter attacks. Twice the BRM driver briefly got back in front, on laps 32 and 35, but otherwise Surtees just about remained in charge with his combatant tucked in his slipstream. Towards the halfway mark (lap 55), a mounting bracket on the left-hand side of the BRM's

rear anti-roll bar broke, causing Hill to lose ground while he drove around his car's sudden and severe understeer.

Now Surtees had a comfortable lead and the Scuderia's only cause for concern was Bandini's performance. The Italian had made a bad start but had laboriously fought his way back up the field from 11th to eighth place, which duly became sixth when problems afflicted two Coopers up ahead on consecutive laps, Bruce McLaren's going out on lap 75 with fuel injection problems and Jo Bonnier's then heading into the pits for a replacement shock absorber.

Surtees had bitter memories of what followed just six laps later: 'I had the race won and I was already looking forward to seeing the chequered flag when my engine died.' Actually, it was not that close to the end of the race, for there were still 27 of the 110 laps to go, but his disappointment was real enough and caused, it was later found, by a blown piston said to have been affected by fuel-injection malfunctioning. Hill was left to lead Ginther home to BRM's second double of the season, while Clark finished third after a magnificent drive from the back. Jack Brabham came home fourth after carburation problems for most of the race and Bandini was fifth.

A race to forget

Mexican Grand Prix, 27th October

Would Jim Clark win in Mexico and join Alberto Ascari and Juan Manuel Fangio as six-time winners in a Grand Prix season? The Scot got his weekend off to a good start by setting the fastest time in Friday's session at 1m 58.8s. This proved that Lucas had

◀ **Mexican Grand Prix.** Surtees returns to the pits after a few exploratory laps at the wheel of the 156 monocoque that he placed on the front row alongside Jim Clark's Lotus. Bruce McLaren, watching from his perch on the pit counter, started on the third row in the #3 Cooper-Climax parked at his feet.

▼ **Mexican Grand Prix.** The Scuderia arrived in Mexico with two monocoques, including a new one that arrived straight from Maranello for Bandini, and also brought two 156s with regular chassis.

➤ **Mexican Grand Prix.** Scuderia mechanics, including Giulio Borsari on the right, work on Bandini's new monocoque 156. The clutch is located between the engine and the six-speed gearbox.

▾ **Mexican Grand Prix.** At the wheel of his new 156 monocoque, Lorenzo Bandini receives final instructions from Mauro Forghieri with Ener Vecchi listening in.

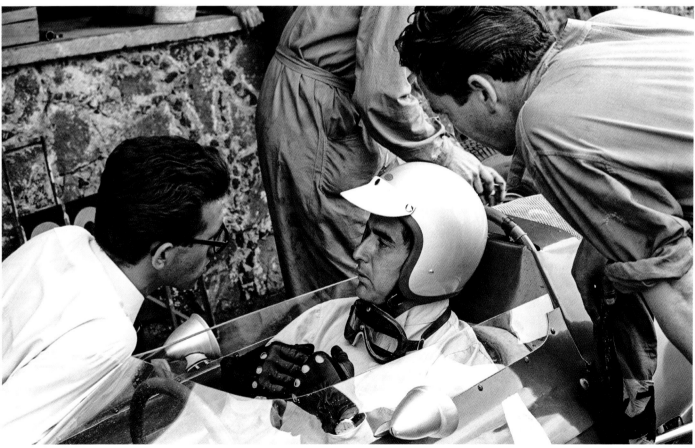

made the right decision in equipping the injection system on the Coventry Climax V8s with special camshafts to mitigate the carburation problems experienced at a circuit situated more than 6,000 feet above sea level. It was no surprise that Surtees (2m 0.5s) in his monocoque 156 from Monza seemed to be the driver most likely to take the fight to Clark although Graham Hill's BRM was just a whisker behind (2m 0.6s). In comparison, Brabham's Dan Gurney (2m 1.6s) and BRM's Richie Ginther (2m 1.8s) almost seemed reduced to playing the undeserved role of second fiddles. Bandini's performance again disappointed Ferrari, for he had available his own monocoque 156 newly arrived from Maranello but was almost two seconds slower than his team leader. The next day, a tropical rainstorm caused by a cyclone over the West Indies ruled out any further improvements for most of the field and its aftermath lingered into the next day when the race began under threatening skies.

It was well known that Surtees was an intractable character. A true perfectionist, he was a very egocentric individual and, like many champions of his calibre, always convinced that his

▾ **Mexican Grand Prix.** On the grid, Surtees, after his brief spat with Mauro Forghieri about tyre pressures, has a few final words with Giulio Borsari. At far left, Colin Chapman, wearing pale trousers, gives Jim Clark some last-minute instructions. On the second row, Graham Hill is about to climb into his BRM while Dan Gurney is already behind the wheel of his Brabham.

approach was the right one. Denis Jenkinson wrote: 'John's idea of the perfect team is one in which Surtees is the owner, Surtees is the designer, Surtees is the engineer, Surtees is the team manager and Surtees is the driver; that way he could be certain of one hundred percent team effort from his staff.' But the future would show us, and Surtees, that even when all these conditions could indeed be combined, it was not always enough to guarantee success. To his credit, it could be said that he was single-minded in his dedication to Ferrari, although in this respect a certain amount of nuance was also necessary. Returning to the front row of the grid in Mexico, *Sport Auto*'s correspondent, Bob Dumpitt, reported that Surtees had a violent argument with Mauro Forghieri about tyre pressures. The driver wanted lower pressures because he knew that his car, set up for wet conditions, would otherwise understeer too much on a track that remained dry as the start time approached. The engineer refused. What ensued turned out to be a big source of regret for the Scuderia.

Once again Clark made a perfect start and cruised off to his sixth victory of the season. Surtees began in second place but very quickly slipped to third, unable to fight off Gurney. He then lost touch with the American and found himself having to fend off Brabham. 'His Ferrari was lurching dangerously all over the track,' wrote Bernard Cahier. 'On the long fast curve before the pits he was understeering to such an extent that blue smoke was pouring from his left front tyre for almost 200 yards towards the end of the bend,' wrote *Motor Sport*. On lap 19, four laps after Brabham overtook him, Surtees stopped

MEXICAN GRAND PRIX

Mexico City, 27th October 1963, 65 laps (3.107 miles/5.000km), 201.946 miles/325.000km Starters 21, finishers 11

RACE				PRACTICE	
1st	Jim Clark	Lotus 25 Climax V8	2h 9m 52.1s	1st	1m 58.8s
2nd	Jack Brabham	Brabham BT7 Climax V8	+1m 41.1s	10th	2m 03.6s
3rd	Richie Ginther	BRM P57 BRM V8	+1m 54.7s	5th	2m 01.8s
4th	Graham Hill	BRM P57 BRM V8	64 laps	3rd	2m 00.6s
5th	Jo Bonnier	Cooper T66 Climax V8	62 laps	8th	2m 02.6s
6th	Dan Gurney	Brabham BT7 Climax V8	62 laps	4th	2m 01.6s
DNF	Lorenzo Bandini	Ferrari 156 V6 120°	36 laps (engine)	7th	2m 02.4s
DSQ	John Surtees	Ferrari 156 V6 120°	82 laps (outside help)	2nd	2m 00.5s

Pole position: Clark, 1m 58.8s, 94.147mph/151.515kph **Fastest race lap:** Clark, 1m 58.1s, 94.705mph/152.413kph **Winner's average speed:** 93.283mph/150.125kph **Drivers' championship:** 1st Clark 54, 2nd Ginther 29, 3rd Hill 25, 4th Surtees 22, 11th Bandini 4, 15th Scarfiotti 1 **Constructors' championship:** 1st Lotus-Climax 54, 2nd BRM 36, 3rd= Ferrari & Brabham-Climax 24

to have the rear tyre pressures reduced. Once that was done, the starter motor refused to work. In the heat of the moment, the mechanics pushed the Ferrari but stewards immediately stepped in to forbid it. Surtees's race ended there and then with disqualification. Progressive collapse of the front suspension was the reason given for the erratic handling of his car.

At that point, Bandini lay sixth, sandwiched between McLaren and Hill, and he was still there when electrical failure ended his race on lap 36. Ferrari had hoped to redeem itself in Mexico but instead had endured yet another fiasco. Meanwhile, Clark had indeed won his sixth race of the season.

An admission of powerlessness

South African Grand Prix, 28th December

After a two-month wait, the only real question surrounding the final round of the World Championship at South Africa's East London circuit was who would finish 'best of the rest' behind Clark.

Surtees, perhaps? A fortnight earlier at Kyalami, Ferrari had entered two cars for the Rand Grand Prix and finished 1–2, Surtees beating Bandini. True, it was a victory not to be taken at face value for the only serious rivals in a field of mainly local drivers had been two works Lotuses, but both Clark and Trevor Taylor had gone out when their fuel injection pumps gave problems. Dan Gurney? He had run second for a long

time in Mexico before being slowed by fuel-feed problems and had then been sprayed in petrol after forcing the tap on his Brabham's second fuel tank, forgetting that it had been closed with sealing tape; he had had to stop at his pit to have the tap closed and saw the flag in sixth place. Jack Brabham? His second place in Mexico had been his best result of the season. The BRM men? Richie Ginther now looked a better bet than Graham Hill because his self-confidence had grown and he was also 'best of the rest' in the points standings after a nice run of results, with two second places and a third in the past three races.

On Thursday morning, Surtees warmed up with a 1m 32.0s before sprinting to the fastest lap of the session at 1m 29.8s in the monocoque 156, despite visible understeer. Pundits asked themselves if the reinforcements added since his previous appearances in the new car had altered its roadholding but that assessment was proved wrong when Surtees revealed later that the fuel-injected V6 delivered its power with such a bang that it was difficult to steer the car through corners using the throttle. Bandini was unable to do better than 1m 33.4s with his monocoque 156 so fell back on the Aero, in which his 1m 31.0s was not too far behind Brabham (1m 30.1s), Gurney (1m 30.2s) and Clark (1m 30.2s). But these relatively satisfactory Ferrari times were a mirage as the next day Surtees and Bandini had to be content with positions on the second row of the grid, for 'Big John' was unable to improve while Bandini edged closer with a 1m 30.2s. Meanwhile, three others all dipped below 1m 30s to occupy the front row, Clark (1m 28.9s) on pole alongside Brabham (1m 29.0s) and Gurney (1m 29.1s).

Several reporters, including *Motor Sport*'s, judged this the dullest race of the season and some said that the curtain-raisers

◄ South African Grand Prix. Just after the start, Surtees and Brabham run neck and neck along one of the East London circuit's straights against a dramatic coastal backdrop. Neither driver finished the race.

were far more exciting. Although Brabham made a meteoric start, Clark overtook him on the first lap and never looked back. Gurney installed himself in second place after seven laps and stayed there. Surtees, who briefly ran second, was let down by his engine on lap 43, gifting third place to Graham Hill. Behind, McLaren and Bandini played follow my leader from lap 49 until the chequered flag. Brabham fell back after his engine suffered a broken valve spring but managed to stay with Bandini until his retirement on lap 70 when a stone disembowelled his fuel tank after a spin. Ginther went out with a broken driveshaft on lap 43, surrendering the runner-up spot in the championship to Hill.

All in all, it was a snooze-inducing finale to a Formula 1 World Championship in which Surtees ended up fourth in the driver rankings. Clark concluded his season with a record seven victories from ten races, a winning total that would not be beaten for 25 years, until Ayrton Senna won eight out of 16 in 1988.

SOUTH AFRICAN GRAND PRIX

East London, 28th December 1963, 85 laps (2.436 miles/3.920km), 207.041 miles/333.200km Starters 20, finishers 14

RACE					PRACTICE	
1st	Jim Clark	Lotus 25 Climax V8	2h 10m 36.9s		1st	1m 28.9s
2nd	Dan Gurney	Brabham BT7 Climax V8	+1m 06.8s		3rd	1m 29.1s
3rd	Graham Hill	BRM P57 BRM V8	84 laps		6th	1m 30.3s
4th	Bruce McLaren	Cooper T66 Climax V8	84 laps		9th	1m 31.2s
5th	**Lorenzo Bandini**	**Ferrari 156 V6 120°**	**84 laps**		**5th**	**1m 30.2s**
6th	Jo Bonnier	Cooper T66 Climax V8	83 laps		11th	1m 32.0s
DNF	**John Surtees**	**Ferrari 156 V6 120°**	43 laps (engine)		4th	1m 29.8s

Pole position: Clark, 1m 28.9s, 98.636mph/158.740kph **Fastest race lap:** Gurney, 1m 29.1s, 98.400mph/158.360kph **Winner's average speed:** 95.100mph/153.049kph **Drivers' championship:** 1st Clark 54 (73)[1], 2nd= Hill 29, 2nd= Ginther 29 (34)[1], 4th Surtees 22, 9th Bandini 6, 15th Scarfiotti 1 **Constructors' championship:** 1st Lotus-Climax 54 (74)[1], 2nd BRM 36 (45)[1], 3rd Brabham-Climax 28 (30)[1], 4th Ferrari 26

[1] Figure in brackets indicates all points scored; only the best six results counted towards the championship

Formula 1 World Championship (Drivers) *Top three plus Ferrari drivers*

	1st Jim Clark	2nd Graham Hill	3rd Richie Ginther	4th John Surtees	9th Lorenzo Bandini	15th Ludovico Scarfiotti
Monaco GP	0	9	6	3	–	–
Belgian GP	9	0	3	0	–	–
Dutch GP	9	0	–2	4	–	1
GP de l'ACF (France)	9	0	0	0	0	–
British GP	9	4	–3	6	2	–
German GP	–6	0	4	9	0	–
Italian GP	9	0	6	0	0	–
United States GP	–4	9	6	0	2	–
Mexican GP	9	3	4	0	0	–
South African GP	–9	4	0	0	2	–
Total	54	29	29	22	6	1

Formula 1 World Championship (Constructors)

	1st Lotus-Climax	2nd BRM	3rd Brabham-Climax	4th Ferrari
Monaco GP	–1	9	0	3
Belgian GP	9	–3	4	0
Dutch GP	9	–2	6	4
GP de l'ACF (France)	9	0	3	0
British GP	9	4	0	6
German GP	–6	4	0	9
Italian GP	9	6	–2	0
United States GP	–4	9	3	2
Mexican GP	9	4	6	0
South African GP	–9	–4	6	2
Total	54	36	28	26

International Championship for GT Manufacturers

	1st Ferrari	2nd Jaguar	3rd Shelby
Daytona Three Hours	9	1	3
Sebring 12 Hours	27	9	3
Targa Florio	18	–	–
Spa 500Km	–9	–	–
Nürburgring 1,000Km	18	4	–
Coppa della Consuma hillclimb	–9	–	–
Le Mans 24 Hours	27	6	9
Trophées d'Auvergne	–9	–	–
Fribourg–Schauinsland hillclimb	–9	–	–
Tourist Trophy	–9	4	–
Ollon–Villars hillclimb	–9	–1	–
Coppa Inter-Europa	–6	–	–
Tour de France	27	–	–
Bridgehampton 500Km	0	4	9
Total	126	28	24

Although 1963 was supposed to have been the year of Ferrari's reconquest of Formula 1, led by John Surtees, the outcome proved otherwise. With just a single victory, the fruits of the season were pretty meagre. On the other hand, the successes in GT racing were a source of satisfaction in Maranello, with the omnipresent 250 GTO reigning supreme over all rivals and winning every title possible. And, for Enzo Ferrari, another victory at Le Mans was worth more than anything.

But what about the future? Lotus was spreading its wings and planning to race in more branches of the sport. BRM had persevered with its monocoque in Formula 1 and continued to look competitive. There were strong rumours of Honda's imminent arrival in Grand Prix racing. In addition, Ford was preparing to avenge its defeats at the beginning of the year with a GT that would be ready for the Sebring 12 Hours.

Enzo Ferrari, however, was never stronger than when he had his back to the wall while possessing a good card up his sleeve that could put him a step ahead of his rivals. He was about to expand on all this in January of the coming year.

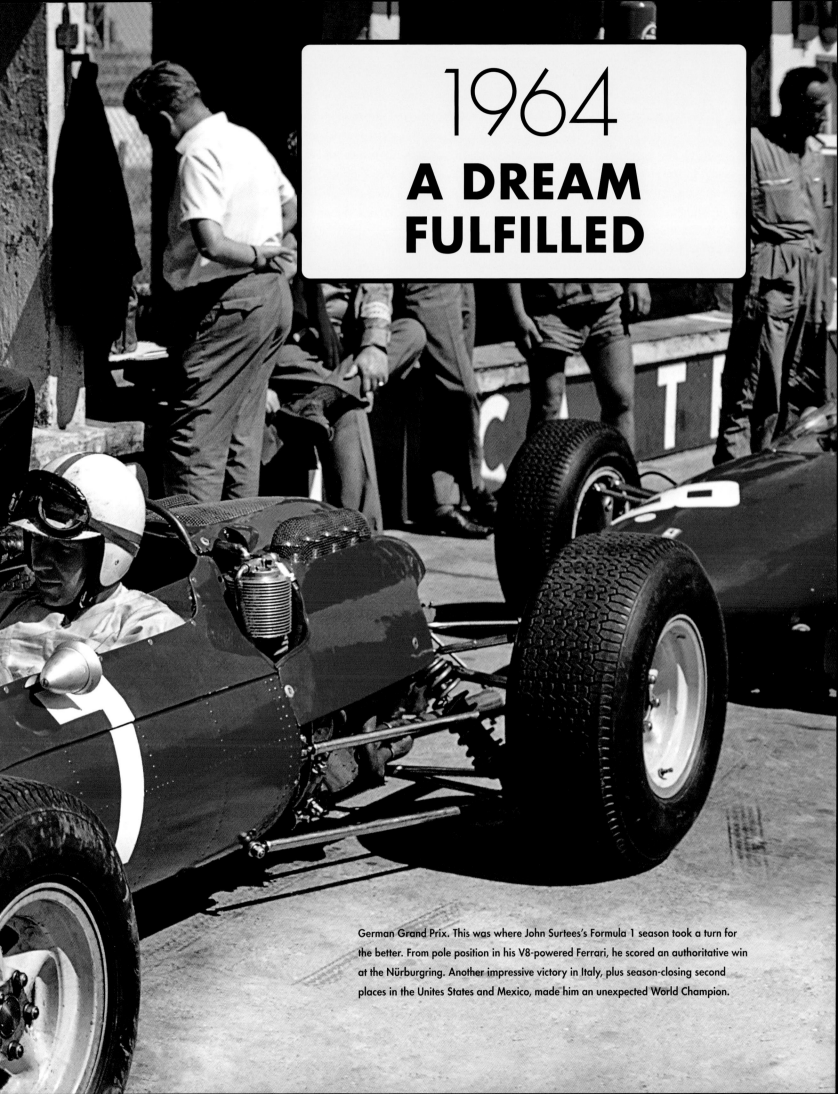

1964
A DREAM FULFILLED

German Grand Prix. This was where John Surtees's Formula 1 season took a turn for the better. From pole position in his V8-powered Ferrari, he scored an authoritative win at the Nürburgring. Another impressive victory in Italy, plus season-closing second places in the Unites States and Mexico, made him an unexpected World Champion.

Make no mistake: if the presentation of the new 330 GT production model in Modena on 11th January served as a pretext for the usual annual press conference, it was really all about the sporting programme.

Would Enzo Ferrari show himself in a new light? Not really. Consummate actor that he was, he dodged embarrassing questions and, as always, remained vague in certain areas. The proof? While the Scuderia's activities would not depend on any official championship, its cars would take part in the main events of the season 'because of technical or indeed commercial necessity' or quite simply because of the excellent relations that Maranello had always enjoyed with certain organisations. However, Formula 1 Grands Prix would be given priority over endurance racing, which, without being sacrificed, would be of secondary importance. Thanks to Ferrari's usual abundance of resources, John Surtees and Lorenzo Bandini, who had been reconfirmed as drivers, would have no fewer than six cars available to them, powered by three different engines: two 156s with the familiar V6, two 158s with the V8 that had already been glimpsed at Monza, and two with a new flat-12. This newest engine, which was claimed to be putting out around 220bhp, would be used at faster circuits in alternation with the V8, a strategy that would have an important consequence.

Concerning the prototypes, Ferrari remained as tight-lipped as ever. The 330 P, as seen at Reims and Silverstone the previous year, would be back racing alongside a 275 P derived from the 250 P that had been victorious at Sebring, the Nürburgring and Le Mans. So who would drive these cars? Ferrari did not mention those drivers who were officially under contract — Surtees, Bandini and Parkes — and instead announced the names of those who might join them. His list contained a few surprises taking into account the fact that politics and matters of the moment always played a role in Maranello. While the return of Ludovico Scarfiotti, now recovered and having postponed his retirement plans, was expected, as was that of Umberto Maglioli, Giancarlo Baghetti's reappearance after his departure from Ferrari for ATS, where he had had a truly dreadful season, had not been predicted. Of course, it was true that we were talking about prototypes, not Formula 1, and Baghetti's propensity for enjoying the good things of life had not yet blunted his speed. Carlo Mario Abate and Jean Guichet were also possibilities because Willy Mairesse and Nino Vaccarella had still not recovered the full use of their injured arms. And while there was no doubting Abate's talent, especially in GTs, it came as a surprise to see him under Eugenio Dragoni's orders as Porsche wanted him to drive its new 904. As for Guichet, many saw his presence as a just reward for having been a loyal Ferrari customer who was as brilliant as he was discreet.

In addition to this effort aimed at thwarting the ambitions of Ford as much as consolidating the export markets that received 70 percent of Ferrari's road-car production, the Scuderia would also support its long-time partner teams — the North American Racing Team (NART), Maranello Concessionaires and Ecurie Francorchamps — in being its representatives in the International Championship for GT Manufacturers. Maranello committed to ensuring that its best customers would benefit from the latest tweaks made to the 250 GTOs, four of which would be converted to a new body style and renamed GTO 64. The aging GTO was supposed to fight off the Ford offensive, a factor that obsessed Maranello, because the 250 LM presented at the previous year's Paris Salon as the rival to the American car had not met with the expected customer take-up. Just three 250 LMs were under construction on 11th January out of the 100 necessary for homologation in the GT category. Ferrari's declaration that the cars would be built within the time frame came as a surprise, especially as Porsche had announced that 100 units of its 904 would be finished by the spring. Ferrari in collaboration with Scaglietti had also constructed three new GTOs (identified in these pages as GTO 64s like the four rebodied examples) whose height complied with the standards of Appendix J, but they could hardly be described as a novelty because homologation criteria prevented any major modifications.

A cakewalk

Daytona 2,000Km, 16th February

Less than a month later at Daytona, which hosted the first round of the International Championship for GT Manufacturers, Ferrari very quickly realised that cosmetic makeovers of cars had their limits. In practice, despite giving their all at the wheel of their NART-entered 250 GTO 64, Pedro Rodríguez/Phil Hill (2m 9.8s) were unable to match the pace of the Cobras as the Bob Holbert/Dave MacDonald coupé (2m 8.8s) and the Tommy Hitchcock/Zourab Tchkotoua roadster (2m 9.0s) were both quicker on a circuit combining the infield track and the oval. This was a below-par Ferrari performance, which Hill claimed was due to repeated problems that the fourth-placed David Piper/Lucien Bianchi 250 GTO (2m 9.9s) had been able to evade. Was there anything to worry about as the event was run over 2,000km (1,243 miles), a distance imposed by the FIA to give it a high coefficient in the complicated new points system? 'Whoever leads in the opening hours won't win the race,' predicted Mike

Salmon, Roy Salvadori's team-mate in the Aston Martin DP214 that had won at Monza the previous year and was sixth on the grid (2m 13.2s) ahead of the Charlie Kolb/A.J. Foyt GTO (which was subsequently disqualified) and the Cobra roadsters of Dan Gurney/Bob Johnson and Jo Schlesser/Jean Guichet.

Holbert's race in the impressive Shelby-built coupé got off to a perfect start. He led from the 10.00am flag-fall followed by Rodríguez and these two remained at the front for the first five hours, the American car ahead except for a brief period before the first pitstops. Behind them, Salvadori's Aston was an early casualty, going out with engine failure on lap 34, but otherwise things remained fairly steady with the Piper/Bianchi GTO holding off the Gurney/Johnson and Schlesser/Guichet Cobra roadsters. It got even better for the sleek new coupé just after 3pm when the second-placed Ferrari, with Rodríguez at the wheel, threw a tread on its left-front tyre on the straight opposite the pits. The time it took Pedro to reach his pit driving on the wheel rim with a wing torn off, followed by repairs, dropped him from second place to fourth behind Piper/Bianchi and Gurney/Johnson. Meanwhile, the race had lost the Schlesser/Guichet Cobra when its overheating engine, caused by a broken fan belt, eventually brought about a piston failure.

Rodríguez/Hill set about their comeback and in due course returned to second place, picking off the Gurney/Johnson Cobra when it slowed because of engine problems, then passing the Piper/Bianchi GTO while it lost half an hour receiving a fresh alternator. The leading Cobra coupé was also ailing because it had to stop every ten laps to have oil added to the rear axle to prevent it overheating because its cooling pump had gone on the blink. The Cobra coupé's pitstop on lap 209 should have been just a routine halt for refuelling but suddenly disaster struck. When the tank had been filled, the petrol that the refueller had inadvertently sprayed over the rear of the car caught fire on contact with the overheated rear axle that mechanic John Ohlsen was inspecting while lying on his back. He suffered burns to his arms and face and owed his life to the prompt intervention of fire marshals. It was curtains for the new Cobra.

The race was now all over bar the shouting for Rodríguez/Hill. As they were no longer under any threat, they stopped for a long time for further patching up of bodywork damaged by the tyre blow-out, including making good a headlight that would be useful in the final stages of the race after dusk. There were also no worries for the Piper/Bianchi GTO, which finished a secure second with yet another GTO, the 330 LM lookalike that Schlesser had driven on the Tour de France five months earlier, nursed home in third place by Walt Hansgen/Bob Grossman. Gurney/Johnson finished fourth after spending most of the race with their engine firing on only seven cylinders.

Despite this 1–2–3 success for the GTOs, the race was a wake-up call for Ferrari. Before their Cobra coupé went up in flames, Holbert/MacDonald had been four and a half laps ahead of the winning Ferrari, and yet it was mechanically identical to a Cobra roadster. In addition, the previous day's American Challenge Cup, run over 250 miles, had seen a disappointing performance from the NART 250 LM driven by Rodríguez. Fifth after practice, it was dominated until its retirement by its American rivals as well as Gurney's Lotus 19 powered by a 4.7-litre Ford V8 just like the one installed in the Cobra coupé.

DAYTONA 2,000KM

Daytona, 16th February 1964, 327 laps (3.810 miles/6.132km), 1,244.560 miles/2,002.925km • Starters 43, classified finishers 24

1st	Pedro Rodríguez/Phil Hill	Ferrari 250 GTO 64 (5571 GT) *(1st Div III)*	327 laps
2nd	David Piper/Lucien Bianchi	Ferrari 250 GTO (4491 GT)	323 laps
3rd	Walt Hansgen/Bob Grossman	Ferrari 250 GTO (4713 GT)	319 laps
4th	Bob Johnson/Dan Gurney	Shelby Cobra (4th Div III)	311 laps
5th	Ulf Norinder/John Cannon	Ferrari 250 GTO (3445 GT)	311 laps
6th	Edgar Barth/Herbert Linge/Jo Bonnier	Porsche 356B 2000 GTS	311 laps
9th	Chuck Dietrich/M.R.J. Wylie	Ferrari 250 GT SWB	302 laps
11th	Bill Eve/Larry Perkins	Ferrari 250 GTO (3223 GT)	293 laps
12th	Eduardo Dibos/Mario Callabatisti	Ferrari 250 GT SWB	280 laps
DSQ	Charlie Kolb/A.J. Foyt	Ferrari 250 GTO	–

Fastest race lap: Dave MacDonald (Shelby Cobra Daytona), 2m 08.2s, 106.989mph/172.182kph **Winner's average speed:** 98.199mph/158.036kph **FIA World Sports Car Championship (GT Division III, over 2,000cc):**[1] 1st Ferrari 11.7, 2nd Shelby 3.9

[1] *Scoring system for the top six places in this event was 9–6–4–3–2–1 multiplied by coefficient 1.3; only the manufacturer's highest-placed car scored points*

Wake-up call

Sebring 12 Hours, 21st March

With three consecutive wins, Ferrari was the hot favourite for the 13th running of the Sebring 12 Hours, at least in the overall classification. In the prototype category there seemed to be no real challengers to the works 330 P of John Surtees/Lorenzo Bandini, the Maranello Concessionaires entry of Graham Hill/Jo Bonnier and the NART car of Pedro Rodríguez/John 'Buck' Fulp, plus the two works 275 Ps of Michael Parkes/Umberto Maglioli and Ludovico Scarfiotti/Nino Vaccarella, and additionally the underperforming 250 LM run by NART for Tom O'Brien/ Charlie Kolb. An experimental Cobra roadster, powered by a 7-litre Ford Galaxie engine and driven by Ken Miles/John Morton, was an unknown quantity, while the usual cohort of Chevrolet Corvettes, including three Grand Sports, one driven by Roger Penske/Jim Hall, were not in the same ballpark. In addition, Ford's début had been put off until the Le Mans test weekend because of an aerodynamic concern that caused front-end lift, especially when buffeted by side winds, an unfortunate trait that had supposedly been dealt with by the addition of a transverse upswept spoiler across the top of the tail.

Ferrari's position was weaker in the over-3-litre GT category. The rebuilt Shelby-entered Daytona Coupe (the name given to it by the press after the 2,000Km event) was again entrusted to Bob Holbert/Dave MacDonald, backed up by roadsters driven by Dan Gurney/Bob Johnson and Bob Bondurant/Lew Spencer. Under the Ford France banner Jo Schlesser teamed up with Phil Hill in another Cobra. There was not much that three aging GTOs and two GTO 64s driven by Jean Guichet/Carlo Mario Abate (entered by the factory) and David Piper/Mike Gammino (NART) could do about this American opposition. The field also contained five of Porsche's new 904 GTS models, entered in the prototype category.

The powerlessness of Ferrari's GTs was underlined in practice when the Guichet/Abate GTO 64 got round in only 3m 21.4s compared with 3m 12.8s for the Daytona Coupe and 3m 15.4s for the Gurney/Johnson Cobra roadster. Furthermore, the best of the Porsches, driven by Richie Ginther/Ronnie Bucknum, was not far behind the Ferrari at 3m 23.2s. On the other hand, the Ferrari 330 Ps showed their expected superiority with the works example coming out on top (3m 4.2s) followed by those of Maranello Concessionaires (3m 6.6s) and NART (3m 8.6s). The best the Penske/Hall Corvette Grand Sport could do was 3m 13.8s.

The outcome of the race was either positive or negative for Ferrari, depending on the category. Everything turned out as expected in the prototype class with a well-deserved but slightly

◄ **Sebring 12 Hours.** Three of Ferrari's Italian works drivers: from left, Ludovico Scarfiotti, Nino Vaccarella and Carlo Mario Abate. While the first two put in a good performance at Sebring in the quicker of the Scuderia's 275 Ps, Abate had a lacklustre race at the wheel of a GTO 64 that was completely outpaced by the Shelby Cobras.

➤ **Sebring 12 Hours.** As Mauro Forghieri approaches, tall Michael Parkes inserts himself behind the wheel of the 275 P he shared with Umberto Maglioli.

▼ **Sebring 12 Hours.** The fastest of the GTOs in practice and in the race, 5573 GT driven by Carlo Mario Abate/Jean Guichet was unable to threaten the American GTs. The car never got higher than 11th and was disqualified shortly after half distance for an illegal battery change out on the circuit.

lucky victory for Parkes/Maglioli after their 275 P's gearbox packed up in the final corner, leaving the car to be manhandled onto the victory podium. They headed a Prancing Horse 1–2–3 followed by Scarfiotti/Vaccarella and Surtees/Bandini, the latter pairing—in the only surviving 330 P—having led for eight hours until darkness, when they were forced to stop to have defective lights fixed. On the negative side, the British and American 330 Ps retired with gearbox and engine trouble respectively, although Hill/Bonnier had at least taken the fight to Surtees/Bandini and snatched the lead briefly in the seventh hour.

As for the GTs, Ferrari suffered a major setback because the GTOs never posed a threat to the dominant Cobras. The Holbert/MacDonald Daytona Coupe finished fourth followed by the Bondurant/Spencer and Schlesser/Hill roadsters. Even

more seriously, the GTO 64 driven by Guichet/Abate never ran higher than 11th and ended up being disqualified for 'assistance' after its starter motor stopped working. The best GTO finisher, the Piper/Gammino car, its drivers aided by Rodríguez after his 330 P dropped out, came home seventh, eight laps behind the best Cobra. The 250 LM retired when it caught fire out on the circuit but provided some small consolation because O'Brien turned in a lap at 3m 21.0s, quicker than Abate's best of 3m 22.6s.

Nonetheless, it was a big night for Parkes because this was his maiden international victory, an important step for the Englishman who was appreciated in Maranello as much for his engineering skills as for his talent behind the wheel. He owed his arrival at Ferrari to the experience he had acquired in managing the design of the Hillman Imp, a popular English car produced by the Rootes Group, which he had joined as a trainee in the winter of 1949. This experience proved to be very valuable when he was asked to oversee the medium-scale production of the 330 GT which, he admitted, had taken up most of his time since starting work in Maranello. Alongside his engineering acumen, he usually drove as quickly as his team-mates despite often having rather less track time in competitive conditions.

Due to his wide-ranging role at Ferrari, he did raise hackles, particularly with Surtees, who went so far as to observe that his fellow Englishman was 'very ambitious and had his finger

➤ **Sebring 12 Hours.** Nearly two hours into the race, Surtees confers with Bandini, who is ready to replace him at the wheel of the leading 330 P. The car is being refuelled under the eagle eye of Parkes, who is observing the steward (wearing pith helmet) as he prepares to seal the fuel tank.

▼ **Sebring 12 Hours.** After five hours of racing, Umberto Maglioli is at the wheel of the winning 275 P that he shared with Michael Parkes, leaving Carel Godin de Beaufort's lapped Porsche 904 GTS in his wake. The car receiving attention at trackside is Al Pease's Austin-Healey 'Sebring' Sprite.

◄ **Sebring 12 Hours.** Umberto Maglioli, pictured with Mauro Forghieri, had every reason to smile after winning. As well as the victory being a major success in his career résumé, it marked his best performance since an accident that had almost cost him his legs seven years earlier.

▼ **Sebring 12 Hours.** Englishmen at Ferrari: Michael Parkes and John Surtees did not get on but at least they respected each other as team-mates, both being very quick drivers.

SEBRING 12 HOURS

Sebring, 21st March 1964, 214 laps (5.200 miles/8.369km), 1,112.800 miles/1,790.878km • Starters 66, classified finishers 26

1st	Michael Parkes/Umberto Maglioli	Ferrari 275 P (0812)	214 laps
2nd	Ludovico Scarfiotti/Nino Vaccarella	Ferrari 275 P (0820)	213 laps
3rd	John Surtees/Lorenzo Bandini	Ferrari 330 P (0822)	212 laps
4th	Bob Holbert/Dave MacDonald	Shelby Cobra Daytona (1st Div III)	209 laps
5th	Bob Bondurant/Lew Spencer	Shelby Cobra	205 laps
6th	Jo Schlesser/Phil Hill	Shelby Cobra	203 laps
7th	David Piper/Mike Gammino/Pedro Rodríguez	Ferrari 250 GTO 64 (5571 GT) (4th Div III)	201 laps
15th	Bob Grossman/Dick Thompson	Ferrari 250 GTO (4713 GT)	186 laps
27th	Bill Eve/Larry Perkins	Ferrari 250 GTO (3223 GT)	158 laps
28th	Ed Cantrell/Harry Heuer/Don Yenko	Ferrari 250 GTO (3767 GT)	154 laps
DNF	Graham Hill/Jo Bonnier	Ferrari 330 P (0818)	139 laps (gearbox)
DSQ	**Carlo Mario Abate/Jean Guichet**	**Ferrari 250 GTO 64 (5573 GT)**	**113 laps (assistance)**
DNF	Pedro Rodríguez/John 'Buck' Fulp	Ferrari 330 P (0810)	40 laps (engine)
DNF	Tom O'Brien/Charlie Kolb	Ferrari 250 LM (5149)	30 laps (fire)

Fastest practice lap: Surtees, 3m 04.2s, 101.629mph/163.556kph **Fastest race lap:** Surtees, 3m 06.2s, 100.537mph/161.799kph **Winner's average speed:** 92.723mph/149.223kph **FIA World Sports Car Championship (GT Division III, over 2,000cc):**[1] 1st Shelby 18.3, 2nd Ferrari 16.5

[1] Scoring system for the top six places in this event was 9–6–4–3–2–1 multiplied by coefficient 1.6; only the manufacturer's highest-placed car scored points

in every pie'. While Parkes and Surtees had in common a very definite but disparate grasp of all things mechanical together with exceptional ability as development drivers, it is difficult to imagine two more contrasting people. Haileybury-educated Parkes, who was very tall at 6 feet 3 inches, came from an affluent background, his father having become chairman of Alvis, a respected Coventry-based engineering company that made high-quality cars, aircraft engines and military vehicles. By contrast, Surtees grew up in modest circumstances and left school at 15 to become an apprentice with Vincent, the prelude to his rise to fame on two wheels. While at Ferrari, Parkes based himself in a bachelor flat in Modena, while Surtees, married to Pat, continued to live in England. While it is not possible to pinpoint quite how, when and why their mutual resentment began, it poisoned the atmosphere within the Scuderia — but at least the conflict was put on hold when they raced together.

Once Sebring was over, each assumed his separate duties. Parkes absorbed himself in preparing for the Le Mans test weekend while Surtees went to Sicily for the Syracuse Grand Prix to give the 158 its racing début on 12th April. Although this turned out well, with victory for the new car while Bandini finished second in the V6 Aero, it raised a few questions. As the only serious opposition came from the Lotuses of Peter Arundell and Mike Spence, the race was really a stroll in the park for 'Big John'. Ferrari would have to wait until Monaco to find out where it really stood.

Absolute domination

Le Mans test weekend, 18–19 April

Meanwhile, Le Mans was the centre of attention on 18–19th April and teams turned up in force with 33 cars present compared with just 14 the previous year. Ferrari brought along a 330 P, a 275 P and a 250 LM. Ford arrived with two prototypes sent directly from Slough plus a Cobra Daytona Coupe from Shelby. To these were added as possible podium contenders a third iteration of the Maserati *Tipo* 151 and two lightweight E-types from Jaguar. While the British cars were certainly worthy of interest, the first Ford/Ferrari duel focused everybody's attention. It was proof yet again that innovation, even with a big budget and a powerful organisation behind it, could not overcome hard-earned experience.

On Saturday in the rain, Jo Schlesser on his first outing in the new Ford lost control when the car hit a pool of water coming out of the kink on the *Hunaudières* straight. It veered off the track, jumped the earth bank and stopped some 50 yards further on with its front and rear ripped off. Schlesser remained at the wheel in the intact cockpit and owed his life to the exceptional rigidity of the chassis. The next day, Roy Salvadori at the wheel of the other Ford had a similar experience a few hundred yards further on, under braking for *Mulsanne*, this time with only the

> **Le Mans test weekend.**
Michael Parkes was third fastest in this experimental 250 LM with its streamlined rear section. He just peeps into shot at the right, waiting with Mauro Forghieri for the weather to improve.

⌄ **Le Mans test weekend.** Mauro Forghieri and Michael Parkes share an umbrella. The Italian engineer was behind the arrival of the Englishman at Ferrari shortly after they first met at Brands Hatch in 1962. They got on really well, both professionally and personally, and over time became good friends.

front end damaged. Shortly afterwards, Schlesser climbed into the Cobra Daytona Coupe and judged it, unsurprisingly, much easier to drive than the new Ford. He then signed an agreement with Carroll Shelby to take part in some European events.

Either ignoring the rain or dodging the showers, Ferrari humiliated Ford when Ludovico Scarfiotti set the fastest lap of the weekend in 3m 43.8s at the wheel of the 275 P, although Carlo Mario Abate then crashed the car and ended up in hospital. The Ford's maximum speed was claimed to be 320kph (199mph) and Surtees, whose best time in the 330 P was 3m 45.9s, came quite close to that when timed at 312kph (194mph) on the *Hunaudières*

straight. Another source of satisfaction for Maranello came when Parkes achieved 3m 47.1s, the third-fastest time of the weekend, in an experimental 250 LM with teardrop-shaped cockpit bodywork that extended right to the back of the car. Meanwhile, Schlesser lapped in 4m 2.3s and almost hit 305kph (190mph) on the straight to put the Cobra Daytona Coupe at the top of the GT timesheets.

Lessons to be learned

Targa Florio, 26th April

The Targa Florio provided a golden opportunity for the Cobras because they promised to be well suited to the Sicilian challenge and Carroll Shelby entered four roadsters in his own colours. Enzo Ferrari decided to give the event a miss, either because of the crowded calendar or as a protest about new levies imposed on the Italian car industry. Now the Texan's ambitions on the international stage had officially become those of Ford as well, for Detroit was now financing his European campaign, allowing him to put forward a top-class driver line-up in the guise of Dan Gurney/Jerry Grant, Phil Hill/Bob Bondurant and Masten Gregory/Innes Ireland, plus local duo Vito Coco/Vincenzo Arena in the fourth entry. Opposition to the American

Targa Florio. With no works Ferraris present, it was up to customers to defend Maranello's interests. Taking advantage of the retirement of successive leaders, the 250 GTO 64 of Luigi Taramazzo/Corrado Ferlaino finished fifth overall and first in the large-capacity GT category, helping Ferrari to retake the lead in the International Championship for GT Manufacturers from Shelby.

Targa Florio. Jean Guichet at the wheel of the 250 GTO 64 he shared with Carlo Facetti still has everything to hope for. They were second on laps 2 and 3, third on lap 4 and second again on lap 5 after a brief spell in the lead. So it was all going swimmingly until the transmission failed just before the end of lap 6.

TARGA FLORIO

Piccolo Madonie, 26th April 1964, 10 laps (44.7 miles/72.0km), 447.4 miles/720.0km • Starters 64, classified finishers 27

1st	Antonio Pucci/Colin Davis	Porsche 904 GTS	7h 10m 53.6s
2nd	Gianni Balzarini/Herbert Linge	Porsche 904 GTS	7h 23m 15.6s
3rd	Roberto Bussinello/Nino Todaro	Alfa Romeo Giulia TZ	7h 27m 07.0s
4th	'Kim'/Alfonso Thiele	Alfa Romeo Giulia TZ	7h 27m 38.4s
5th	Luigi Taramazzo/Corrado Ferlaino	Ferrari 250 GTO 64 (3413 GT) *(1st Div III)*	7h 28m 25.0s
6th	Edgar Barth/Umberto Maglioli	Porsche 904/8	7h 29m 16.8s
9th	Ulf Norinder/Picko Troberg	Ferrari 250 GTO (3445 GT)	7h 40m 44.0s
10th	Claude Bourillot/Michel de Bourbon-Parme	Ferrari 250 GTO (3909 GT)	7h 46m 45.0s
12th	Egidio Nicolosi/Abramo Zanardelli	Ferrari 250 GTO (3705 GT)	9 laps
13th	Baldassare Taormina/Pasquale Tacci	Ferrari 250 GT Lusso	9 laps
DNF	Jean Guichet/Carlo Facetti	Ferrari 250 GTO 64 (4675 GT)	6 laps (transmission)
DNF	'Ulisse' (Luigi Mosca)/'Fortinbras' (Enrico Mosca)	Ferrari 250 GTO (3647 GT)	–
DNF	Leandro Terra/Cesare Toppetti	Ferrari 196 S	–

Fastest race lap: Davis, 41m 10.4s, 65.196mph/104.922kph **Winner's average speed:** 62.296mph/100.256kph **FIA World Sports Car Championship (GT Division III, over 2,000cc):**[1] 1st Ferrari 30.9, 2nd Shelby 27.9

[1] *Scoring system for the top six places in this event was 9–6–4–3–2–1 multiplied by coefficient 1.6; only the manufacturer's highest-placed car scored points*

attack came from six GTOs, including two GTO 64s entered by Scuderia Sant'Ambroeus for Luigi Taramazzo/Corrado Ferlaino and Jean Guichet/Carlo Facetti, while Porsche was represented by four works cars led by Jo Bonnier/Graham Hill (718 WRS) and Edgar Barth/Umberto Maglioli (904/8), supplemented by Antonio Pucci/Colin Davis and Gianni Balzarini/Herbert Linge in 904 GTS models newly homologated in the 2-litre GT category.

What remained of these hopes some 8,000 corners later? The outcome was another victory for Porsche thanks to Pucci, a Sicilian baron, and Davis, an Englishman resident in Italy. Fifth place for the Taramazzo/Ferlaino GTO gave Ferrari victory in Division III, putting Maranello back in the lead of the International Championship for GT Manufacturers following Shelby's points haul in Florida. There were setbacks for Porsche, whose prototypes retired with transmission problems after dominating for the first four laps, initially with Bonnier/Hill, then Barth/Maglioli. Then Guichet, on fine form, led briefly in his GTO 64 only for his transmission to let him down sixth time round.

As for the Cobras, this outing was a lesson in humility for Shelby, who declared: 'To win, you have to learn and draw lessons from your setbacks. See you at the Nürburgring.' Even though only one of his cars finished, he felt confident because Hill and Gurney, his two most combative drivers, never lost contact with the leading Porsche. The single surviving Cobra, the Gurney/Grant car, finished in eighth place after collapsed rear suspension forced Gurney to trundle very slowly around the last lap.

Lost illusions

Monaco Grand Prix, 10th May

When John Surtees and Lorenzo Bandini took part in the first practice session, it seemed a very long time since Ferrari's previous victory in Monaco, back in 1955 with Maurice Trintignant, especially as this Thursday afternoon gave little cause for optimism despite appearances. Although Surtees, concerned about lack of torque at low revs in the new 158, topped the timesheets at 1m 35.0s, there were reasons to view this with perspective. The main one was that Jim Clark and Dan Gurney were absent because they had been trying to qualify for the Indianapolis 500, although they were now on their way back, and the Lotus camp in any case was having to make do with two of the previous year's 25s updated to latest Type 33 specification because Clark had wrecked his new 33 during the Aintree 200 three weeks earlier. Bandini in a V6 car was one second behind his team leader, a good performance, although Jack Brabham (Brabham) and Graham Hill (BRM) beat the Italian with laps in 1m 35.1s and 1m 35.3s respectively.

On Friday, Surtees had more cause to be dissatisfied. Gearbox trouble with the 158 forced him to fall back on the spare 156, in which he posted a 1m 36.0s, while Bandini in his usual car went quicker (1m 35.5s). But Clark, seemingly unaffected by

➤ **Monaco Grand Prix.** Lorenzo Bandini has good reason to be worried at the wheel of a 156 with a recalcitrant gearbox that left him two seconds slower than his team leader after the final practice session. But there was still the race to come on a circuit he liked.

▼ **Monaco Grand Prix.** John Surtees had an up-and-down time in practice with his 158 also suffering from a troublesome gearbox, so he lapped in the spare 156 as well. He set the fastest time on the first day, matching the pace of Graham Hill's BRM P261, but in the end he was not quick enough to worry Jim Clark in his Lotus 25B.

Monaco Grand Prix. Surtees arrives on the grid in company with Jo Bonnier's Rob Walker Cooper T66 (#19), followed by other privately entered cars in the form of Peter Revson's Lotus 24 and Maurice Trintignant's BRM P57. The car disappearing out of shot is Graham Hill's BRM, which went on to win the race, while Surtees was an early retirement with gearbox failure.

Monaco Grand Prix. Bandini made a bad start and slipped down to tenth before fighting back over the next 18 laps to his original position of seventh on the grid. He had a long scrap with Phil Hill in his Cooper and retired on lap 68 with gearbox trouble when lying fourth.

MONACO GRAND PRIX

Monaco, 10th May 1964, 100 laps (1.954 miles/3.145km), 195.421 miles/314.500km • Starters 16, finishers 6

RACE					PRACTICE	
1st	Graham Hill	BRM P261 BRM V8	2h 41m 19.5s		3rd	1m 34.5s
2nd	Richie Ginther	BRM P261 BRM V8	99 laps		8th	1m 35.9s
3rd	Peter Arundell	Lotus 25 Climax V8	97 laps		6th	1m 35.5s
4th	Jim Clark	Lotus 25 Climax V8	96 laps		1st	1m 34.0s
5th	Jo Bonnier	Cooper T66 Climax V8	96 laps		11th	1m 37.4s
6th	Mike Hailwood	Lotus 25 BRM V8	96 laps		15th	1m 38.5s
10th	Lorenzo Bandini	Ferrari 158 V8	68 laps (gearbox)		7th	1m 35.5s
DNF	John Surtees	Ferrari 156 V8	15 laps (gearbox)		4th	1m 34.5s

Pole position: Jim Clark (Lotus 25 Climax V8), 1m 34.0s, 74.842mph/120.447kph **Fastest race lap:** Hill, 1m 33.9s, 74.922mph/120.575kph
Winner's average speed: 72.645mph/116.910kph **Drivers' championship:**[1] 1st Hill 9, 2nd Ginther 6, 3rd Arundell 4 **Constructors' championship:**[2] 1st BRM 9, 2nd Lotus-Climax 4, 3rd Cooper-Climax 2

[1] Scoring system for the top six places was 9–6–4–3–2–1 [2] Scoring system for the top six places was 9–6–4–3–2–1; only the manufacturer's highest-placed car scored points

any jet lag, set the fastest-ever lap of the street circuit (1m 34.0s) after a prolonged ding-dong with Brabham (1m 34.1s), while Gurney was next best (1m 34.7s) ahead of Graham Hill (1m 34.8s). Saturday unfolded in similar fashion. Surtees got round in 1m 34.5s, which equalled Graham Hill's improved time, and both ended up on the second row of the two-by-two grid behind Clark and Brabham, who did not better their previous day's efforts. Bandini dug into his reserves and landed a place on the fourth row alongside Richie Ginther (BRM), who was suffering from a fractured jaw and sore ribs after a spectacular roll at Aintree. Perhaps it was some consolation for the Scuderia to see that the Coopers that had once reigned in Monaco were now on the fifth row in the hands of Bruce McLaren and Phil Hill.

For Surtees, the lack of torque and gearbox woes experienced in practice sowed the seeds of his disappointment in the race. On lap 12, he was fifth in the 158 while Clark, who had made a meteoric start, led from Brabham, Gurney and Graham Hill. Three laps later the Ferrari quit when the expected transmission stubbornness reared its ugly head. Bandini, skilful and pugnacious, circulated behind Ginther for a long time before becoming involved in a battle with Phil Hill, but he too eventually succumbed to transmission problems, on lap 68 while running fourth.

After the race, which ended with a BRM 1–2, Hill a lap ahead of Ginther, many people at Ferrari were asking themselves if the victory in Syracuse might have been a red herring. It was a concern that Clark, who finished fourth in Monaco, had spent most of the race in the lead despite his Lotus lacking a functioning rear anti-roll bar after it broke away from its mountings. In addition, the BRMs now had a particularly rigid

and strong monocoque, as had been demonstrated at Aintree by how well it withstood Ginther's crash. And there remained the potential of the Lotus 33 that Clark had briefly revealed at Aintree as he reeled in Jack Brabham after a poor start until his sudden retirement at Melling Crossing.

An uncontested victory

17th May, Spa 500Km

The Spa 500Km, squeezed between Monaco and Zandvoort, was of major interest as the fourth round of the International Championship for GT Manufacturers in Divisions II and III. Carroll Shelby, who wanted to make up for his Sicilian setback, sent a Daytona Coupe and three roadsters for Phil Hill, Jo Schlesser, Innes Ireland and Bob Bondurant. Ferrari's answer consisted of four customer-run GTO 64s for Michael Parkes, Jean Guichet, Lucien Bianchi and Lorenzo Bandini, plus a raft of GTOs led by David Piper's example with modified 'low-line' bodywork. The E-types of Dick Protheroe and Peter Sutcliffe were outsiders capable of springing a surprise and the Porsche 904 GTSs of Edgar Barth and Ben Pon were possible top-six finishers.

The hierarchy established by the fastest times in Friday's practice session did not bode well for Shelby. Spa's high-speed character penalised the roadsters to such an extent that none appeared among the front-runners and Hill even judged the closed version to be 'undriveable'. However, it was probably his experience at Ferrari that inspired the addition of an improvised

▲ Spa 500Km. Obvious proof that the Cobra Daytona was now a serious rival to Ferrari was provided by the sight of Phil Hill's car sandwiched between the 250 GTO 64s of pole-sitter Michael Parkes (#20) and Jean Guichet (#21), whose registration number indicates that it raced in the Targa Florio. The makeshift spoiler mounted on the rear of the American car is impressively large.

◄ Spa 500Km. Although Pierre Noblet had finished second in the previous year's race in this aging GTO, this time, up against four GTO 64s as well as the well-tuned E-types of Peter Sutcliffe and Dick Protheroe, he came home 13th.

SPA 500KM

Spa-Francorchamps, 17th May 1964, 36 laps (8.761 miles/14.100km), 315.408 miles/507.600km • Starters 45, classified finishers 26

1st	Michael Parkes	Ferrari 250 GTO 64 (4399 GT) *(1st Div III)*	2h 32m 05.2s
2nd	Jean Guichet	Ferrari 250 GTO 64 (4675 GT)	+1m 08.9s
3rd	Lorenzo Bandini	Ferrari 250 GTO 64 (5573 GT)	+2m 15.2s
4th	David Piper	Ferrari 250 GTO (4491 GT)	+4m 13.6s
5th	Edgar Barth	Porsche 904 GTS	35 laps
6th	Gérald Langlois van Ophem	Ferrari 250 GTO (4153 GT)	32 laps
13th	Pierre Noblet	Ferrari 250 GTO (3943 GT)	29 laps
DNF	Ulf Norinder	Ferrari 250 GTO (3445 GT)	–
DNF	Lucien Bianchi	Ferrari 250 GTO 64 (5575 GT)	–
DNF	Chris Kerrison	Ferrari 250 GT Drogo (2735 GT)	–
DNF	Peter Clarke	Ferrari 250 GTO (3757 GT)	–
DNF	Xavier Boulanger	Ferrari 250 GTO (4757 GT)	–
DNF	Manfred Ramminger	Ferrari 250 GTO (4115 GT)	–
DNS	Francis van Lysbeth/Gustave Gosselin	Ferrari 250 GT Drogo (2053 GT)	– (accident in practice)

Fastest practice lap: Parkes, 4m 09.0s, 126.670mph/203.855kph **Fastest race lap:** Phil Hill (Shelby Cobra Daytona), 4m 04.5s, 129.001mph/207.607kph **Winner's average speed:** 124.432mph/200.254kph **FIA World Sports Car Championship (GT Division III, over 2,000cc):**[1] 1st Ferrari 42.6, 2nd Shelby 29.2

[1] *Scoring system for the top six places in this event was 9–6–4–3–2–1 multiplied by coefficient 1.3; only the manufacturer's highest-placed car scored points*

spoiler, which Phil Remington made overnight and mounted on the rear of the Daytona Coupe. This initiative immediately propelled Hill (4m 9.2s) to a place on the front row between Parkes (4m 9.0s) and Guichet (4m 12.0s) and would go on to play a crucial role at Le Mans.

What happened next was a disaster for Hill. While Parkes installed himself in the lead of the race, the American was plagued by fuel starvation around the first lap, bringing about a series of pitstops that cost him three laps in all. This left him to finish only 22nd despite driving like the clappers and pulling back a lap on Parkes, a glorious performance that saw him break the lap record four times, leaving it at 4m 4.5s (giving an average speed of just over 129mph) compared with the winner's best of 4m 6.8s.

As for the cause of the Daytona Coupe's early problems, the fuel filters were found to be partially blocked by a strange fibrous material. In the words of Peter Brock, the car's designer, 'sabotage was suspected but never proved'. While Ferraris filled the first four places with Guichet, Bandini and Piper finishing behind Parkes, it was undeniable that the Daytona Coupe was the quicker car on a circuit with average speeds that were comparable to those achieved at Le Mans. Before the shoot-out in the Sarthe, therefore, Ferrari was intent on clinching a third GT world title at the Nürburgring.

A glimmer of hope

Dutch Grand Prix, 24th May

Would Surtees be able to stop Clark winning at Zandvoort? The question preoccupied the Scuderia, especially as Bandini was due to have his own 158 and hopefully could finally play his role of riding shotgun to his team leader. Friday morning's practice provided no answers. As Bandini's 158 was not yet ready, he had to fall back on a 156 and the best he could do was to equal the 1m 36.6s posted by Bruce McLaren (Cooper). Surtees matched Jack Brabham's 1m 33.8s but both were much slower than Dan Gurney, who got his Brabham round in 1m 31.6s but was erroneously credited with Clark's time of 1m 31.2s. The afternoon session did little to calm the agitation at Ferrari, for Surtees could only improve to 1m 32.8s before he had to park with an oil leak from an inaccessible union at the front of the V8. Although Bandini made up some ground with a 1m 35.0s, his 156's performance highlighted the progress made by Ferrari's rivals in two years, especially when Clark turned in a remarkable 1m 31.3s. The only driver to come close was Graham Hill, whose demon lap in 1m 31.4s put his BRM on the front row alongside the Lotus. The next day the sun promised for the weekend finally appeared but did

▲ **Dutch Grand Prix.** John Surtees was back in the 158 seen in Monaco. He had below-par practice sessions and started on the second row, six tenths of a second behind Dan Gurney's Brabham and Jim Clark's Lotus.

▲ **Dutch Grand Prix.** Lorenzo Bandini was at the wheel of a 158 for the first time in a Grand Prix. His race could be summed up as a slide to the back of the field followed by retirement due to engine problems that had plagued him since his arrival at Zandvoort.

not change anything. Surtees's car sprung another leak, water this time, and Bandini spent his time getting to grips with his new 158.

The lap chart for the 80-lap race did not really reflect the way it unfolded. Clark shot into the lead and was never threatened, leaving his rivals to sort out the remaining points-scoring places among themselves. Behind him, Hill, Surtees and Gurney battled away, until the American driver pitted on lap 23 with

his Brabham feeling odd, due, it was found, to a crack in his steering wheel. At about the same time, Hill's BRM began to misfire, allowing Surtees to slip past into second place, where he remained for the rest of the race. By lap 51, Hill had had enough of his engine's recalcitrant behaviour and decided to call at the pits, where it was found that an overheating pressure pump had been causing intermittent fuel starvation. He resumed in sixth

◄ **Dutch Grand Prix.** Jim Clark took full advantage of his pole position and led throughout without ever being challenged. Either side of him here, Dan Gurney (at the far side of the track) and Graham Hill already trail, while directly behind John Surtees has again fluffed his start.

place and, with the engine running smoothly again, picked off Chris Amon (Lotus) and McLaren to finish fourth.

Surtees second! It did not really matter that he finished 53.6 seconds behind Clark and that engine problems almost spoiled his party. At least the gearbox had worked perfectly, so the bearing issues that had been found to lie behind the trouble in Monaco had been cured. The only blot on Ferrari's copybook was Bandini's lacklustre showing in his new 158. Right from the start, his V8 ran badly, due to the fuel pump's drive belt not being tight enough, and he limped along near the back of the field before quitting on lap 21.

▲ **Dutch Grand Prix.** Surtees had a very encouraging race. Pictured when running third, soon after passing Dan Gurney's Brabham on lap 10, he moved up to second place when the engine in Graham Hill's BRM began to lose power and stayed there to the chequered flag.

After eight months of gloom surrounding Ferrari's efforts to make progress in Formula 1, Surtees's performance was the proverbial ray of sunshine. Everyone in Maranello was now convinced that once their preoccupations with Le Mans were over, they would enjoy a long spell of sunshine.

DUTCH GRAND PRIX

Zandvoort, 24th May 1964, 80 laps (2.605 miles/4.193km), 208.433 miles/335.440km • Starters 17, finishers 12

RACE				PRACTICE	
1st	Jim Clark	Lotus 25 Climax V8	2h 7m 35.4s	2nd	1m 31.3s
2nd	**John Surtees**	**Ferrari 156 V8**	**+53.6s**	**4th**	**1m 32.8s**
3rd	Peter Arundell	Lotus 25 Climax V8	79 laps	6th	1m 33.5s
4th	Graham Hill	BRM P261 BRM V8	79 laps	3rd	1m 31.4s
5th	Chris Amon	Lotus 25 BRM V8	79 laps	13th	1m 35.9s
6th	Bon Anderson	Brabham BT11 Climax V8	78 laps	11th	1m 35.4s
DNF	**Lorenzo Bandini**	**Ferrari 158 V8**	20 laps (engine)	10th	1m 35.0s

Pole position: Dan Gurney (Brabham BT7 Climax V8), 1m 31.2s, 102.845mph/165.513kph **Fastest race lap:** Clark, 1m 32.8s, 101.072mph/162.659kph **Winner's average speed:** 98.017mph/157.743kph **Drivers' championship:** 1st= Hill & Clark 12, 3rd Arundell 8, 4th Surtees 6 **Constructors' championship:** 1st Lotus-Climax 13, 2nd BRM 12, 3rd Ferrari 6

Not without a scare

Nürburgring 1,000Km, 31st May

When practice began at the Nürburgring, the men from Dearborn again discovered the reality of the challenge they faced. This time they brought only a single Ford prototype, with revised aerodynamics involving a redesigned front end and a rear spoiler, and with Phil Hill and Bruce McLaren the assigned drivers. It qualified second with a time of 9m 4.7s but this owed as much to the American's in-depth knowledge of the track as to the prowess of the car, which, as a singleton entry, looked vulnerable against rivals that had turned up in force.

The strongest opponent, of course, was Ferrari with 275 Ps claiming three of the first five places in the starting line-up. Way out in front with a time of 8m 57.9s was the John Surtees/Lorenzo Bandini example, while Ludovico Scarfiotti/Nino Vaccarella (9m 5.9s) and Graham Hill/Innes Ireland (9m 9.9s) were split by the Porsche 904/8 of Jo Bonnier/Richie Ginther (9m 8.8s). Two 250 LMs, which were now known as 275 LMs because they used the 3.3-litre V12 from the spyders, were also potential contenders for victory in the hands of 'Beurlys'/Pierre Dumay (9m 30.3s) and Umberto Maglioli/Jochen Rindt (9m 31.4s); as

they were awaiting their homologation for the GT category, they raced in the prototype class.

Among the GTs, the odds seemed to favour four Cobra roadsters, although this was perhaps a misleading impression. Without underestimating the skills of Tommy Hitchcock/Günter Thiel and Paul Hawkins/Bob Olthoff, it was clear that the combined talents of Jo Schlesser/Richard Attwood and Bob Bondurant/Jochen Neerpasch at the wheel of works entries would have a tough job on their hands fighting off seven GTOs, two of which were 1964 models driven by Lucien Bianchi/Gérald Langlois van Ophem and Michael Parkes/Jean Guichet, the latter a works entry. In the role of possible interlopers were four Peters in Lightweight E-types — Lindner/Nöcker and Sargent/Lumsden — and the little Porsche 904 GTSs of Ben Pon/Gerhard Koch and Gerhard Mitter/Herbert Linge.

Given the weakness of the opposition, was a Ferrari victory a mere formality? When Bandini opened the second round of refuelling stops on lap 27 by coming in before his scheduled stop, the Italian driver heaved a sigh of relief, as did Surtees, because their fear of running out of fuel had been allayed. Their 275 P was second, sandwiched between those of Ireland and Vaccarella, but the ex-motorcycle champion was quicker than his co-driver and knew that reclaiming the lead would not be a problem. During Surtees's earlier stint, he had owned the race. On only the second lap, he had lowered the record to 9m 9.0s and

◄ **Nürburgring 1,000Km.** Nino Vaccarella (far right) is about to get behind the wheel of the 275 P he shared with John Surtees. It is an important moment for the Italian, whose career had almost ended after crashing here a year earlier. Note the Peugeot 404 estate car used by Ferrari as a service vehicle.

pulled away from his rivals, so that by the quarter-distance mark (lap 11) he headed Graham Hill, Scarfiotti, Phil Hill, Maglioli and Parkes. What happened next thinned the ranks and swayed the odds further in his favour. The Ford, having held its own against the Maranello spyders, was pushed into the dead car park on lap 15 with a broken weld in the rear suspension as well as emerging transmission problems. Three laps earlier, there had been another significant departure when the Bondurant/ Neerpasch Cobra, which had looked a threat to the GTOs, went out with engine problems.

Then Lady Luck suddenly deserted the Italian camp. On lap 29, while Dragoni deliberately held up Scarfiotti's departure after a pitstop until Surtees had gone by, Ireland ran out of fuel a good quarter of a mile short of the pits and arrived on foot. Although the regulations stated that a car could only be refuelled in the pits and at least one race steward pointed that out, Ireland's co-driver, Graham Hill, took a can of petrol to the stranded 275 P and drove it back for a proper fill-up prior to rejoining the race. The consequence was inevitable: the Maranello Concessionaires Ferrari was disqualified for illegal refuelling. Ferrari lost one of its front-runners, which at least relieved Dragoni of having to juggle with the ambitions of Colonel Ronnie Hoare, proprietor of the Maranello Concessionaires team.

Lap 30. With no rivals breathing down his neck, Surtees was comfortably installed in the lead ahead of Scarfiotti, whose ardour had just been reined in by team orders. Dragoni, though, had little time to enjoy his team's 1–2 supremacy. Just two laps later, Surtees had the left-rear hub break without warning, causing his spyder to plunge into the thickets bordering the climb up to the *Flugplatz*, thankfully without injuring him. Another blow struck Maranello a few laps later. A sudden shower soaked the track in the area around the *Karussell*, taxing the concentration of the most experienced drivers, including Maglioli, whose 250 LM ended up in a ditch. Nonetheless, Ferraris still ran first and second, with Scarfiotti/Vaccarella 275 P a lap ahead of the Parkes/Guichet GTO 64, and that was how they finished, with the other GTO 64, the Bianchi/Langlois van Ophem car, in fourth place.

When it came to adding up the points, it was looking good for Maranello, but there were still numerous questions that required answers with less than a month to go before Le Mans. The main one was that only one of the three spyders had survived seven hours at the Nürburgring and that did not bode well for durability over 24 hours at Le Mans. Furthermore, although victory was always a source of satisfaction, it had been sealed with some scares along the way, underlining the fact that by wanting to do things through strength in numbers, it was maybe the case that Ferrari was spreading its resources a

▲ **Nürburgring 1,000Km.** After the premature retirement of Ford's singleton GT40, the race turned into a high-speed parade of 275 Ps. In this photo, taken near the half-distance mark, Nino Vaccarella leads Lorenzo Bandini and Innes Ireland. He soon pulled away.

▼ **Nürburgring 1,000Km.** Innes Ireland went really well in the Maranello Concessionaires 275 P and here keeps Lorenzo Bandini at bay in the works car with which John Surtees had established a good lead. The British team's boss, Colonel Ronnie Hoare, understandably refused Eugenio Dragoni's request that he should rein in his driver and allow the factory car to prevail.

➤ **Nürburgring 1,000Km.** When Innes Ireland's 275 P ran out of fuel little more than a quarter of a mile short of the pits, Graham Hill, his co-driver, took a can of petrol out to it in the vain hope that they could remain in the race. As can be seen, he ignored a steward's attempt to remind him that refuelling could only take place in the pits, and disqualification was the inevitable consequence.

▼ **Nürburgring 1,000Km.** Having poured his can of petrol into the stranded Maranello Concessionaires 275 P, Graham Hill arrives in the pits to refuel properly and rejoin the race. Two laps later the clerk of the course showed him the black flag.

little too thinly. Once again fuel consumption had been wrongly calculated and then there was the matter of the hub breakage.

As for the opposition, the Porsches had posed the most dangerous threat, but at least Le Mans would not suit them. On the other hand, the fact that the Ford prototype had matched the pace of the winning car came as a surprise. At Le Mans, where Dearborn personnel would be turning up in force with three cars, their aspirations would be much higher. It was a similar story for the Shelby team, which was expected to bring three Daytona Coupes to Le Mans and do well with them, unlike at the Nürburgring with the roadsters, which really were lagging now in terms of performance despite the best efforts of their top drivers. The car Bondurant shared with Neerpasch went out after a string of problems (a puncture following a collision, a broken shock absorber and finally the loss of a wheel), while Schlesser/Attwood managed to at least win their category, albeit in 23rd place, after their own catalogue of setbacks (a broken ignition coil wire and throttle linkage issues). In contrast, it was a disappointing race for Jaguar because neither Lightweight E-type was in contention and both retired, but as Coventry refused to enter cars officially, Sargent and Lindner could only rely on themselves.

> **Nürburgring 1,000Km.** At two-thirds distance, Jean Guichet walks away from the factory-entered GTO 64 after handing it over to Michael Parkes, who is about to roar off and seal a fine result with second place overall.

NÜRBURGRING 1,000KM

Nürburgring, 31st May 1964, 44 laps (14.173 miles/22.810km), 623.633 miles/1,003.640km • Starters 81, classified finishers 46

1st	Ludovico Scarfiotti/Nino Vaccarella	**Ferrari 275 P (0820)**	7h 08m 27.0s
2nd	**Michael Parkes/Jean Guichet**	**Ferrari 250 GTO 64 (5573 GT)** *(1st Div III)*	**43 laps**
3rd	Gerhard Koch/Ben Pon	Porsche 904 GTS	43 laps
4th	Lucien Bianchi/Gérald Langlois van Ophem	Ferrari 250 GTO 64 (5575 GT)	43 laps
5th	Jo Bonnier/Richie Ginther	Porsche 904/8	42 laps
6th	Herbert Müller/André Knörr	Porsche 904 GTS	42 laps
7th	David Piper/Tony Maggs	Ferrari 250 GTO (4491 GT)	42 laps
18th	Gustave Gosselin/Francis van Lysbeth	Ferrari 250 GTO (4153 GT)	40 laps
20th	Manfred Ramminger/Herbert Schander	Ferrari 250 GTO (4115 GT)	40 laps
26th	Hans-Peter Koepchen/Erich Bitter	Ferrari 250 GT SWB	39 laps
28th	Peter Clarke/Dan Margulies	Ferrari 250 GTO (3757 GT)	38 laps
39th	Umberto Maglioli/Jochen Rindt	Ferrari 250 LM (5909)	34 laps
46th	**John Surtees/Lorenzo Bandini**	**Ferrari 275 P (0802)**	**31 laps (accident)**
DNF	Graham Hill/Innes Ireland	Ferrari 275 P (0818)	28 laps (illegal refuelling)
DNF	'Beurlys' (Jean Blaton)/Pierre Dumay	Ferrari 250 LM (5843)	9 laps (suspension)
DNF	Picko Troberg/Chris Amon	Ferrari 250 GTO (3445 GT)	4 laps (accident)

Fastest practice lap: Surtees, 8m 57.9s, 94.859mph/152.660kph **Fastest race lap:** Surtees, 9m 09.0s, 92.957mph/149.600kph **Winner's average speed:** 87.333mph/140.549kph **FIA World Sports Car Championship (GT Division III, over 2,000cc):**[1] 1st Ferrari 57.0, 2nd Shelby 30.8

[1] *Scoring system for the top six places in this event was 9–6–4–3–2–1 multiplied by coefficient 1.6; only the manufacturer's highest-placed car scored points*

When every drop counts!

Belgian Grand Prix, 14th June

The calendar being what it was, the Belgian Grand Prix was held just a week before the Le Mans 24 Hours, the most important race of the year for Ferrari, and must have marked a particular pressure point for Maranello's multi-faceted racing programme.

After a Friday session run in blazing sunshine, Surtees was second quickest (3m 55.2s) and Bandini third (3m 59.2s), but the pace of their cars suffered because of the effect of the day's heat on their fuel-injection systems. Dan Gurney, though, was in scintillating form in his flying Brabham. His 3m 50.9s not only unofficially beat the outright lap record held since 1960 by Jack Brabham in a 2.5-litre Cooper but also left all his rivals open-mouthed in astonishment because he was so dominant, fully five seconds quicker than 'Big John', six faster than Richie Ginther and Graham Hill in their BRMs, and seven ahead of Jim Clark's Lotus. The following afternoon the weather was hotter still and Ferrari found itself in even deeper trouble with its fuel injection. With Surtees unable to cover a single flying lap reliably,

Hill and Brabham displaced him to the second row, alongside Peter Arundell (Lotus). Bandini, although slightly quicker than the previous day (3m 58.8s), was relegated to the fourth row as Clark, McLaren and Ginther all produced quicker laps.

Despite all that, the race got off to a good start for the Scuderia. Surtees was sixth as the cars tackled the *Raidillon* at *Eau Rouge* and at the end of the lap flashed past the pits in second place behind Gurney. The uncertainty caused by the drops of rain that fell around 10 minutes before the start was forgotten. There had been no last-minute tyre changes at Ferrari, unlike at Lotus, where

▲ **Belgian Grand Prix.** During Friday practice, Surtees did well despite fuel-injection problems due to hot weather, but the following day, in even higher temperatures, he was unable to complete a single flying lap and ended up four seconds slower. Sharing his worry are Eugenio Dragoni (leaning over the cockpit), Giulio Borsari and Mauro Forghieri.

◄ **Belgian Grand Prix.** Pat Surtees's notes probably made discouraging reading for Bandini. Unlike her husband, he at least improved his times on the second day of practice despite his V8 engine not pulling all its revs, but he could only qualify on the fourth row, alongside débutant Peter Revson in a Lotus-BRM.

➤ Belgian Grand Prix. After a start given using a dummy grid, Jack Brabham leads away, just ahead of Peter Arundell (Lotus) in the centre and a slightly hesitant Graham Hill (BRM) on the right. After one of his usual poor getaways, Surtees is directly behind the leader

➤ Belgian Grand Prix. Surtees's race at Spa was short but sweet. Putting all the disappointments of practice behind him in cooler and more favourable weather, he finished the first two laps in second place and briefly led the third only to head for his pit to retire after the fourth.

BELGIAN GRAND PRIX

Spa-Francorchamps, 14th June 1964, 32 laps (8.761 miles/14.100km), 280.363 miles/451.200km • Starters 18, finishers 8

RACE				PRACTICE	
1st	Jim Clark	Lotus 25 Climax V8	2h 6m 40.5s	6th	3m 56.2s
2nd	Bruce McLaren	Cooper T73 Climax V8	+3.4s	7th	3m 56.2s
3rd	Jack Brabham	Brabham BT7 Climax V8	+48.1s	3rd	3m 52.8s
4th	Richie Ginther	BRM P261 BRM V8	+1m 58.6s	8th	3m 57.2s
5th	Graham Hill	BRM P261 BRM V8	31 laps (out of fuel)	2nd	3m 52.7s
6th	Dan Gurney	Brabham BT7 Climax V8	31 laps (out of fuel)	1st	3m 50.9s
DNF	**Lorenzo Bandini**	**Ferrari 158 V8**	**11 laps (engine)**	**9th**	**3m 58.8s**
DNF	**John Surtees**	**Ferrari 158 V8**	**3 laps (engine)**	**10th**	**3m 55.2s**

Pole position: Gurney, 3m 50.9s, 136.599mph/219.835kph **Fastest race lap:** Gurney, 3m 49.2s, 137.612mph/221.465kph **Winner's average speed:** 132.793mph/213.709kph **Drivers' championship:** 1st Clark 21, 2nd Hill 14, 3rd Ginther 9, 5th Surtees 6 **Constructors' championship:** 1st Lotus-Climax 22, 2nd BRM 15, 3rd Cooper-Climax 8, 4th Ferrari 6

Colin Chapman had decided that Clark's Lotus should race on unused tyres rather than the partly worn ones that his star driver always favoured on a dry track. In addition, the temperature had fallen thanks to an overnight storm and in the cool conditions the 158 was running like a train, as confirmed on lap 2. This time Surtees was all over Gurney as they raced past the pits. He shot past him approaching *Malmedy* and next time round the Ferrari led the Brabham by 1.5 seconds. Then it all went south. Halfway round the fourth lap, the Ferrari suddenly slowed: a piston had let go. Gurney, Clark and Hill all overtook the ailing 158 in an instant and by the time it had limped round the rest of the lap and pitted under its own momentum the rest of the field had left it far behind. Bandini's 158 lasted until lap 12, when it also coasted into the pits with a sick engine, its ignition timing and lubrication system both awry. In less than an hour, Ferrari's hopes had evaporated.

But before turning the page on the 24th running of the Belgian Grand Prix, it is worth describing the end of the race. Gurney and Hill both ran out of petrol on the last lap, depriving them one after the other of victory. That left McLaren in the lead but his Cooper was in the process of having an electrical meltdown and by the time he reached *La Source* he had a dead engine too. He was freewheeling down to the finishing line and an unlikely win when Clark flashed past him just a few car lengths before the chequered flag to snatch victory.

All in all, the dice had certainly rolled in the Scot's favour as he now led Hill in the points standings, 21 versus 14, while Surtees had only six. People were beginning to ask themselves if the championship title battle might be nearly done and dusted as Clark, in addition to his prodigious talent, seemed to have luck on his side.

No worries about other rivals

Le Mans 24 Hours, 20th–21st June

Jean Guichet was happy after the first practice session and even more so after the second session the next day. His apprenticeship in the 275 P he shared with Nino Vaccarella on his seventh Le Mans outing was passing off without a hitch. Shortly after his victory in the previous year's Tour de France, he had decided that he had had enough of being a Maranello customer and henceforth would only race factory cars. One morning he was having coffee in his native Marseille with Johnny Rives from *L'Equipe* and told him: 'I want to have a prototype Ferrari to win Le Mans.' Enzo Ferrari promised to fulfil that wish but Guichet had to wait until the very last moment for it to come true.

However, the Guichet/Vaccarella Ferrari was far from quickest in practice, particularly on the Thursday, when Surtees (3m 42.0s) in his 330 P fended off Ginther in the fastest GT40 (3m 45.3s). As the race approached, what was important was that Guichet's strategy, decided with his co-driver, had been given the green light by Eugenio Dragoni. They would lap at around the four-minute mark 'without worrying about their rivals', who, in the Ferrari camp, comprised three other works prototypes in the shape of the aforementioned 330 P of John Surtees/Lorenzo Bandini and two more 275 Ps for Michael Parkes/Ludovico Scarfiotti and Giancarlo Baghetti/

Umberto Maglioli, while in addition there were customer 330 Ps for Graham Hill/Jo Bonnier (Maranello Concessionaires) and Pedro Rodríguez/Skip Hudson (NART). The Fords, which the regulations deemed to be prototypes despite their 'GT' designation, were crewed by Richie Ginther/Masten Gregory, Jo Schlesser/Richard Attwood and Phil Hill/Bruce McLaren. Neither did Guichet rule out contenders from the GT category as potential adversaries, notably a pair of 250 LMs (still awaiting their official homologation) and four GTO 64s, these Ferraris the main rivals to two Cobra Daytona Coupes in the hands of Dan Gurney/Bob Bondurant and Jochen Neerpasch/Chris Amon.

Sunday 21st June. Dawn. Although Guichet knew that it is never over at Le Mans until 'the fat lady sings', he was savouring his lead, even if it was far from secure because the Surtees/Bandini 330 P followed only a lap behind with the Hill/Bonnier 275 P a further four laps down. For the time being, the situation confirmed what Guichet had said to Rives just before the start: 'I think the 3.3-litre is the car that will win rather than the 4-litre versions.' Paul Frère shared this point of view, reckoning that the 330 Ps were 'barely quicker' than the 275 Ps and had to refuel more often. Frère also expressed reservations about the strength of the 330 P's transmission because it had to 'cope with engine torque out of proportion to the general dimensions of the engine internals'. True to these judgements, the 275 P had indeed performed faultlessly, the only setback of any kind due to Guichet's inattention during one of his rest periods. Just before midnight, while having a bite to eat, he relaxed so much that he forgot to get ready in time to relieve his team-mate on schedule, leaving Vaccarella having to drive another 25-lap stint.

▲ **Le Mans 24 Hours.** The works spyders line up in numerical order for the public to admire, with the single 330 P on the left in company with three 275 Ps. The drivers were John Surtees/Lorenzo Bandini (#19), Jean Guichet/Nino Vaccarella (#20), Michael Parkes/Ludovico Scarfiotti (#21) and Giancarlo Baghetti/Umberto Maglioli (#22).

▼ **Le Mans 24 Hours.** Now a works driver, Jean Guichet opted for a 275 P because he reckoned that it was a more reliable prospect than a 330 P to fulfil his ambition of an outright Le Mans victory after two successive wins in the GT category. He had every reason to be satisfied with his seventh-fastest time during practice and hit it off right away with co-driver Nino Vaccarella thanks to the Sicilian's no-nonsense approach and sheer speed.

▲ **Le Mans 24 Hours.** Pedro Rodríguez won the sprint across the tarmac to lead away in his 330 P (#15) followed by Graham Hill's 330 P (#14) and Michael Parkes's 275 P (#21), while John Surtees's 330 P (#19) and Jean Guichet's 275 P (#20) are just setting off. Among those yet to get moving are the Fords of Richie Ginther (#11), Phil Hill (#10) and Jo Schlesser (#12), while Dan Gurney's Cobra Daytona Coupe (#5) is just starting to nose out.

He apologised and his co-driver continued to get the job done, never letting Surtees gain significant advantage.

The Fords had had their fair share of trouble. After Phil Hill flooded his GT40's carburettors at the start, Ginther played the role of 'hare' and did so in style for more than an hour. After that, the car fell behind the Surtees/Bandini Ferrari and went out when its fragile gearbox developed terminal problems during the evening, soon after Attwood had had to park his sister car near *Mulsanne* with flames licking from the engine compartment. While Surtees/Bandini consolidated a lead they held for nine hours, Hill/McLaren attempted to save the day for Ford and put on a stunning display, fighting their way back from 44th place to sixth during eight hours of flat-out driving. Ford's boast back in April that it had produced the fastest car in the world now seemed not so far off the mark and certainly Phil Hill

had never driven so quickly in the Sarthe. And he was soon to go even faster. Just after 5am on Sunday, as the cold morning air numbed flesh and bone, the commentator announced that Hill, by then in fourth place, had covered the 187th lap in a record 3m 49.2s at an average speed of 131mph. That was as good as it got. Five laps later, the Ford's Colotti gearbox decided that it could not cope with the stress any longer.

Over at Shelby, the Amon/Neerpasch Daytona Coupe had begun well, briefly holding fourth place during the opening hours, but then an illegal battery change brought disqualification. The Gurney/Bondurant entry, however, was doing well, running fourth in fairly close company with the third-placed Maranello Concessionaires 330 P. Another Cobra coupé, a version created especially for the race by AC Cars and driven by Peter Bolton/Jack Sears, had experienced early delay with fuel-pump problems due to dirt in the tank and then had a tyre blow out just before midnight in one of the curves following *Arnage*, ending up upside-down. This crash also took out the Baghetti/Maglioli 275 P, which had never featured because Baghetti cooked its clutch at the start and took an hour to complete his first lap. The Parkes/Scarfiotti 275 P had also had its problems early on, misfiring from only the fourth lap due to malfunctioning ignition that took several pitstops to resolve.

Rodríguez, poorly backed up by Hudson, quit in the early evening with a blown cylinder head gasket.

Guichet/Vaccarella took over the lead shortly before dawn when the Surtees/Bandini 330 P faltered. The car had been experiencing some loss of water but the more serious delay, which cost 23 minutes, occurred when the pick-up pipe inside the fuel tank broke halfway up, which meant that the fuel pump could only extract half the contents and therefore obliged the drivers to make refuelling stops twice as often. Through breakfast time, optimism among Guichet/Vaccarella supporters ratcheted up another notch when the only significant non-Ferrari rival left in the race, the surviving Cobra Daytona Coupe, needed a longer-than-usual stop for fresh brake pads and tyres before returning to the pits twice more, first for replacement of a holed oil line, then for installation of a makeshift pipe to bypass a leaking oil radiator, all of which cost half an hour.

At 10am Guichet began to breathe more freely. Not only was daybreak over with its patchy mist that seemed to vary in density each time round, but the fresh oysters given to him by Jean Noaille from the Shell-Berre competition service had also done his eyesight a power of good. In the chasing 330 Ps, Hill/Bonnier were now seven laps behind after a succession of problems and Surtees/Bandini were ten laps down. If there

▲ ▼ **Le Mans 24 Hours.** Heading into the low sun of early evening, the Ferrari 330 Ps that finished second and third round the tight corner at *Mulsanne*, driven by Jo Bonnier (#14) and Lorenzo Bandini (#19).

◄ **Le Mans 24 Hours.** Overall, the GTO 64s put on a below-par performance. During the first third of the race, the Maranello Concessionaires entry of Innes Ireland/Tony Maggs (pictured) was the best of them, before the Ecurie Francorchamps car of Lucien Bianchi/'Beurlys' moved ahead. Both survived to the finish, the Belgian entry fifth, the British one sixth, both beaten by the class-winning Cobra Daytona Coupe.

▼ **Le Mans 24 Hours.** Jean Guichet/Nino Vaccarella were fifth at the end of the first hour, then ran steadily in the top three before taking the lead at 4am. They really deserved the post-race acclaim because the Le Mans 24 Hours had rarely provided such a display of cool-headedness and speed combined with abundant good humour. Here Guichet carefully negotiates the usual trackside route to the official victory celebrations while his co-driver and two factory mechanics enjoy the ride. Behind is the Dan Gurney/Bob Bondurant Cobra Daytona Coupe that finished fourth overall and won the GT category.

LE MANS 24 HOURS

Le Mans, 20th–21st June 1964, 348 laps (8.364 miles/13.461km), 2,917.530 miles/4,695.310km • Starters 55, classified finishers 24

1st	Jean Guichet/Nino Vaccarella	Ferrari 275 P (0816)	348 laps
2nd	Jo Bonnier/Graham Hill	Ferrari 330 P (0818)	343 laps
3rd	John Surtees/Lorenzo Bandini	Ferrari 330 P (0822)	336 laps
4th	Dan Gurney/Bob Bondurant	Shelby Cobra Daytona *(1st Div III)*	333 laps
5th	Lucien Bianchi/'Beurlys' (Jean Blaton)	Ferrari 250 GTO 64 (5575 GT) *(2nd Div III)*	332 laps
6th	Innes Ireland/Tony Maggs	Ferrari 250 GTO 64 (4399 GT)	327 laps
9th	Fernand Tavano/Bob Grossman	Ferrari 250 GTO 64 (5573 GT)	314 laps
16th	Pierre Dumay/Gérald Langlois van Ophem	Ferrari 250 LM (5843)	297 laps
DNF	Ed Hugus/José Rosinski	Ferrari 250 GTO 64 (5571 GT)	114 laps (differential)
DNF	Michael Parkes/Ludovico Scarfiotti	Ferrari 275 P (0820)	71 laps (oil pump)
DNF	Giancarlo Baghetti/Umberto Maglioli	Ferrari 275 P (0812)	68 laps (accident)
DNF	Pedro Rodríguez/Skip Hudson	Ferrari 330 P (0810)	58 laps (engine)
DNF	David Piper/Jochen Rindt	Ferrari 250 LM (5909)	– (oil pipe)

Fastest practice lap: Surtees, 3m 42.0s, 135.637mph/218.286kph **Fastest race lap:** Phil Hill (Ford GT40), 3m 49.2s, 131.376mph/211.429kph **Winner's average speed:** 121.564mph/195.638kph **FIA World Sports Car Championship (GT Division III, over 2,000cc):**[1] 1st Ferrari 69.0, 2nd Shelby 48.8

[1] Scoring system for the top six places in this event was 9–6–4–3–2–1 multiplied by coefficient 2.0; only the manufacturer's highest-placed car scored points

was a fly in the ointment, it concerned Ferrari's prospects in the GT category, for the Daytona Coupe, despite its delay, had got back on the same lap as the fourth-placed Fernand Tavano/Bob Grossman GTO 64 and was soon to pass it, while two other GTO contenders, the cars of Lucien Bianchi/'Beurlys' and Innes Ireland/Tony Maggs, sat a lap behind. But it soon seemed to be all over bar the shouting as Gurney/Bondurant motored on as best they could without overheating their engine's oil, while the GTOs held station or retired.

Ferrari pretty much swept the board. Guichet/Vaccarella secured Maranello's fifth victory in a row and also won the Index of Performance. Ferrari's three surviving prototypes finished first, second and third, and there were two more Ferraris in the top six. Frère and Guichet had been right: whereas the 330 Ps had hit problems, the winning 275 P had run so smoothly that it had required only fuel, four litres of oil and two new rear wheels — and it had not even needed any water added to the radiator.

In terms of championship points, however, Ford was the main winner thanks to the class-winning Daytona Coupe, particularly as Le Mans was the most generous event of the year with its 'coefficient 2' status, which meant double points awarded in Division III of the International Championship for GT Manufacturers, allowing Shelby with 48.8 points to close the gap to Ferrari on 69. The Reims 12 Hours looked like it would be a humdinger.

Bitter disillusion

Grand Prix de l'ACF, 28th June

When Surtees and Bandini failed to appear for the first practice session at Rouen-Les Essarts, it almost seemed to be a sign that preparations for Le Mans and faltering performances in Formula 1 had sapped both body and mind at Maranello. Meanwhile, Dan Gurney, on top form after his stunning performance at Spa and very much at ease at the wheel of his Brabham, liked the Rouen circuit's layout and gave Jim Clark a run for his money in the quest for fastest time, only conceding it right at the end of the session.

Next morning, however, the Ferraris were present, although with a few regrets. One was that the team's absence the previous day left it with insufficient time to evaluate the benefits of a relocated fuel filter, which was now placed outside the bodywork and fitted with cooling fins because it was thought that overly warm fuel could have been the reason for the injection problems that had been so troublesome at the previous races. Despite having missed a day of practice, Surtees did well to claim a place on the front row alongside Clark and Gurney, while Bandini shared the third row with Bruce McLaren (Cooper) and Graham Hill (BRM), held slightly back by a sluggish engine and his aversion to the fast downhill section leading to the *Nouveau Monde* hairpin.

▲ **Grand Prix de l'ACF.** Ferrari arrived at Rouen-Les Essarts hoping that it had found a remedy for the fuel-injection problems that had been plaguing the team. It was thought that the fuel filter had been getting too hot so it was now mounted in the air flow and given cooling fins.

▲ **Grand Prix de l'ACF.** After matching Dan Gurney's pace in the second practice session, Surtees might have regretted that he had not been able to take part in the first session because of the Ferrari team's late arrival. In the end he lined up third on the grid, alongside Gurney and pole-sitter Jim Clark.

On Sunday evening, the Maranello camp was in a state of complete despondency after a double setback. At the start, Clark and Gurney pulled away from Surtees, who was able to keep them in sight for only two laps before a sick-sounding engine sent him into the pits at the end of the third lap. An oil line to the fuel-injection pump was found to be leaking within the engine vee. Although it was repaired, he retired after another three laps with the ignition now playing up because escaped oil had seeped into the distributors. At least Bandini finished the race, but only in ninth place with his engine emitting strange noises.

With four of ten races run, Surtees had only six championship points while Bandini's scorecard read zero, so the Scuderia had a growing crisis that it had to resolve urgently or renounce any remaining title ambitions. By painful comparison, Clark was leading the title chase on 21 points, even though he had not finished this race, leaving Gurney to secure the second Grand Prix victory of his career. Graham Hill, who finished second at Rouen, was just one point behind Clark, Richie Ginther and Peter Arundell were joint third with 11 points each, and Gurney's tally was 10.

GRAND PRIX DE L'ACF

Rouen-Les Essarts, 28th June 1964, 57 laps (4.065 miles/6.542km), 231.706 miles/372.894km • Starters 17, finishers 12

RACE				PRACTICE	
1st	Dan Gurney	Brabham BT7 Climax V8	2h 7m 49.1s	2nd	2m 10.1s
2nd	Graham Hill	BRM P261 BRM V8	+24.1s	6th	2m 12.1s
3rd	Jack Brabham	Brabham BT7 Climax V8	+24.9s	5th	2m 11.8s
4th	Peter Arundell	Lotus 25 Climax V8	+1m 10.6s	4th	2m 11.6s
5th	Richie Ginther	BRM P261 BRM V8	+2m 12.1s	9th	2m 13.9s
6th	Bruce McLaren	Cooper T73 Climax V8	56 laps	7th	2m 12.4s
9th	**Lorenzo Bandini**	**Ferrari 158 V8**	**55 laps**	**8th**	**2m 12.8s**
DNF	**John Surtees**	**Ferrari 158 V8**	**6 laps (engine)**	**3rd**	**2m 11.1s**

Pole position: Jim Clark (Lotus 25 Climax V8), 2m 9.6s, 112.917mph/181.722kph **Fastest race lap:** Brabham, 2m 11.4s, 111.370mph/179.232kph **Winner's average speed:** 108.767mph/175.042kph **Drivers' championship:** 1st Clark 21, 2nd Hill 20, 3rd= Ginther & Arundell 11, 8th Surtees 6 **Constructors' championship:** 1st Lotus-Climax 25, 2nd BRM 21, 3rd Brabham-Climax 14, 5th Ferrari 6

Grand Prix de l'ACF. Despite how it looked at the 'off', this race was not done and dusted. After leading for just over half the distance, Jim Clark was denied victory when his Lotus's Climax engine suffered a piston breakage, thought to have been brought about by a stone ingested into the cylinder. Dan Gurney, whose Brabham is seen nosing ahead of Surtees's Ferrari to take up second place, went on to win. Meanwhile, *Il Grande John* headed for the pits after only three laps and was out of the race after six.

Grand Prix de l'ACF. Seen at the cobbled *Nouveau Monde* hairpin, Lorenzo Bandini had a long battle with Innes Ireland's BRP and Bruce McLaren's Cooper before his engine began to lose power. He finished ninth, two laps behind victorious Dan Gurney.

'Breathless'

Reims 12 Hours, 5th July

The Reims 12 Hours was back on the calendar after a break since 1958 and now counted for a world championship for the first time as a round of the International Championship for GT Manufacturers in Division III. In the points reckonings, the race was strangely watered down in importance by being assigned a coefficient of only 1.0, the figure normally attributed to a hillclimb, even though there were shorter races on the calendar with values of 1.3 and 1.6, but the event nonetheless had an impact.

Following Le Mans, the Reims race was an extension of the Ford/Ferrari duel with the difference that Maranello left its customers to represent the company. It was a finely balanced contest in which the 250 LMs of Graham Hill/Jo Bonnier (Maranello Concessionaires), John Surtees/Lorenzo Bandini (NART) and Gérald Langlois van Ophem/'Beurlys' (Ecurie Francorchamps) took on the works Fords of Phil Hill/Bruce McLaren, Richie Ginther/Masten Gregory and Richard Attwood/Jo Schlesser. In the GT ranks, the GTO 64s driven by Michael Parkes/Ludovico Scarfiotti, Pedro Rodríguez/Nino Vaccarella, Bob Grossman/Skip Hudson and Lucien Bianchi/

Pierre Dumay went head-to-head with the Cobra Daytona Coupes of Dan Gurney/Bob Bondurant and Innes Ireland/Jochen Neerpasch. And while the GTOs of David Piper/Tony Maggs and Chris Amon/Jackie Stewart tipped the balance in favour of the Italians, Dearborn's hopes of victory were raised because its prototypes had shown at Le Mans that they should be capable of holding their own in a race of half the distance.

Right from the midnight start, Ford believed that its ambitions would be fulfilled. Ginther came round in first place at the end of lap one and traded punches with the 250 LMs of Surtees and Hill during the first hour. Behind came McLaren and Attwood in their Fords, happy to let Ginther make the running. Although Parkes was sixth, already a lap in arrears, he was encouraged by the longish stops of Amon and Rodríguez, and above all by that of Gurney, who was immobilised by a broken fan belt for 10 minutes when leading the GT category. Then the clamour of the large contingent of American soldiers in the grandstands suddenly faded. What happened next shut them up as problems in the Ford camp suddenly accumulated. Gurney's Cobra returned to its pit at 1.08am. Fifteen minutes later Ginther, also let down by his gearbox, parked at *Thillois* and took off his helmet, his retirement officially confirmed at 1.25am.

When the time came for the first round of refuelling stops,

◀ **Reims 12 Hours.** Uniquely, this race started at midnight, so those spectators filling the main grandstand were a hardy and committed lot, keen to see another skirmish in the Ford/Ferrari battle. Twelve hours later at midday, all those present felt they had just watched a Grand Prix rather than an endurance race.

▶ **Reims 12 Hours.** By this stage of the race, with early-morning sun casting long shadows, the GT40s had fallen by the wayside and the Surtees/ Bandini 250 LM held a narrow lead over this Maranello Concessionaires version in the hands of Graham Hill/Jo Bonnier. Standing on the pit counter, Hill waits to get into the car while the team's proprietor, urbane Colonel Ronnie Hoare, can be seen behind it in his overcoat, suit and tie.

those for the 250 LMs of Bandini and Graham Hill were as short as possible, while that of the Phil Hill/McLaren Ford seemed to go on forever and it slipped back from fourth place to 24th. Its retirement was announced over the public address at 2am but that was a mistake. At the same time as the pit balconies crackled with applause to welcome the arrival of Ginther, who had walked back from *Thillois*, Phil Hill set off to try to reduce a deficit that had reached 10 laps.

Three hours. Phil Hill was 17th. Graham Hill led with Bandini struggling to stay in touch. The Attwood/Schlesser Ford was third, on the same lap as the leading pair. The Ireland/Neerpasch Cobra lay fourth, a heartening sign for Dearborn that all hope of GT victory was not yet lost, while the Parkes/Scarfiotti GTO 64 was fifth. Shortly after 4am, however, Attwood/Schlesser pitted for two 16-minute stops before falling back to 20th place and retiring with gearbox failure.

A veil of silence descended upon the American contingent — and nothing developed to boost their morale. Insidiously, then more obviously, the surviving Ford that had set a new lap record at a speed of 131.24mph was running out of steam. In four laps its average speed fell from 130.48mph to 125.51mph. After briefly running in tandem with the Ireland/Neerpasch Cobra, it conceded 200 metres in a single lap. At 4.45am its retirement with a broken gearbox was confirmed. The only consolation

remaining for Ford and Shelby was that the Ireland/Neerpasch Daytona Coupe now ran third, two laps in front of the Parkes/ Scarfiotti GTO 64, which was having trouble with its carburettors icing up due to the chill of early morning. Immediately behind came the Piper/Maggs GTO ahead of four Porsche 904 GTSs while in the depths of the classification Bianchi/Dumay, Rodríguez/Vaccarella, Amon/Stewart and Grossman/Hudson were squabbling among themselves, and the Langlois van Ophem/'Beurlys' 250 LM was about to retire.

The Shelby team's hopes were soon dashed. Shortly after 5am, the remaining Daytona Coupe came into the pits and Ireland, who had been seen gesticulating when passing on the previous lap, tumbled out of a cockpit filled with smoke. Flames were beginning to lick the floor as the exhaust manifold on one bank of cylinders was coming apart. The 40 minutes required to fit a replacement manifold borrowed from the abandoned Gurney/ Bondurant car turned out to be merely a pointless prelude to retirement just seven laps later with a cracked gearbox casing.

Just before 6am, after Bandini and Hill had indulged in a particularly cut-and-thrust battle, setting lap record after lap record, Surtees went faster than both of them and took command. As the first rays of sunshine began to dissipate the morning cold, these leading Ferraris continued to trade blows in a battle that only fluctuated when they stopped to refuel. At 7am, Hill/

▲ **Reims 12 Hours.** Leaving the 250 LMs to duke it out at the front, Michael Parkes/Ludovico Scarfiotti added to the joy at the Maranello Concessionaires team by finishing third overall and first in the GT class in their GTO 64. Their biggest problem had been carburettor icing during the coldest part of the night, a trait that their mechanics had tried to address by distorting the air intake on the bonnet in a vain attempt to make it admit less air.

▼ **Reims 12 Hours.** While the Champagne region bathes in bright morning sunlight, Surtees, delayed by an unexpected change of brake pads, hunts down the Hill/Bonnier 250 LM, which is less than 90 seconds in front with just over an hour of the race to go. His efforts proved to be in vain when a left-front tyre blow-out under braking for *Thillois* intervened, but he still managed to get his car back to the pits for a fresh wheel and resume without losing second place.

Bonnier were in front of Surtees/Bandini, but they swapped places just before 8am when the next driver changes intervened. Behind, Parkes/Scarfiotti took advantage of the brake issues that affected the Piper/Maggs GTO and consolidated their claim to the bottom step of the podium.

By 10am, Hill/Bonnier had eked out a 39-second lead. Twenty minutes later, Hill wanted to leave his co-driver a little breathing space before handing over so he banged in a new lap record at a speed of 133.408mph. When the Swede rejoined, the gap to Surtees in the lead was 32 seconds. Suddenly Lady Luck made her choice. For five consecutive laps, 'Big John' waved his arms each time he passed the pits but nobody could understand why until, at 10.40am, he finally came in. He had virtually no brakes because the team had failed to check and replace the pads at the previous pitstop. Once this error had been rectified, Surtees rejoined but he was now 1m 44s behind the Maranello Concessionaires Ferrari. He stepped on it and by the time the 11th hour struck, with one hour remaining, he had closed the gap to 1m 26s — the fight was on.

Ten minutes later all bets were off. Such were the relative track positions of the two dominant Ferraris that when Bonnier passed the grandstands on a given lap, Surtees could be seen in the far distance speeding along the road towards Soissons. If all was well, he would then roar over the start/finish line about three quarters of a minute before Bonnier's reappearance. This time, however, Surtees was nowhere in sight. Finally he appeared, limping down the pitlane with the front of the 250 LM dragging along the tarmac. The left-front tyre, which his

REIMS 12 HOURS

Reims-Gueux, 5th July 1964, 296 laps (5.158 miles/8.301km), 1,521.696 miles/2,448.933km • Starters 37, classified finishers 20

1st	Graham Hill/Jo Bonnier	Ferrari 250 LM (5907)	296 laps
2nd	John Surtees/Lorenzo Bandini	Ferrari 250 LM (5909)	295 laps
3rd	Michael Parkes/Ludovico Scarfiotti	Ferrari 250 GTO 64 (4399 GT) *(1st Div III)*	279 laps
4th	David Piper/Tony Maggs	Ferrari 250 GTO (4491 GT)	273 laps
5th	Andrea Vianini/Nasif Estéfano	Porsche 904 GTS	273 laps
6th	Gerhard Koch/Gerhard Mitter	Porsche 904 GTS	271 laps
9th	Lucien Bianchi/Pierre Dumay	Ferrari 250 GTO 64 (5575 GT)	269 laps
16th	Pedro Rodríguez/Nino Vaccarella	Ferrari 250 GTO 64 (5571 GT)	264 laps
DNF	Chris Amon/Jackie Stewart	Ferrari 250 GTO (3445 GT)	248 laps
DNF	Gérald Langlois van Ophem/'Beurlys' (Jean Blaton)	Ferrari 250 LM (5843)	–
DNF	Bob Grossman/Skip Hudson	Ferrari 250 GTO 64 (5573 GT)	–

Fastest practice lap: Surtees, 2m 19.2s, 133.397mph/214.681kph **Fastest race lap:** Hill, 2m 19.2s, 133.397mph/214.681kph **Winner's average speed:** 126.808mph/204.077kph **FIA World Sports Car Championship (GT Division III, over 2,000cc):**[1] 1st Ferrari 78.0, 2nd Shelby 48.8

[1] *Scoring system for the top six places in this event was 9–6–4–3–2–1 (coefficient 1.0); only the manufacturer's highest-placed car scored points*

crew had not replaced at the previous pitstop, exploded under braking for *Thillois*. A fresh wheel was quickly fitted and the former motorcycle world champion rejoined, but now, despite another brilliant display, he had no hope of victory unless the Maranello Concessionaires car stumbled. When the chequered flag fell, his only satisfaction was that he had at least got himself back on the same lap as Colonel Ronnie Hoare's car.

In the GT category, the Parkes/Scarfiotti GTO 64's winning run to third place overall allowed Ferrari to pull away in the points standings after the Shelby team failed to add to its tally. Of course, it was far from over for Shelby and Ford, but as the International Championship for GT Manufacturers was now moving into the second half of the season, they no longer had room for error and would have to earn points wherever possible.

Hope springs eternal

British Grand Prix, 11th July

Six days later, Brands Hatch hosted its inaugural British Grand Prix, which was also awarded the honorary title of European Grand Prix. During the first day of practice on Thursday, Maranello proved that it was still trying to catch up as Surtees and Bandini shared a 156 while awaiting the arrival of the 158 reserved for the English driver. This did not prevent him equalling Graham Hill's fastest time before Dan Gurney got round in 1m 38.4s to win the 100 bottles of champagne awarded

to the day's quickest driver. The next day, however, the battle for pole position made the previous day's activities look like a vicarage tea party. After frenetic efforts, Clark's Lotus (1m 38.1s), Hill's BRM (1m 38.3s) and Gurney's Brabham occupied the front row, but it certainly looked like Ferrari had made worthwhile progress because Surtees (1m 38.7s) came close to those times in the 158 to share the second row with Jack Brabham (1m 38.5s).

Post-race, the Scuderia was torn between disappointment and hope. Clark had scored a typical flag-to-flag victory with Hill close behind, while Surtees had established his place on the podium from only the third lap and finished the race as the only other man on the same lap as the leaders. Even more encouraging was that Surtees's fastest lap (1m 39.6s) was only eight tenths slower than the Scot's best and that Bandini, who had traded blows with Brabham, finished a well-deserved fifth. Hope is often fed by weakness in an opponent and it was clear that Clark, at the wheel of a Lotus 25B modified to the extent that it was a 33 in all but name, could never pull away from Hill apart from a brief moment mid-race when the BRM slowed because of fluctuating oil pressure. Proof of the intensity of the battle between the two drivers was that Clark set the lap record on lap 73 and was just 2.8 seconds in front of Hill at the chequered flag.

Could Surtees win the World Championship with only five Grands Prix to go? Barring a miracle, the answer was surely 'no'. He was 20 points behind Clark and 16 behind Hill. And, just a week after Brands Hatch, on 19th July, Clark again proved that he was a cut above his rivals by winning the Solitude Grand

◄ **British Grand Prix.** While Mauro Forghieri is locked in conversation during Friday's practice with John Surtees and two mechanics, Lorenzo Bandini calls on his skills as a former mechanic to help with adjustments (seemingly to the anti-roll bar) on the old 156 that he will drive in the race. That choice of car was apparently down to Eugenio Dragoni and definitely left him at a disadvantage.

▼ **British Grand Prix.** Not for the first time, Jim Clark immediately took the lead and stayed there for the entire 80 laps. Dan Gurney (right) challenged him briefly for two laps before Graham Hill emerged as the only driver capable of keeping the Scot in sight. In the far distance, Chris Amon has stalled his Lotus and caused Jo Siffert (Brabham) to collect Frank Gardner (Brabham), whose race ended there and then with a wheel torn off his car.

◄ **British Grand Prix.** John Surtees was fourth first time round at Brands Hatch and then third behind Graham Hill and the uncatchable Jim Clark for the rest of the race. Here the Ferrari driver holds off Jack Brabham (Brabham) and Bruce McLaren (Cooper).

▼ **British Grand Prix.** Lap 66 and Jack Brabham has just passed Lorenzo Bandini's 156, leaving him scrapping over fifth place with Bob Anderson's privately entered Brabham, powered by a two-year-old Climax V8. Bandini remained fifth at the chequered flag.

Prix, even if he was helped by a collision and several 'offs' on the first lap that changed the face of the race by eliminating most of the front-runners, including Lorenzo Bandini, Jack Brabham, Graham Hill and Innes Ireland among others. Surtees established a 20-second lead in pouring rain but Clark pulled that back on a drying track and overtook to claim victory by just over 10 seconds. While it was difficult to believe that the Scot owed his superiority to his Lotus 33, it was equally doubtful that Surtees had been able to fend him off due to the merits of the 158 alone. Later, Mauro Forghieri would state that he now considered these drivers to be equal in terms of speed. At the time, few would have agreed with him.

BRITISH GRAND PRIX

Brands Hatch, 11th July 1964, 80 laps (2.650 miles/4.265km), 212.000 miles/341.200km • Starters 23, finishers 14

RACE					PRACTICE	
1st	Jim Clark	Lotus 25 Climax V8	2h 15m 07.0s		1st	1m 38.1s
2nd	Graham Hill	BRM P261 BRM V8	+2.8s		2nd	1m 38.3s
3rd	**John Surtees**	**Ferrari 158 V8**	**+1m 20.6s**		**5th**	**1m 38.7s**
4th	Jack Brabham	Brabham BT7 Climax V8	79 laps		4th	1m 38.5s
5th	**Lorenzo Bandini**	**Ferrari 156 V6 Aero**	**78 laps**		**8th**	**1m 40.2s**
6th	Phil Hill	Cooper T73 Climax V8	78 laps		15th	1m 42.6s

Pole position: Clark, 1m 38.1s, 97.253mph/156.514kph **Fastest race lap:** Clark, 1m 38.8s, 96.560mph/155.398kph **Winner's average speed:** 94.140mph/151.504kph **Drivers' championship:** 1st Clark 30, 2nd Hill 26, 3rd= Brabham, Ginther & Arundell 11, 6th Surtees 10, 9th Bandini 2 **Constructors' championship:** 1st Lotus-Climax 34, 2nd BRM 27, 3rd Brabham-Climax 17, 5th Ferrari 10

The 'Ring cycle

German Grand Prix, 2nd August

Neither Clark nor Surtees was the star of the first practice session for the 26th German Grand Prix because Honda arrived and stole the limelight. The Japanese car was certainly a most impressive machine and captivated everyone. Its 60-degree V12 engine, which delivered a claimed 230bhp at 12,000rpm, not only had four overhead camshafts and four valves per cylinder but was also mounted transversely. The driver, Ronnie Bucknum, was also a newcomer to Formula 1 and found it hard going, ending up the last qualifier, nearly a minute adrift of the pole-

▼ **German Grand Prix.** Lorenzo Bandini has just made a blinder of a start from the far side of the front row and rocketed out of frame. Next up are Dan Gurney's Brabham (#5), Jim Clark's Lotus (#1) and John Surtees's Ferrari (#7), the latter once again caught napping. Forming a tidy four-car row behind them are Richie Ginther's BRM (#4), Bruce McLaren's Cooper (#9), Jack Brabham's eponymous car (#6) and Graham Hill's BRM (#3). Tucked behind, we can make out Jo Siffert's Brabham, its driver's trademark helmet with Swiss flag clearly visible, with Chris Amon's Lotus (#14) alongside and Maurice Trintignant's BRM (#22) behind.

position time. Although the Honda retired from the race after an accident on lap 11 before the *Karussell*, it was officially classified 13th. There was better to come.

On Friday morning, while Clark swapped between his Solitude-winning Lotus 33 and a brand-new car as well as the 25B, Graham Hill (8m 44.4s) topped the timesheets without shrugging off Surtees (8m 45.2s), who set this time in a 158 with a fresh engine as the second 158 at his disposal had a somewhat tired V8. Bandini posted an encouraging 8m 47.8s with a 156 and then did better still in the afternoon session when he emerged quickest of all at 8m 42.6s. The next day Surtees came out on top with a lap of 8m 39.2s in the morning and drove home his advantage with an 8m 38.4s in the afternoon to secure pole, while Bandini's previous day's time was good enough for fourth place in the line-up. Without going into ecstasy, the Scuderia was rather pleased to see red cars sandwiching Clark's Lotus and Gurney's Brabham on the four-car front row.

When the race started at 2pm, it was quite a surprise to see Bandini hit the front after getting the jump on Surtees, who had one of his typically tardy getaways. Clark closed in on the Italian in the *Südkehre* and slipped in front as the cars screamed down the straight behind the pits. He led first time round, but without pulling away from Surtees and Gurney, who had Graham Hill (BRM) hot on their heels. Now Bandini was back in seventh

place, trailing Jack Brabham and — surprise — Phil Hill's works Cooper, which had started on the third row but was destined to last only one more lap before engine failure intervened. As in 1963, when Surtees had claimed that all-important first victory, he overtook Clark for the lead on the second lap but what followed made this race a rather different one.

Around the third lap, Clark encountered problems with the Lotus's gear-selector mechanism, finding it taking him straight from second gear to fifth, so he had to give way to Gurney. The American was intent on snatching the lead and when Surtees tackled the *Nordkehre* shortly after the start of the fourth lap the American was level with him. Gurney continued to push and

used a slight off-line moment by Surtees in the following wooded section to grab the lead. Next time round the Englishman fought back on the straight by pulling out of the Brabham's slipstream to put his Ferrari in front again. At that stage, Graham Hill was quite a close third with Clark, Brabham and Bandini following, but over the next few laps the leading pair began to open up a gap as Hill's BRM engine became sluggish and Clark continued to struggle, the Scot eventually going out after seven laps when an exhaust valve stuck open in his Climax engine.

The duel between the leaders was so intense on the sixth lap that they both set the same time of 8m 47.5s. None of the 310,000 spectators wanted to see any end to this spellbinding battle for the lead but it began to wane in intensity. Gurney's gauges warned him that both water temperature and pressure were rising and he was forced to back off a little. Surtees twisted the knife by setting the fastest lap so far in 8m 45.1s and lowered that to 8m 43.0s eighth time round. By the end of the ninth lap, Surtees had increased his lead to 16 seconds, but Gurney had not yet thrown in the towel and on lap 10 set the fastest lap so far at 8m 42.9s before bringing his Brabham into the pits for water replenishment. Meanwhile, fourth-placed Jack Brabham, unable to catch Graham Hill, had eased off to conserve his car, allowing Bandini to close up. In a rare moment of misjudgement, 'Black Jack' thought the red car behind him was the race leader, so

▲ **German Grand Prix.** Lorenzo Bandini put on a great show in practice, his old 156 seemingly no handicap at the Nürburgring. Come the race, he was seventh first time round, sixth for a long spell, fourth at the two-thirds mark and third by the end, behind Graham Hill.

➤ **German Grand Prix.** After leading most of the way, Surtees scored his second successive Formula 1 victory at the Nürburgring. The Ferrari driver's toughest rival, Dan Gurney, fell back after his Brabham's water temperature went sky high.

GERMAN GRAND PRIX

Nürburgring, 2nd August 1964, 15 laps (14.173 miles/22.810km), 212.602 miles/342.150km • Starters 22, finishers 10

RACE				PRACTICE	
1st	John Surtees	Ferrari 158 V8	2h 12m 04.8s	1st	8m 38.4s
2nd	Graham Hill	BRM P261 BRM V8	+1m 15.6s	5th	8m 43.8s
3rd	Lorenzo Bandini	Ferrari 156 V6 Aero	+4m 52.8s	4th	8m 42.6s
4th	Jo Siffert	Brabham BT11 BRM V8	+5m 23.1s	10th	8m 56.9s
5th	Maurice Trintignant	BRM P57 BRM V8	14 laps (battery)	14th	9m 06.8s
6th	Tony Maggs	BRM P57 BRM V8	14 laps	16th	9m 09.8s

Pole position: Surtees, 8m 38.4s, 98.427mph/158.403kph **Fastest race lap:** Surtees, 8m 39.0s, 98.302mph/158.200kph **Winner's average speed:** 96.561mph/155.400kph **Drivers' championship:** 1st Hill 32, 2nd Clark 30, 3rd Surtees 19, 9th Bandini 6 **Constructors' championship:** 1st Lotus-Climax 34, 2nd BRM 33, 3rd Ferrari 19

he moved over and waved it by, only to realise his blunder. Bandini stayed ahead for two laps before Brabham reclaimed the surrendered place, only to grind to a halt at the *Karussell* with a broken crown wheel and pinion.

The insatiable Surtees lowered the lap record again on lap 11, leaving it at 8m 39.0s, and went on to score a first victory of the season, with Bandini third behind Graham Hill. With four races to go, the title chase was back on with a vengeance, Surtees now on 19 points against Hill's 32 points and Clark's 30.

▾ **German Grand Prix.** Surtees can relax at last: to the delight of his team, he has just secured his first victory of the season and thrown open the championship chase. One of the bystanders is Raymond Mays (the tall man on the right wearing a suit), who had been the driving force behind the creation of BRM.

Ideal timing

Austrian Grand Prix, 23rd August

On Friday 21st August, most of the drivers had their first taste of the Zeltweg circuit laid out on a military airport that had remained in use right up to the day before the first practice session. The place was a real shock. Laid out on a typical aerodrome surface of concrete slabs, the 1.9-mile track comprised just three curves and a hairpin linked by two parallel straights bordered with straw bales. It looked like an ice hockey stick. Because the lap was so short, there would be 105 of them, making it a bit like Monaco in that single respect, if no others. A London bus brought in the previous day served as a timekeeping box.

Graham Hill soon made himself at home in his BRM. He was quickest in the first session at just over 1m 10s before going on to secure pole the next day with a time of 1m 9.84s. Joining him on the front row were Surtees (1m 10.12s), who had his usual pair of 158s, Clark (1m 10.21s) and Gurney (1m 10.40s). Bandini, although satisfied with his 156, was slower at 1m 10.63s and lined up on the second row with Brabham and Ginther, who was rumoured to be on his way from BRM to Honda for the 1965 season.

On race morning, torrential rain hit the Steyr valley in which the village of Zeltweg nestled, but it cleared and gave way to a sunny afternoon. As the start time approached, Ferrari discovered that one of the injectors in the engine of the 158 that Surtees had chosen for the race needed to be changed, but when that was done the V8 still refused to fire up and the Ferrari had to be pushed to the dummy grid, where it finally sprung into life. When the flag fell, Gurney and Surtees roared away in front while Bandini took advantage of the fact that both Clark and

> **Austrian Grand Prix.** Lorenzo Bandini took the lead just before the halfway mark after the favourites had all fallen by the wayside and went on to claim his first Formula 1 World Championship victory. Here, in the foreground, Phil Hill keeps well out of the way in his Cooper.

Hill made really sluggish starts to grab third. Any threat that Brabham might have posed to the Italian was soon neutralised as his car was plagued with fuel-feed problems and he pitted at the end of the lap for an extended stop. The Scuderia had another stroke of good fortune when Surtees took the lead on the second lap by exploiting a momentary lift by Gurney, who, like many others, was concerned about the solidity of his Brabham's suspension on the rough track, having experienced a collapse during practice when a front upright broke. On the fifth lap, Hill had his engine cut out on the back straight and coasted round to the pits, where the BRM mechanics found that the distributor drive had sheared. The championship leader's demise brought optimism at the Scuderia but it was short-lived.

When Surtees braked for the hairpin leading on to the main straight on the eighth lap, his Ferrari wallowed like an overloaded galleon in a storm and its right-rear corner fell to the ground, sending up dust and sparks — a 'unibal' bearing on the lower wishbone had broken. Leaving his stranded car, he ran the short distance to his pit and returned with a jack, tools and a replacement wishbone to carry out repairs as best he could. After almost an hour, he climbed in, fired up the engine and delivered his battle-scarred Ferrari to base and officially retired. In the meantime, while Gurney now led from Bandini, Clark's tardy start had left him 13th but he had been fighting his way back up the order and was now homing in on the surviving Ferrari, passing it on the ninth lap.

For the next 30 laps or so the race turned into a procession with Gurney some 10 seconds ahead of Clark, followed by Bandini, Bruce McLaren (Cooper) and Ginther. Suddenly, the contest burst into life when Clark free-wheeled into his pit at the end of lap 40 to retire, the Lotus's left-hand driveshaft broken. Three laps later, McLaren pulled out with a damaged engine,

AUSTRIAN GRAND PRIX

Zeltweg, 23rd August 1964, 105 laps (1.988 miles/3.200km), 208.781 miles/336.000km • Starters 20, finishers 9

RACE				PRACTICE	
1st	Lorenzo Bandini	Ferrari 156 V6 Aero	2h 06m 18.23s	7th	1m 10.63s
2nd	Richie Ginther	BRM P261 BRM V8	+6.18s	5th	1m 10.40s
3rd	Bob Anderson	Brabham BT11 Climax V8	102 laps	14th	1m 12.04s
4th	Tony Maggs	BRM P57 BRM V8	102 laps	19th	1m 12.40s
5th	Innes Ireland	BRP Mk2 BRM V8	102 laps	11th	1m 11.60s
6th	Jo Bonnier	Brabham BT7 Climax V8	101 laps	10th	1m 11.59s
DNF	John Surtees	Ferrari 158 V8	9 laps (suspension)	2nd	1m 10.12s

Pole position: Graham Hill (BRM P261 BRM V8), 1m 09.84s, 102.553mph/165.043kph **Fastest race lap:** Dan Gurney (Brabham BT7 Climax V8), 1m 10.56s, 101.571mph/163.462kph **Winner's average speed:** 99.202mph/159.650kph **Drivers' championship:** 1st Hill 32, 2nd Clark 30, 3rd Surtees 19, 5th Bandini 15 **Constructors' championship:** 1st BRM 36, 2nd Lotus-Climax 34, 3rd Ferrari 28

some valve springs having broken shortly after a stop for a plug change. Another three laps later, Gurney came in to have his Brabham's front suspension examined, rejoined and covered one more lap before stopping for good because a radius arm had pulled away from its chassis mounting.

This left Bandini in the lead at half distance, 16 seconds ahead of Ginther and 26 in front of Jo Bonnier in his Rob Walker-entered Brabham. With the awful track surface inflicting so much damage on suspensions and chassis, Ferrari people held their breath every time the Italian passed the pits, but they need not have worried. Bandini crossed the finishing line to win a World Championship Grand Prix for the first time, by six seconds from Ginther. While it was obvious that the Italian had taken advantage of the retirements of so many front-runners, he had still had to hang in there to secure his victory, rather as Clark had done when taking his fortuitous win at Spa two months earlier. After this success by an Italian driver in an Italian car, the organisers of the next race, the Italian Grand Prix, must have been rubbing their hands with glee.

Before we leave Austria, we should note that a former Ferrari driver was also a casualty of car-breaking Zeltweg. The first practice session had come to a sudden halt when Phil Hill, after an error of judgement, had crashed his Cooper heavily into straw bales, breaking its front suspension. Come the race, his rear suspension collapsed on lap 59, leaving him powerless as the Cooper again ploughed into straw bales, this time through no fault of his own, and caught fire. He escaped safely but John Cooper gave him an angry reception back in the pits and a divorce that had been brewing for a long time finally came about. Hill only learned from the press that John Love would replace him for the next race, at Monza, although the Rhodesian never made it onto the grid after suffering a blown engine early in practice. While Hill did race for Cooper in the last two Grands Prix of the season, it was down to contractual obligations rather than any desire to do so.

Complicated calculations

Tourist Trophy, 29th August

Six days later, on 29th August, the 29th edition of the famous Tourist Trophy at Goodwood was as important to the destiny of Division III of the International Championship for GT Manufacturers as the Italian Grand Prix was about to be for Formula 1's title contenders. The Fribourg–Schauinsland Hillclimb on 9th August had seen GT victory go to Bob Bondurant's fourth-placed Shelby Cobra roadster from Ludovico Scarfiotti's GTO 64 in fifth place while Porsche, thanks to Edgar Barth, came out on top in the overall classification. As the German event's coefficient was 1.0, Ferrari came away on 84.0 points compared with 57.8 for Shelby. And knowing that the coefficient of the Goodwood race was 1.3, followed by values of 1.0 for the Sierre–Montana Hillclimb, 1.6 for the Tour de France, 1.3 for the Bridgehampton 500Km and 1.6 for Paris 1,000Km, anything was still possible.

Representing Ferrari at Goodwood, Graham Hill with the 330 P in which he had finished second at Le Mans and David Piper at the wheel of his 250 LM were in the prototype category, while the GT contenders were John Surtees and Innes Ireland in GTO 64s and Tony Maggs and Richie Ginther in 'regular' GTOs that were beginning to show their age. Shelby opposition comprised two works Daytona Coupes for Dan Gurney and Phil Hill as well as privately entered Cobras in the form of roadsters for Jack Sears and Roy Salvadori and the Willment team's home-grown coupé for Bob Olthoff. The 25 starters also included Jim Clark (Lotus 30) and Bruce McLaren (Cooper-Oldsmobile) in the sports category.

Unfortunately, the expected duels soon fizzled out with McLaren's retirement on lap 18 through clutch failure and Clark's on lap 113, just 17 laps from the end, with engine, steering and suspension troubles just when he looked to have the race sewn up. This handed victory to Graham Hill with Piper second, a lap behind. It was almost the same story in the GT 'race within a race' in which the GTO 64s dug their own grave, the worst moment being Surtees's 'off'. In trying to avoid a spinning Ireland, he clipped the verge and then harpooned Tony Lanfranchi's Elva-BMW, putting himself in hospital for a few days. By the time Ireland had made up for his blunder and its consequences, Salvadori, Gurney and Sears had pulled away, leaving Ginther and Maggs to rue their powerlessness or their errors. In the end, after taking advantage of a quick pitstop to snatch the class lead, Gurney fended off attacks from fellow Cobra drivers and assorted Ferrari men to finish behind Piper, but above all first of the GTs in front of Sears and Olthoff. Ireland finally came home sixth overall and only fourth in the class. So, with an additional 11.7 points for Shelby and only 3.9 for Ferrari, the outcome of the championship was more uncertain than ever.

The suspense intensified a little in Switzerland the very next day. Scarfiotti won the Sierre–Montana Hillclimb in a 250 LM and Bondurant in his Cobra took first place in GT Division III and the nine points that went with it. As Swiss privateer Pierre

FRIBOURG–SCHAUINSLAND HILLCLIMB

Germany, 9th August 1964, hillclimb (6.959 miles/11.200km), 13.919 miles/22.400km • Starters 46, classified finishers 43

1st	Edgar Barth	Porsche 718 RS Spyder	13m 49.58s
4th	Bob Bondurant	Shelby Cobra *(1st Div III)*	14m 02.75s
5th	Ludovico Scarfiotti	Ferrari 250 GTO 64 (5573 GT) *(2nd Div III)*	14m 05.79s
29th	Charly Müller	Ferrari 250 GT Lusso	15m 51.15s

FIA World Sports Car Championship (GT Division III, over 2,000cc):[1] 1st Ferrari 84.0, 2nd Shelby 57.8

[1] *Scoring system for the top six places in this event was 9–6–4–3–2–1 (coefficient 1.0); only the manufacturer's highest-placed car scored points*

TOURIST TROPHY

Goodwood, 29th August 1964, 130 laps (2.400 miles/3.862km), 312.000 miles/502.115km • Starters 25, classified finishers 16

1st	Graham Hill	Ferrari 330 P (0818)	3h 12m 43.6s
2nd	David Piper	Ferrari 250 LM (5897)	129 laps
3rd	Dan Gurney	Shelby Cobra Daytona *(1st Div III)*	129 laps
4th	Jack Sears	Shelby Cobra	127 laps
5th	Bob Olthoff	Shelby Cobra Willment coupé	126 laps
6th	Innes Ireland	Ferrari 250 GTO 64 (4399 GT) *(4th Div III)*	125 laps
9th	Richie Ginther	Ferrari 250 GTO (3729 GT)	123 laps
10th	Tony Maggs	Ferrari 250 GTO (4491 GT)	123 laps
DNF	John Surtees	Ferrari 250 GTO 64 (5573 GT)	8 laps (accident)

Fastest practice lap: Bruce McLaren (Cooper-Oldsmobile), 1m 23.2s, 103.846mph/167.124kph **Fastest race lap:** McLaren, 1m 23.8s, 103.010mph/165.923kph **Winner's average speed:** 97.130mph/156.316kph **FIA World Sports Car Championship (GT Division III, over 2,000cc):**[1] 1st Ferrari 87.9, 2nd Shelby 69.5

[1] *Scoring system for the top six places in this event was 9–6–4–3–2–1 multiplied by coefficient 1.3; only the manufacturer's highest-placed car scored points*

➤ **Sierre–Montana Hillclimb.** Driving a Scuderia Filipinetti 250 LM, Ludovico Scarfiotti won this event, a round of both the European Hillclimb Championship and the International Championship for GT Manufacturers. Behind is Swiss driver Edgar Berney's ISO Grifo, which finished tenth.

SIERRE–MONTANA HILLCLIMB

Switzerland, 30th August 1964, two climbs (6.835 miles/11.000km), 13.670 miles/22.000km

1st	Ludovico Scarfiotti	Ferrari 250 LM (5899)	13m 26.0s
4th	Bob Bondurant	Shelby Cobra *(1st Div III)*	13m 54.0s
6th	Jo Schlesser	Shelby Cobra	13m 59.6s
8th	Jochen Neerpasch	Shelby Cobra	14m 04.0s
17th	Gotfrid Köchert	Ferrari 250 LM (5905)	14m 43.7s
19th	Pierre Sudan	Ferrari 250 GTO (3809 GT) *(4th Div III)*	15m 06.8s
28th	Walter Ringgenberg	Ferrari 250 GT	15m 43.2s
33rd	Charly Müller	Ferrari 250 GT Lusso	16m 00.3s
36th	Armand Boller	Ferrari 250 GTO (3527 GT)	16m 15.5s

Winner's average speed: 61.058mph/98.263kph **FIA World Sports Car Championship (GT Division III, over 2,000cc):**[1] 1st Ferrari 90.9, 2nd Shelby 78.3

[1] *Scoring system for the top six places in this event was 9–6–4–3–2–1 (coefficient 1.0); only the manufacturer's highest-placed car scored points*

Sudan's GTO finished behind the Cobras of Jo Schlesser and Jochen Neerpasch, Ferrari scored only three points, Shelby now had 78.5 compared with 90.9 for Maranello. With only three rounds left, a world title was still on the cards for Ford with the reservation that only the best six race results plus the best hillclimb placing would count towards the final standings.

▼ **Italian Grand Prix.** The flat-12 Ferrari's disastrous lap times on Friday meant that its scream did not echo through Monza's woodland for very long. Enzo Ferrari and John Surtees both championed the car but Mauro Forghieri was unenthusiastic. He thought that its extra 10bhp was not worth the increase in weight, bulk and fuel consumption compared with the eight-cylinder model, and he was to be proved right.

Force of belief

Italian Grand Prix, 6th September

Monza echoed to the anger of Enzo Ferrari, who went ballistic like never before when he learned that the CSI had refused to homologate the 250 LM. It was the correct decision because only 14 of the required 100 cars had been produced at the time of Ferrari's request for official approval, and ultimately only 32 were built in any case. To add to Mr Ferrari's ire and make the walls of Maranello shake still more, the CSI had showed itself to be rather more lenient with some of his rivals, Jaguar and Aston Martin in particular, even if homologation of the Cobra brooked no doubts because Shelby had manufactured the roadster version in the required numbers before even seeking official confirmation. This amounted to a very bitter pill for *Il Commendatore* to swallow in view of his well-known past propensity for bending governing bodies to his will.

Whether or not it had anything to do with the foregoing, the organisers of the Italian Grand Prix certainly managed to favour Maranello through their late decision to reduce the length of the race from 86 laps to 78, a convenient change because the distance originally scheduled — the longest on the calendar — would have obliged the Ferraris to stop for a fuel top-up. The Scuderia was present in force with 158s for John Surtees and Lorenzo Bandini and a 156 for Ludovico Scarfiotti. Although the team leader was still not fully recovered after his accident in the Tourist Trophy, he hammered home his credentials as a World Championship contender by posting a stunning lap of 1m 37.4s, which neither of the title favourites, Graham Hill (1m 38.7s) and Jim Clark (1m

Italian Grand Prix. The front row of the grid forms up with Graham Hill's BRM P261 nearest the camera, Dan Gurney's Brabham BT7 in the centre and John Surtees's Ferrari 158 at the far side. Hill's clutch let him down and left him stranded on the grid, putting a severe dent in his title chances.

Italian Grand Prix. Surtees and Gurney swapped the lead numerous times in an awesome duel that lasted most of the race, until the American began to slip back with low fuel pressure and eventually had to make a pitstop. That left Surtees to take an authoritative victory.

39.1s), were able to match, while Dan Gurney (1m 38.2s) was second quickest for Brabham. Bandini (1m 39.8s), the *tifosi*'s new hero, was the last of seven drivers to break the 1m 40s barrier but Scarfiotti (1m 41.6s) was some way back in 16th spot. The next day, Surtees had every reason to be satisfied as the second session was run mostly in pouring rain so his previous day's time remained good enough for pole position. Another point of interest was that Bandini gave the flat-12 car (variously called the 512 F1 or 1512)

a first public run for a few laps on an almost dry track but no times were announced; the exercise was described by the team as 'promising' but for the moment the car had no immediate future.

After a couple of Coppa Inter-Europa races, there was a surprise at the start of the main event of the day when Hill's BRM remained motionless on the grid with clutch failure, so Gurney, Surtees, McLaren and Clark raced off into the distance without him and left his prospects of a second World Championship title

ITALIAN GRAND PRIX

Monza, 6th September 1964, 78 laps (3.573 miles/5.750km), 278.685 miles/448.500km • Starters 20, finishers 13

RACE				PRACTICE	
1st	John Surtees	Ferrari 158 V8	2h 10m 51.8s	1st	1m 37.40s
2nd	Bruce McLaren	Cooper T73 Climax V8	+1.06s	5th	1m 39.40s
3rd	Lorenzo Bandini	Ferrari 158 V8	77 laps	7th	1m 39.80s
4th	Richie Ginther	BRM P261 BRM V8	77 laps	9th	1m 40.40s
5th	Innes Ireland	BRP Mk2 BRM V8	77 laps	13th	1m 41.00s
6th	Mike Spence	Lotus 33 Climax V8	77 laps	8th	1m 40.30s
9th	Ludovico Scarfiotti	Ferrari 156 V6 Aero	77 laps	16th	1m 41.60s

Pole position: Surtees, 1m 37.40s, 132.058mph/212.526kph **Fastest race lap:** Surtees, 1m 38.80s, 130.186mph/209.514kph **Winner's average speed:** 127.775mph/205.634kph **Drivers' championship:** 1st Hill 32, 2nd Clark 30, 3rd Surtees 28, 5th Bandini 19 **Constructors' championship:** 1st Ferrari 37, 2nd BRM 36, 3rd Lotus-Climax 35

looking rather less hopeful. For the first third of the race, Surtees battled with Gurney and Clark, the three taking turns in front, while McLaren hung on for dear life. The Ferrari driver took up the running when Clark stopped at his pit, rejoined and then retired with a blown piston, dampening his hopes of a second world title. This left McLaren in a solitary third place.

Tough as it was at the front, with the lead continuing to flit between Surtees and Gurney, there was now a big slipstreaming battle of similar intensity for fourth place involving Bandini, Jack Brabham (Brabham), Richie Ginther (BRM), Innes Ireland (BRP), Jo Bonnier (Rob Walker Brabham), Giancarlo Baghetti (Centro-Sud BRM), Jo Siffert (his own Brabham), Mike Spence (Lotus) and Ronnie Bucknum (Honda). The last-named was the first to drop out, let down by his engine and brakes, with Bonnier the next to hit trouble, pitting on lap 51 for a battery change after his alternator failed. Brabham departed with a blown engine on lap 59, by which time Baghetti, Siffert and Spence had been outpaced. This was also about the time when Ireland, handicapped by poor handling, left Bandini and Ginther to get on with their fight at the head of what remained of the group.

Now Gurney's Brabham was also ailing. From lap 62, his engine began to stutter, causing him to lose the tow to Surtees, and on lap 68 he pulled into his pit with falling fuel pressure. Although he resumed and reached the finish, it was only as an also-ran.

Surtees in the lead! Had Bandini not been locked in battle with Ginther over third place, 70,000 *Tifosi* would have had eyes only for the Englishman's Ferrari. Instead, their attention was riveted to the Italian's car, whose every move was greeted with thunderous applause. The clamour intensified at the end of the final lap when Bandini, eyes on his mirrors, emerged from the *Parabolica* in front of Ginther. It mattered not a jot that the Italian,

seeing his rival try to squeeze past on the right, veered towards the pit wall to force him to jink to the left. At the finish line they were separated by just a tenth of a second. That they were a good third of a lap behind second-placed McLaren was of no importance. For the delirious spectators, screaming with joy as they poured onto the track, Bandini was the hero of the day, even though Surtees had just won the race for their beloved Ferrari.

But that did not bother *Il Grande John*. With 28 points against 30 for Clark and 32 for Hill, winning the world title was now a very real possibility, even if four races earlier that prospect had looked absurd. It was also encouraging that in the past three years the winner of the Italian Grand Prix had gone on to become the World Champion.

Experience pays off

Tour de France, 11th–20th September

On the day the Tour de France began, the talk was of whether it had lost some of its interest even before it had started. Rumours had led enthusiasts to believe that John Surtees, Michael Parkes and Ludovico Scarfiotti would be taking part and it was certainly a mouth-watering prospect to have the Scuderia's top drivers tackle a marathon of nearly 3,750 miles. Unfortunately, at the start of the first 130-mile leg in Lille, they were nowhere to be seen because Maranello, following the CSI's refusal to homologate the 250 LM, had left its customers with GTOs to defend its colours in this vital round of the International Championship for GT Manufacturers. So, there were no works drivers to take on three Daytona Coupes driven by Bob Bondurant/Jochen Neerpasch,

▲ **Tour de France.** At Reims just before the start of the race that rounded off the first leg from Lille, Maurice Trintignant prepares to board the Cobra Daytona Coupe he shared with Bernard de Saint-Aubin. Other drivers mingling on the grid include Annie Soisbault (red helmet), driver of the #170 Ferrari 250 GTO 64, and André Simon (far right), standing behind his #186 Daytona Coupe.

▼ **Tour de France.** At the Reims start, Jean Guichet prepares to return to *parc fermé* with his GTO, which has just suffered a sudden loss of power because of flooded spark plugs; he later discovered that this had been caused by incorrect valve timing. Once the plugs had been changed, Guichet was able to embark, three laps in arrears. Victory in the race fell to the Bob Bondurant/Jochen Neerpasch Cobra Daytona Coupe that sits on the far side of the front row while the Lucien Bianchi/ Georges Berger GTO in the middle went on to win the event overall.

▲ **Tour de France.** The front row of the grid at Rouen-Les Essarts comprises the Daytona Cobras of Bob Bondurant (#187) and Maurice Trintignant (#188) and the Ferrari GTO of Lucien Bianchi (#172); behind, Jean Guichet can be seen leaning on the roof of his GTO. Bondurant was halted by a detached throttle cable but the other drivers took the top three places, Trintignant first, Guichet second and Bianchi third.

▼ **Tour de France.** Immediately after the start of the race at Le Mans, the GTOs of Lucien Bianchi (#172) and Claude Dubois (#175) sandwich the Daytona Cobras of André Simon (#186), Maurice Trintignant (#188) and Jochen Neerpasch (#187) as they roar into the Dunlop curve. By the end of the next day, all three American cars were out.

Maurice Trintignant/Bernard de Saint-Auban and André Simon/Maurice Dupeyron. But chargers like Lucien Bianchi, Jean Guichet, Fernand Tavano and David Piper hardly fell short of the works aces in terms of talent and experience. Furthermore, one must not overlook the role played by their co-drivers, those overlooked figures whose fields of competence ranged from navigation to knowledge of the regulations and now were also obliged to take the wheel in two hillclimbs. The men with these duties in the aforementioned Ferraris were respectively Georges Berger, Michel de Bourbon-Parme, Marcel Martin and Jo Siffert.

Victory in the hour-and-a half race at Reims and the Bramont hillclimb that followed in darkness went to the same Cobra, with Neerpasch driving it at Reims and Bondurant at Bramont. At Rouen-Les Essarts, Trintignant came out on top with Bianchi's GTO second, while Bondurant had the setback of a broken throttle cable that stranded him at trackside until, with a bit of smart thinking, he reset the carburettors for an idle speed of 3,000rpm and completed the race like that, albeit way down in 16th place. Shelby's mechanics still needed to replace the throttle cable, however, and by the time the competitors reached Le Mans, the first race of the third leg, Trintignant led the overall classification from Bianchi, Tavano and Simon, with the Bondurant/Neerpasch Daytona seventh. Guichet, who had been delayed by plug problems before the start at Reims, was not even in the top ten.

Trintignant had to settle for third place at Le Mans after a puncture left him well behind the winner, Guichet, and second-placed Bianchi, but elsewhere in the Shelby camp things had taken a worse turn because Neerpasch's engine had broken its crankshaft during the race. Before long, the other two Daytona Coupes were also out. The left-front wheel bearing of Trintignant's car seized during the overnight run to the following day's one-hour race on the Cognac circuit, where Simon's car had a piston destroy itself. That was certainly a double whammy for Ford and its Shelby team, which had just learned that ambition and resources were not enough to compensate for lack of knowledge of regulations and the specific requirements of a particularly arduous event on which frequent improvisation was the norm.

The rest of the Tour de France became a straight fight between two GTOs, the Ecurie Francorchamps car of Bianchi/Berger that in the end clinched victory over the works entry of Guichet/de Bourbon-Parme. With that, Ferrari sealed Division III of the International Championship for GT Manufacturers. On the same day as the Tour de France reached its climax, the final round of the championship took place on the other side of the Atlantic. In the absence of any GTOs, Ken Miles's fourth place in the Bridgehampton 500Km in a Shelby-run Cobra gave him GT class honours.

▲ **Tour de France.** During the fourth leg between Pau and Aurillac, Lucien Bianchi (left) and Jean Guichet (right) have a quick chat before the Albi race. By this stage in the Tour de France, these two were vying for overall victory. In this race, Bianchi led comfortably until shock-absorber problems intervened, leaving Guichet to cruise to victory.

▼ **Tour de France.** Leaving Albi behind, the Ecurie Francorchamps GTO of Lucien Bianchi/Georges Berger heads for Aurillac along the N603 proudly wearing the yellow ribbon that denoted the event leader.

TOUR DE FRANCE

France, 11th–20th September 1964, six stages, total distance 3,734.441 miles/6,010.0km • Starters 117, classified finishers 36

1st	Lucien Bianchi/Georges Berger	Ferrari 250 GTO (4153 GT) *(1st Div III)*	1,368.292 miles/2,202.053km
2nd	Jean Guichet/Michel de Bourbon-Parme	Ferrari 250 GTO (5111 GT)	1,354.686 miles/2,180.155km
8th	Claude Dubois/Philippe de Montaigu	Ferrari 250 GTO (3607 GT)	1,198.672 miles/1,929.075km
9th	Annie Soisbault/Nicole Roure	Ferrari 250 GTO 64 (5575 GT)	1,188.201 miles/1,912.224km
DSQ	David Piper/Jo Siffert	Ferrari 250 GTO 64 (4399 GT)	Illegal refuelling
DNF	Sylvain Garant/Jacques Lanners	Ferrari 250 GTO (3769 GT)	Accident
DNF	Fernand Tavano/Marcel Martin	Ferrari 250 GTO (5095 GT)	Piston failure

FIA World Sports Car Championship (GT Division III, over 2,000cc):[1] 1st Ferrari 105.3, 2nd Shelby 78.3

[1] *Scoring system for the top six places in this event was 9–6–4–3–2–1 multiplied by coefficient 1.3; only the manufacturer's highest-placed car scored points*

BRIDGEHAMPTON 500KM

Bridgehampton, 20th September 1964, 110 laps (2.860 miles/4.603km), 314.619 miles/506.330km • Starters 28, classified finishers 16

1st	Walt Hansgen	Scarab MkIV	3h 20m 54.1s
2nd	Pedro Rodríguez	Ferrari 275 P (0812)	110 laps
3rd	Bob Grossman	Ferrari 250 LM (5909)	108 laps
4th	Ken Miles	Shelby Cobra	107 laps
5th	John 'Buck' Fulp	Ferrari 330 P (0810)	107 laps
6th	Ronnie Bucknum	Shelby Cobra	107 laps
13th	Stephen A. McClellan Jr/Tom Pietre	Ferrari 196 SP (0804)	98 laps
DNF	Ludovico Scarfiotti	Ferrari 330 P (0824)	– (engine)
DNF	Augie Pabst	Ferrari 250 LM (6047)	– (rear axle)

Fastest practice lap: Scarfiotti, 1m 43.4s, 99.961mph/160.872kph **Fastest race lap:** Hansgen, 1m 44.6s, 98.432mph/158.411kph **Winner's average speed:** 93.956mph/151.208kph **FIA World Sports Car Championship (GT Division III, over 2,000cc):**[1] 1st Ferrari 84.6 (105.3)[2], 2nd Shelby 78.3 (90.2)[2]

[1] *Scoring system for the top six places in this event was 9–6–4–3–2–1 multiplied by coefficient 1.3; only the manufacturer's highest-placed car scored points*
[2] *Figure in brackets indicates all points scored; only the six best circuit results and the best hillclimb result counted towards the championship*

While rewriting history is a futile exercise, it is fair to say that Guichet could have won the Tour de France but for his initial setback at Reims, a handicap that affected him for the rest of the event, his only other problems being two changes of windscreen wipers in the deluge during the Pau race and persistent brake trouble when the itinerary ventured briefly into Italy with a race at Monza. All the same, Bianchi never played a waiting game and enjoyed a consistent advantage after the departure of the Daytona Coupes, notwithstanding shock-absorber problems at Albi and Monza. Proof that his exploits were much appreciated in Maranello came at Monza, where Enzo Ferrari was in attendance and congratulated the Belgian driver. That was a fitting accolade for a talented racer who had long been overshadowed by his more successful compatriot, Olivier Gendebien, or the victim of too much bad luck.

The title can wait

US Grand Prix, 4th October

Enzo Ferrari never stopped saying that as long as he was alive his cars would always be called Ferraris and would be painted Italian red. However, there have been exceptions, the most notable of which remain the last two Grands Prix of 1964 when the cars carried the white-and-blue colours of the North American Racing Team (NART) because Mr Ferrari, still fulminating about the denial of homologation for the 250 LM, decided that he did not want them run under the works banner. In the end, the livery was unimportant.

After the first of the two four-hour practice sessions, Surtees, using both of the 158s at his disposal, posted a lap in 1m 13.63s, which was almost as quick as Jim Clark's Lotus (1m 13.23s) while Graham Hill, at the wheel of the BRM that had let him down at Monza, was unable to get below 1m 14s. Lorenzo Bandini in the 12-cylinder Ferrari (1m 14.15s) was faster than Ronnie Bucknum's improving Honda (1m 14.90s).

The stakes being what they were, the next day's proceedings in better weather saw the three championship rivals fighting for pole position with Dan Gurney muscling in as well on home territory. Gurney laid down a marker (1m 13.20s), Clark went quicker (1m 12.65s), the American's best response fell short (1m 12.90s) and Hill got close (1m 12.92s). At the end of a hotly contested session, Surtees, who tried the 156 as well as his 158s and found it quicker on the straights, produced a 1m 12.78s in one of the V8 cars to put himself on the two-strong front row alongside Clark. Bandini (1m 13.83s) took a place on the fourth row alongside Jack Brabham, providing proof that the 1512 was beginning to meet expectations, apart from a few cooling problems that required the fitting of additional radiators.

Like Stirling Moss, Surtees had achieved his finest Formula 1 victories so far in cars bearing #7, and both men had done so at the Nürburgring, in Surtees's case twice. Here at Watkins Glen, Surtees again carried #7. Following a lightning start by Clark that gave him a brief advantage, Surtees led for 12 laps before the Lotus driver upped his game, passed the Ferrari and

▲ **United States Grand Prix.** Pictured waiting to take part in Friday's practice session at Watkins Glen, three of the four Ferraris entered by NART for John Surtees (#7T and #7) and Lorenzo Bandini (#8T) wore an unfamiliar white-and-blue livery.

▼ **United States Grand Prix.** After Surtees led the first 12 laps, Jim Clark took over at the front and remained there until his Lotus faltered 30 laps later. Graham Hill went on to win with Surtees second, leaving a three-way showdown for the championship title at the last round in Mexico.

UNITED STATES GRAND PRIX

Watkins Glen, 4th October 1964, 110 laps (2.300 miles/3.701km), 252.966 miles/407.110km • Starters 19, finishers 8

RACE				PRACTICE	
1st	Graham Hill	BRM P261 BRM V8	2h 16m 38.0s	4th	1m 12.92s
2nd	**John Surtees**	**Ferrari 158 V8[1]**	**+30.5s**	**2nd**	**1m 12.78s**
3rd	Jo Siffert	Brabham BT11 BRM V8	109 laps	12th	1m 14.65s
4th	Richie Ginther	BRM P261 BRM V8	107 laps	13th	1m 14.67s
5th	Walt Hansgen	Lotus 33 Climax V8	107 laps	17th	1m 15.90s
6th	Trevor Taylor	BRP Mk2 BRM V8	106 laps	15th	1m 15.30s
DNF	**Lorenzo Bandini**	**Ferrari 1512 F12[1]**	58 laps (engine)	8th	1m 13.85s

Pole position: Jim Clark (Lotus 25 Climax V8), 1m 12.65s, 113.956mph/183.394kph **Fastest race lap:** Clark, 1m 12.70s, 113.866mph/183.250kph **Winner's average speed:** 111.076mph/178.760kph **Drivers' championship:** 1st Hill 39, 2nd Surtees 34, 3rd Clark 30, 5th Bandini 19 **Constructors' championship:** 1st Ferrari 43, 2nd BRM 42, 3rd Lotus-Climax 36

[1] Entered by North American Racing Team (NART)

pulled away, leaving the white-and-blue car in the sights of Hill and Gurney. After that, a familiar pattern unfolded. By lap 40 of the 110, Clark had a six-second lead over his three pursuers and seemed to be on course for victory and a possible second title. Unknown to him, however, the filter in the Lotus's injection pump was beginning to break up, allowing impurities to pass. Clark found his lead swiftly transformed into a deficit and by lap 44 he had dropped to fourth. What happened next was a kind of prolonged agony that saw him stop, resume, slip back to last but one, then finally retire six laps later.

Colin Chapman called in Mike Spence, who was lying fourth, to hand over his Lotus to the team leader. Although Clark would not be eligible for points in a substitute car, the hope was that he might displace one or even both of his championship rivals and deny them some points. When the Scot rejoined, Hill led with Surtees close behind and Gurney third. After Gurney's retirement on lap 70 with oil leaking from his Brabham, Clark found himself in third place behind Surtees, and closer than he might have expected because the Ferrari driver, most uncharacteristically, had lost time with a spin, probably on the Brabham's oil. Then Clark began to lose ground in his Lotus with another fuel-feed problem and finally retired on lap 102, although he was credited with seventh place in the final classification.

So Hill won from Surtees, with Jo Siffert a lap down in third place with Rob Walker's Brabham. Bandini drove a good race and lay fifth behind Spence for a long time before bowing out after 58 laps, Ferrari citing a flat battery as the reason before admitting that the flat-12 engine had failed.

In Bourne, Cheshunt and Maranello, everyone pored over the points and permutations. Hill's victory put him on 41 points,

although in reality his score was 39 because only the best six results could count and therefore he had to drop the two points he had earned in Belgium. Surtees had 34 points and Clark 30, the latter now in need of a miracle at the final round.

A logical result

Paris 1,000Km, 11th October

With both Ford and Shelby absent, there was not a great deal left to attract spectators to Montlhéry for the Paris 1,000Km, the 20th and last round of the International Championship for GT Manufacturers, especially as the title outcome had already been decided. There was, though, the Trophée France-Amérique, which remained unresolved in the GT category. This little-known contest comprised three events and after the first two — the Daytona 2,000Km and the Reims 12 Hours — Pedro Rodríguez, David Piper and Tony Maggs were in the running in the drivers' standings while NART and Piper had the entrants' award at stake.

Enthusiasts hoped that this Paris 1,000Km would relive fine Ferrari battles of the past, such as those between Willy Mairesse/ Wolfgang von Trips and Olivier Gendebien/Lucien Bianchi in 1960, Mairesse/Bianchi against the Rodríguez brothers in 1961, or those same Mexican prodigies against John Surtees/Michael Parkes in 1962. There was certainly a plethora of Ferraris on the entry list, headed by the Maranello Concessionaires 330 P of Graham Hill/Jo Bonnier. Five 250 LMs were in the hands of Jean Guichet/Nino Vaccarella, Jackie Stewart/Ludovico Scarfiotti, Willy Mairesse/'Beurlys', Guy Ligier/Annie Soisbault

➤ **Paris 1,000Km.** Graham Hill, mischievous as always, takes up a conker challenge with a slightly apprehensive Jackie Stewart just before the start of the Montlhéry race. Both men drove cars entered by Maranello Concessionaires, Britain's Ferrari importer, Hill a 330 P with Jo Bonnier, Stewart a 250 LM with Ludovico Scarfiotti.

➤ **Paris 1,000Km.** Seen with Jo Bonnier getting ready to rejoin after a routine pitstop, the Maranello Concessionaires 330 P he shared with Graham Hill led throughout, other than during brief reshuffles at staggered refuelling stops when the sister 250 LM of Jackie Stewart/Ludovico Scarfiotti briefly hit the front, until steering problems caused it to slip back.

and Hermann Müller/Armand Boller, while the strongest of five GTOs was driven by Pedro Rodríguez/Jo Schlesser. With only a mixed bag of rivals, including the Peter Lindner/Peter Nöcker Lightweight E-type Jaguar, the Maurice Trintignant/André Simon Maserati *Tipo* 151 and a fleet of Porsches headed by the eight-cylinder version of Edgar Barth/Colin Davis, it really looked like Maranello's cars would dominate. In all, 38 cars turned up for the two practice sessions and on Sunday 37 lined up to tackle the 129 laps of the treacherous 4.8-mile layout, which combined the road circuit and the banked oval.

The first practice session took place in execrable weather and the best times seemed to promise a no-holds-barred fight between Ferraris as expected, with the quickest of them belonging to Vaccarella/Guichet (3m 6.4s), Stewart/Scarfiotti (3m 7.4s) and Hill/Bonnier (3m 8.7s). Mairesse, making his racing comeback after injury, was in prudent mood on a very slippery track as proved by his lap in a modest 3m 15.3s. In the GT category, Lindner/Nöcker (3m 12.8s) led Rodríguez/Schlesser (3m 14.7s).

Improved weather on Saturday morning saw much faster times, Hill (2m 43.6s) coming out on top followed by Vaccarella (2m 45.5s), Mairesse (2m 46.7s) and Stewart (2m 47s), the Belgian reassuring both himself and his friends that his speed was undiminished, while the Scottish newcomer's performance was admirable not just for his pace but also the ease with

which he adapted to an unfamiliar car. The GT benchmark was now set by GTOs, the 'regular' one driven by Lucien Bianchi/Gérald Langlois van Ophem (2m 52.9s) narrowly beating the 1964 example of Rodríguez/Schlesser (2m 53.0s). Piper, who was wearing a plaster truss following a crash at Snetterton two weeks earlier, was way back on the penultimate row of the grid in his 'low-line' GTO shared with Maggs.

Pre-race hype predicted that the race would be a thriller but this was not the case as far as the winners were concerned, for Hill screamed off into the lead and he and Bonnier were never threatened. Mairesse hit engine problems and retired after only four laps. Guichet took over from Vaccarella, who had done his best to keep Stewart in sight, but threw in the towel within a few laps in a cloud of steam because his 250 LM's radiator had been stoved in when his co-driver rammed the back of the Claude Dubois/Gustave Gosselin GTO 64. Müller/Boller lay an impressive third at one point but retired because of clutch problems while the Trintignant/Simon Maserati, delayed early on by a broken condenser wire, went out when the oil pump bracket fractured. As for Stewart, whom Christian Moity described as 'the most adventurous of hunters', steering problems brought him into the pits shortly after half distance and thereafter he and Scarfiotti tumbled down the order, but at least he went home with the consolation of fastest lap.

◄ **Paris 1,000Km.** After finishing a fine second at Montlhéry with their NART GTO 64, Jo Schlesser (cap) and Pedro Rodríguez (helmet) enjoy the glory. They had won not only the GT category but also the little-known Trophée France-Amérique.

PARIS 1,000KM

Montlhéry, 11th October 1964, 129 laps (4.837 miles/7.784km), 623.941 miles/1,004.136km • Starters 37, classified finishers 22

1st	Graham Hill/Jo Bonnier	Ferrari 330 P (0818)	6h 32m 53.1s
2nd	Pedro Rodríguez/Jo Schlesser	Ferrari 250 GTO 64 (5573 GT) *(1st Div III)*	127 laps
3rd	Edgar Barth/Colin Davis	Porsche 904/8	126 laps
4th	David Piper/Tony Maggs	Ferrari 250 GTO (4491 GT)	126 laps
5th	Lucien Bianchi/Gérald Langlois van Ophem	Ferrari 250 GTO (4153 GT)	125 laps
6th	Ron Slotemaker/David van Lennep	Porsche 904 GTS	124 laps
10th	Jackie Stewart/Ludovico Scarfiotti	Ferrari 250 LM (5095)	120 laps
12th	Oddone Sigala/Edoardo Lualdi	Ferrari 250 GTO 64 (4675 GT)	120 laps
13th	Gustave Gosselin/Claude Dubois	Ferrari 250 GTO (5575 GT)	117 laps
18th	Annie Soisbault/Guy Ligier	Ferrari 250 LM	111 laps

Fastest practice lap: Hill, 2m 43.6s, 106.438mph/171.296kph **Fastest race lap:** Stewart, 2m 45.1s, 105.472mph/169.740kph **Winner's average speed:** 95.392mph/153.518kph **Trophée France-Amérique:** 1st North American Racing Team (NART), 2nd David Piper

Rodríguez/Schlesser took advantage of the ill-fortune of their rivals as well as their own sterling efforts to finish second. This allowed them to proudly lift the Trophée France-Amérique, even if Piper/Maggs put up a good fight to claim fourth place with Bianchi/Langlois van Ophem fifth. When Lindner lost control of his E-type in pouring rain on the exit from the oval and crashed, the accident claimed not only his life but also those of Italian driver Franco Patria (Abarth) and three marshals.

One point decides it

Mexican Grand Prix, 25th October

From time to time in the history of the Formula 1 World Championship, the outcome has kept everyone on tenterhooks until the very end, sometimes even up to the last lap of the last race. Mike Hawthorn won the 1958 title in the dying minutes thanks to Phil Hill obeying team orders, while Hill himself triumphed in tragic circumstances three years later. In 1959, Jack Brabham, despite running out of fuel on the last lap at Sebring, was crowned after Stirling Moss had been let down by his car and Tony Brooks had been unable to finish in a high enough position. In 1962, fans had had to wait until the final round in East London to discover the name of the champion. And now, in Mexico in 1964, the suspense of the title battle between Graham Hill, John Surtees and Jim Clark lasted the entire meeting.

The circuit's altitude, at 2,500 metres above sea level, added uncertainty to the proceedings because it affected carburation and tyre pressures, so during the first practice session everybody tried to find ways to offset the repercussions. Clark again hesitated between his cars (25B and 33) before setting his time of 1m 57.6s in the newer Lotus equipped with a Climax engine with side-exiting exhausts. After evaluating the two 158s at his disposal and having the engine fail in one, Surtees fell back on his other car, found that it was running less well and posted a 1m 58.7s that left him displeased. Hill in the older of his P261s was further off the pace at 1m 59.8s, which was slower than Dan Gurney's Brabham (1m 58.5s) and Lorenzo Bandini's Ferrari 1512 (1m 58.6s). Pedro Rodríguez had a third Ferrari entry, a 156, either through NART's generosity or because his father paid for it, and managed 2m 0.9s.

On Saturday the pressure began to build and each of the potential championship winners naturally tried to do better than the previous day but with mixed fortunes on a greasy track. Using the 33, Clark initially got round in 1m 58.6s and was surprised that his revs on the straight were no higher than the day before even though an overnight gearbox change should have helped, but then his crew found that this gearbox had been wrongly labelled and was not the one he wanted. Surtees tried to go quicker but to no avail. And Hill dissipated his efforts by trying to address his newer P261's understeer with changes of tyre pressures but ended up slower than on Friday.

The session continued. With the correct gearbox installed, Clark stunned everybody with a lap in 1m 57.24s. Surtees got round in only 1m 59.68s in one of his 158s and this made him slower than Bandini in the 1512, whose indirect Lucas fuel injection coped better with the altitude. Hill was again the slowest of the trio at 2m 0.10s after engine trouble for both of his P261s, first a broken valve on one, then falling oil pressure on the other. After everyone had given their best, the grid line-up was Clark and Gurney on the front row, Surtees and Bandini on the second, and Hill and Mike Spence (Lotus) on the third. Rodríguez equalled his Friday time and shared the fifth row with Bruce McLaren (Cooper).

The outcome looked to be decided straight away when Clark, after another magnificent start, shot past the pits two seconds ahead of Gurney with Bandini third, while the other title combatants immediately faltered. Surtees almost stalled at the start because his plugs had fouled after inordinate delay on the dummy grid, while Hill had a problem with the elastic strap of his goggles just as the flag was about to drop and had not got them properly over his eyes nor first gear selected when the cars moved off. Consequently, both men were a long way down the field first time around, in only 13th and 10th places respectively, although they made up ground to eighth and sixth after four laps. Up at the front, Clark was now five seconds ahead of Gurney and continued to ease away at the rate of a second a lap, while Bandini was a further five seconds back, with Spence and Brabham battling away behind him and Hill closing in on them. Then the BRM driver gained three places within four laps, overtaking Brabham on the eighth, Spence on the tenth and Bandini on the 12th to put himself third — a position that would assure him of the world title if nothing else changed. Meanwhile, Surtees was making similar progress, so that by the

18th lap he was fifth behind his team-mate.

And then came the incident that has been talked about ever since. It happened on lap 31. Bandini had been on Hill's tail for several laps and this time round neither driver gave way at the very tight hairpin, Bandini on the inside line and Hill taking a wide entry. They rounded the apex side by side and very close together before widening their trajectories on the exit, both trying to avoid any collision. But Bandini could not hold the Ferrari on the necessary line and its left-front wheel tangled with the BRM's right-rear. Hill lost the back end and grazed the barrier, damaging both exhaust pipes, while Bandini briefly came to rest with his path blocked by the BRM. Just as both drivers were gathering themselves together to resume, Surtees came round the hairpin and nipped ahead. Hill called at his pit where the crumpled ends of the exhausts were torn off with jack handles and hacksaws before he rejoined in 13th place, a lap down. For him, the title was probably lost.

'Further proof of Bandini's reckless driving,' thundered Bill Gavin in *Sport Auto*. Bernard Cahier, reporting for *L'Automobile* among others, witnessed the incident first-hand and was more objective. After interviewing those involved, he stated that the 'Italian driver had no intention of hindering, much less eliminating, the driver who at that moment was the title winner'

▾ **Mexican Grand Prix.** It did not really matter that the spark plugs were the problem when Bernard Cahier took this photo on the second day of practice. Despite Surtees's efforts to beat his previous day's best time, he ended up on the second row of the grid in part because the Bosch/Ferrari injection system was affected by the circuit's altitude.

▾ **Mexican Grand Prix.** The 12-cylinder engine was equipped with a new camshaft and shorter inlet trumpets sent by air from Maranello. Compared with the V8, this engine was less sensitive to the altitude because of its Lucas indirect injection system. This turned out to be a decisive factor in the battle for the title.

▲ **Mexican Grand Prix.** As the start approaches, the three title contenders — John Surtees, Jim Clark and Graham Hill — have a chat, joined by Dan Gurney. Hill was the one with the best chance: he only needed to finish third to claim the crown regardless of the outcome for his two rivals.

➤ **Mexican Grand Prix.** Hill's BRM had just got round Bandini's Ferrari on the outside of the hairpin when the pair clipped wheels. Here the sliding BRM is about to crumple its exhaust pipes against the guardrail. Although both resumed, Hill's car needed a pitstop — and his title hopes were dashed.

MEXICAN GRAND PRIX

Mexico City, 25th October 1964, 65 laps (3.107 miles/5.000km), 201.946 miles/325.000km • Starters 19, finishers 14

RACE				PRACTICE	
1st	Dan Gurney	Brabham BT7 Climax V8	2h 9m 50.32s	2nd	1m 58.10s
2nd	**John Surtees**	**Ferrari 158 V8[1]**	**+1m 08.94s**	**4th**	**1m 58.70s**
3rd	**Lorenzo Bandini**	**Ferrari 1512 F12[1]**	**+1m 09.63s**	**3rd**	**1m 58.60s**
4th	Mike Spence	Lotus 25 Climax V8	+1m 21.86s	5th	1m 59.21s
5th	Jim Clark	Lotus 33 Climax V8	64 laps	1st	1m 57.24s
6th	**Pedro Rodríguez**	**Ferrari 156 V6 Aero[1]**	**64 laps**	**9th**	**2m 00.90s**

Pole position: Clark, 1m 57.24s, 95.400mph/153.531kph **Fastest race lap:** Clark, 1m 58.37s, 94.489mph/152.066kph **Winner's average speed:** 93.321mph/150.185kph **Drivers' championship:** 1st Surtees 40, 2nd Hill 39 (41)[2], 3rd Clark 32, 5th Bandini 23, 19th Rodríguez 1 **Constructors' championship:** 1st Ferrari 45, 2nd BRM 42 (51)[2], 3rd Lotus-Climax 37 (40)[2]

[1] Entered by North American Racing Team (NART) [2] Figure in brackets indicates all points scored; only the best six results counted towards the championship

and added that Lorenzo was very sorry 'and had just apologised to his victim'. At that moment the title really did seem to be destined for Clark, who, although level-pegging with Hill on points, had scored more victories.

▼ **Mexican Grand Prix.** Surtees has every reason to express his joy as he has just become Ferrari's fifth Formula 1 World Champion. Although Dan Gurney looks downcast, he has just inherited a surprise victory, a fair reward after a season marked by misfortune.

Three laps later, on lap 34, Bandini used his 12-cylinder power to get back in front of Surtees so that the order became Clark, Gurney, Bandini, Surtees, Rodríguez and Spence. For much of the second half of the race there were no changes to those positions other than Spence swapping places with Rodríguez on lap 45. Then, some 10 laps from the finish, Clark saw a thin trail of oil at the hairpin and took a wider line. Next time round, there was another streak on that wider line, so he knew the oil must be spilling from his car. A flexible pipe had split and lubricant was

Formula 1 World Championship (Drivers) *Top three plus other Ferrari drivers*

	1st	2nd	3rd	4th	9th
	John Surtees	Graham Hill	Jim Clark	Lorenzo Bandini	Pedro Rodríguez
Monaco GP	0	9	3	0	–
Dutch GP	6	3	9	0	–
Belgian GP	0	–2	9	0	–
GP de l'ACF (France)	0	6	0	0	–
British GP	4	6	9	2	–
German GP	9	6	0	4	–
Austrian GP	0	0	0	9	–
Italian GP	9	0	0	4	–
United States GP	6	9	0	0	–
Mexican GP	6	0	2	4	1
Total	40	39	32	23	1

Formula 1 World Championship (Constructors)

	1st	2nd	3rd
	Ferrari	BRM	Lotus-Climax
Monaco GP	0	9	4
Dutch GP	6	–3	9
Belgian GP	0	–3	9
GP de l'ACF (France)	0	6	3
British GP	–4	6	9
German GP	9	6	0
Austrian GP	9	6	0
Italian GP	9	–3	–1
United States GP	6	9	–2
Mexican GP	6	0	3
Total	45	42	37

International Championship for GT Manufacturers

	1st	2nd	3rd
	Ferrari	Shelby	Jaguar
Daytona 2,000Km (1.3)[1]	11.7	3.9	–
Sebring 12 Hours (1.6)	–4.8	14.4	–
Targa Florio (1.6)	14.4	9.6	–
Spa 500Km (1.3)	11.7	–1.3	0
Nürburgring 1,000Km (1.6)	14.4	–1.6	0
Le Mans 24 Hours (2.0)	12	18	–
Reims 12 Hours (1.0)	–9	0	4
Fribourg Schauinsland hillclimb (1.0)	6	9	–
Tourist Trophy (1.3)	–3.9	11.7	2.6
Sierre–Montana hillclimb (1.0)	–3	–9	0
Tour de France (1.3)	14.4	0	–
Bridgehampton 500Km (1.3)	0	11.7	–
Total	84.6	78.3	6.6

[1] *Figures in brackets indicate coefficients used for scoring system*

slowly seeping away. Gurney was 17 seconds behind.

Hoping that he could keep going for those final laps and that Gurney might not realise he was in trouble, Clark made no signals to his pit each time he passed. This lasted until the end of the penultimate lap, when his Climax engine's oil pressure dropped away sharply in the banked 180-degree turn leading onto the start/finish straight. He passed his pit at a snail's pace with his hands in the air, gifting victory to Gurney. At Ferrari, where all personnel were massed at the side of the track, they realised that the destiny of the title now depended upon Bandini moving over and surrendering his second place to Surtees. The Italian duly did just that and a lap later *Il Grande John* became the fifth Ferrari driver to become Formula 1 World Champion, by a

single point and without having had any chance of that precious outcome for 64 of the 65 laps.

One could quibble endlessly about the merits of regulations that give preference to victories over points-scoring finishes. But for Hill having had to surrender two points earned from his fifth place in Belgium, he would have been crowned champion, with Surtees a point behind. But that is of little importance because victory is all that counts.

As ever in motor racing, everybody focused their attention on what was to come. None of the British constructors had any intention of letting Ferrari build on a title that they felt had been won in exceedingly fortuitous circumstances.

Italian Grand Prix. After qualifying on the front row, John Surtees's Ferrari developed a clutch problem and he dropped to 13th place by the end of the first lap. His comeback drive, which was cruelly terminated by total clutch failure, was described by David Phipps as 'one of the highlights of the season and maybe of the formula itself'. Here he leads Graham Hill (BRM), Jim Clark (Lotus), Lorenzo Bandini (Ferrari), Dan Gurney (Brabham) and Mike Spence (Lotus).

1965
RUNNING OUT OF STEAM

Modena, Saturday 12th December 1964. Even though his cars had won both Formula 1 world titles (drivers and constructors), the International Trophy for GT Manufacturers in Division III, the Prototype World Championship and the Trophée France-Amérique, Enzo Ferrari remained faithful to his press conference rituals, including the inevitable diatribe against the governing body's rules that penalised him. There was, however, a surprise. While everyone still remembered the FIA's refusal to homologate the 250/275 LM, which was still being built, he simply regretted the fact that the 'direct consequences of this decision would lead to the absence of works GTs in championship events'. In fact, there was nothing really new about this as it was often Maranello's policy to leave privateers to win for Ferrari.

Il Commendatore was more expansive about prototype sports cars. He was keenly aware that more needed to be done if he was going to thwart Ford's ambitions. So, while the 275 P2 and 330 P2 followed in the footsteps of the previous models, they had received some significant modifications. The main ones were more flowing bodywork with wider front and rear wings to accommodate bigger tyres and a chassis derived from Formula 1 practice with a tubular structure reinforced by riveted aluminium panels. In the engine room, although cubic capacities remained unchanged, the supposed power outputs were now around 360bhp (275 P2) and over 400bhp (330 P2), although these figures were not actually announced. Here, there was an important break with Ferrari's V12 heritage in that these engines had two overhead camshafts per cylinder bank, something previously only seen on an experimental supercharged engine back in 1949. In addition, a small number of 365 Ps or 365 P2s would be built for a few select customers, with capacity enlarged to 4,390cc (by increasing cylinder bore) but only a single overhead camshaft per bank, giving a power output about the same as that of the updated 4-litre engine.

In Formula 1, the 158 and particularly the 1512 spearheaded Ferrari's attack, with the flat-12 version now likely to be the quicker of the two at many circuits, enabling John Surtees and Lorenzo Bandini to take the fight to their British rivals in, according to Raymond Miomandre, 'a serene state of mind'. Financial prudence being the watchword, Ferrari limited its participation in both Formula 1 and endurance to two-car entries entrusted to four in-house test/racing drivers. Besides Surtees and Bandini, the chosen men were Michael Parkes and Jean Guichet, although this did not exclude the occasional outing for a few others.

Finally, Maranello decided not to build a single-seater for the 1-litre Formula 2, which the CSI had extended by one more year until the end of 1966. Instead, the 1.6-litre rules due to come into force in 1967 looked a much more enticing proposition, especially as the engine in question had to come from a production road car. The result was the presentation in the spring of a car called the Dino 166. This GT, powered by a V6 derived from the Formula 1 V8, would also be built in prototype form.

As this press conference was not accompanied by the time-honoured static presentation of cars in Maranello, visiting journalists were invited to see the 330 P2 in action at the Modena *aerautodromo*. Surtees seemed reasonably satisfied as he took a mere 57 seconds to cover the 1.53-mile circuit on the outskirts of Modena in a car that differed from the familiar guise in having a lower windscreen and no roll-over bar. Four days later this same 330 P2 did a series of tests at Monza before a 1,000km run at Vallelunga near Rome. It was a vital stage in preparation for the first world championship round for sports cars, the Daytona 2,000Km, scheduled for 28th February.

Scottish supremacy

South African Grand Prix, 1st January

As this first showdown in the 1965 Formula 1 World Championship took place at the East London circuit just two months after the last race of 1964 and nearly five months before the next one in Monaco, there was little innovation to be seen among the cars.

The Ferraris were back in their usual red livery but entered under Eugenio Dragoni's name because Enzo Ferrari had not yet obtained his own entrant's licence. John Surtees chose a 158, which would become his preference, so the 1512 was entrusted to Lorenzo Bandini. As the reigning World Champion's principal aim was to defend his title, he did not want to waste time developing an engine that, although promising, he judged to be insufficiently reliable. Jim Clark's Lotus 33, unlike that of team-mate Mike Spence, was powered by an even more 'square' Coventry Climax V8 than the previous year's version. The BRM P261s of Graham Hill and newcomer Jackie Stewart had centrally mounted exhaust systems. The works Cooper T73s of Bruce McLaren and Jochen Rindt appeared with just a few minor tweaks. At Brabham, both Jack Brabham and Dan Gurney now had BT11s, the new model that the boss had tried for the last four races of 1964.

The main technical interest lay in tyres. Goodyear, whose ambitions hitherto had been limited to prototypes, sports cars and occasionally Formula 2, was enlarging its field of operations

South African Grand Prix. Although John Surtees was the reigning World Champion, he could do nothing about the Lotuses of Jim Clark, who led from start to finish, and Mike Spence, who ran second for the first half of the race. With his Ferrari 158 back in its familiar red, Surtees came home second behind Clark.

to include Formula 1. After dipping a toe in the water at Monza a few months earlier by equipping Mario Cabral's ATS with Blue Streak rubber, the American company now linked itself contractually to Brabham in a sure sign that this was a long-term project. Dunlop, which still supplied the rest of the field, reacted by introducing R6 tyres made of softer rubber while continuing to experiment with the R7, which was promised to be quick in all track conditions, dry or wet. It seemed that there might be a tyre war in prospect.

The first of three practice sessions took place in warm sunshine on Wednesday afternoon and involved 16 invited entries that were guaranteed a start along with nine others vying for the last four places. Hill joined the Brabham drivers in evaluating Goodyear's offering but in the end Gurney, who had a personal contract with the tyre company, was the only one who persevered and raced with Akron-made rubber. Although Jim Clark was having to wear a corset to protect his back after suffering a slipped disc when skiing in Cortina d'Ampezzo,

he silenced doubters and reassured his own team by lapping quickest in 1m 27.6s, with Surtees not far off on 1m 28.2s. Bandini's 1512 only arrived on the morning of practice and he soon found himself far behind, unable to do any better than 1m 33.6s, which put him in the same ballpark as the 'non-invited' drivers, mainly locals, who were fighting to qualify.

The first of the next day's two sessions kicked off in cool, still conditions at 6am and saw the expected improvements in times. Clark got down to 1m 27.2s to confirm his pole position while Surtees (1m 28.1s) and Brabham (1m 28.3s) lined up alongside on the front row, with Spence (1m 28.3s) and Hill (1m 28.6s) on

SOUTH AFRICAN GRAND PRIX

East London, 1st January 1965, 85 laps (2.436 miles/3.920km), 207.041 miles/333.200km • Starters 20, finishers 16

RACE				PRACTICE	
1st	Jim Clark	Lotus 33 Climax V8	2h 06m 46.0s	1st	1m 27.2s
2nd	**John Surtees**	**Ferrari 158 V8**	**+29.0s**	**2nd**	**1m 28.1s**
3rd	Graham Hill	BRM P261 BRM V8	+31.8s	5th	1m 28.6s
4th	Mike Spence	Lotus 33 Climax V8	+54.4s	4th	1m 28.3s
5th	Bruce McLaren	Cooper T77 Climax V8	84 laps	8th	1m 29.4s
6th	Jackie Stewart	BRM P261 BRM V8	83 laps	11th	1m 30.5s
15th	**Lorenzo Bandini**	**Ferrari 1512 F12**	**65 laps**	**6th**	**1m 29.3s**

Pole position: Clark, 1m 27.2s, 100.560mph/161.835kph **Fastest race lap:** Clark, 1m 27.6s, 100.097mph/161.091kph **Winner's average speed:** 97.970mph/157.668kph **Drivers' championship:**[1] 1st Clark 9, 2nd Surtees 6, 3rd Hill 4 **Constructors' championship:**[2] 1st Lotus-Climax 9, 2nd Ferrari 6, 3rd BRM 4

[1] Scoring system for the top six places was 9–6–4–3–2–1 [2] Scoring system for the top six places was 9–6–4–3–2–1; only the manufacturer's highest-placed car scored points

the second row. Bandini improved dramatically to sixth fastest with a time of 1m 29.3s. Gurney (1m 29.5s), struggling with his Goodyears, had to make do with tenth on the grid alongside Rindt, the new boy. Wind blew up in the afternoon and most drivers settled for their morning times.

Clark dominated the race. Over the 85 laps, he put on yet another display of his formidable talent to beat Surtees by 29 seconds. The end brought some confusion when the man with the chequered flag waved it at Clark a lap too soon, leaving the Scot confused and somewhat agitated because his pit had just told him that he had one more lap to go. He covered the 'extra' lap quite slowly because he feared that the track might be invaded by spectators but meanwhile the officials determined that there was indeed one more lap and the chequered flag was put away until Clark came round once more. Spence, Clark's team-mate, had emphasised Lotus's supremacy by running second until lap 60, when he spun for a second time on spilled oil and allowed both Surtees and Hill to pass. Bandini was not quite so fortunate. He circulated in the mid-field before stopping on lap 34 to have all 12 spark plugs changed, rejoining 14th, then stopped again with continuing ignition problems on lap 67 and this time stayed put. Was Surtees right about the reliability of the flat-12? Mauro Forghieri now had five months to prove him wrong.

< South African Grand Prix.
Lorenzo Bandini was less fortunate than Surtees. He never got any higher than seventh in his 12-cylinder 1512 and then fell to the back of the field with persistent ignition problems.

Warning shot

Daytona 2,000Km, 28th February

After spending time at Modena testing a new 158, which was really only a modified version of the car seen in South Africa, John Surtees travelled to Daytona to co-drive with Pedro Rodríguez the only 330 P2 in the field, jointly entered by the Scuderia and the North American Racing Team (NART), with Mauro Forghieri and works mechanics on hand. There were two other NART entries, a 330 P for Walt Hansgen/David Piper and a 275 P for Bob Grossman/John 'Buck' Fulp. They were up against a pair of Ford GT40s driven by Bob Bondurant/Richie Ginther and Ken Miles/Lloyd Ruby along with four Cobra Daytona Coupes run by Shelby American for Ed Leslie/Allen Grant, Bob Johnson/Tom Payne, Jo Schlesser/Harold Keck and Rick Muther/John Timanus. Added to these potential contenders for victory, Dan Gurney's team, All American Racers, put forward a Lotus 19 powered by a 5.3-litre Ford V8 with Gurney himself and Jerry Grant as drivers. This initiative is worth noting because it added momentum to the trend of Formula 1 drivers becoming constructors, Jack Brabham being the first and best known.

From his position on the fifth row of the grid, Gurney (2m 11.0s) only needed two laps to overtake Surtees, who had qualified on pole position (2m 0.6s) alongside the Bondurant/Ginther Ford (2m 1.8s). Ferrari's first setback came on lap 14 when third-placed Hansgen's 275 P ran over debris scattered in front of the grandstands by a Jaguar E-type's blown-up engine,

leaving the American with a shredded right-front tyre and no choice but to take to an escape road and retire. This prompted Carroll Shelby to call in the two Ford GTs from third and fourth places for their tyres to be checked and changed if necessary, causing them to slip back before gradually returning to those same positions. The top two remained unchanged through the first pitstops, which saw Surtees hand over to Rodríguez while Gurney stayed put for a second stint.

A cascade of incidents then ruined the race for Ferrari. The left-rear tyre on the 330 P2 punctured suddenly while Surtees was driving and then exploded with Rodríguez at the wheel, leaving the car stranded with a damaged battery. The Mexican had to run almost a mile to his pit for a fresh battery and return with it to carry out repairs that cost 20 laps. With Surtees back behind the wheel, the left driveshaft then broke, probably because of the stresses imposed during the previous incidents, and the car was out after 116 laps. At about the same time, NART suffered a final blow when its other 275 P retired with clutch failure while lying third, having completed 130 laps. The only Prancing Horse left now was Peter Clarke's three-year-old GTO in which he had invited Charlie Hayes and Bob Hurt to join him. Despite some trouble with its brakes and starter motor, they did well to finish seventh overall and fourth in the Division III GT category.

Ford reigned that day. The GT40s finished first and third, Miles/Ruby the winners, while three of the Daytona Coupes came in second, fourth and sixth, the Johnson/Payne example having gone out with piston failure. That meant a Cobra 1–2–3 finish in Division III, the best possible start to Shelby's assault on the International Championship for GT Manufacturers.

DAYTONA 2,000KM

Daytona, 28th February 1965, 327 laps (3.810 miles/6.132km), 1,244.560 miles/2,002.925km • Starters 43, classified finishers 21

1st	Ken Miles/Lloyd Ruby	Ford GT40	12h 27m 09.0s
2nd	Jo Schlesser/Harold Keck/Bob Johnson	Shelby Cobra Daytona (1st Div III)	322 laps
3rd	Bob Bondurant/Richie Ginther	Ford GT40	318 laps
4th	Rick Muther/John Timanus	Shelby Cobra Daytona	317 laps
5th	Charlie Kolb/Roger Heftler	Porsche 904 GTS	313 laps
6th	Ed Leslie/Allen Grant	Shelby Cobra Daytona	312 laps
7th	Bob Hurt/Peter Clarke/Charlie Hayes	Ferrari 250 GTO (3757 GT) (4th Div III)	308 laps
DNF	Bob Grossman/Walt Hansgen/Pedro Rodríguez/David Piper	Ferrari 275 P (0814)	130 laps (clutch)
DNF	John Surtees/Pedro Rodríguez	Ferrari 330 P2 (0826)	116 laps (rear axle)
DNF	Walt Hansgen/David Piper	Ferrari 330 P (0820)	18 laps (driveshaft)

Fastest practice lap: Surtees, 2m 00.6s Fastest race lap: Hansgen (Ferrari 330 P), 2m 01.8s, 114.680mph/184.560kph Winner's average speed: 99.849mph/160.691kph FIA World Sports Car Championship (GT Division III, over 2,000cc):[1] 1st Shelby 14.4, 2nd Ferrari 4.8

[1] Scoring system for the top six places in this event was 9–6–4–3–2–1 multiplied by coefficient 1.6; only the manufacturer's highest-placed car scored points

Water world!

Sebring 12 Hours, 27th March

The outcome at Sebring was a wake-up call for Ferrari. The fact that Enzo Ferrari had refused to enter works cars made the prospect of defeat all the more likely, especially as the American threat was now boosted by the arrival of General Motors in the form of its support for Jim Hall's two Chaparrals. This was GM's first step to counter Ford. The previous December, the latest Chaparral 2A had made mincemeat of its rivals at the Bahamas Speed Week when winning the Nassau Trophy, the team's seventh victory of the season. More recently Hall and his associate, Hap Sharp, had booked Sebring for private testing with an A2 in preparation for the 12 Hours and had lapped in

▼ **Sebring 12 Hours.** The 330 P entered by the Mecom Racing Team for Pedro Rodríguez and Graham Hill made a good start but never threatened the winning Chaparral. Pictured with Rodríguez at the wheel, the Ferrari retired just before the two-thirds mark with clutch failure.

record times. With GM's backing, Chaparral was now far more than the plaything of well-off Texans who had decided to build their own cars rather than buy them from others.

Hall was a clever engineer who had graduated from the California Institute of Technology and gone into racing, soon to make good use of his fortune by founding Chaparral Cars. He formed a mutually productive relationship with the top brass of GM's Technical Center in Detroit, helping them in their pursuit of automotive advances, and quite quickly — and very unofficially — obtained their technical support for his racing endeavours. Even if the now-proven A2 had a conservative approach to power, using a 5.3-litre Chevrolet V8 that put out around 435bhp, it was otherwise an innovative machine for its time with a semi-monocoque chassis using reinforced glass-fibre and a GM semi-automatic two-speed transmission.

The Chaparrals were up against nine Ferraris which, in the sports category, included the NART-owned 330 P entered by the Mecom Racing Team for Pedro Rodríguez/Graham Hill and a 275 P shared by Umberto Maglioli/Giancarlo Baghetti in the colours of Kleiner Racing Enterprises. In the prototype category were two 330 Ps driven by Bob Grossman/Skip Hudson and Charlie Kolb/John 'Buck' Fulp and two 275 Ps for Ed Hugus/Tom

▲ **Sebring 12 Hours.** Texas-based Kleiner Racing Enterprises entered Umberto Maglioli/Giancarlo Baghetti in this 275 P, which finished the race in eighth place after a delay caused by a defective throttle linkage.

O'Brien and Willy Mairesse/Lucien Bianchi. In addition, there were a couple of 250 LMs for Walt Hansgen/Mark Donohue and David Piper/Tony Maggs, the Englishman back again with his indispensable South African team-mate.

As the two American races took place only four weeks apart, there were no novelties on show at Sebring. The Prancing Horse's main opposition came from the two Ford GT40s already seen at Daytona driven by Phil Hill/Richie Ginther (together for the first time as team-mates in a sports car since 1954) and Ken Miles/Bruce McLaren, the two Chaparrals driven by Hall/Sharp and Ronnie Hissom/Bruce Jennings, plus the Dan Gurney/Jerry Grant Lotus 19. In light of their previous result, the four Cobra Daytona Coupes from the Daytona 2,000Km could also be added to the list of potential winners, especially the one shared by Jo Schlesser and Bob Bondurant.

After Hall concluded a scintillating performance in practice with pole position at 2m 57.6s, he got the better of Gurney in a no-holds-barred battle and led the race at the end of the first hour. In suffocating heat, the Fords suffered a few early setbacks including Bondurant's stop for some bodywork repair and Ginther's at the end of the first lap to replace a wheel that was rubbing against a brake. Rodríguez's 330 P, sandwiched between Hissom's Chaparral and Miles's Ford, was third. In two of the 275 Ps, both Maglioli and Mairesse got off to a bad start and tumbled down the order after attention to, respectively, throttle linkage and transmission. Two hours later, under a darkening sky, Hall/Sharp still led with the Rodríguez/Hill Ferrari now second, three laps behind, while the other Chaparral was third, the Miles/McLaren Ford fourth and the Kolb/Fulp 330 P fifth. Ginther had retired, regretting the fact that a broken suspension mounting point had cut short his reunion with Phil Hill. Gurney had parked his Lotus after 43 laps with oil pump failure.

As the leading Chaparral cruised onwards, the rout continued. At 4pm, half distance, the white car led the Mecom 330 P duo by five laps and after one more hour the gap had stretched to seven laps. It looked like Hall/Sharp had the race in the bag when a storm broke at 5.30pm. Its violence was extraordinary and the sudden deluge turned the track into a lake. Equipment was swept away in the pits and water came up to drivers' waists in some of the open cockpits. Some cars took as long as 20 minutes to complete a lap. Plenty went off, the worst of the incidents occurring when Mike Gammino, blinded by rain and spray, went off in his ISO Grifo and smashed into a footbridge, leaving

▲ Sebring 12 Hours. The Charlie Kolb/'Buck' Fulp 330 P leads the David Piper/Tony Maggs 250 LM as they race along Sebring's concrete expanses. The 330 P went out with gearbox trouble after making a good start but the 250 LM soldiered on through the race's challenges, including a violent storm that left the track under water, to finish third.

◄ Sebring 12 Hours.. At the height of the storm, the Bob Grossman/Skip Hudson 330 P ploughs through standing water, its driver straining forward to try to see better. The car retired with a differential problem.

him miraculously uninjured despite the car being literally cut in two. The Chaparrals, with no wet-weather Firestone tyres on hand, slowed almost to a standstill. On the other hand, some of the Porsche 904s, Alfa Romeos and Austin-Healey Sprites, equipped with narrow tyres and driven by crews with rallying experience, found themselves in their element and moved up the order. Another who did so was Miles, for his GT40 was on Goodyear rain tyres prepared in anticipation of the rain and he overtook the Rodríguez/Hill Ferrari. Piper/Maggs, helped by the Dunlop R7s on their 250 LM and their own doggedness, kept the Schlesser/Bondurant Daytona at bay.

Once the storm had blown over, the surviving runners were able to assess the consequences. The Rodríguez/Hill Ferrari was one of the cars from Maranello still circulating but its V12 had frequently drowned in the rain and the Mexican's efforts to restart it tortured the clutch and brought about the car's retirement on lap 133. Grossman/Hudson did not go much further because their 330 P's differential failed. Third-placed Piper/Maggs were unable to muster enough speed in their 250 LM to take advantage of McLaren's lengthy stop for his GT40's windscreen wipers to be repaired. Nothing much changed in the remaining hours of the race, run in persistent rain with the track still soaking wet, except that the dominant Chaparral's supremacy was not as absolute as before the storm and its winning margin ended up at four laps. Shelby told his drivers to lift off in order to secure

a second successive 'double' in the prototype and GT categories, with Miles/McLaren second and Schlesser/Bondurant fourth.

Although the opinion in Maranello was that the Fords were not unbeatable and that the Daytona Cobra's fourth place owed a lot to the skills of its drivers, the need to react was obvious. As the Chaparral would not be present at Le Mans, the Scuderia was determined to make a big impact at the test weekend in April.

Meanwhile, it was no surprise that Enzo Ferrari was once again bickering with the CSI, this time about the homologation of the 275 GTB, a grand touring production car that was as faithful to the spirit and the letter of the law as the international governing body could wish. The 3.3-litre front-engined Berlinetta with a rear axle/gearbox ensemble and independent suspension on all four corners, plus a cut-off rear end topped by a small spoiler, was more like the 250 GTO than the 250 LM. By 16th March, Maranello stated, the factory had built 147 examples and they were being delivered to customers, so on the face of it there was absolutely no reason for a new dispute. However, the delegates entrusted with agreeing its homologation were taken aback when they saw that the dry weight of 1,050kg (2,315lb) announced in the brochure for the production car was rather different from the 850kg (1,874lb) quoted by Ferrari in the homologation papers.

SEBRING 12 HOURS

Sebring, 27th March 1965, 196 laps (5.200 miles/8.369km), 1,019.200 miles/1,640.243km • Starters 66, classified finishers 43

1st	Jim Hall/Hap Sharp	Chaparral 2A	196 laps
2nd	Ken Miles/Bruce McLaren	Ford GT40	192 laps
3rd	David Piper/Tony Maggs	Ferrari 250 LM (5897)	190 laps
4th	Bob Bondurant/Jo Schlesser	Shelby Cobra Daytona (1st Div III)	187 laps
5th	Luke Underwood/Günther Klass	Porsche 904 GTS	185 laps
6th	Joe Buzzetta/Ben Pon	Porsche 904 GTS	185 laps
8th	Umberto Maglioli/Giancarlo Baghetti	Ferrari 275 P (0812)	184 laps
11th	Walt Hansgen/Mark Donohue	Ferrari 250 LM (6047)	183 laps
12th	Ed Hugus/Tom O'Brien/Charlie Hayes/Paul Richards	Ferrari 275 P (0814)	182 laps
23rd	Willy Mairesse/Lucien Bianchi	Ferrari 275 P (0816)	171 laps
34th	Bob Grossman/Skip Hudson	Ferrari 330 P (0810)	143 laps (differential)
37th	Pedro Rodríguez/Graham Hill	Ferrari 330 P (0820)	133 laps (clutch)
DNF	Charlie Kolb/John 'Buck' Fulp	Ferrari 330 P (0822)	104 laps (gearbox)
DNF	Skip Scott/Peter Clarke	Ferrari 250 GTO (3757 GT)	35 laps (clutch)

Fastest practice lap: Hall, 2m 57.6s, 105.405mph/169.633kph **Fastest race lap:** Hall, 2m 59.3s, 104.410mph/168.031kph **Winner's average speed:** 84.723mph/136.349kph **FIA World Sports Car Championship (GT Division III, over 2,000cc):**[1] 1st Shelby 28.8, 2nd Ferrari 4.8

[1] Scoring system for the top six places in this event was 9–6–4–3–2–1 multiplied by coefficient 1.6; only the manufacturer's highest-placed car scored points

What happened next was farcical. A Ferrari representative claimed that a secretary had made a mistake when typing the text for the brochure. When a delegate suggested that the 275 GTB on display at the Geneva motor show, where it rubbed shoulders with a 250 LM in American colours, should be weighed, Ferrari declined. What the CSI did not want was to repeat the loose application of its rules that had allowed the 250 GTO to be homologated even though the necessary 100 examples had never been built, so on 29th March the homologation of the 275 GTB was turned down on the grounds of the weight discrepancy. Inevitably the situation escalated.

In a press release, Enzo Ferrari, demonstrating a rather selective memory, denounced the 'irregularities that had been committed in homologations to the advantage of other firms' and announced his withdrawal from the International Championship for GT Manufacturers. Perhaps Carroll Shelby, who was known to be something of a 'cowboy' when it came to business, had whispered in the ear of the CSI to pay close attention to the homologated weight of the new Berlinetta, as Denis Jenkinson hinted in *Motor Sport*. Certainly, a weight difference was allowed between a production model on sale to the public and its racing version and that of the 275 GTB did not seem too excessive. Ford, of course, was delighted. And Ferrari, perhaps without being aware of it, was putting its own interests in a perilous situation.

The 275 GTB's homologation was not the only problem affecting Ferrari: the Formula 1 158 had revealed worrying flaws in its first European race of the season, the Race of Champions at Brands Hatch on 13th March. John Surtees's hopes of fighting on a level playing field with the best British teams vanished in practice with a defective V8 that had to be replaced by another one flown in from Maranello. The race was run in two heats: Jim Clark won the first with Surtees only sixth; in the second, the Ferrari expired after only five laps with a fuel leak and soon afterwards Clark crashed out during a furious duel for the lead with Dan Gurney's Brabham, leaving Mike Spence to win not only the heat but also the race overall. Both Clark and Spence were driving Lotus 33s and already this model looked like being the season's class of the field.

Three weeks later, any further doubts were dispelled in the Syracuse Grand Prix when Clark, who started from pole with Surtees alongside, won again, although Jo Siffert (Brabham) was the star of the race and looked on course for the win until he over-revved his BRM engine when the car took off over a bump. Although Surtees drove a good race, twice taking the lead, his Ferrari finished on six cylinders and with defective brakes.

Lorenzo Bandini qualified an encouraging fifth in the 1512 but was never able to break into the top three despite his car's supposed advantage in top speed.

Ferrari red shines

Le Mans test weekend, 10th–11th April

Ferrari had every reason to be satisfied after its performance at the Le Mans test weekend. Although rain disrupted Saturday's activities, both days went off like a dream for the Scuderia. The 330 P2 and the 275 P2 in which John Surtees and Lorenzo Bandini spent the most time were the quickest of the Maranello cars and proved to be faster than their rivals. They basically enjoyed untroubled running apart from erratic roadholding on the *Hunaudières* straight that was readily corrected by the addition of a larger tail spoiler. Another reason to be satisfied was that the 365 P entered by Scuderia Filipinetti for Swiss driver Tommy Spychiger, having his first outing in the car, was quicker than the fastest Fords. Only the performance of the Ecurie Francorchamps 250 LM failed to live up to expectations due to its front end tending to become airborne on the straight.

Surtees at the wheel of the 330 P2 was a cut above everyone and got round in a new record time of 3m 35.1s compared with 3m 36.8s for Michael Parkes, 3m 37.6s for Ludovico Scarfiotti, 3m 38.0s for Vaccarella and 3m 39.5s for Bandini. The fact that Bandini was slower than Parkes would become quite significant when it came to Eugenio Dragoni's decisions about his driver line-ups and Surtees's views about his potential co-drivers.

This overall satisfaction for Ferrari, however, should be tempered by the fact that Ford, with four GTs in attendance, including the two from Sebring without any overhaul, was present to learn rather than to search for out-and-out performance. A particular task was to test different types of radiator openings and to assess a new ZF gearbox. Richard Attwood's 3m 40.9s and Bob Bondurant's 3m 42.9s were enough to at least reassure John Wyer that he need not be too worried by the Ferraris' performance even if he was not entirely satisfied with how his own cars had performed. Come June, though, a larger 5.3-litre engine would be available, and perhaps even a 7-litre version.

The weekend also brought a fatality when 'Lucky' Casner's Maserati *Tipo* 151, now in its fourth and final iteration, suddenly shot off the track on the approach to *Mulsanne*.

▲ **Le Mans test weekend.** Swiss
entrepreneur and sponsor
Georges Filipinetti poses in
Geneva with three Ferraris
carrying his name. Beyond him
is the 365 P2 in which Tommy
Spychiger set the sixth-fastest time
at the test weekend; there is a 250
GTO just visible behind it and a
250 LM sits in the foreground.

➤ **Le Mans test weekend.** Georges
Filipinetti has every reason to be
happy. Tommy Spychiger (left)
and Herbert Müller were very
quick on their first outing in the
365 P2, with Spychiger quicker
than everyone except John Surtees
during rain on the Saturday.

Low key

Monza 1,000Km, 25th April

The Monza 1,000Km, which counted for the International Trophy for Prototypes and the International Championship for GT Manufacturers (Divisions I, II and III), was an obligatory first dress rehearsal for the Le Mans 24 Hours. Knowing how much was at stake, Ferrari entered two 330 P2s and a 275 P2 plus some lightweight back-up in the form of a prototype version of the Dino 166 P, making its first official appearance driven by Giancarlo Baghetti/Giampiero Biscaldi. John Surtees, strangely enough, asked that he be paired with Ludovico Scarfiotti in one of the 330 P2s while the other such car was entrusted to Lorenzo Bandini/Nino Vaccarella, with Michael Parkes/Jean Guichet in the 275 P2. As well as five 250 LMs, the nine other Ferraris present included a 330 P entered by Maranello Concessionaires for Jo Bonnier/David Piper and the Scuderia Filipinetti 365 P2 of Herbert Müller/Tommy Spychiger. Against this Ferrari armada, there were two Ford GTs crewed by Bruce McLaren/Ken Miles (in a Sebring car) and Umberto Maglioli/Chris Amon, plus two Cobra Daytona Coupes for Bob Bondurant/Allen Grant and Jack Sears/John Whitmore.

Practice performances on the combined road circuit and

oval indicated a Ferrari victory unless Ford had kept a card up its sleeve. Parkes emerged fastest of the red cars with a lap of 2m 46.9s that just pipped Surtees's 2m 47.0s and Bandini's 2m 47.1s, with the Bonnier/Piper 330 P a more distant fourth on 2m 51.2s. Also well placed, sixth and seventh respectively, were the Müller/Spychiger 365 P2 (2m 54.8s) and the best of the 250 LMs, the Ecurie Francorchamps entry of Willy Mairesse/Lucien Bianchi (2m 55.3s). The quicker of the Fords, the McLaren/Miles car (2m 53.5s), was fifth fastest while Maglioli/Amon (2m 55.4s) lined up eighth.

Surtees was determined to stamp his authority on the 100-lap race and led the first 10 laps while Parkes and Müller followed with McLaren in tow. Baghetti's Dino 166 P went out with engine failure after only one lap, a precursor to a long list of retirements whose frequency and gravity would culminate in tragedy. Tenth time round, Bonnier (tyre and suspension) and Vaccarella (steering) also joined the dead car park. Shortly afterwards, Surtees came in for a four-minute stop with a tyre problem; he resumed in seventh place and set about clawing back lost time before handing over to Scarfiotti.

It was a surprise that Scarfiotti, although a very useful driver, had been Surtees's choice of partner because Bandini was quicker and *Il Grande John* remained as hungry for success as ever. The Englishman's temperament dictated that quest, of course, but unrelenting determination was also beginning to

◄ **Monza 1,000Km.** Watched by Romolo Tavoni (far right) and Lucien Bianchi (arms folded), Jean Guichet sets off in practice in the 275 P2 he shared with Michael Parkes. They took advantage of setbacks for the Surtees/Scarfiotti 330 P2 to score an untroubled victory. The #73 car is the Ecurie Francorchamps 250 LM that Bianchi shared with Willy Mairesse.

become necessary to keep his relationship with Enzo Ferrari, who treated him almost like a son, on an even keel. Surtees had no intention of limiting himself to being 'just' a driver. Given his obsessive desire for perfection, he liked to control the whole show. His vision of the ideal team was one in which he oversaw the car he wanted from conception to victory. That urge was exemplified by the fact that, with Mr Ferrari's agreement, he had just bought a Lola T70 to run himself under his Team Surtees banner. First time out with it, at Silverstone on 20th March, he had finished second to Jim Clark's Lotus 30 in pouring rain.

Back at Monza, meanwhile, Parkes/Guichet held a comfortable lead at one-third distance while Surtees/Scarfiotti had reached fourth place behind the Maglioli/Amon Ford and the Müller/Spychiger 365 P2. That became third when Müller stopped to refuel, change tyres and hand over to his team-mate. Tragedy came less than a lap later. Seemingly without its driver applying the brakes, the Scuderia Filipinetti Ferrari left the track on the approach to the *Parabolica*, hit the bank, ploughed into nearby woods and caught fire. Spychiger was thrown out and killed instantly.

After that catastrophe, the rest of the race comprised just a series of minor happenings of which the most notable were the retirements of the Mairesse/Bianchi 250 LM with terminal steering failure after earlier attempts to fix it and of the Maglioli/Amon Ford with broken suspension when firmly ensconced

⌃ **Monza 1,000Km.** Tommy Spychiger prepares for a practice session in the Scuderia Filipinetti 365 P2 that he shared with Herbert Müller. Come the race, he crashed fatally just after taking over from his team-mate.

⌄ **Monza 1,000Km.** Twelfth in qualifying, the Dino 166 P entrusted to Lorenzo Bandini/Giampiero Biscaldi was by far the fastest 1.6-litre car on the grid but a first-lap engine failure stopped it from showing its prowess in the race.

▲ Monza 1,000Km. On the formation lap, blue Fords and red Ferraris prepare for battle. On the American side of the track, the #69 GT40 of Bruce McLaren/Ken Miles heads the Daytona Coupes of Bob Bondurant/Allen Grant (#48) and Jack Sears/John Whitmore (#49). The three most prominent Ferraris are the Jo Bonnier/David Piper 330 P (#67), the Herbert Müller/Tommy Spychiger 365 P2 (#66) and the Lorenzo Bandini/Giampiero Biscaldi Dino 166 P (#53), the latter with the yellow 250 LM of Willy Mairesse/Lucien Bianchi close behind, alongside the Innes Ireland/Mike Salmon 250 LM (#76).

◄ Monza 1,000Km. The Maranello Concessionaires 330 P, seen with Jo Bonnier at the wheel, was slower in practice than the factory cars and was one of the first victims of the banked oval's punishing surface. The car was delayed by tyre problems from the outset and retired with broken suspension.

in third place. Parkes/Guichet avoided all the pitfalls to claim victory, their second together, after a steady drive under the eagle eye of Enzo Ferrari. Surtees/Scarfiotti closed the gap to less than two minutes to finish second, joined on the podium by McLaren/Miles. The GT40 had never run lower than fifth and its dependable performance was no doubt regarded in Dearborn as a satisfactory outcome, especially as it was bolstered by the eighth-placed Bondurant/Grant Daytona Coupe's success in winning the Division III GT category. Bondurant had found it a frustrating day because Alan Mann, the English team owner who was now in charge of the Shelby campaign in Europe, had instructed him to drive at a pre-determined pace, a requirement that was doubly demeaning for this highly skilled racer because he considered that his record of achievement in America, including with Cobras, deserved better. Feeling that the team manager was favouring his English drivers with this policy, Bondurant made a point of slowing down at the finish to take the chequered flag just in front of the sister Daytona of Sears/Whitmore.

➤ **Monza 1,000Km.** John Surtees shot into the lead at the start but fell back to seventh place after a long pitstop. With Ludovico Scarfiotti's help, he embarked on an impressive comeback that brought the 330 P2 back to second place, where it stayed until the finish.

MONZA 1,000KM

Monza, 25th April 1965, 100 laps (6.214 miles/10.000km), 621.371 miles/1,000.000km • Starters 34, classified finishers 18

1st	Michael Parkes/Jean Guichet	Ferrari 275 P2 (0836)	4h 56m 08.0s
2nd	John Surtees/Ludovico Scarfiotti	Ferrari 330 P2 (0828)	+1m 51.8s
3rd	Bruce McLaren/Ken Miles	Ford GT40	96 laps
4th	Ben Pon/Rob Slotemaker	Porsche 904 GTS	92 laps
5th	Pierre Noblet/Mario Casoni	ISO Grifo A3C	92 laps
6th	Innes Ireland/Mike Salmon	Ferrari 250 LM (5895 or 5907)	91 laps
10th	Oddone Sigala/Luigi Taramazzo	Ferrari 250 LM (6173)	89 laps
11th	Vincenzo Nember/Marino Bonomi	Ferrari 250 GTO 64 (4675 GT) *(3rd Div III)*	88 laps
DNF	Armand Boller/Dieter Spoerry	Ferrari 250 GTO (3527 GT)	62 laps (withdrawn)
DNF	Willy Mairesse/Lucien Bianchi	Ferrari 250 LM (6023)	42 laps (steering)
DNF	Herbert Müller/Tommy Spychiger	Ferrari 365 P2 (0824)	34 laps (fatal accident)
DNF	Annie Soisbault/Gérald Langlois van Ophem	Ferrari 250 LM (5843)	17 laps (gearbox)
DNF	**Lorenzo Bandini/Nino Vaccarella**	**Ferrari 330 P2 (0802)**	**9 laps (suspension)**
DNF	Jo Bonnier/David Piper	Ferrari 330 P (0818)	9 laps (tyres and suspension)
DNF	Gustave Gosselin/Jean-Claude Franck	Ferrari 250 LM (6313)	4 laps (engine)
DNF	**Giancarlo Baghetti/Giampiero Biscaldi**	**Ferrari Dino 166 P (0834)**	**1 lap (engine)**

Fastest practice lap: Parkes, 2m 46.9s, 135.369mph/217.855kph **Fastest race lap:** Surtees, 2m 47.2s, 133.788mph/215.311kph **Winner's average speed:** 125.897mph/202.611kph **FIA World Sports Car Championship (GT Division III, over 2,000cc):**[1] 1st Shelby 40.5, 2nd Ferrari 10.0

[1] *Scoring system for the top six places in this event was 9–6–4–3–2–1 multiplied by coefficient 1.3; only the manufacturer's highest-placed car scored points*

TOURIST TROPHY

Oulton Park, 1st May 1965, 138 laps (2.761 miles/4.443km), 380.984 miles/613.134km • Starters 24, classified finishers 15

1st	Denny Hulme	Brabham BT8 Climax	4h 03m 01.4s
2nd	David Hobbs	Lola T70	137 laps
3rd	David Piper	Ferrari 250 LM (5897)	133 laps
4th	John Whitmore	Shelby Cobra roadster *(1st Div III)*	130 laps
5th	Peter Sutcliffe	Ferrari 250 GTO (4491 GT) *(2nd Div III)*	130 laps
6th	Allen Grant	Shelby Cobra roadster	128 laps
12th	Mike Salmon	Ferrari 250 GTO 64 (4399 GT)	114 laps

Fastest practice lap: John Surtees (Lola T70), 1m 36.6s, 102.890mph/165.585kph **Fastest race lap:** Bruce McLaren (McLaren Elva Mk1), 1m 39.0s, 100.400mph/161.578kph **Winner's average speed:** 94.069mph/151.389kph **FIA World Sports Car Championship (GT Division III, over 2,000cc):**[1] 1st Shelby 52.2, 2nd Ferrari 17.8

[1] *Scoring system for the top six places in this event was 9–6–4–3–2–1 multiplied by coefficient 1.3; only the manufacturer's highest-placed car scored points*

Eyes wide shut

Targa Florio, 9th May

On 1st May, six days after the Monza 1,000Km, Surtees was at Oulton Park to race his Lola T70 in the Tourist Trophy, which had transferred from Goodwood and was now being run as two heats with an aggregated result. From pole position, he rocketed away to lead the first heat but dropped out just four laps later with a broken steering arm, leaving Denny Hulme (Brabham BT8) to win. Although David Hobbs (Lola T70) prevailed in the second heat, Hulme came out on top in the final classification.

A week later, the 49th Targa Florio was run without Surtees. The Scuderia was represented by three 275 P2s for Nino Vaccarella/Lorenzo Bandini, Ludovico Scarfiotti/Michael Parkes and Jean Guichet/Giancarlo Baghetti together with a lightened 275 GTB entered as a prototype for Giampiero Biscaldi/Bruno Deserti. This works quartet was backed up by Ferrari privateers with four 250 LMs, three 250 GTOs and a GTO 64, plus diverse oddballs in the form of a 500 TRC and even a 250 GT Lusso. Porsche's weapons against this stampede of Prancing Horses comprised a works 904/8 (Jo Bonnier/Graham Hill), a 904/6 (Umberto Maglioli/Herbert Linge), a 904 GTS (Antonio Pucci/Günther Klass) and a new 904/8 spyder (Colin Davis/Gerhard Mitter) that was both powerful at around 225bhp and ultra-light at just 600kg (1,323lb). Even though Ford had nothing to learn or to prove, it entered its prototype GT40 roadster, as seen at the Le Mans test weekend, for Bob Bondurant/John Whitmore in the name of Ford Advanced Vehicles (FAV), its Slough-based subsidiary.

When it came to winning the Targa Florio, it was a big advantage to have intimate knowledge of the twists and turns of the *Piccolo Madonie* circuit, especially if that was combined with prodigious driving talent. Vaccarella, whose meticulous professional approach was on a par with that of Surtees, possessed these twin requirements in abundance. In practice he demonstrated this by becoming the first driver to break the 40-minute barrier with a lap in 39m 30s, a feat described by Bernard Cahier as 'a dominant display that was head and shoulders above those of his rivals'. Everyone else could only follow at some distance, in the order Scarfiotti (40m 56s), Bondurant (41m 46s), Bonnier (42m 5s), Davis (42m 35s) and Maglioli (42m 49s).

On Sunday, Vaccarella showed off his skills in front of 200,000 exuberant Sicilians roaring themselves hoarse. He covered the first lap in 40m 5s to open up a margin of nine seconds over Scarfiotti, with Bondurant third and Bonnier fourth, and a circumspect Guichet sixth. Vaccarella completed the second lap in 39m 21s, a new record, to put Scarfiotti 50 seconds behind and very much on the ragged edge, with Guichet now third. Next time round, Vaccarella stopped to hand over to Bandini with a much bigger advantage of 4m 48s over the second-placed car, which was now the Guichet/Baghetti 275 P2. Parkes was supposed to have taken over from Scarfiotti at the same time but his co-driver never appeared, having wrecked their 275 P2's steering after clipping a kerb, thereby denying the Englishman the possibility of back-to-back victories. The GT40 was now third, with Whitmore in the driving seat, while Bonnier headed a batch of Porsches.

Bad luck? Race incidents? What happened next was a boon to the leaders. On the fourth lap, Bonnier was delayed by his throttle linkage acting up. Next time round, Whitmore had the Ford's left-front Halibrand wheel part company at high speed

➤ **Targa Florio.** Lorenzo Bandini's season had got off to a low-key start with retirements from three Formula 1 races as well as a premature departure from the Monza 1,000Km. He needed to score a good result in Sicily, where he had previously done well with a second and a third.

▾ **Targa Florio.** At first everything went well for Ludovico Scarfiotti, running second to Nino Vaccarella. Third time round, though, he hit a kerb and retired his 275 P2 with broken steering before co-driver Michael Parkes even had a chance to get behind the wheel.

TARGA FLORIO

Piccolo Madonie, 9th May 1965, 10 laps (44.7 miles/72.0km), 447.4 miles/720.0km • Starters 59, classified finishers 30

1st	Nino Vaccarella/Lorenzo Bandini	Ferrari 275 P2 (0828)	7h 01m 12.5s
2nd	Colin Davis/Gerhard Mitter	Porsche 904/8	7h 05m 34.0s
3rd	Umberto Maglioli/Herbert Linge	Porsche 904/6	7h 06m 58.0s
4th	Jo Bonnier/Graham Hill	Porsche 904/8	7h 10m 08.0s
5th	Antonio Pucci/Günther Klass	Porsche 904 GTS	7h 11m 07.0s
6th	Hans Herrmann/Leo Cella	Abarth 1600 OT Spyder	7h 17m 23.0s
8th	Luigi Taramazzo/Oddone Sigala	Ferrari 250 LM (6173)	7h 37m 15.0s
12th	Clemente Ravetto/Gaetano Starrabba	Ferrari 250 GTO 64 (4091 GT) *(1st Div III)*	7h 50m 57.2s
14th	Antonio Nicodemi/Francesco Lessona	Ferrari 250 LM (5891)	7h 57m 02.0s
30th	Luigi Mosca/Tullio Sergio Marchesi	Ferrari 250 GTO (3647 GT)	9 laps
NC	Franco Tagliavia/Silvestre Semilia	Ferrari 500 TRC	9 laps (over time limit)
NC	**Giampiero Biscaldi/Bruno Deserti**	**Ferrari 275 GTB (6885)**	**8 laps (over time limit)**
NC	'Bouchon'/Jean-Claude Sauer	Ferrari 250 GT Lusso	7 laps (over time limit)
DNF	Sergio Bettoja/Andrea De Adamich/Mario Casoni	Ferrari 250 LM	– (battery)
DNF	**Jean Guichet/Giancarlo Baghetti**	**Ferrari 275 P2 (0832)**	**– (battery)**
DNF	Ignazio Capuano/Ferdinando Latteri	Ferrari 250 GTO (3765 LM)	–
DNF	Cesare Toppetti/Maurizio Grana	Ferrari 250 LM	– (accident)
DNF	Michel de Bourbon-Parma/Claude Bourillot	Ferrari 250 GTO (3909 GT)	– (accident)
DNF	**Ludovico Scarfiotti/Michael Parkes**	**Ferrari 275 P2**	**– (accident)**

Fastest practice lap: Vaccarella, 39m 30.0s, 67.958mph/109.367kph **Fastest race lap:** Vaccarella, 39m 21.0s, 68.217mph/109.784kph **Winner's average speed:** 63.729mph/102.562kph **FIA World Sports Car Championship (GT Division III, over 2,000cc):**[1] 1st Shelby 52.2, 2nd Ferrari 32.2

[1] *Scoring system for the top six places in this event was 9–6–4–3–2–1 multiplied by coefficient 1.6; only the manufacturer's highest-placed car scored points*

◄ **Targa Florio.** After taking over the second-placed 275 P2 from Jean Guichet at the end of the fourth lap, Giancarlo Baghetti sets off for his Sicilian stint. Battery failure halted the car three laps later.

▲ **Targa Florio.** With all of Sicily rooting for him, Nino Vaccarella rejoins after taking over from Lorenzo Bandini for a final stint with a handsome lead. The final laps were a formality and he brought the 275 P2 safely home to a popular victory.

but nonetheless managed to get back to the pits after fitting the spare, even though a search was needed to find the missing three-eared central fixing to secure it. This left the Porsches of Davis/Mitter third and Maglioli/Linge fourth, joined a lap later by yet another Stuttgart-built car when Pucci/Klass slotted into fifth place, with the Bonnier/Hill car recovering fast.

The smiles in the Ferrari camp turned to frowns on the seventh lap when second-placed Baghetti suffered battery failure and parked his 275 P2 at the side of the road near Cerda. The consistent Porsches in distant pursuit all moved up a place, although the light, powerful Abarth 1600 of Hans Herrmann/ Leo Cella was now harassing them. The eighth lap brought no changes in the top six but Vaccarella, back in for his second stint, was now more concerned with consolidating his position than lowering the lap record. The crowd's fervour intensified, especially around Cerda, as the race headed towards its conclusion with Vaccarella completing his triumphant last lap in a very cautious 43 minutes. The day ended on a low note for Ford as the GT40 roadster finished up in a ditch after Bondurant spun off when approaching Cerda on the last lap.

Enzo Ferrari was able to breathe a little easier because his prototypes had now beaten Ford's twice in a fortnight while Porsche's management were delighted that their four works cars had finished in line astern behind the winning Ferrari. But there was no time to relax in Maranello with the next four weekends bringing the International Trophy at Silverstone, the Spa 500Km, the Nürburgring 1,000Km and the Monaco Grand Prix. Was this pile-up of commitments the reason why Surtees had not been in Sicily? There was no evidence to prove it but Denis Jenkinson, for one, was asking the question.

John Surtees arrived at Silverstone for the International Trophy with his usual pair of 158s and Lorenzo Bandini with his regular 1512. The results obtained in the absence of Jim Clark and Dan Gurney, who were seeking to qualify for the Indianapolis 500, were rather disappointing. The Ferraris shared the four-strong front row of the grid with two BRMs that had out-qualified them in the hands of Graham Hill (1m 31.4s) and new recruit Jackie Stewart (1m 31.6s), with Surtees (1m 32.1s) a little ahead of Bandini (1m 32.3s). After the retirements of Hill (valve gear) and Jack Brabham (gearbox), Stewart outpaced Surtees to claim victory, although the Ferrari finished only three seconds behind and Surtees also set a new lap record. Bandini, however, put in an under-par performance and never broke out of a mid-field pack, finishing a lap behind in seventh place. More would be expected of him in Monaco.

'Big John' continued to widen the scope of his activities by competing in the day's 25-lap sports car race at the wheel of his Lola T70. He had to cede victory to a delighted Bruce McLaren in the Elva-Oldsmobile that the New Zealander had carefully developed and improved, perhaps giving the English perfectionist food for thought.

A good omen!

Nürburgring 1,000Km, 23rd May

As the Nürburgring 1,000Km was the curtain-raiser for the Le Mans 24 Hours, Ferrari and Ford took it very seriously.

Of 14 Ferraris, four were works entries, each a different model. The Scuderia's mainstays were John Surtees/Ludovico Scarfiotti in a 330 P2 and Michael Parkes/Jean Guichet with a 275 P2. As

back-up, the factory put Giampiero Biscaldi/Giancarlo Baghetti in the 275 GTB that had débuted on the Targa Florio, again as a prototype but with this status about to change because the homologation would be granted on 1st June. The Dino 166 P, also a works entry, was crewed by Lorenzo Bandini/Nino Vaccarella in the hope that its race would last longer than its single lap at Monza. Other strong contenders were the Maranello Concessionaires 275 P2 of Graham Hill/Jackie Stewart and 250 LMs in the hands of David Piper/Tony Maggs (entered by Piper) and Willy Mairesse/'Beurlys' (Ecurie Francorchamps). The Belgian entry deserves special mention because 'Wild Willy' was back to his belligerent best. Driving this very car, he had not only won the Spa 500Km just a week earlier but also the Angola Grand Prix the previous November. Parkes had led at Spa in a 330 P run by Maranello Concessionaires until its fuel pump played up after 17 laps, allowing Mairesse to win.

Ford arrived with four GT40s still classed in the prototype category. The two entered by Shelby for Phil Hill/Bruce McLaren and Chris Amon/Ronnie Bucknum were those seen in Florida at the beginning of the season although Hill/McLaren now benefited from a more powerful 5.3-litre V8. The other GT40s were entrusted to European pairings, with Frenchmen Maurice Trintignant/Guy Ligier in a Ford France entry and Englishmen John Whitmore/Richard Attwood in the roadster run by FAV.

Battle still raged in the International Championship for GT Manufacturers between Ford and Ferrari but it was far from plain sailing for Dearborn. Before the previous round, 20 points

SPA 500KM

Spa-Francorchamps, 16th May 1965, 36 laps (8.761 miles/14.100km), 315.408 miles/507.600km • Starters 27, classified finishers 17

1st	Willy Mairesse	Ferrari 250 LM (6023)	2h 29m 45.7s
2nd	David Piper	Ferrari 250 LM (5897)	+1m 57.8s
3rd	Ben Pon	Porsche 904 GTS	+2m 37.2s
4th	Peter Sutcliffe	Ferrari 250 GTO (4491 GT) *(1st Div III)*	+2m 58.1s
5th	Bob Bondurant	Shelby Cobra Daytona *(2nd Div III)*	+3m 04.1s
6th	Mike Salmon	Ferrari 250 GTO 64 (4399 GT)	35 laps
8th	Jean-Claude Franck	Ferrari 250 LM (6313)	35 laps
9th	Michael Parkes	Ferrari 330 P (0818)	34 laps
16th	'Bouchon'	Ferrari 250 GT Lusso	29 laps
DNF	Annie Soisbault	Ferrari 250 LM (5843)	21 laps (fuel pump)
DNF	Gérald Langlois van Ophem	Ferrari 250 GTO (4153 GT)	19 laps (transmission)
DNF	Xavier Boulanger	Ferrari 275 GTB	–

Fastest practice lap: Parkes, 3m 59.7s, 131.771mph/212.065kph **Fastest race lap:** Parkes, 4m 01.3s, 130.712mph/210.360kph **Winner's average speed:** 126.301mph/203.262kph **FIA World Sports Car Championship (GT Division III, over 2,000cc):**[1] 1st Shelby 60.0, 2nd Ferrari 43.9

[1] Scoring system for the top six places in this event was 9–6–4–3–2–1 multiplied by coefficient 1.3; only the manufacturer's highest-placed car scored points

▲ **Nürburgring 1,000Km.** John Surtees's 330 P2 rightly carried #1. Quickest in practice, he led from start to finish with flawless support from Ludovico Scarfiotti.

➤ **Nürburgring 1,000Km.** By finishing second, less than a minute behind the Surtees/ Scarfiotti 330 P2, Jean Guichet, seen rejoining after a routine pitstop for his 275 P2, could only regret the precious seconds lost in the pits for a wheel change after co-driver Michael Parkes's collision with a tailender.

▲ Nürburgring 1,000Km. Two weeks after their Sicilian triumph, the task for Lorenzo Bandini and Nino Vaccarella was to prove that the Dino 166 P, despite its setback at Monza, could take the fight to the six-cylinder Porsches. They did so in style. Despite fuel starvation towards the end, the car finished fourth and beat its Stuttgart rivals convincingly.

had separated Shelby's Cobras from the score notched up by privately run GTOs, but suspect reliability and bad luck for the Daytona Coupes had brought the gap down to 16.1 at Spa. There, Bob Bondurant's down-on-power car had lost out on fourth place by just six seconds to Peter Sutcliffe's class-winning GTO while John Whitmore's race had been ruined when Harry Digby's Cobra roadster strayed into his path and left him unable to avoid hitting it. For the Nürburgring, three Daytona Coupes joined the fray, two entered by Alan Mann Racing for Bondurant/Jochen Neerpasch and Jack Sears/Frank Gardner, the other in Ford France colours for Jo Schlesser/André Simon.

Porsches were becoming an increasingly serious threat and ten of them lined up for the usual Le Mans-style start. The works effort was spearheaded by a 904/8 for Jo Bonnier/Jochen Rindt with solid support from three 904/6s in the hands of Umberto Maglioli/Herbert Linge, Colin Davis/Gerhard Mitter and Peter Nöcker/Günther Klass, while a Porsche GB-entered 904 GTS

shared by Gerhard Koch and Ben Pon, who had finished third in the Spa 500Km, was not to be overlooked.

Surtees dominated practice with a time of 8m 53.1s in the 330 P2 followed by Graham Hill (8m 58.8s), Parkes (9m 0.1s) and Phil Hill (9m 0.2s). Bandini, wanting to prove that he was as quick as his team leader, also had a go in the 330 P2 and got it round in a splendid 8m 53.9s, and then opened everyone's eyes with an equally impressive 9m 11.1s in the Dino 166 P, a remarkable turn of speed for a 1.6-litre car that was almost as quick as Bonnier's Porsche and faster than the much more powerful cars of Trintignant, Mairesse and Bondurant.

If there were any Doubting Thomases concerning Surtees's prospects in the race, he immediately put them in their place by taking the lead in the *Südkehre*, opening up a significant advantage by *Quiddelbacher Höhe*, getting almost out of reach at *Breidscheid* and reaching the *Karussell* completely on his own. When he shot past the pits at the end of the lap, he was 18 seconds in front of Phil Hill with the other Hill next, followed by Amon and Parkes. On his first flying lap, *Il Grande John* then turned in a 8m 50.5s, which was quicker than his practice best despite having a full tank of fuel, and now his margin over Phil Hill was 27 seconds. Thereafter, the tide turned a little, for the American slipped back by only four more seconds third time round and then began to fight back, reducing the deficit on each of the next three laps in turn to 28, 26 and 21 seconds. At the same time, he pulled away from his namesake, leaving the Maranello Concessionaires Ferrari 49 seconds behind after six laps and now under threat from Parkes.

That was as good as it got for the Ford. It coasted to a halt with a driveshaft failure on the seventh lap, leaving its driver to trek back to the pits on foot. Phil's explanation for his up-and-down race went like this: during the first lap he realised that he had not properly buckled his safety harness and slowed down to sort it out; then, realising that his pursuers were quickly catching up, he hit the loud pedal to get away and twisted a driveshaft, which survived for a while before eventually breaking, just as had happened during practice.

In the 275 P2s, meanwhile, Parkes kept up the pace and got past Graham Hill on lap eight, but the Maranello Concessionaires car stayed in very close contact for another two laps before grinding to a halt thanks to a short circuit in its alternator. With Surtees still romping away up at the front, the race now became rather monotonous until the first refuelling stops. These went without a hitch for the leading trio but Amon missed his signal to stop and went round again only for the Ford to run dry just before it reached the pits. Somehow, he pushed the car to its pit, on the

brink of exhaustion by the time he arrived, whereupon team manager Carroll Smith re-assigned it to McLaren/Hill, who climbed back up the leader board to finish eighth. Although it had run perfectly, investigation afterwards revealed a deep knife cut in a plug lead that had caused the exposed wire to short against the engine until vibration had shaken the lead clear. That raised a big question mark because anyone could have accessed the car, or any others, during their previous night in an unguarded *parc fermé*. The other two Fords lasted little more than half distance. A sluggish start meant that the Trintignant/Simon car never got higher than 15th before it had to retire due to a broken engine mount on the 23rd lap. Three laps later, Whitmore stopped unexpectedly at the pits, rejoined at a snail's pace and then threw in the towel for the same reason.

With three Ferraris in the top three places, Surtees/Scarfiotti in the lead from Parkes/Guichet and the irrepressible Bandini/Vaccarella Dino, the result now looked to be a foregone conclusion. And so it turned out except that the Dino dropped back a place after lapsing onto five cylinders, which gifted the last podium position to the Bonnier/Rindt Porsche.

But Ferrari was not spared setbacks, in particular with the retirement of the Mairesse/'Beurlys' 250 LM on lap 25

NÜRBURGRING 1,000KM

Nürburgring, 23rd May 1965, 44 laps (14.173 miles/22.810km), 623.633 miles/1,003.640km • Starters 63, classified finishers 32

1st	John Surtees/Ludovico Scarfiotti	Ferrari 330 P2 (0828)	6h 53m 05.4s
2nd	Michael Parkes/Jean Guichet	Ferrari 275 P2 (0832)	+44.8s
3rd	Jo Bonnier/Jochen Rindt	Porsche 904/8	+7m 54.2s
4th	Lorenzo Bandini/Nino Vaccarella	Ferrari Dino 166 P (0834)	43 laps
5th	Umberto Maglioli/Herbert Linge	Porsche 904/6	43 laps
6th	Peter Nöcker/Günther Klass	Porsche 904/6	43 laps
13th	Gianni Biscaldi/Giancarlo Baghetti	Ferrari 275 GTB (6885)	41 laps
15th	Peter Sutcliffe/Peter Lumsden	Ferrari 250 GTO (4491 GT) *(4th Div III)*	41 laps
16th	David Piper/Tony Maggs	Ferrari 250 LM (5897)	40 laps
22nd	Peter Ettmüller/Peter Harper	Ferrari 250 LM (6119)	39 laps
23rd	Werner Lindermann/Manfred Ramminger	Ferrari 250 GTO (4115 GT)	39 laps
29th	Karl vom Kothen/Karl-Friedrich Kronenberg	Ferrari 250 GT SWB	36 laps
DNF	Willy Mairesse/'Beurlys' (Jean Blaton)	Ferrari 250 LM (6023)	25 laps (gearbox)
DNF	Mike Salmon/Chris Kerrison	Ferrari 250 GTO 64 (4399 GT)	22 laps (engine)
DNF	Gérald Langlois van Ophem/Xavier Boulanger	Ferrari 250 LM (6313)	13 laps (accident)
DNF	Graham Hill/Jackie Stewart	Ferrari 275 P2 (0826)	9 laps (electrics)
DNF	Gustave Gosselin/Pierre Dumay	Ferrari 250 LM (5843)	7 laps (gearbox)
DNF	Rollo Feilding/Peter Clarke	Ferrari 250 GTO (3757 GT)	0 laps (con rod)

Fastest practice lap: Surtees, 8m 53.1s, 95.713mph/154.035kph **Fastest race lap:** Surtees, 8m 50.5s, 96.064mph/154.600kph **Winner's average speed:** 90.658mph/145.900kph **FIA World Sports Car Championship (GT Division III, over 2,000cc):**[1] 1st Shelby 74.4, 2nd Ferrari 48.7

[1] Scoring system for the top six places in this event was 9–6–4–3–2–1 multiplied by coefficient 1.6; only the manufacturer's highest-placed car scored points

with gearbox trouble after an early delay for a change of fuse in its fuel pump. Parkes also seemed on the point of losing everything when he collided with a backmarker, luckily getting away with needing only a replacement front wheel. Another disappointment was the performance of the 275 GTB, which lost too much time for a change of brake pads and was never really able to match the pace of the well-driven Daytona Coupes, in particular the Bondurant/Neerpasch car that finished seventh and won the GT category. However, with only four weeks to go before Le Mans, there were more worries in Dearborn than in Maranello.

Above all, the glory lay with Surtees, who joined Rudolf Caracciola, Alberto Ascari, Juan Manuel Fangio and Stirling Moss as a three-times winner at the fabulous Nürburgring.

Hill at the summit

Monaco Grand Prix, 30th May

The absence of Jim Clark and Dan Gurney, who were racing in the Indy 500, had its effect on the Monaco Grand Prix. At Lotus, Colin Chapman wanted to bring in Pedro Rodríguez as Clark's substitute but the organisers would not guarantee a starting position for two entries, Mike Spence being the other, so Chapman withdrew both cars. At Brabham, Denny Hulme,

an emerging star in Formula 2, made his début as Gurney's replacement.

As for Ferrari, some observers wondered why John Surtees was still using a 158 when Lorenzo Bandini had a 1512 and another example for Surtees was ready in Maranello, simply awaiting assembly, but the reason was that the reigning World Champion preferred to defend his title in a car with a tried-and-tested engine rather than a complicated new one that he reckoned was not yet fully raceworthy. Bill Gavin wondered in *Sport Auto* why the V8s in the two cars at Surtees's disposal also lacked the Lucas fuel injection that had been successfully grafted onto the 12-cylinder engine and wrongly deduced that 'Bandini was favoured in the team for national political reasons'.

Just as Thursday's practice session opened, rain began to fall and then intensified, leaving only those who were quick off the mark able to set respectable times, Bandini (1m 37.5s) among them with the second-best lap. Although far slower, Surtees (1m 49.3s) splashed around fairly consistently, assessing two different types of Dunlop rain tyres on his pair of 158s. In perfect weather the next morning, at an ungodly hour that would have rudely awakened Monégasques from their dreamless sleep, Bandini (1m 33.2s) continued to be quicker than Surtees (1m 34.0s), the Italian beaten only by the BRMs of Graham Hill and Jackie Stewart, the latter slightly quicker than his team leader. The final session on Saturday broadly provided confirmation of

◀ **Monaco Grand Prix.** Although Lorenzo Bandini inherited the lead on lap 30 after Jackie Stewart spun his BRM, Jack Brabham put him under relentless pressure, as seen at the exit from the Station hairpin. Within four laps, the Australian driver was in front.

Monaco Grand Prix. Another challenge for Bandini was to hold off his team leader. The Ferraris ran in close company (above) for much of the middle phase of the race, except for a spell between laps 53 and 65 (right) when they were separated by Graham Hill, who was charging back up the order in his BRM after an incident at the chicane.

the previous one, except that Jack Brabham (1m 32.8s) inserted himself between Hill (1m 32.5s) on pole position and Stewart, who did not improve on his previous day's time. 'Black Jack' was certainly getting the best out of the new four-valve Coventry Climax V8 that at this stage was still for his exclusive use. Both Bandini (1m 33.0s) and Surtees (1m 33.2s) went a little quicker to line up fourth and fifth but the day's efforts were disappointing for 'Big John' because he had to fall back on his spare car after the V8 in his usual 158 exploded. The Italian was brimming with confidence for the race, especially as the use of a shortened nose for his 1512 brought about a 10°C reduction in running temperature, which was most helpful in view of the flat-12's tendency to overheat.

As ever, starting from pole position in Monaco provided a major step towards victory and Hill confirmed that by beating Stewart into the first corner, after which the two BRMs gradually

▾ **Monaco Grand Prix.** For most of the final third of the race, Surtees ran second, ahead of Bandini. As the end approached, he tried harder and harder to catch Graham Hill's BRM. But for a few drops of petrol, he would have finished just a few seconds behind the winner, but at least he salvaged some points with fourth place.

pulled away at nearly a second per lap from the Ferraris, Bandini heading Surtees, with Brabham fifth. On lap 25, however, the race was turned on its head when Hill emerged from the tunnel and had to take to the escape road at the chicane to avoid hitting Bob Anderson's privateer Brabham crawling along after a driveshaft breakage. By the time Hill had climbed out of the BRM, pushed it to a position where he could rejoin and restarted the engine, 33 seconds had elapsed and he was now fifth behind Brabham with his young team-mate in the lead.

Everyone at Ferrari, whose cars were now running second and third, hoped that Stewart might make an error and he duly obliged on lap 30 when he threw away his comfortable lead with a wild spin at *Ste-Dévote*. The BRM went backwards onto a pavement, sustaining a chipped wheel rim and some rear-suspension damage, but at least Stewart was able to rejoin, just ahead of Hill, whom he quickly allowed to pass. Now Bandini led from Brabham, who had managed to outfox Surtees three laps earlier and was now right on the 12-cylinder Ferrari's tail. The Australian launched his attack at the *Gazomètre* hairpin on lap 34 and pulled it off with a huge opposite-lock slide. The winner of the 1959 race now led the Ferraris and pulled away.

Brabham was having to change gear 'by ear' because his rev counter had packed up and this did not do his special Climax

MONACO GRAND PRIX

Monaco, 30th May 1965, 100 laps (1.954 miles/3.145km), 195.421 miles/314.500km • Starters 16, finishers 9

RACE				PRACTICE	
1st	Graham Hill	BRM P261 BRM V8	2h 37m 39.6s	1st	1m 32.5s
2nd	**Lorenzo Bandini**	**Ferrari 1512 F12**	**+1m 04.0s**	**4th**	**1m 33.0s**
3rd	Jackie Stewart	BRM P261 BRM V8	+1m 41.9s	3rd	1m 32.9s
4th	**John Surtees**	**Ferrari 158 V8**	**99 laps (out of fuel)**	**5th**	**1m 33.2s**
5th	Bruce McLaren	Cooper T77 Climax V8	98 laps	7th	1m 34.3s
6th	Jo Siffert	Brabham BT11 BRM V8	98 laps	10th	1m 36.0s

Pole position: Hill, 1m 32.5s, 76.059mph/122.400kph **Fastest race lap:** Hill, 1m 31.7s, 76.831mph/123.647kph **Winner's average speed:** 74.339mph/119.637kph **Drivers' championship:** 1st Hill 13, 2nd= Surtees & Clark 9, 4th Bandini 6 **Constructors' championship:** 1st BRM 13, 2nd Ferrari 12, 3rd Lotus-Climax 9

engine much good, especially as he could not ease up and risk surrendering his lead. Despite all his skill and experience, it was impossible not to over-rev the engine from time to time in the heat of battle and it finally succumbed on lap 43. Meanwhile, Hill, on a charge, was now only four seconds behind Surtees and gaining. Ferrari supporters held their breath. The BRM driver pounced on lap 53, so now it was up to Bandini to hold him back. The Italian did his best until lap 65, when Hill, who had almost got past on the previous lap in the *Gazomètre* hairpin, successfully pulled off his next attempt.

Now Surtees dug deep to try to salvage the race for Ferrari. He caught Bandini and overtook on lap 77. Hill, aware of the threat, went quicker than ever, breaking his own string of lap records on lap 82 with a remarkable 1m 31.7s, which was nearly a whole second better than his pole-position time. Meanwhile, Bandini was advised from the pits that his flat-12's fuel consumption, which was marginal in any case, was likely to leave him dry before the end of the race after such a furious pace, so he eased off a little, without letting fourth-placed Stewart get too close.

While Hill maintained his lead, Surtees was never more than six seconds behind and kept Maranello's hopes alive, although they faded as the laps counted down. Little did he know it, but his V8 was also marginal on fuel and it spluttered approaching *Tabac* corner on the penultimate lap. Using the starter motor, he limped to the finish and stopped just over the line under the amused gaze of Louis Chiron who, in his role as clerk of the course, had stationed himself there to receive the winner.

Might the outcome have been different if Surtees had not been forced to fall back on his spare car before the completion of fuel-consumption tests in his regular one? Maybe, but that question only served to distract from a fine victory. Everyone agreed that Graham Hill had driven one of his greatest races.

No excuses

Belgian Grand Prix, 13th June

A week before Le Mans, it was not surprising that the Ferraris presented for this race, which was given the honorary title of European Grand Prix, were unchanged from those seen in Monaco other than each having an additional fuel tank above the engine. Jim Clark was back after his historic victory in the Indianapolis 500 and he and Mike Spence had the use of three Lotus 33s, including one with a four-valve Coventry Climax V8. At Brabham, Dan Gurney was also back from his Indy excursion, which had seen him qualify his Lotus on the front row but retire from the race. BRM brought three P261s for Graham Hill and Jackie Stewart, one with its seat trimmed in the Scot's tartan. Cooper and Honda completed the works teams.

As anticipated, a recurrent problem of starting money and status reared its head in Friday's practice. Of the 21 drivers entered, only those in the 12 works cars took part that day. The nine 'independents', although assured of a position on the grid, unlike at Monaco, rebelled against the decision of the organisers to give starting money only to the four quickest among them. While waiting for the parties to come to an agreement, Hill once again displayed scintillating form by ending the session with a time of 3m 48.0s, followed by Stewart and Surtees. Among the 12-cylinder cars, Richie Ginther and Ronnie Bucknum in their Hondas sandwiched Bandini at the wheel of a 1512 that had been somewhat detuned to improve its fuel consumption. More worrying for the Scuderia was that the next day's session saw Surtees pushed back to the third row alongside the Rob Walker-run Brabhams of Jo Bonnier (Climax-powered BT7) and

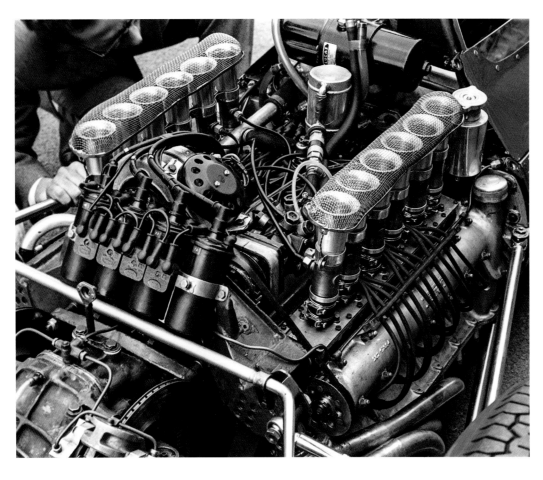

◀ **Belgian Grand Prix.** At Spa, a circuit that favoured powerful cars, Lorenzo Bandini's flat-12 proved to be rather less effective than Surtees's V8, and his 1512 was also slower than the Hondas with their V12 engines.

▼ **Belgian Grand Prix.** While on his way to his Ferrari 158 on the third row of the grid, John Surtees pauses for a few words with Honda's Richie Ginther, while the Japanese team's number two, Ronnie Bucknum, appears to enjoy the exchange. Two Brabham men are among the bystanders, wearing matching team jackets: driver Dan Gurney checks out the back of the Honda RA272 while designer Ron Tauranac smiles at the banter.

Belgian Grand Prix. While Graham Hill (#7 BRM) made the best start, Jim Clark (#17 Lotus) soon took the lead. Closest behind Clark is Jackie Stewart's BRM, while the next four cars, from left, are Jo Siffert's Brabham (#21), Dan Gurney's Brabham (#15), Richie Ginther's Honda (#10) and John Surtees's Ferrari (#1).

Belgian Grand Prix. Pushing very hard in wet conditions, with his inside front wheel almost clear of the track, Surtees ran as high as third before going out after only six laps with a blown piston. Note the additional fuel tank fitted above the engine.

◄ **Belgian Grand Prix.** Bandini had a big problem adapting to the wet weather at a circuit he disliked. In one of the worst performances of his career, he spent the entire race near the back of the field and came home ninth, three laps behind the winner.

Jo Siffert (BRM-powered BT11), cars that really were not in the same league as the Ferrari and, due to their 'independent' status, had not even run the previous day. To make matters even worse, Bandini, who disliked the high-speed Spa circuit, shared the sixth row with Jochen Rindt's works Cooper. Considering that Ginther was fourth fastest with Honda's V12 engine, perhaps Surtees was wrong to be spurning Ferrari's flat-12, especially as he had played a part in its creation.

To add to the Scuderia's woes, rain poured down 15 minutes before the 3.30pm start and upset the odds. After everyone switched to their most suitable tyres for the conditions, the race got under way on a soaked track in lower temperatures than those that had prevailed during practice. Clark sprinted away to an uncontested victory with Stewart an equally convincing second, these two drivers finishing the race a lap ahead of everyone else. Surtees began well but did not last long. Fourth first time round, he was third by lap 5 with only Clark and Stewart in front of him, but at the end of lap 6 he coasted into the pits with a piston failure in his V8, seemingly provoked by the sensitivity of the Bosch fuel-injection system to the drop in ambient temperature. At that moment, Bandini, his 1512 struggling like a ship in a storm, was 14th, which by the end became 10th, two laps down. It was an unsatisfactory performance that the Italian, unable to get to grips with the difficult track conditions, acknowledged without seeking to make any excuses.

BELGIAN GRAND PRIX

Spa-Francorchamps, 13th June 1965, 32 laps (8.761 miles/14.100km), 280.363 miles/451.200km • Starters 19, finishers 13

RACE				PRACTICE	
1st	Jim Clark	Lotus 33 Climax V8	2h 23m 34.8s	2nd	3m 47.5s
2nd	Jackie Stewart	BRM P261 BRM V8	+44.8s	3rd	3m 48.8s
3rd	Bruce McLaren	Cooper T77 Climax V8	31 laps	9th	3m 51.3s
4th	Jack Brabham	Brabham BT11 Climax V8	31 laps	10th	3m 51.5s
5th	Graham Hill	BRM P261 BRM V8	31 laps	1st	3m 45.4s
6th	Richie Ginther	Honda RA272 Honda V12	31 laps	4th	3m 49.0s
9th	**Lorenzo Bandini**	**Ferrari 1512 F12**	**30 laps**	**15th**	**3m 54.0s**
DNF	**John Surtees**	**Ferrari 158 V8**	5 laps (engine)	**6th**	**3m 49.5s**

Pole position: Hill, 3m 45.4s, 139.933mph/225.200kph **Fastest race lap:** Clark, 4m 12.9s, 124.716mph/200.711kph **Winner's average speed:** 117.160mph/188.550kph **Drivers' championship:** 1st Clark 18, 2nd Hill 15, 3rd Stewart 11, 4th Surtees 9, 5th Bandini 6 **Constructors' championship:** 1st BRM 19, 2nd Lotus-Climax 18, 3rd Ferrari 12

Seeds of discord

What was perhaps more serious than Ferrari's poor results after the first three Formula 1 World Championship rounds was the increasingly poisonous atmosphere within the team. In an article in *Motor Sport* titled 'Belgian Grand Prix Reflections', Denis Jenkinson provided the lowdown. Shortly after the Monaco Grand Prix, an English newspaper for which Surtees occasionally provided ghosted columns had published an article that was very derogatory about Ferrari and presented it as if in the driver's own words, although it had been knocked together by an irresponsible journalist without any consultation. Of course, it served only to ramp up the tensions that some people in Maranello nursed in relation to the World Champion's inclination to diversify his activities.

On 5th June, Surtees was at Mosport in Canada winning the Player's 200 in his Lola T70. Meanwhile, the Italian specialist press, which was never reticent about inflaming a situation, especially when it revolved around Ferrari, made matters worse just at a time when Surtees was on the other side of the Atlantic and unable to defend himself. Added aggravation came when *Auto Italiana* published a three-page illustrated article by David Phipps in which Surtees's 'hobby' with his Lola was described as not only driving it but also being involved in its development. What happened next was embarrassing for the Englishman. As explained by Luca Dal Monte in *Ferrari Rex*, his in-depth biography of Enzo Ferrari, *Il Commendatore* consulted Mauro Forghieri about the matter and they concluded that the Lola bore a certain resemblance to the 330 P and 330 P2. Beyond that, no more is known about what went on in Mr Ferrari's mind.

Tossed by waves but still afloat

Le Mans 24 Hours, 19th–20th June

The Le Mans 24 Hours produced an evenly matched battle between Maranello and Dearborn, even if the results ultimately did not reflect that. Both supplied 11 cars, in Ferrari's case ten prototypes and a GT, while Ford's tally was six prototypes and five GTs. The sheer weight of numbers and level playing field provided a mouth-watering prospect. The other potential contenders for outright victory were seven Porsches and a singleton Maserati.

The factory contributions to the showdown were two 330 P2s and a 275 P2 from Ferrari and two 7-litre Mk IIs from Ford via Shelby American. It was obvious that both manufacturers were determined to win without judging it useful to provide other examples of their latest weapons to their respective customer teams, even if the best of them undoubtedly had the resources and expertise to run them. In the Ferrari camp, there were five such supporting operations: from England, Maranello Concessionaires provided a 365 P2 and a 250 LM; the North American Racing Team (NART) matched that with its 365 P2 and 250 LM; Ecurie Francorchamps of Belgium entered a 250 LM and a 275 GTB; and Scuderia Filipinetti of Switzerland and French privateer Pierre Dumay each supplied a 250 LM. And Ford? Back-up to the works Mk IIs was provided by four GT40s, comprising two with 5.3-litre engines from the Filipinetti and Rob Walker teams and two with 4.7-litre versions entered by Ford Advanced Vehicles (FAV) and Ford France, to which were added five Cobra Daytona Coupes entered in American, English, French and Swiss colours.

Wednesday's practice session was cancelled due to severe weather rolling in from the west so only on Thursday did it become possible to assess the potential of the different teams. John Surtees was the first to lay down a marker with a lap of 3m 38.1s in the 330 P2 he shared with Ludovico Scarfiotti. Bob Bondurant (3m 38.7s) and Herbert Müller (3m 39.2s), respective partners of Umberto Maglioli and Ronnie Bucknum, were next up in the Walker and Filipinetti GT40s. The drivers of the 7-litre Mk IIs found them very unstable on the *Hunaudières* straight, but next morning, in an extra practice session laid on to replace the cancelled Wednesday one, the big Fords showed their prowess after overnight attention that involved adding various improvised appendages to make them behave at high speed. Fortuitously, this was the ideal time for the 7-litre monsters to stretch their legs because plenty of teams, including the Scuderia, were now holding back for the race, so the track was relatively free of traffic.

Speed tests by Ford at the Michigan speedway had seen the Mk IIs lap at an average speed of 201.5mph and reach a top speed of 210mph. Full 24-hour endurance tests had also been run at Riverside in California without any mechanical setbacks. But the layout of Riverside, a short track of 2.6 miles where a benchmark average race speed for a competitive sports car was around 95mph, was completely different from Le Mans, where the previous year's race average had exceeded 120mph. After a year of experimentation, testing and development, Ford set off for the Sarthe with double the personnel it had deployed the previous year, aiming to lap the circuit at between 3m 30s and

◄ **Le Mans 24 Hours.** The race has just got under way. At *Mulsanne*, the Lucien Bianchi/Mike Salmon 250 LM leads Jo Siffert in the Maserati *Tipo* 65 he shared with Jochen Neerpasch. The Maranello Concessionaires entry was the first of the Ferraris to depart the race, shortly before 11pm when 12th.

▼ **Le Mans 24 Hours.** Again at *Mulsanne*, now at about the two-hour mark, second-placed John Surtees gives the impression that his 330 P2 is towing the Bob Bondurant/Umberto Maglioli Ford GT40 in its wake but in fact the American car is several laps behind and soon to retire. The beached car is an Alfa Romeo TZ2 that Teodoro Zeccoli, his helmet visible, is trying to dig out of the sand.

> **Le Mans 24 Hours.** Lorenzo Bandini, winner in 1963 and third in 1964, shared this 275 P2 with Giampiero Biscaldi. At midnight they were lying second and looking on course to take the lead, but the disc-brake problems that afflicted Ferrari's prototypes during the night dropped them out of the running and eventually a breakage in their engine's valve gear ended their race.

3m 35s without going over 6,200rpm, even though the big V8 could run up to 7,000rpm without comprising reliability. Henry Ford II would be present at Le Mans with his new wife Cristina to see his cars succeed.

Phil Hill had masses of Le Mans experience and was also an expert when it came to taming large-capacity cars. And he proved it. With a few minutes to go to the end of the Friday session, when none of the opposition would be able to hit back, he turned in a lap at 3m 33.0s, which equated to an unprecedented average speed of 141.368mph. Stunning! Ford was in seventh heaven. Bruce McLaren added to the delight when he got round in 3m 38.9s to make it two Mk IIs in the top four. So, the two 7-litre Fords, with Chris Amon partnering Hill and Ken Miles with McLaren, sandwiched the Surtees/Scarfiotti 330 P2 and the Bondurant/ Maglioli GT40 in the starting line-up. However, doubts remained. The GT40 in third position and that of Bucknum/Müller in fifth had both suffered failures of their 5.3-litre engines in practice and would race with 4.7-litre versions.

On Saturday at 7pm, after three hours of racing, Ferraris occupied the top five places followed by the first of the Fords driven by McLaren/Miles in sixth. Jean Guichet/Michael Parkes led in their works 330 P2 with the Surtees/Scarfiotti example in hot pursuit. Behind them came Jo Bonnier/David

Piper (Maranello Concessionaire 365 P2) and Lorenzo Bandini/ Giampiero Biscaldi (works 275 P2) on the same lap as the leaders. Henry Ford II, seething with frustration, had already left the circuit.

Everything had begun as expected for Ford. To make the headlines, the two 7-litre cars came round in the lead at the end of the first lap, McLaren in front of Amon, while Surtees and Guichet followed in their Ferraris. Bondurant's GT40 was sixth, the NART 250 LM of Jochen Rindt (sharing with Masten Gregory) was seventh and Dan Gurney (partnered by Jerry Grant) was eight in his Daytona Coupe. An hour later, with McLaren and Amon still in front, it was all going according to plan for Dearborn. But then the 7-litre cars came in to refuel, leaving the Ferraris to take up the running. Of course, the Italian cars would need fuel too, but with the big Fords obliged to stop every hour compared with 90 minutes for their rivals, it became obvious after two hours of racing that Ford needed to open up a bigger advantage than the mere 22 seconds that separated the leader, McLaren, from Surtees.

To that painful reality was added an extended pitstop during the second hour for the Amon/Hill Mk II for repairs to its gearbox at the cost of 12 laps. Furthermore, the Ford France GT40 roadster of Maurice Trintignant/Guy Ligier had already gone

⌃ Le Mans 24 Hours. Jean Guichet, pictured at the wheel of the 330 P2 he shared with Michael Parkes, was lying fourth two hours into the race. Here at *Mulsanne* he leads a mixed bag comprising the Ronnie Bucknum/ Herbert Müller Ford GT40, the Carlo Zuccoli/'Geki' Alfa Romeo TZ2 and the Jean-Jacques Thuner/ Simo Lampinen Triumph Spitfire.

◂ Le Mans 24 Hours. After five hours, the top two finishers in the GT category — the Willy Mairesse/'Beurlys' 275 GTB run by Ecurie Francorchamps and the Jack Sears/Dick Thompson Daytona Coupe entered by AC Cars — battle for tenth place. By the end the Ferrari was a strong third overall while the Cobra limped home in eighth place.

> **Le Mans 24 Hours.** Delayed
at the start when the NART 365
P2's engine refused to fire, Pedro
Rodríguez was only 10th after an
hour's racing, but he and Nino
Vaccarella brought the car up to
third place by midnight before
brake trouble and a misfiring
engine dropped them to seventh
at the end. Here the Italian driver
rejoins in midday sunshine as
Mauro Forghieri, providing factory
support, shouts last-minute advice.

out just before 5pm, the one-hour mark, with gearbox failure, while 6.15pm saw the almost simultaneous retirements of both 4.7-litre GT40s, victims of leaking cylinder-head gaskets. And to crown it all, Miles had to quit in the other 7-litre Ford shortly after its third refuelling stop with a transmission breakage brought on by having to supplement deteriorating brakes by using the gearbox to help arrest the car from high speeds.

Thus, at 7pm, Ferrari led a race that looked like it would become rather a procession. The main interest that remained for Ford was to seal the International Championship for GT Manufacturers in a very uneven contest between its five Daytona Coupes and a single Ferrari in the guise of the Willy Mairesse/'Beurlys' 275 GTB. At this time, Gurney/Grant led the Cobra onslaught but very soon fluctuating oil pressure forced their car to make a lengthy pitstop and by 10pm it had dropped to tenth place. After the retirement of the Innes Ireland/John Whitmore GT40 due to an overheating engine and the impending demise of the delayed 7-litre Ford with terminal gearbox problems, the task of rescuing something from the Dearborn debacle fell to the seventh-placed Jack Sears/Dick Thompson Daytona Coupe, the very car that had won the class and finished fourth overall a year earlier.

Just when spectators were becoming resigned to an uneventful race, it all began to go wrong for Ferrari. The first blow for

Maranello, a relatively minor one, had come after only two laps with the expiry of the works Dino 166 P of Giancarlo Baghetti/Mario Casoni after a missed gearchange by Baghetti sent its little V6's revs sky high, causing terminal valve damage. Ferrari's game plan began to unravel after nightfall when, shortly before 11pm, the Surtees/Scarfiotti 330 P2 had to surrender its lead with a 20-minute pitstop for replacement of a broken spring in the right-front suspension. At much the same time, both Maranello Concessionaires entries hit trouble, the Lucien Bianchi/Mike Salmon 250 LM with gearbox failure and the third-placed Bonnier/Piper 365 P with a cracked exhaust manifold.

The first indication of a pattern of brake problems for Ferrari occurred half an hour after midnight when Pedro Rodríguez arrived in the pits with the third-placed NART 365 P2 he shared with Nino Vaccarella. As on the other Ferrari prototypes, the brake discs were of a new ventilated design with radial slots and it was found that the right-front disc had cracked. The car lost 45 minutes while replacement brakes of the old type were assembled and fitted, the car rejoining seventh. Very soon afterwards, the Bandini/Biscaldi 275 P2 stopped for the same reason, to be followed eventually by the 330 P2s of Guichet/Parkes and Surtees/Scarfiotti.

At 1am, the 330 P2s were in control of the race, Guichet/

Parkes leading Surtees/Scarfiotti by six laps, with the Pierre Dumay/Gustave Gosselin 250 LM and the Mairesse/'Beurlys' 275 GTB each a further lap down in third and fourth places. Then Parkes had to stop when the same brake problem occurred on his car, delaying it by 50 minutes. That left Surtees/Scarfiotti back in front, where they had been four hours earlier, only for their car to suffer the same affliction, losing 47 minutes. By 3am, privately run Ferraris occupied the top three places: Dumay/Gosselin (250 LM) and Mairesse/'Beurlys' (275 GTB) were first and second, while Gregory/Rindt (250 LM) were now third after early problems with their car's starter motor and distributor had dropped them to 18th place. Recovering after its delay, the Guichet/Parkes 330 P2 was fourth and Gurney/Jerry Grant in the quickest of the Daytona Coupes were fifth.

The Cobras were also falling by the wayside and by breakfast time they no longer posed any threat to Ferrari's prototypes. The first to go, soon after midnight, was the Ford France entry of Jo Schlesser/Allen Grant, victims of clutch failure after a long period of severe vibration. Within an hour, Scuderia Filipinetti's car driven by Peter Sutcliffe/Peter Harper went out in clouds of steam when a cylinder-head gasket failed. Then the Shelby entry of Bob Johnson/Tom Payne vanished at dawn with an overheated engine. When the fastest of them all, the Gurney/Jerry Grant car, exited the race at 7.37am, just one survivor remained, the 12th-placed Jack Sears/Dick Thompson entry run by AC Cars.

By 8am, Guichet/Parkes were briefly back in second place between the 250 LMs of Dumay/Gosselin and Gregory/Rindt, but Surtees/Scarfiotti were now too far behind to be a contender for a top-six finish, while the Bandini/Biscaldi 275 P2 gave up the ghost at 8.40am. At NART, Rodríguez/Vaccarella in their 365 P2, stuck in eighth place, had no aim other than to make it to the chequered flag. The Gregory/Rindt 250 LM was now second, having taken advantage of the 275 GTB's extended stop for fresh tyres and brake pads, and was gaining on the Dumay/Gosselin car.

At this point, we should digress briefly to the matter of a third driver who claimed to have driven one stint in the NART 250 LM as a stand-in for Masten Gregory. The story emerged in 1999 when the driver concerned, Ed Hugus, who was part of the NART team, told János L. Wimpffen, author of the book *Time and Two Seats*, that he had discreetly stepped in because his fellow American was concerned about his night vision. Ever since this dubious revelation, the claim has received extra credence by being repeated in print from time to time, such that historian Doug Nye decided to look into it. His article, 'The Mystery of the Third Man', was published in the July 2020 issue of *Motor Sport* and concluded: 'We emerge from this investigation 99 per cent sure that Ed Hugus's claim simply cannot stand.'

At 9am, with Rindt at the wheel, the red NART 250 LM was only 22 seconds behind the yellow Ecurie Francorchamps version. But as the refuelling stops imposed their rhythm, that gap stretched to become the best part of a lap by 10am, when Gregory took over from Rindt. At 11.30am, after a stop lasting 1m 35s, Rindt rejoined just as Dumay shot past the pits, but could not make up ground against the swift Frenchman. At 12.10pm, Gosselin, who was slower than his team-mate, took over from Dumay and now Rindt, although lapping slightly less quickly than in his previous stint, was able to start reeling in the yellow 250 LM. Suddenly, Gosselin stopped at his pit and then set off again almost immediately, reducing his advantage to 53 seconds on the track, but more in reality because his car needed only one more refuelling stop compared with two for the challenger. In fact, calculations of fuel consumption for the Index of Thermal Efficiency showed that Gregory/Rindt were turning in a significantly worse average of 37.84 litres per 100km (7.47mpg) compared with the 33.84 litres per 100km (8.35mpg) achieved by Dumay/Gosselin.

Suddenly Gosselin's times went haywire and he began to lose as much as 12 seconds per lap. There were suspicions that he may have flat-spotted his rear tyres under braking. At 12.53pm the loudspeakers announced that the yellow 250 LM was limping along the *Hunaudières* straight. A tyre had exploded. While Rindt was in the pits handing over to Gregory, the Ecurie Francorchamps car arrived with its right-rear wheel grinding along on the rim and adjacent bodywork torn apart by flying rubber.

Seven minutes later, the NART 250 LM went back out with new tyres and front brake pads. Meanwhile, the Ecurie Francorchamps car received rudimentary bodywork repairs and a fresh wheel, after which Gosselin did one exploratory lap to check that the car felt satisfactory, then pitted again to have the other tyres changed. By the time he could resume in anger, Gregory had pulled out a five-lap lead. And that is how the race concluded. Come 4pm, Gregory and Rindt delivered Ferrari's sixth consecutive Le Mans 24 Hours victory, a record that at the time was considered unbeatable. As the entrant of the winning car, Luigi Chinetti celebrated a fourth victory following the three he had achieved as a driver. And Goodyear claimed its first win.

As for the works 330 P2s, the last survivor, the Guichet/Parkes car, officially retired at 2.41pm due to gearbox failure, having completed 90 laps more than the Surtees/Scarfiotti version, also the victim of a broken gearbox. Despite the various Ferrari

⌃ Le Mans 24 Hours. With just over three hours to go, Gustave Gosselin was driving the Ecurie Francorchamps 250 LM at top speed down the *Hunaudières* straight when its right-rear tyre exploded. That was the moment when he and Pierre Dumay lost a race they had led since 3am.

➤ Le Mans 24 Hours. At about the time Bernard Cahier took this photo, the Masten Gregory/ Jochen Rindt 250 LM had been gifted the lead. It is 1pm, new tyres and brake pads have been fitted and both fuel tanks filled, and Gregory is about to pull away and drive to victory.

◄ **Le Mans 24 Hours.** Masten Gregory (left) and Jochen Rindt have a quick chat during their last handover at lunchtime on Sunday. Despite their disagreement over strategy — the Austrian wanted to push hard whereas the American preferred a more cautious approach — nothing cast a shadow over their unexpected success.

▼ **Le Mans 24 Hours.** With just an hour to go, the Jean Guichet/ Michael Parkes 330 P2 is pushed away, its gearbox *hors de combat.* It had led by six laps during the night until struck by the works team's disc-brake woes.

LE MANS 24 HOURS

Le Mans, 19th–20th June 1965, 347 laps (8.364 miles/13.461km), 2,906.221 miles/4,677.110km • Starters 51, classified finishers 14

1st	Masten Gregory/Jochen Rindt	Ferrari 250 LM (5893)	347 laps
2nd	Pierre Dumay/Gustave Gosselin	Ferrari 250 LM (6313)	341 laps
3rd	Willy Mairesse/'Beurlys' (Jean Blaton)	Ferrari 275 GTB (6885) *(1st Div III)*	338 laps
4th	Herbert Linge/Peter Nöcker	Porsche 904/6	334 laps
5th	Gerhard Koch/Anton Fischhaber	Porsche 904 GTS	324 laps
6th	Dieter Spoerry/Armand Boller	Ferrari 250 LM (6119)	323 laps
7th	Pedro Rodríguez/Nino Vaccarella	Ferrari 365 P2 (0838)	319 laps
DNF	**Jean Guichet/Michael Parkes**	**Ferrari 330 P2 (0836)**	**315 laps (gearbox)**
DNF	**John Surtees/Ludovico Scarfiotti**	**Ferrari 330 P2 (0828)**	**225 laps (gearbox)**
DNF	**Lorenzo Bandini/Giampiero Biscaldi**	**Ferrari 275 P2 (0832)**	**221 laps (valve)**
DNF	'Elde' (Léon Dernier)/Gérald Langlois van Ophem	Ferrari 250 LM (6023)	146 laps (clutch)
DNF	Jo Bonnier/David Piper	Ferrari 365 P2 (0826)	101 laps (ignition/brakes)
DNF	Lucien Bianchi/Mike Salmon	Ferrari 250 LM (5895)	99 laps (gearbox)
DNF	**Giancarlo Baghetti/Mario Casoni**	**Ferrari Dino 166 P (0834)**	**2 laps (valve)**

Fastest practice lap: Phil Hill (Ford Mk II), 3m 33.0s, 141.368mph/227.509kph **Fastest race lap:** Phil Hill (Ford Mk II), 3m 37.5s, 138.443mph/222.803kph **Winner's average speed:** 121.093mph/194.880kph **FIA World Sports Car Championship (GT Division III, over 2,000cc):**[1] 1st Shelby 95.4, 2nd Ferrari 66.7

[1] Scoring system for the top six places in this event was 9–6–4–3–2–1 multiplied by coefficient 2.0; only the manufacturer's highest-placed car scored points

setbacks, all five of the Maranello-built cars that finished were in the top seven. The two cars that brought up the rear swapped positions in the final hour, Dieter Spoerry/Armand Boller in their Scuderia Filipinetti 250 LM snatching sixth place from the NART 365 P2 of Rodríguez/Vaccarella. The Swiss-entered car had never been among the front-runners, but thanks to its consistency and the attrition of others, it steadily worked its way up through the field despite a few clutch problems.

Thanks to the third-placed Mairesse/'Beurlys' 275 GTB, Ferrari scored 18 points in the International Championship for GT Manufacturers compared with the 12 that Shelby picked up with its sole surviving Daytona Coupe, the Sears/Thompson car in eighth place overall and second in the GT rankings. But with four rounds to go, Ferrari's points deficit remained large, at 28.7, especially as a week earlier at the Rossfeld hillclimb Bondurant had won the GT category and finished 10th overall in a Cobra roadster. It seemed strange that two runs totalling just 7.5 miles could be worth only three points less than the runner-up's score at Le Mans, which had involved covering a distance of 2,532.783 miles.

The next rendezvous would be at Reims where some of the cars that had raced at Le Mans would be competing. But with just three elderly GTOs to take on two Daytona Coupes and a third Cobra coupé in the form of the one-off that John Willment had built, the championship outcome looked set in stone.

Another Clark masterclass

Grand Prix de l'ACF, 27th June

After his victories in South Africa and Belgium, it seemed that nothing could interfere with Jim Clark's domination because those two events had been so different, in terms of both circuit character and weather conditions. Now came more variety, for the Grand Prix de l'ACF had transferred to another home and was being held for the first time on the Charade circuit in the Auvergne, not far from Clermont-Ferrand. Laid out on sinuous public roads around the base of an extinct volcano, the five-mile track was likened to a mini-Nürburgring.

In torrid heat on Friday, it was a surprise to see Clark arrive in the pits astride the back of John Surtees's Ferrari 158. His Lotus 33, powered by a four-valve Coventry Climax V8, had gone off following the collapse of its rear suspension because a screw had not been properly tightened. While the Scot got used to the spare Lotus with a regular two-valve Climax engine, Surtees equalled the time of 3m 22.1s set by Jackie Stewart (BRM), but Brabham's new driver was faster than both of them by a tenth of a second. As a works driver for Brabham in Formula 2, Denny Hulme had

◄ Grand Prix de l'ACF. Lorenzo Bandini and Dan Gurney (Brabham) arrive back at the pits after some laps of the Charade circuit during the half-hour warm-up provided before the start. Bandini qualified on the front row of the grid with Jim Clark (Lotus) and Jackie Stewart (BRM) while Gurney sat alongside Surtees on the second.

▼ Grand Prix de l'ACF. Jim Clark (Lotus) took advantage of his pole position to head the field into the first corner and went on to score an untroubled victory. Lorenzo Bandini is second and Jackie Stewart (BRM) third, while John Surtees (with a front wheel on the white line) and Dan Gurney (Brabham) follow, with Richie Ginther (Honda) next.

▲ Grand Prix de l'ACF. Pictured during practice, Bandini spent most of the race in fifth place behind Denny Hulme's Brabham before bowing out three laps from the end when a broken driveshaft caused him to crash.

➤ Grand Prix de l'ACF. Surtees, also seen during practice, endured a misfire for most of the race thanks to an alternator problem and did well to finish third.

GRAND PRIX DE L'ACF

Clermont-Ferrand, 27th June 1965, 40 laps (5.005 miles/8.055km), 200.206 miles/322.200km • Starters 17, finishers 9

RACE					PRACTICE	
1st	Jim Clark	Lotus 33 Climax V8	2h 14m 38.4s		1st	3m 18.3s
2nd	Jackie Stewart	BRM P261 BRM V8	+26.3s		2nd	3m 18.8s
3rd	**John Surtees**	**Ferrari 158 V8**	**+2m 33.5s**		**4th**	**3m 19.1s**
4th	Denny Hulme	Brabham BT11 Climax V8	+2m 53.1s		6th	3m 20.5s
5th	Graham Hill	BRM P261 BRM V8	39 laps		13th	3m 23.7s
6th	Jo Siffert	Brabham BT11 BRM V8	39 laps		14th	3m 25.2s
8th	**Lorenzo Bandini**	**Ferrari 1512 F12**	36 laps (accident)		**3rd**	**3m 19.1s**

Pole position: Clark, 3m 18.3s, 90.865mph/146.233kph **Fastest race lap:** Clark, 3m 18.9s, 90.590mph/145.791kph **Winner's average speed:** 89.216mph/143.580kph **Drivers' championship:** 1st Clark 27, 2nd= Hill & Stewart 17, 4th Surtees 13, 6th Bandini 6 **Constructors' championship:** 1st Lotus-Climax 27, 2nd BRM 25, 3rd Ferrari 16

beaten Stewart to win the previous year's Trophées d'Auvergne at this circuit and, unlike most of the more experienced drivers on the grid, already knew the track — which is why Jack Brabham decided to stand down for this race and give the young New Zealander another outing following his encouraging début in Monaco. What impressive use Hulme made of his head start!

Lorenzo Bandini (3m 24.6s) was slower than his team leader that day but made up for it on Saturday. As Surtees was still reluctant to drive the 12-cylinder Ferrari, it was again entrusted to Bandini, who took it round in 3m 19.1s, good enough for a place on the front row. Although the reigning World Champion in his 158 equalled his team-mate's best time just two laps later, it still left observers wondering what he might have achieved with a 1512. Meanwhile, Clark was comfortably cocooned in his own bubble. After again having to abandon his favoured car, this time because its four-valve engine had broken, the Scot went out in the spare Lotus and clinched pole with a lap in 3m 18.3s. Scotland's other ace, Stewart (3m 18.8s), lined up second, while in the Brabham camp Gurney (3m 19.8s) battled away to make sure Hulme (3m 20.5s) did not hog the limelight, the pair fifth and sixth in the rankings. At BRM, Graham Hill (1m 23.7s) was far from his best, especially as his efforts on Friday had ended with a big shunt when his engine's throttle slides had failed to close properly, sending him off the track and into a rock face.

Clark took advantage of his pole position on the left-hand side of the track to make the best start and lead into the first corner. He was still in front at the end of the lap, three seconds clear of Bandini, Stewart, Gurney and Surtees. Second time round, he was five seconds ahead of Stewart, who had got the better of Bandini, while Surtees was searching for a way past Gurney. Within three more laps, Clark had established a stranglehold

on the race and led Stewart by nine seconds with Surtees next, a further six seconds down. Thereafter, the podium positions remained fixed, Surtees holding on to his third place despite having to put up with a severe top-end misfire. Caused by a defective alternator, the handicap was so bad at times that he even made a brief pitstop at the end of lap 16 but was swiftly sent on his way again.

And Bandini? Although he made a good start, he slipped down the order to seventh place before fighting back. He ran fifth behind Hulme for over half the race but three laps from home crashed heavily, without hurting himself, when a driveshaft broke just as Clark was about to lap him.

M aybe it was time for Surtees to finally get behind the wheel of a 1512? With the British Grand Prix looming, Ferrari had to do something to help the World Champion defend his title. With four races run and six to go, Clark's score from his three starts was a 'full house' of 27 points, while Hill and Stewart had 17 and Surtees trailed with 13. Of course, there was no guarantee that the Lotus driver would continue to be so dominant, but if that were to be the case he could potentially be crowned after three more races. With only the six best results allowed to count, six victories would give him the maximum possible points total.

Surtees continued to put some of his energy into non-Ferrari activities. A week later, the Reims 12 Hours was to be followed by the Reims Grand Prix, a Formula 2 race for which Ken Tyrrell offered a seat in one of his Cooper-BRMs alongside regular driver Jackie Stewart, following on from a previous outing at Crystal Palace four weeks earlier. In fact, the former motorcycle champion experienced two broken con rods in rapid succession that rendered him a non-starter. Surtees was also strengthening his relationship with Eric Broadley and agreed to race a Formula 2 Lola as well as the T70 whenever there was a gap in his diary.

A well-deserved title

Reims 12 Hours, 3rd–4th July

The night-time start of the Reims 12 Hours was brought forward by an hour, to 11pm, to provide more time in the subsequent schedule of follow-up races for Formula 2 and Formula 3 single-seaters. With Ford licking its wounds after the disappointments at Le Mans two weeks earlier, the company's big GTs were absent. In fact, the field was pretty thin, with 10 privately entered Ferraris facing only 12 other starters.

John Surtees and Michael Parkes shared a 365 P2 run by Maranello Concessionaires but entered under the Team Surtees banner. Their toughest rivals were another of Colonel Ronnie Hoare's cars, a 330 P for Graham Hill/Jo Bonnier, and a 365 P2 run by NART for Pedro Rodríguez/Jean Guichet. As at Le Mans, a 250 LM could always spring a surprise and four were present for Pierre Dumay/Gustave Gosselin, Willy Mairesse/'Beurlys', David Piper/Richard Attwood and Gérald Langlois van Ophem/

Annie Soisbault. In the GT entry, three elderly 250 GTOs faced three Cobras, two of them Daytona Coupes assigned to Bob Bondurant/Jo Schlesser and Jack Sears/John Whitmore, the other the Willment coupé of Frank Gardner/Innes Ireland.

After a couple of practice periods in which the drivers found their bearings, Friday's sessions confirmed Surtees's worst fears when he qualified only third (2m 20.8s), put in the shade by Rodríguez/Guichet (2m 18.2s) and Hill/Bonnier (2m 19.7s). The four 250 LMs headed the Schlesser/Bondurant Daytona.

The first hour of the race reassured Surtees because the 330 P was no quicker. When Hill covered the 23rd lap in a time of 2m 19.1s, Surtees responded next time round with 2m 19.0s. While the smaller-engined Maranello Concessionaires car led by just five seconds, at least Surtees was able to keep Rodríguez, on his tail since the start, at arm's length. Clearly pitstops were going to play a big part in the race if the top three continued to be so evenly matched and indeed there was a reshuffle at the first round of refuelling, with the NART crew putting Rodríguez in front by turning him around more swiftly than the Maranello Concessionaires crews could manage (1m 7s versus 1m 15s).

Needless to say, the English drivers had no intention of letting the NART team's advantage persist. Surtees was the one who upped the tempo, twice setting new lap records in the space of just 10 minutes. At 12.30am he led Hill by just 100 yards

> **Reims 12 Hours.** After his success at Le Mans, Luigi Chinetti (behind the car, wearing jacket and tie) has no reason to be worried at Reims, where Pedro Rodríguez (near the pit counter, helmet in hand) qualified fastest in the 365 P2 he shared with Jean Guichet.

▲ **Reims 12 Hours.** Graham Hill brakes for *Thillois* at the wheel of the Maranello Concessionaires 330 P he co-drove with Jo Bonnier. Winners of this race a year earlier, they had two spells in the lead before going out in the ninth hour with transmission failure.

▼ **Reims 12 Hours.** During a sensational comeback performance after a long delay at dawn, John Surtees rather eclipsed co-driver Michael Parkes by staying behind the wheel of their 365 P2 longer than scheduled, producing a display of brio on a 'power' circuit that offered few opportunities for a driver to make the difference.

but noted that Rodríguez had vanished from his mirrors. Next time round, he saw why. The Mexican's 365 P2 was parked at its pit with the tail section open: the clutch had failed and the NART mechanics were setting about fitting a replacement. The car rejoined at 12.56am in 15th place and 15 laps down.

Now Surtees could focus on defending himself from Hill, who remained only a few car lengths behind. The next pitstops brought driver changes for both cars and the picture began to change. Surtees knew that Parkes, despite their differences, was a quick and consistent partner, and the tall Englishman soon demonstrated this by pulling away from Bonnier at quite a rate, by as much as five seconds a lap. By the end of the third hour, Parkes had consolidated the break from the 330 P, while Rodríguez, still at the wheel of the NART 365 P2, had risen to eighth place with such determination and pace that he now held the lap record. Surtees was in an increasingly relaxed frame of mind by the time Parkes handed the 365 P2 back to him shortly after the four-hour mark, all the more so when he saw that the rival 330 P was delayed at its refuelling stop, immobilised while mechanics investigated a clutch problem.

By half distance, the race had become a procession. Surtees/Parkes led Hill/Bonnier by three laps with Piper/Attwood third and Rodríguez/Guichet up to fourth. But drama lay just around the corner.

Ten minutes later, at 5.10am, Surtees stopped to refuel. He was concerned about a lack of power and asked his crew if they could identify the reason. He lost a few minutes before rejoining. Hardly had he settled into his usual rhythm when, approaching the pit area at 5.20am, he suddenly took to the slowing-down lane and stopped just after the timekeepers' box. He leaped out of the cockpit, grabbed the nearest fire extinguisher and sprayed it at the back of his 365 P2 just as flames started to appear. Most unusually, a rocker arm had broken in the engine's valve gear, causing a blow-back in the carburettors that had caught alight. But all was not lost: there was no significant damage and the rocker arm could be replaced.

Now Hill/Bonnier led Piper/Attwood by two laps. In their wake came Rodríguez/Guichet, the Sears/Whitmore Cobra, the Mairesse/'Beurlys' 250 LM and the Schlesser/Bondurant Cobra.

Surtees rejoined at 6.02am, in seventh place and 15 laps behind the leader. In the early-morning sunshine, the hardy spectators — small in number but big in dedication — now hoped to see the reigning World Champion perform at his stubborn best. He did not disappoint. With his big Ferrari again firing on all cylinders, 'Big John' began lapping three seconds quicker than Hill, the race leader. Although Surtees was still seventh an hour later, at two-thirds distance, his determination had enabled him to significantly close the gap on those ahead,

helped by some of them starting to falter. The NART 365 P2 needed another long pitstop for a tyre change and renewed attention to its transmission while the Piper/Attwood 250 LM was experiencing gearbox and brake trouble. During the next hour, the flying #2 Ferrari disposed of the Sears/Whitmore and Schlesser/Bondurant Cobras to reach fifth place.

Although Hill/Bonnier still led, their 330 P's transmission was causing concern. Bonnier expressed his agitation for several laps in succession by gesticulating as he passed the pits before limping into the pitlane with no third gear and a ruined clutch. The Piper/Attwood 250 LM now led followed by the Rodríguez/Guichet 365 P2 with the Mairesse/'Beurlys' 250 LM third and Surtees/Parkes fourth. Perhaps there would be a rerun of Le Mans with LMs stealing the glory? It may have looked like that but the reality was very different. Piper/Attwood were struggling, the health of their gearbox deteriorating, and were about to surrender the lead to Rodríguez/Guichet, while Mairesse/'Beurlys' had no intention of risking a strong result by trying to fight off the flying 365 P2 behind them. At 10am on the dot, with one hour to go, Surtees set a final and decisive lap record at 2m 17.9s — nearly three seconds better than his qualifying time for a sensational average speed of 134.666mph — and shot past the green LM, which no longer had fifth gear.

Parkes took over for the final hour and, not wanting to be

➤ **Reims 12 Hours.** Although Pedro Rodríguez spent the lion's share of time behind the wheel of NART's 365 P2, he helped Jean Guichet, already a winner at Monza, to score his second big success of the year. This proved to be NART's last victory in a world championship sports car race.

REIMS 12 HOURS

Reims-Gueux, 3rd–4th July 1965, 296 laps (5.158 miles/8.301km), 1,469.825 miles/2,365.454km • Starters 22, classified finishers 14

1st	Pedro Rodríguez/Jean Guichet	Ferrari 365 P2 (0838)	284 laps
2nd	John Surtees/Michael Parkes	Ferrari 365 P2 (0826)	282 laps
3rd	Willy Mairesse/'Beurlys' (Jean Blaton)	Ferrari 250 LM (6023)	279 laps
4th	David Piper/Richard Attwood	Ferrari 250 LM (5897)	273 laps
5th	Bob Bondurant/Jo Schlesser	Shelby Cobra Daytona (1st Div III)	270 laps
6th	Paul Hawkins/Mike De Udy	Porsche 904 GTS	261 laps
11th	Graham Hill/Jo Bonnier	Ferrari 330 P (0818)	231 laps
DNF	Pierre Dumay/Gustave Gosselin	Ferrari 250 LM (6313)	– (gearbox)
DNF	Peter Sutcliffe/William Bradley	Ferrari 250 GTO (4491 GT)	– (steering)
DNF	Allen Grant/Guy Ligier	Ferrari 250 GTO (4153 GT)	– (engine)
DNF	Gérald Langlois van Ophem/Annie Soisbault	Ferrari 250 LM (5843)	– (accident)
NC	Peter Clarke/Rollo Feilding	Ferrari 250 GTO (3757 GT)	– (starter motor)

Fastest practice lap: Rodríguez, 2m 18.2s, 134.362mph/216.234kph **Fastest race lap:** Surtees, 2m 17.9s, 134.666mph/216.724kph **Winner's average speed:** 122.485mph/197.121kph **FIA World Sports Car Championship (GT Division III, over 2,000cc):**[1] 1st Shelby 109.8, 2nd Ferrari 66.7

[1] Scoring system for the top six places in this event was 9–6–4–3–2–1 (coefficient 1.6); only the manufacturer's highest-placed car scored points

overshadowed by his team-mate, continued the charge, pulling back as much as eight seconds a lap on the NART 365 P2. Although he unlapped himself once, it was all in vain despite the fireworks because the leading car survived to receive the chequered flag from Raymond Roche with a two-lap advantage. Following Luigi Chinetti's victory at Le Mans, this win provided his team with a second blaze of glory in the space of a fortnight.

The United States had something else to celebrate because Ford, thanks to Shelby American, clinched the International Championship for GT Manufacturers in Division III. One can gloss over the fact that this conquest had been made that much easier by the questionable refusal of the authorities to homologate the 250 LM and their delay in agreeing to approve the 275 GTB. The fifth place achieved by the Schlesser/Bondurant Daytona Coupe added 14.4 points to Shelby's score and made it unassailable. With three rounds to go, Shelby now had 109.8 points compared with 66.7 for Ferrari. The Coppa Città di Enna, Ollon–Villars hillclimb and Bridgehampton 500Km all helped Shelby to increase its total score to 133.2 against 84.8 for Ferrari, but after taking into account the fact that only the best six results plus the highest hillclimb placing could be counted, the official standings concluded at 90.3 points for the Americans and 71.3 for the Italians.

◄ Ludovico Scarfiotti won two hillclimbs with this Dino 206 P spyder during August, at Fribourg on the 8th and Ollon–Villars (pictured) on the 29th. The Dino 206 P was powered by a 1,998cc double-overhead-camshaft V6.

◄ **British Grand Prix.** With practice in full swing, Mauro Forghieri gives the impression that he has personally taken in hand the development of John Surtees's 1512. His input probably paid off because the car started on the second row having set the same time as Richie Ginther's Honda and Jackie Stewart's BRM.

▼ **British Grand Prix.** In the wake of his disappointing performance at Spa and his crash at Charade, Bandini was able to choose between two 158s, neither of which was to his liking. He started the race on the third row and did not manage to complete a full flying lap before suffering his second engine failure of the weekend.

Scottish resourcefulness

British Grand Prix, 10th July

In Thursday morning's first practice session at Silverstone, Surtees had a 12-cylinder Ferrari at his disposal while Bandini was given a 158 for the first time this season. Had *Il Grande John* been told to try the 1512 in the hope of turning round Maranello's diminishing championship prospects? After taking out the spare 158 for comparison, Surtees was indeed faster in the 1512, but his best lap of 1m 32.0s was only seven tenths of a second quicker than Bandini's. By the afternoon, with the 12-cylinder car now equipped with Dunlop R7 tyres rather than R6s, he widened the margin by improving to 1m 31.7s while his team-mate slipped slightly to 1m 32.9s. But — and it was a big 'but' — the Englishman set his best time of the day, 1m 31.4s, in an R6-shod V8. This equalled Jackie Stewart's fastest for BRM but put him behind Jim Clark (1m 31.1s) and Graham Hill (1m 31.0s) at the top of the timesheets.

The fact that the Ferrari 12-cylinder engine did not provide the expected advantage was a source of frustration when measured against the progress Honda had been making with its V12. After comparing the two Hondas at his disposal, Richie Ginther confirmed the Japanese car's prowess on fast circuits by getting round in 1m 31.6s in that afternoon session. Next day, Surtees did manage to tease a little more from his 12-cylinder car, as did Ginther, both of them ending up on 1m 31.3s, a time also posted by

Stewart, while Clark and Hill continued to head the order, now on 1m 30.8s and 1m 31.0s respectively. For Surtees, there was added frustration because he set his time after Ginther and Stewart, so he would have to start the race behind them on the second row. Bandini ended up on the third row after engine failure in his 158 forced him to use the spare car, which had some brake trouble.

Saturday dawned in threatening weather but the sun came out for the race. When Ginther surged away neck and neck with Clark, there was a brief prospect that he and his Honda might spice up the race. The American just about kept his white car ahead through Copse and Maggots but Clark imposed his will at Becketts and established himself in his customary position at the head of the field as they roared down Hangar Straight. At the end of the lap, Clark led Ginther, Hill, Stewart and Surtees, but next time round there was a reshuffle behind the escaping

▲ **British Grand Prix.** Richie Ginther set off like a scalded cat in his #11 Honda, making the most of its V12 power, but within half a lap Jim Clark's #5 Lotus was back in its familiar place at the head of the field. Close behind are the BRMs of Graham Hill (#3), who nearly snatched victory from the Scot in the final stages when the Lotus's Climax engine faltered, and Jackie Stewart (#4).

◀ **British Grand Prix.** Pursued for much of the race by Mike Spence's Lotus, Surtees finished third without ever being able to threaten second-placed Graham Hill. He did not have great memories of his first race in the 1512: he considered the car a big disappointment despite his earlier prediction that the 12-cylinder engine had 'a great future'.

BRITISH GRAND PRIX

Silverstone, 10th July 1965, 80 laps (2.927 miles/4.711km), 234.182 miles/376.880km • Starters 21, finishers 13

RACE				PRACTICE	
1st	Jim Clark	Lotus 33 Climax V8	2h 05m 25.4s	1st	1m 30.8s
2nd	Graham Hill	BRM P261 BRM V8	+3.2s	2nd	1m 31.0s
3rd	**John Surtees**	**Ferrari 158 V8**	**+27.6s**	**5th**	**1m 31.3s**
4th	Mike Spence	Lotus 33 Climax V8	+39.6s	6th	1m 31.7s
5th	Jackie Stewart	BRM P261 BRM V8	1m 14.6s	4th	1m 31.3s
6th	Dan Gurney	Brabham BT11 Climax V8	79 laps	7th	1m 31.9s
DNF	**Lorenzo Bandini**	**Ferrari 1512 F12**	2 laps (engine)	8th	1m 32.7s

Pole position: Clark, 1m 30.8s, 116.060mph/186.780kph **Fastest race lap:** Hill, 1m 32.2s, 114.289mph/183.930kph **Winner's average speed:** 112.021mph/180.280kph **Drivers' championship:** 1st Clark 36, 2nd Hill 23, 3rd Stewart 19, 4th Surtees 17, 6th Bandini 6 **Constructors' championship:** 1st Lotus-Climax 36, 2nd BRM 31, 3rd Ferrari 20

leader with the order now Hill, Surtees, Ginther, Stewart. As at Charade, that pretty much settled the top three for the rest of the race, although Mike Spence (Lotus) put some pressure on Surtees and had two very brief spells in front of him (on laps 36 and 41) before settling for fourth place. Ginther, after his moment of glory, slipped back with fuel-injection trouble and retired before one-third distance. Bandini never featured, bowing out after two laps with a blown piston.

Yet again, Clark was at the top of his game, but this time he had to call upon all of his reserves when his lead melted away during the last third of the race. He was nearly half a lap up on Hill when his Climax engine developed a misfire, causing the gap to shrink little by little. As Hill edged closer, he got the bit between his teeth and drove harder. Clark's difficulties worsened in the closing laps when his engine started losing oil as well, forcing him to coast through corners to preserve at least some oil pressure. The last few laps were very tense but the Scot, using all his skill and guile, managed to hang on to take the chequered flag 3.2 seconds to the good.

Unstoppable

Dutch Grand Prix, 18th July

When Surtees tackled this sixth round of the World Championship with 17 points against Clark's 36, he had to win to retain any hope of retaining his crown as well as requiring the Lotus man to miss out on points and the BRM drivers to underplay their hands too. This scenario did not look at all likely, especially when taking into account Zandvoort's reputation for punishing cars.

▼ **Dutch Grand Prix.** On Saturday at Zandvoort, Bandini had good reason to look miffed. Neither of the two 158s at his disposal had enabled him to stand out from his rivals the previous day. Now, the victim of an engine failure, he is having to fall back on his spare car. Come the race, he gave the impression of being completely overwhelmed, finishing ninth behind Mike Spence's Lotus.

Friday's practice took place in winter temperatures in the morning and pouring rain in the afternoon, so it was only the Saturday session that provided any useful preparation for Sunday's race. While Graham Hill topped the timesheets by just three tenths of a second from the trio of Clark, Ginther and Surtees, all credited with 1m 31.0s, it was so close that at least the race looked like being more open than of late. Clark had to abandon his four-valve engine after oil loss and was unhappy about having to fall back again on one of the old two-valve units,

▾ **Dutch Grand Prix.** As at Silverstone, Richie Ginther used the Honda V12 engine's prodigious power to beat Graham Hill's BRM (#10) into the first corner but the English driver got ahead two laps later. The Ferraris are in the middle of the pack, the 1512 of John Surtees (#2) visible on the left behind Jackie Stewart's BRM (#12). The eventual winner, Jim Clark's Lotus, is partly concealed behind the Honda while the Brabhams of Denny Hulme (#14) and Dan Gurney (#16) are prominent behind.

while Ginther's performance, despite his qualities as a driver and the power of his 12-cylinder engine, was generally thought to owe a great deal to the generosity of the timekeepers. Surtees racked up laps in the 1512 and deliberated about which tyres, R6s or R7s, were best suited to improving its roadholding. Bandini, yet again the victim of a V8 engine failure that had the Ferrari engineers scratching their heads, could do no better than 12th.

The race began badly for Surtees. While Ginther reprised his Silverstone exploits by leading for two laps, the Englishman found himself stuck in seventh place in company with Mike Spence's Lotus and Denny Hulme's Brabham. This time he had a significant problem with his 1512. While the flat-12 provided satisfactory performance, it did not give him any advantage in terms of flexibility compared with the Climax V8s of the Lotus and Brabham rivals with whom he battled lap after lap. Once past Spence and in sixth place, his next target was the Honda, for Ginther had gradually slipped back after his explosive start.

Hulme, however, had other ideas and overtook both Spence and Surtees in quick succession, pushing the Ferrari driver back to seventh place again. Now Surtees was really wrestling with his 1512, enduring worsening all-round grip, especially at the front end, as his chosen R7 tyres deteriorated in the sunny warmth of afternoon. He regained a place when Ginther spun at *Hunzerug* but the two 12-cylinder cars slugged it out and by the end Ginther was ahead again, leaving Surtees a dispirited seventh, not even in the points and lapped by the top four. The day went no better for Bandini, who crossed swords with Spence for more than half the race but eventually lost out, only just surviving to the finish with his gearbox stuck in second on the final lap.

▲ **Dutch Grand Prix.** Surtees hoped that Dunlop R7 tyres would solve his 1512's mediocre road-holding problems at Zandvoort but he had a disappointing race and finished only seventh.

It was another disappointing race for Ferrari and even more so for Surtees. Clark scored his fifth victory of the season, making it virtually certain that he would become World Champion. All Surtees could do at the next round at the Nürburgring would be to try to win and perhaps postpone the inevitable. Bandini's task, after a string of below-par performances, was to put himself in a good light at a circuit where he had always shone.

DUTCH GRAND PRIX

Zandvoort, 18th July 1965, 80 laps (2.605 miles/4.193km), 208.433 miles/335.440km • Starters 17, finishers 13

RACE				PRACTICE	
1st	Jim Clark	Lotus 33 Climax V8	2h 03m 59.1s	2nd	1m 31.0s
2nd	Jackie Stewart	BRM P261 BRM V8	+8.0s	6th	1m 31.4s
3rd	Dan Gurney	Brabham BT11 Climax V8	+13.0s	5th	1m 31.2s
4th	Graham Hill	BRM P261 BRM V8	+45.1s	1st	1m 30.7s
5th	Denny Hulme	Brabham BT11 Climax V8	79 laps	7th	1m 32.0s
6th	Richie Ginther	Honda RA272 Honda V12	79 laps	3rd	1m 31.0s
7th	**John Surtees**	**Ferrari 1512 F12**	**79 laps**	**4th**	**1m 31.0s**
9th	**Lorenzo Bandini**	**Ferrari 158 V8**	**79 laps**	**12th**	**1m 33.1s**

Pole position: Hill, 1m 30.7s, 103.412mph/166.426kph **Fastest race lap:** Clark, 1m 30.6s, 103.525mph/166.608kph **Winner's average speed:** 100.865mph/162.326kph **Drivers' championship:** 1st Clark 45, 2nd Hill 26, 3rd Stewart 25, 4th Surtees 17, 6th Bandini 6 **Constructors' championship:** 1st Lotus-Climax 45, 2nd BRM 37, 3rd Ferrari 20

The end of the illusions

German Grand Prix, 1st August

On Friday morning, Ferrari seemed to have the equipment to postpone Jim Clark's coronation because for the first time Ferrari provided two 1512s for John Surtees with a 158 for Lorenzo Bandini. However, the truth of the matter, at least according to Eugenio Dragoni, was that the second 1512 was merely a chassis fitted with a spare flat-12 engine that had been brought to previous races but kept in the back of the truck. Although Ferrari had announced that the 12-cylinder engine would receive revised cylinder heads for the Nürburgring, this had been postponed until Monza, a delay that raised questions about the usefulness of the update considering that the end of the 1.5-litre formula was rapidly approaching.

Surtees was not going to give up his title without a fight and in the original 1512 he got close to the 8m 30s barrier with a lap in 8m 33.8s. This performance was not entirely unexpected because he had always excelled at the Nürburgring and in addition a part of the circuit had been levelled and resurfaced, helping lap times to tumble. In the afternoon, 'Big John' went even quicker with a 8m 27.8s but the Scottish clan was also running amok. Jackie Stewart

had emerged on top in the morning with a lap in 8m 30.6s but in the afternoon Clark trounced that with a stunning 8m 22.7s. Stewart, whose BRM was now exhibiting an intermittent ignition fault, had no answer to that, although his senior team-mate, Graham Hill, produced a flyer at 8m 26.8s to elevate himself above Surtees. When Saturday morning's session opened on a damp track, not everyone ventured out and few of them were able to improve their times, although Stewart somehow managed to defy the conditions and go round in 8m 26.1s, giving him a place on the front row alongside Clark, Hill and Surtees. Bandini at the wheel of the 158 was another to do better on Saturday, improving to 8m 33.8s from Friday's 8m 39.3s to put himself on the second row with Mike Spence (Lotus) and Dan Gurney (Brabham).

The following day, Surtees's illusions were shattered from the very start of the race. While Clark sprinted away with Hill, Gurney and Stewart trying to keep up, the Ferrari driver dropped to the back. He had accelerated away from the grid only for the 1512's gear selectors to go awry and leave him almost at a standstill before he could finally engage a gear. A bearing from the selector slide had fallen into the gearbox, depriving him of the use of second and fourth, and by the time he had limped round the very long lap and reached his pit, Clark had already passed him twice. It was the end of any hopes he may have entertained of delaying Clark's accession to the Formula 1 throne. Still, he was not going

◄ **German Grand Prix.** John Surtees had huge trouble with his gearbox at the start and dropped far behind everyone else before pitting at the end of the first lap. Always keen to excel at the Nürburgring, he resumed and put on a fine show before calling it a day after 11 laps.

► **German Grand Prix.** After being hit from behind by Jochen Rindt's Cooper at the *Karussell*, Bandini had to vacate his car and break off a damaged exhaust pipe before he could get going again. He did well to fight back from 12th place to sixth at the finish.

GERMAN GRAND PRIX

Nürburgring, 1st August 1965, 15 laps (14.173 miles/22.810km), 212.602 miles/342.150km • Starters 19, finishers 8

RACE				PRACTICE	
1st	Jim Clark	Lotus 33 Climax V8	2h 07m 52.4s	1st	8m 22.7s
2nd	Graham Hill	BRM P261 BRM V8	+15.9s	3rd	8m 26.8s
3rd	Dan Gurney	Brabham BT11 Climax V8	+21.4s	5th	8m 29.0s
4th	Jochen Rindt	Cooper T77 Climax V8	+3m 29.6s	8th	8m 37.5s
5th	Jack Brabham	Brabham BT11 Climax V8	+4m 41.2s	14th	8m 44.9s
6th	Lorenzo Bandini	Ferrari 158 V8	+5m 08.6s	7th	8m 33.8s
DNF	John Surtees	Ferrari 1512 F12	11 laps (gearbox)	4th	8m 27.8s

Pole position: Clark, 8m 22.7s, 101.501mph/163.350kph **Fastest race lap:** Clark, 8m 24.1s, 101.221mph/162.900kph **Winner's average speed:** 99.792mph/160.600kph **Drivers' championship:** 1st Clark 54, 2nd Hill 30, 3rd Stewart 25, 4th Surtees 17, 7th Bandini 7 **Constructors' championship:** 1st Lotus-Climax 54, 2nd BRM 39, 3rd Ferrari 21

to give up and when Maranello's mechanics restored all five gears to working order, *Il Grande John* rejoined the race to appreciative applause from the big grandstand opposite the pits. Although a distant tailender, he was determined to put on a show, especially after his pit informed him that Clark had set a new record of 8m 24.1s on his tenth lap. Surtees responded with a 8m 27.0s before deciding to withdraw from the race because his gearbox was showing signs of playing up again — and it was never wise to

set out on another lap of the Nürburgring if there was a good probability of being stranded many miles away at its far side.

Left to fly the Ferrari flag on his own, Bandini started the race in seventh place and rose to fifth by the end of the first lap, locked in a ferocious battle with Mike Spence's Lotus and the Coopers of Jochen Rindt and Bruce McLaren. Plunging into the *Karussell* third time round, Bandini followed McLaren and Spence through the long, banked turn with Rindt very close to his tail.

Too close in fact. The Cooper hit the back of the Ferrari, twisting one of its exhaust megaphones and pitching the car into a spin. After climbing out to tear off the damaged pipe with his bare hands, Bandini resumed and attempted a comeback. From 12th place, he ascended the order, mainly through the retirements of others ahead of him, to claim one point for sixth place, a little bitter that his afternoon's work had not yielded more.

Yet again, Clark led from start to finish to claim his sixth victory from six starts and confirm his status as the undisputed World Champion. As for poor Surtees, it was especially tough for him to lose his crown at a circuit where he felt he could have won and in doing so match Alberto Ascari and Juan Manuel Fangio as three-time winners of the German Grand Prix — and therefore the ultimate '*Ringmeisters*'.

▼ **Italian Grand Prix.** Nino Vaccarella's presence at Monza was doubly notable. It was the last of his four Grand Prix starts and, what was more, his only one at the wheel of a Ferrari. Engine failure eliminated him from the race.

John Surtees was increasingly involved with Lola. On 30th August, four weeks after the German Grand Prix, he was at Brands Hatch driving not one but two of Eric Broadley's cars. The first was an updated version of the T70 sports car in which he won the Guards Trophy. The second was a Formula 2 T60 run by the Midland Racing Partnership in the British Eagle Trophy, a race that saw him make uncharacteristic mistakes, spinning out of third place and then crashing on the last lap after a spirited attempt to catch up again. Meanwhile, fellow Formula 1 stars took the top four places in the order Jim Clark, Denny Hulme, Jack Brabham and Graham Hill.

As that quartet of names confirms, Surtees was far from alone among top-line drivers in taking part in other forms of racing, but he was the only one whose Formula 1 employer also involved him in a full programme of sports car racing. And now, in addition, he very definitely had a committed Lola two-seater operation running in parallel under the aegis of his own Team Surtees. Perhaps he was planning to become a constructor in his own right? Time would tell, but this was certainly becoming a trend, for Bruce McLaren and Dan Gurney were on the point of following in Jack Brabham's footsteps.

High hopes

Italian Grand Prix, 12 September

If John Surtees's relationship with Eric Broadley presented food for thought in Maranello, Enzo Ferrari had to acknowledge that it did not affect his number-one driver's determination to defend Ferrari's colours at every opportunity. In the days leading up to the Italian Grand Prix, Surtees could be found at Monza carrying out multiple test sessions. When official practice opened on Friday, that effort seemed to bear fruit as he set the fastest lap of the three-and-a-half-hour session at 1m 37.0s before a rain shower prevented his rivals from hitting back.

This performance was not unexpected because Surtees was at the wheel of the newest and most powerful of the three 1512s present, complete with the vaunted new cylinder heads. Lorenzo Bandini got round in 1m 38.4s in one of the 1512s seen at the Nürburgring, while Nino Vaccarella's third Ferrari entry, the latest version of the 158, lapped in 1m 40.2s. Unfortunately, the next day, with the sun shining again upon another three-and-a-half-hour speedfest, there was double Scottish trouble in store. While Surtees turned in a fine 1m 36.1s, Jim Clark trumped it with a stunning 1m 35.9s to put his Lotus on pole position while Jackie Stewart (BRM) took the other place on the three-car front row at

➤ **Italian Grand Prix.** Jackie Stewart's BRM (left) and John Surtees's Ferrari have barely left the line while Jim Clark's Lotus, out of shot, has taken off like a dragster. What happened next was most unfortunate for Surtees, for a slipping clutch meant that he ended the first lap down in 13th place.

▼ **Italian Grand Prix.** Second time around, the clutch in Surtees's Ferrari stopped slipping but now would not disengage. Although forced to make clutchless gearchanges, he put on a stirring performance and charged back up through the field. Here, on the eighth lap, he has just shot past Mike Spence's Lotus and is about to overtake team-mate Bandini on the inside. He went on to enjoy three brief turns in the lead before his ailing clutch gave up on lap 35.

◄ **Italian Grand Prix.** After Surtees's retirement, Bandini continued his prolonged duel with Dan Gurney's Brabham. The American driver finally got past and finished third, while the Italian slipped to nearly a minute behind him in fourth place.

1m 36.6s. Bandini did well, producing a 1m 37.2s to join the second row with Graham Hill's BRM on 1m 37.1s. Vaccarella, who lacked track time, shared the sixth row with Jo Bonnier's Brabham.

Once again Surtees was unable to capitalise on his prime starting position, this time because the clutch's hydraulic mechanism gave trouble just before the start. When the flag fell, the Ferrari pulled away sluggishly and its clutch slipped all round the first lap, which Surtees completed in 13th place. Typically for Monza, the field divided into two main groups with a furious Surtees in the second one, now with his clutch ceasing to disengage at all. At least it was no longer slipping, so he pushed on, making clutchless gearchanges and driving as hard as he could. Quite soon he left the second group behind,

put himself in touch with the front-runners and worked his way into the slipstreaming frenzy.

On lap 11, the high point, spectators in the grandstands rose to their feet as one to cheer Surtees onwards as his Ferrari screamed past in first place after briefly dislodging Stewart and Clark from the lead. He hit the front again on laps 13, 15 and 17 but then gradually fell away. For a while he circulated in fifth place, with Bandini behind, before his clutch suddenly surrendered on lap 35, leaving him to crawl round the rest of the lap and throw in the towel.

While all this had been going on, Bandini had been part of the leading group, running from time to time as high as fourth, which was where he finished, never quite able to fulfil the

ITALIAN GRAND PRIX

Monza, 12th September 1965, 76 laps (3.573 miles/5.750km), 271.539 miles/437.000km • Starters 23, finishers 14

RACE				PRACTICE	
1st	Jackie Stewart	BRM P261 BRM V8	2h 04m 52.8s	3rd	1m 36.60s
2nd	Graham Hill	BRM P261 BRM V8	+3.3s	4th	1m 37.10s
3rd	Dan Gurney	Brabham BT11 Climax V8	+16.5s	9th	1m 38.11s
4th	**Lorenzo Bandini**	**Ferrari 1512 F12**	**+1m 15.9s**	**5th**	**1m 37.20s**
5th	Bruce McLaren	Cooper T77 Climax V8	75 laps	11th	1m 38.26s
6th	Richard Attwood	Lotus 25 BRM V8	75 laps	13th	1m 38.85s
12th	**Nino Vaccarella**	**Ferrari 158 V8**	58 laps (engine)	15th	1m 38.91s
DNF	**John Surtees**	**Ferrari 1512 F12**	34 laps (clutch)	2nd	1m 36.10s

Pole position: Jim Clark (Lotus 33 Climax V8), 1m 35.90s, 134.123mph/215.850kph **Fastest race lap:** Clark, 1m 36.40s, 133.427mph/214.730kph **Winner's average speed:** 130.464mph/209.961kph **Drivers' championship:** 1st Clark 54, 2nd Hill 34, 3rd Stewart 33, 4th Surtees 17, 6th Bandini 10 **Constructors' championship:** 1st Lotus-Climax 54, 2nd BRM 42, 3rd Ferrari 24

promise he had shown during practice. By now the crowd had largely deserted the grandstands without a thought for Vaccarella, trying to keep his head above water at the back of the field until eliminated by engine failure. They had no interest in seeing the outcome of the battle for victory between Stewart and Hill after Clark's retirement with 13 laps to go. They had only come to Monza to witness a Ferrari triumph and instead the outcome was a BRM 1–2, Stewart from Hill, with Dan Gurney's Brabham third.

The mood within the Scuderia was very downbeat. The extra six horsepower (at most) that Mauro Forghieri had promised from the new cylinder heads seemed to have gone missing. In fact, Surtees had had to start the race in a second-string 1512 that at one stage had been earmarked for Ludovico Scarfiotti, the outgoing World Champion's chosen car, the newest of the 1512s, having suffered untraceable electrical niggles at the end of practice. In short, the 12-cylinder engine had ultimately proved to be a disappointment, even at the very track at which it had been expected to shine. Judged over the season as a whole, the flat-12 had been unable to eclipse the V8, which although less powerful did benefit from being lighter and more fuel efficient. With only two Grands Prix to go until the end of the season, and of the 1.5-litre era, Ferrari's latest 12-cylinder engine would remain a flop unless a miracle intervened.

During the three-week gap before the United States Grand Prix, John Surtees had two Lola outings on his agenda. At Oulton Park on 18th September, the International Gold Cup was now a Formula 2 race and he won it at the wheel of the Midland Racing Partnership T60, vanquishing rivals such as Denny Hulme (second), Graham Hill (third) and Jim Clark (sixth).

The very next day, he was on the other side of the Atlantic, at Mont-Tremblant in Canada for the first round of the *Autoweek* Championship, a new series for 'big banger' sports cars that turned out to be the forerunner of the following year's inaugural Canadian-American Challenge — the fabled 'Can-Am'. Somehow he was unaffected by jet lag and came out on top in his Team Surtees T70, followed home by David Piper's Ferrari 365 P2.

Five days later, on Friday 24th September, he was at Mosport — scene of his first victory in the T70 back in June — for the Canadian Grand Prix. This was the second round of the *Autoweek* Championship and now his Team Surtees was running a sister T70 for Jackie Stewart. After equalling Bruce McLaren's time in his McLaren-Elva, Surtees transferred to Stewart's car to try to identify a concern that his new team-mate had raised. Something broke in the front suspension and the Lola veered off the track, bounced along a bank and down into a deep culvert where it came to rest upside-down with its driver trapped

beneath. Surtees suffered fractures to his lower vertebrae and pelvis as well as multiple internal lesions. At hospital in Toronto, the diagnosis was grave at first but became more reassuring within a few days, giving hope that he could make a reasonable recovery and be able to race again — but not for at least six months.

At Maranello, once the initial shock had worn off, the aftermath brought mixed feelings. Writing in *Motor Sport*, Denis Jenkinson stated that there was little sympathy within the Scuderia for a man who was widely felt to have been 'freelancing' rather too much. However, Mauro Forghieri, who saw the situation from the inside, observed that Enzo Ferrari was most concerned about his injured driver and talked frequently with him on the telephone. Still, the fact remained that the relationship between *Il Commendatore* and *Il Grande John* would never be quite the same again.

Hill's hat-trick

United States Grand Prix, 3rd October

In John Surtees's absence, Lorenzo Bandini became Ferrari's number one, a role he embraced with some discomfort because he had come to realise that he was not the equal of his English team leader. As the American market was increasingly important to Ferrari and its New York-based agent, Luigi Chinetti, three cars were entered at Watkins Glen. Bandini took over the 1512 that Surtees would have driven and had a spare as well, supported by a 1512 for Pedro Rodríguez and a 158 for Bob Bondurant, the latter making his Grand Prix début and also using Goodyear tyres rather than Ferrari's usual Dunlops. Rodríguez and Bondurant were nominally entered by Chinetti's North American Racing Team (NART) but their cars were tended by Scuderia mechanics and Eugenio Dragoni was in overall charge.

The main focus among their rivals was the fight for the runner-up spot in the World Championship between BRM team-mates Graham Hill (38 points from eight results) and Jackie Stewart (34 from seven), although there was more talk in the paddock about the imminent 3-litre formula, including the enticing prospect that these BRM drivers, both with renewed contracts, would have cars powered by a 16-cylinder 'H' engine that was under development in Bourne. Among other teams, it was said that Jack Brabham was not planning to run a full works effort because of cost but would build a new car to keep his hand in. While pursuing his activities with sports cars of his own construction, Bruce McLaren hoped also to design, build and race his own Formula 1 car provided that he could fund it. Lotus was said to be in talks with Ford and Cosworth Engineering about the design of a new V8 but in the meantime was contemplating a deal with BRM to use the new H16. Dan Gurney, founder with Carroll Shelby of All American Racers, was close to completion of his car, the Eagle, powered by a V12 engine penned by Harry Weslake, the well-known specialist in the design of combustion chambers.

Ferrari put in a low-key performance in the first of the two four-hour practice sessions. While up front the BRMs of Hill (1m 12.50s) and Stewart (1m 12.80s) sandwiched Clark's Lotus (1m 12.70s), Bandini (1m 13.05s) was scarcely quicker than Jo Bonnier's Brabham (1m 13.20s). After Rodríguez (1m 14.90s) put his 1512 in the same bracket as the Hondas of Ronnie Bucknum and Richie Ginther, he spent the rest of the session with Bondurant (1m 15.1s) in his wake to help him learn the circuit. The next day, when everyone improved, brought further proof that the complexity of a 12-cylinder engine, whether in 'vee' or 'boxer' configuration, did not really justify the marginal gain in power compared with the quickest V8s. While Hill (1m 11.25s) claimed pole with Clark (1m 11.35s) alongside on the two-car

front row, Bandini (1m 11.73s) trailed Ginther (1m 11.40s) to line up fifth. Bondurant (1m 12.90s) and Rodríguez (1m 13.00s) were much quicker than the previous day, particularly the American, who racked up more than 150 laps learning the ropes, but they still found themselves towards the back of the grid.

Since first staging the United States Grand Prix in 1961, Watkins Glen had never produced exciting races and the 60,000 spectators who trooped to the circuit despite gloomy weather could only hope that this year would be different. It was not. Hill jumped into the lead at the start from Clark but their promising duel ended on lap 12 when the Lotus retired with engine failure. Thereafter there was little left to cheer, especially as rain had begun to fall and four other cars, including Stewart's BRM, had already left the fray. Still, Bandini was doing well, running third behind Gurney's Brabham after a decent start, although that soon became fourth when Jack Brabham overtook him. It was encouraging to see the Italian properly challenging for a place in the top three, something that had not happened since Monaco, even if he was later lapped twice while remaining fourth at the chequered flag.

◀ **United States Grand Prix.** The grid assembles at Watkins Glen. The first two rows are entirely out of shot, while the two cars on the third row, Lorenzo Bandini's Ferrari and Jackie Stewart's BRM, peep only slightly into view at the bottom of the frame. Then we see Jack Brabham (#7) although his team-mate, Dan Gurney, sharing the fourth row, does not get into the picture. Further back, though, everyone is visible: fifth row — Bruce McLaren's Cooper (#9) and Jo Bonnier's Brabham (#15); sixth row — Jo Siffert's Brabham (#16) and Ronnie Bucknum's Honda (#12); seventh row — Jochen Rindt's Cooper (#10) and Bob Bondurant's Ferrari (#24); eighth row — Pedro Rodríguez's Ferrari (#14) and Richard Attwood's Lotus (#21); ninth row — Moisés Solana's Lotus (#18) and Innes Ireland's Lotus (#22).

➤ **United States Grand Prix.** Bob Bondurant, a first-rate driver in two-seaters, made his Grand Prix début at Watkins Glen with a third Ferrari, a 158. As with Pedro Rodríguez's sister car, NART was the entrant, and both cars carried a broad white stripe overlaid by a thin blue one to honour the connection. Bondurant briefly ran seventh in the race but dropped to ninth by the finish.

Dragoni was delighted with that outcome and it was not his only source of satisfaction. While Bondurant drove cautiously, Rodríguez was in fine form. Fifteenth at the start, he fought his way up to sixth by lap 13, one of his victims being Jochen Rindt (Cooper) after the Mexican's sustained pressure forced him into a spin. Six laps later, Rodríguez picked off Bonnier to put himself fifth, now running in convoy with Bandini. Rindt, who had fallen back to ninth place after a second spin when the track became damp and slippery, gradually regained ground and got back in front of Rodríguez on lap 45, and that was how

they remained until near the end. Urged by his pit to go faster, Rodríguez closed on the Austrian and passed him with seven laps to go, on lap 103. It was the first time since Monaco that two Ferraris had finished in the points.

The second half of the race was no more eventful than the first. Hill won, having led since the fifth lap, while the Brabhams of Gurney and Brabham finished second and third after running in those positions since lap 53. Perhaps the fourth Mexican Grand Prix, the last race to be run under the 1.5-litre regulations, could at least bring a memorable conclusion.

UNITED STATES GRAND PRIX

Watkins Glen, 3rd October 1965, 110 laps (2.300 miles/3.701km), 252.966 miles/407.110km • Starters 18, finishers 13

RACE				PRACTICE	
1st	Graham Hill	BRM P261 BRM V8	2h 20m 36.1s	1st	1m 11.25s
2nd	Dan Gurney	Brabham BT11 Climax V8	+12.5s	8th	1m 12.25s
3rd	Jack Brabham	Brabham BT11 Climax V8	+57.5s	7th	1m 12.20s
4th	**Lorenzo Bandini**	**Ferrari 1512 F12**	**109 laps**	5th	**1m 11.73s**
5th	**Pedro Rodríguez**	**Ferrari 1512 F12**[1]	**109 laps**	15th	**1m 13.00s**
6th	Jochen Rindt	Cooper T77 Climax V8	108 laps	13th	1m 12.90s
9th	**Bob Bondurant**	**Ferrari 158 V8**[1]	**106 laps**	14th	**1m 12.90s**

Pole position: Hill, 1m 11.25s, 116.195mph/186.998kph **Fastest race lap:** Hill, 1m 11.90s, 115.157mph/185.328kph **Winner's average speed:** 107.978mph/173.773kph **Drivers' championship:** 1st Clark 54, 2nd Hill 40, 3rd Stewart 33, 5th Surtees 17, 6th Bandini 13, 12th Rodríguez 2
Constructors' championship: 1st Lotus-Climax 54, 2nd BRM 45, 3rd Ferrari 26

[1] *Entered by North American Racing Team (NART)*

Honda's first

Mexican Grand Prix, 24th October

Statisticians would have had a field day reviewing the end of the 1965 season and, with it, the conclusion of the five-year 1.5-litre era of Formula 1. With one Grand Prix to go and a few adjustments to points scores, it was all over bar the shouting. Jim Clark had already emerged as the outstanding driver of the period with a total of 200 World Championship points while Lotus-Climax was the dominant constructor with 22 Grand Prix victories, all but the first three achieved by Clark. Second in this five-year reckoning were Graham Hill and BRM with respectively 172 points and 11 victories. Then came Ferrari with nine victories and points scores of 79 and 52 for John Surtees and Phil Hill respectively.

After the first practice session in Mexico, it looked highly unlikely that the Scuderia would be able to add to its score, despite again having three entries, all 12-cylinder models, with Ludovico Scarfiotti in the third car this time. Local boy Pedro Rodríguez, driving the 1512 he had raced at Watkins Glen, had not even had time to check out a set of Firestone tyres when a stub-axle breakage sent him flying off the track, damaging the car sufficiently badly for it to play no further part in the weekend.

Scarfiotti had just begun to get to grips with the second 1512 and the unfamiliar circuit when he too was halted, by engine failure. Bandini was trying short exhausts in place of the usual megaphones when he hit the guardrail on the outside of the curve after the pits. With all three Ferrari men having managed only a few flying laps, their times were not too meaningful but for the record they were 1m 57.71s for Bandini, 1m 59.06s for Rodríguez and 2m 1.84s for Scarfiotti. Bandini's time put him seventh, quite far behind the day's best, Dan Gurney's Brabham (1m 56.24s), Jim Clark's Lotus (1m 56.26s) and Richie Ginther's Honda (1m 56.48s), the latter helped by plenty of prior running in three private test sessions.

The next day the Ferrari drivers were determined to improve but their illusions were soon shattered. Rodríguez, now assigned Scarfiotti's car on Eugenio Dragoni's orders, was no quicker than

▼ **Mexican Grand Prix.** First lap at the hairpin. Richie Ginther (Honda), Jackie Stewart (BRM), Mike Spence (Lotus) and Dan Gurney (Brabham) have already gone through, so Lorenzo Bandini, leading this group, is fifth. While Graham Hill (BRM) takes a wide line to avoid any trouble, the Ferrari is pursued by Jack Brabham (#7 Brabham), Pedro Rodríguez (#14 Ferrari), Jim Clark (#5 Lotus), Jo Siffert (#16 Brabham), Bruce McLaren (#9 Cooper), Ronnie Bucknum (#12 Honda) and Jo Bonnier (#15 Brabham).

the previous day, while Bandini posted a small improvement to 1m 57.31s but remained seventh in the rankings. Scarfiotti was allowed a few laps in his surrendered car and ironically made the best improvement by far, setting a 1m 58.93s, quicker than Rodríguez could manage despite 'home advantage'. Dragoni, however, was not sufficiently impressed to let the Italian keep his car so he was destined to sit out the race. With the end of the season beckoning, Ferrari had to resign itself to playing a minor role. Up front, Clark took pole after improving to 1m 56.17s, while Gurney and Ginther lined up next on unchanged times, with Brabham fourth.

While Ginther shot off into the lead at the start and remained there throughout, Ferrari's hopes that Bandini might be able to fight for a podium position quickly faded. Initially fifth behind Gurney, he slipped to sixth on the fourth lap when Graham Hill (BRM) got past. The only consolation at this stage was that Clark was behind the Ferrari after a poor start and was soon to become the first retirement of the race when unhealthy sounding noises emanating from his Climax engine were the prelude to terminal failure after only eight laps. This left Bandini and Rodríguez together on the track and they became locked in a hard-fought dice.

▲ **Mexican Grand Prix.** This is the eighth lap and the long-running Ferrari battle between Lorenzo Bandini and Pedro Rodríguez is about to intensify.

▼ **Mexican Grand Prix.** After their simultaneous pitstops on lap 33, Rodríguez and Bandini tried to keep the crowd entertained with their scrap at the back of the field. Naturally the Mexican spectators were rooting for the man leading here.

Bandini held off his temporary team-mate until lap 14, when Rodríguez delighted the partisan crowd by slipping ahead. However, the Italian had no intention of giving an inch and over the next 12 laps he and the Mexican traded places several times. Directly ahead of them, fifth-placed Jackie Stewart's BRM was now troubled by a slipping clutch and gradually fell into the clutches of the Ferrari pair. Now the battle raged between three cars and the crowd's fervour for their man reached fever pitch. He obliged on lap 28 by getting ahead but two laps later Stewart was back in front.

Then suddenly, at half distance, it all went wrong for Ferrari. Bandini got sideways on lap 33 and bashed the front of his 1512 against one of the white-painted tyres embedded in the ground to mark the edges of the track, forcing him to pit at the end of the lap for a replacement nose. While he was waiting for it to be fitted, Rodríguez happened to arrive as well, his car in need of a fresh battery because of a faulty rectifier. Hush fell over the crowd, their hopes for Rodríguez dashed. With repairs done, both Ferrari drivers rejoined at the back of the field and indulged in a more desultory duel for the rest of the race, finishing three laps behind the winner. Rodríguez passed Bandini on the very last lap when the Italian's car slowed, its engine starting to overheat through loss of water.

An historic result brought down the curtain on a Formula 1 era that had served its purpose but had its day. Richie Ginther delivered a début win for Honda, for Goodyear and for himself, while Dan Gurney finished second for Brabham to make it two American drivers on the top two steps of the podium. Ferrari would have certainly wished for a better result at the twilight of the 1.5-litre Formula 1 but Maranello would be back.

The new 3-litre Formula 1 was about to arrive. Although it had been feared that Coventry Climax's decision to withdraw from racing could have a devasting effect on grids, there now seemed to be enough constructors who wanted to take part. Commitment from Ferrari and BRM was already a given, both manufacturers from the outset having backed plans to double engine capacity when first proposed two years earlier. It seemed that most teams, even Brabham after earlier caution, would continue. In addition, there would be two new teams, both with their own cars built by renowned drivers: Dan Gurney's All American Racers would run its Weslake-powered Eagle and Bruce McLaren would race his own car with a V8 derived from Ford's successful Indianapolis engine. Brabham would turn to a 2.5-litre Oldsmobile V8 bored out by Repco and Cooper would go for a Maserati V12. Little was known about Honda's plans except that the Japanese company was intending to keep going and its car would have a new 3-litre engine.

To discover Ferrari's intentions for the following season, the world would have to wait until the press conference in Maranello on 11th December, when all would be revealed. Enzo Ferrari, a man for all seasons whose backbone stiffened in the

MEXICAN GRAND PRIX
Mexico City, 24th October 1965, 65 laps (3.107 miles/5.000km), 201.946 miles/325.000km • Starters 18, finishers 8

RACE				PRACTICE	
1st	Richie Ginther	Honda RA272 Honda V12	2h 8m 32.10s	3rd	1m 56.48s
2nd	Dan Gurney	Brabham BT11 Climax V8	+2.89s	2nd	1m 56.24s
3rd	Mike Spence	Lotus 33 Climax V8	+1m 00.15s	6th	1m 57.20s
4th	Jo Siffert	Brabham BT11 BRM V8	+1m 54.42s	11th	1m 57.94s
5th	Ronnie Bucknum	Honda RA272 Honda V12	64 laps	10th	1m 57.88s
6th	Richard Attwood	Lotus 25 BRM V8	64 laps	17th	2m 00.61s
7th	**Pedro Rodríguez**	**Ferrari 1512 F12**[1]	**62 laps**	**14th**	**1m 59.06s**
8th	**Lorenzo Bandini**	**Ferrari 1512 F12**	**62 laps**	**7th**	**1m 57.31s**
DNS	**Ludovico Scarfiotti**	**Ferrari 1512 F12**	**–**	**18th**	**1m 58.93s**

Pole position: Jim Clark (Lotus 33 Climax V8), 1m 56.17s, 96.278mph/154.945kph **Fastest race lap:** Gurney, 1m 55.84s, 96.586mph/155.440kph **Winner's average speed:** 94.268mph/151.710kph **Drivers' championship:** 1st Clark 54, 2nd Hill 40 (47)[2], 3rd Stewart 33 (34)[2], 5th Surtees 17, 6th Bandini 13, 14th Rodríguez 2 **Constructors' championship:** 1st Lotus-Climax 54 (58)[2], 2nd BRM 45 (61)[2], 3rd Brabham-Climax 27 (31)[2], 4th Ferrari 26

[1] Entered by North American Racing Team (NART) [2] Figure in brackets indicates all points scored; only the best six results counted towards the championship

Formula 1 World Championship (Drivers) *Top three plus Ferrari drivers*

	1st Jim Clark	2nd Graham Hill	3rd Jackie Stewart	5th John Surtees	6th Lorenzo Bandini	14th Pedro Rodríguez
South African GP	9	4	−1	6	0	–
Monaco GP	–	9	4	3	6	0
Belgian GP	9	−2	6	0	0	–
GP de l'ACF (France)	9	−2	6	4	0	–
British GP	9	6	2	4	0	–
Dutch GP	9	−3	6	0	0	–
German GP	9	6	0	0	1	–
Italian GP	0	6	9	0	3	–
United States GP	0	9	0	0	3	2
Mexican GP	0	0	0	0	0	0
Total	54	40	33	17	13	2

Formula 1 World Championship (Constructors)

	1st Lotus-Climax	2nd BRM	3rd Brabham-Climax	4th Ferrari
South African GP	9	−4	0	6
Monaco GP	0	9	0	6
Belgian GP	9	6	3	0
GP de l'ACF (France)	9	6	−3	4
British GP	9	6	−1	4
Dutch GP	9	−6	4	0
German GP	9	−6	4	−1
Italian GP	0	9	4	3
United States GP	0	9	6	3
Mexican GP	−4	0	6	0
Total	54	45	27	26

International Championship for GT Manufacturers

	1st Shelby	2nd Ferrari	3rd Austin-Healey
Daytona 2,000Km (1.6)[1]	14.4	−4.8	–
Sebring 12 Hours (1.6)	14.4	0	4.8
Monza 1,000Km (1.3)	11.7	5.2	–
Tourist Trophy (1.3)	−11.7	7.8	–
Targa Florio (1.6)	0	14.4	9.6
Spa 500Km (1.3)	−7.8	11.7	–
Nürburgring 1,000Km (1.6)	14.4	−4.8	–
Rossfeld hillclimb (1.0)	9	–	–
Le Mans 24 Hours (2.0)	12	18	–
Reims 12 Hours (1.6)	14.4	0	–
Coppa Città Di Enna (1.3)	−11.7	5.2	–
Ollon–Villars hillclimb (1.0)	–	9	–
Bridgehampton 500Km (1.3)	−11.7	−3.9	1.3
Total	90.3	71.3	15.7

[1] Figures in brackets indicate coefficients used for scoring system

face of adversity, was expected to be even more pugnacious than usual. Formula 1, Formula 2, prototypes, sports cars, GTs — he was involved on multiple fronts and there was also talk that, urged by Luigi Chinetti, he might expand even further by tackling Indianapolis. After all, why not cross swords with Ford at the Brickyard when the American giant had stated more clearly than ever that it wanted to put a spanner in the works for Maranello, especially at Le Mans, where nothing short of victory would satisfy Henry Ford II.

In endurance racing, the new season would kick off on 6th February at Daytona, where the race duration would now be 24 hours, and continue at Sebring on 26th March. In Formula 1, once the non-championship events in South Africa and Sicily were over, Monaco would host the first round of new World Championship on 22nd May.

As he continued to convalesce in England, John Surtees pondered the prospects with interest. There was now little doubt that he would be ready, able and willing to return to driving duties by the spring and Enzo Ferrari would receive him back with optimism.

TECHNICAL SPECIFICATIONS

YEAR	1960				1961			1962				
MODEL	Dino 246[1]	250 TR	Dino 246 S	250 GT[2]	156[3]	156[3]	246 SP	156[4]	250 GTO	196 SP	248 SP	268 SP
TYPE	F1	Open	Open	Berlinetta	F1	F1	Open	F1	Berlinetta	Open	Open	Open
ENGINE												
Number of cylinders	6	12	6	12	6	6	6	6	12	6	8	8
Vee angle	65°	60°	60°	60°	65°	120°	65°	120°	60°	60°	90°	90°
Bore x stroke (mm)	85 x 71	73 x 58.8	85 x 71	73 x 58.8	73 x 58.8	73 x 58.8	85 x 71	73 x 58.8	73 x 58.8	77 x 71	77 x 66	77 x 71
Capacity (cc)	2417.33	2953.21	2417.33	2953.21	1476.60	1476.60	2417.33	1476.60	2953.21	1983.72	2458.70	2644.96
Cylinder displacement (cc)	402.88	246.10	402.88	246.10	246.10	246.10	402.88	246.10	246.10	330.62	307.33	330.62
Compression ratio	9.8:1	9.8:1	9.8:1	9.2:1	9.8:1	9.8:1	9.8:1	9.8:1	9.8:1	9.8:1	9.8:1	9.8:1
Maximum power (bhp)	280	300	250	240-280	185	190	270	190	295/302	210	250	265
Rpm at maximum power	8500	7200	7500	7000	9200	9500	8000	9500	7500	7500	7400	7000
Fuel system	3 Weber	6 Weber	3 Weber	3 Weber	3 Weber	2 Weber	3 Weber	2 Weber	6 Weber	3 Weber	4 Weber	4 Weber
	42 DCN	38 DCN	42 DCN	40 DCL	38 DCN	40 IF3C	42 DCN	40 IF3C	38 DCN	42 DCN	40 IF2C	40 IF2C
Overhead camshafts	2 per bank	2 per bank	1 per bank	1 per bank	2 per bank	2 per bank	2 per bank	2 per bank	1 per bank	1 per bank	1 per bank	1 per bank
TRANSMISSION												
Clutch	Multi-plate	Twin-plate	Multi-plate	Single-plate	Multi-plate	Multi-plate	Multi-plate	Multi-plate	Single-plate	Multi-plate	Multi-plate	Multi-plate
Gearbox	5 + reverse	4 + reverse	5 + reverse	4 + reverse	5 + reverse	5 + reverse	5 + reverse	6 + reverse	5 + reverse	5 + reverse	5 + reverse	5 + reverse
CHASSIS												
Type	Tubular	Tubular	Tubular	Tubular	Tubular	Tubular	Tubular	Tubular	Tubular	Tubular	Tubular	Tubular
Wheelbase (mm)	2350	2350	2160	2400	2320	2320	2320	2320	2400	2320	2320	2320
(inches)	92.52	92.52	85.04	94.49	91.34	91.34	91.34	91.34	94.49	91.34	91.34	91.34
Track front (mm)	1300	1308	1245	1354	1200	1200	1200	1340	1354	1200	1200	1200
(inches)	51.18	51.50	49.02	53.31	47.24	47.24	47.24	52.76	53.31	47.24	47.24	47.24
Track rear (mm)	1300	1300	1205	1349	1200	1200	1200	1320	1350	1200	1200	1200
(inches)	51.18	51.18	47.44	53.11	47.24	47.24	47.24	51.97	53.12	47.24	47.24	47.24
Weight (kg) dry	est 540	800	640	960	460	470	590	460	880	600	640	660
(lbs) dry	est 1190	1764	1411	2116	1014	1036	1301	1014	1940	1521	1411	1698
Tyres front	5.50 x 16	5.50 x 16	5.50 x 15	6.00 x 16	5.25 x15	5.00 x 15	5.50 x 15	5.00 x 15	6.00 x 15	5.25 x 15	5.25 x 15	5.00 x 15
Tyres rear	6.50 x 16	6.00 x 16	6.00 x 15	6.00 x 16	6.00 x 15	6.00 x 15	6.50 x 15	6.00 x 15	7.00 x 15	6.50 x 15	6.50 x 15	7.00 x 15

[1] Also known as 246 F1

[2] SWB (Short Wheelbase)

[3] 156 F1 V 65° and 120° are also known as Dino 156 F1

[4] As per mid-season

1962			1963			1964				1965				
286 SP	330 TR	330 LM	156	250 P	250 LM	158	1512[7]	275 P	330 P	Dino 166 P	275 GTB	275 P2	330 P2	365 P[9]
Open	Open	Berlinetta	F1	Open	Coupé[6]	F1	F1	Open	Open	Coupé	Berlinetta	Open	Open	Open
6	12	12	6	12	12	8	12	12	12	6	12	12	12	12
60°	60°	60°	120°	60°	60°	90°	Flat	60°	60°	65°	60°	60°	60°	60°
90 x 75	77 x 71	77 x 71	73 x 58.8	73 x 58.8	77 x 58.8	67 x 52.8	56 x 50.4	77 x 58.8	77 x 71	77 x 57	77 x 58.8	77 x 58.8	77 x 71	81 x 71
2862.78	3967.44	3967.44	1476.00	2953.21	3285.72	1489.23	1489.63	3285.72	3967.44	1592.57	3285.72	3285.72	3967.44	4390.35
477.13	330.62	330.62	246.10	246.10	273.81	186.15	124.13	273.81	330.62	265.42	273.81	273.81	330.62	365.86
9.5:1	8.8:1	8.8:1	9.8:1	9.5:1	9.7:1	10.5	9.8:1	9.7:1	9.8:1	11.5:1	9.5:1	9.9:1	9.9:1	9.1:1
260	390	390	205	310	320	210	220	320	370	175	300	350	410	380
6800	7500	7500	10,500	7500	7500	11000	12000	7700	7200	9000	7600	8500	8000	7200
3 Weber	6 Weber	6 Weber	Bosch injection	6 Weber	6 Weber	Bosch injection	Lucas injection	6 Weber	6 Weber	3 Weber	6 Weber	6 Weber	6 Weber	6 Weber
42 DCN	42 DCN	42 DCN	Direct	39 DCN	38/40 DCN	Direct	Indirect	38 DCN	38 DCN	40 DCN/2	40 DCN/2	40 DCN/2	40 DCN/2	38 DCN
1 per bank	1 per bank	1 per bank	2 per bank	1 per bank	1 per bank	2 per bank	2 per bank	1 per bank	1 per bank	2 per bank	1 per bank	2 per bank	2 per bank	1 per bank
Multi-plate	Multi-plate	Multi-plate	Multi-plate	Multi-plate	Single-plate	Multi-plate	Multi-plate	Multi-plate	Multi-plate	twin-plate	Single-plate	Multi-plate	Multi-plate	Multi-plate
5 + reverse	5 + reverse	4 + reverse	6 + reverse	5 + reverse	5 + reverse	5 + reverse	5 + reverse	5 + reverse	5 + reverse	5 + reverse	5 + reverse	5 + reverse	5 + reverse	5 + reverse
Tubular	Tubular	Tubular	Tubular	Tubular	Tubular	Semi-monocoque	Semi-monocoque	Tubular	Tubular	Tubular	Tubular	Tubular	Tubular	Tubular
2320	2420	2420	2380	2400	2400	2380	2400	2400	2400	2280	2400	2400	2400	2400
91.34	95.28	95.28	93.70	94.49	94.49	93.70	94.49	94.49	94.49	89.76	94.49	94.49	94.49	94.49
1200	1245	-	1340	1350	1350	1350	-	1350	1350	1392	1377	1400	1400	1400
47.24	49.02	-	52.76	53.15	53.15	53.15	-	53.15	53.15	54.80	54.21	55.12	55.12	55.12
1200	1275	-	1320	1340	1340	1350	-	1340	1340	1414	1426	1370	1370	1370
47.24	49.02	-	51.97	52.76	52.76	53.15	-	52.76	52.76	55.67	56.14	53.94	53.94	53.94
620	820	950	465	760	820	468	490[8]	755	785	586	980	790	820	850
24.41	1808	2094	1025	1976	1808	1032	1080	1665	1731	1292	2161	1742	1808	1874
5.25 x 15	6.00 x 16	6.00 x 15	5.00 x 15	5.50 x 15	5.50 x 15	6.00 x 13	5.50 x 13	5.50 x 15	6.00 x 15	5.50 x 13	5.50 x 15	5.50 x 15	5.50 x 15	5.50 x 15
7.00 x 15	7.00 x 16	7.00 x 15	6.00 x 15[5]	7.00 x 15	7.00 x 15	7.00 x 13	7.00 x 13	7.00 x 15	7.25 x 15	6.50 x 13	6.50 x 15	6.50 x 15	6.50 x 15	6.50 x 15

5 Later on with 7.00 x 15 and magnesium wheels Rear track: 1,380mm
6 As per ferrari.com
7 Also known as 512 F1
8 With liquids
9 Also known as 365 P2

INDEX

Abate, Carlo Mario 28, 30, 128, 131, 134, 137, 142, 143, 144, 155, 162, 185, 186, 187, 189, 194, 202, 203, 211, 212, 214, 227, 228, 229, 230, 240, 242, 243, 244, 248

Allison, Cliff 15, 16, 17, 18, 19, 20, 24, 25, 27, 28, 29, 30, 70, 98

Amon, Chris 213, 214, 216, 257, 265, 266, 272, 273, 276, 278, 312, 313, 320, 322, 323, 333

Anderson, Bob 221, 277, 326

Arena, Vincenzo 248

Arents, George 40

Arundell, Peter 247, 262, 263, 270

Ascari, Alberto 66, 104, 231, 324, 354

Ashmore, Gerry 195

Astle, Derrick 142

Attwood, Richard 202, 258, 260, 265, 266, 272, 273, 310, 320, 343, 344, 345, 358

Baghetti, Giancarlo 74, 76, 78, 89, 90, 94, 97, 100, 102, 103, 104, 105, 106, 113, 114, 115, 116, 123, 126, 134, 135, 136, 138, 140, 141, 142, 143, 150, 153, 155, 158, 161, 166, 167, 169, 171, 172, 173, 185, 186, 195, 201, 207, 240, 264, 265, 266, 286, 306, 307, 312, 316, 318, 319, 320, 335

Baillie, Ian 40, 42, 43, 158

Ballisat, Keith 88

Balzarini, Gianni 250

Bandini, Lorenzo 6, 113, 114, 126, 129, 134, 135, 136, 137, 141, 142, 143, 146, 147, 148, 149, 150, 155, 166, 167, 168, 169, 170, 171, 172, 173, 180, 182, 183, 184, 186, 188, 189, 191, 195, 198, 202, 205, 206, 207, 210, 213, 214, 216, 219, 220, 221, 222, 224, 225, 227, 229, 231, 232, 233, 234, 235, 236, 240, 242, 244, 245, 247, 250, 251, 252, 253, 255, 256, 257, 258, 259, 262, 264, 265, 266, 267, 269, 270, 271, 272, 273, 274, 275, 276, 277, 278, 279, 280, 281, 282, 284, 285, 286, 291, 292, 295, 296, 297, 298, 299, 300, 302, 303, 304, 310, 312, 313, 314, 316, 317, 319, 320, 322, 323, 324, 325, 326, 327, 328, 330, 333, 335, 336, 340, 341, 342, 347, 349, 350, 351, 352, 353, 354, 355, 356, 357, 358, 359, 360, 361, 362

Barberis, Celso Lara 18

Barlow, Roger 64

Barlow, Vic 110

Barth, Edgar 17, 24, 25, 27, 40, 42, 62, 76, 78, 90, 134, 185, 190, 192, 194, 202, 250, 253, 282, 294

Bazzi, Luigi 42, 53

Behra, Jean 70, 141

Behra, José 93, 229

Bellei, Angelo 201

Bellentani, Vittorio 12

Berger, Georges 226, 287, 289

Berney, Edgar 229, 283

'Beurlys' — see 'Blaton, Jean'

Bianchi, Lucien 28, 30, 36, 130, 131, 132, 158, 174, 202, 206, 222, 226, 227, 228, 229, 230, 240, 241, 253, 258, 259, 268, 269, 272, 273, 287, 288, 289, 290, 292, 294, 295, 307, 312, 313, 314, 332, 335

Billi, Giorgio 173

Bini, Umberto 186

Birkin, Sir Henry 'Tim' 206

Biscaldi, Giampiero 312, 313, 314, 316, 320, 333, 335, 336

Bizzarrini, Giotto 122, 128, 129

Black, Duncan 184

Blaton, Jean 28, 36, 158, 161, 202, 203, 205, 206, 258, 268, 269, 272, 273, 292, 320, 323, 334, 335, 336, 339, 343, 345

Blondeau, Marcel 158

Boffa, Mennato 113

Bogart, Humphrey 64

Boller, Armand 294, 339

Bolton, Peter 202, 266

Bondurant, Bob 242, 244, 248, 253, 258, 259, 260, 265, 266, 268, 269, 272, 273, 282, 286, 287, 288, 289, 305, 307, 309, 310, 312, 314, 315, 316, 319, 322, 324, 331, 332, 333, 339, 343, 345, 346, 357, 358, 359

Bonnier, Jo 6, 17, 18, 20, 21, 23, 24, 25, 26, 27, 28, 29, 30, 32, 40, 42, 44, 47, 49, 51, 55, 63, 69, 76, 78, 82, 85, 90, 101, 102, 103, 104, 105, 106, 109, 113, 114, 130, 131, 132, 134, 137, 139, 143, 144, 146, 147, 149, 155, 157, 172, 173, 181, 185, 186, 187, 189, 192, 195, 207, 212, 216, 222, 231, 242, 244, 250, 252, 258, 265, 267, 272, 273, 274, 282, 286, 292, 293, 294, 312, 314, 316, 319, 322, 323, 327, 333, 335, 343, 344, 345, 356, 358, 359, 360

Bordino, Pietro 178

Borsari, Giulio 185, 219, 233, 234, 262

Brabham, Jack 6, 15, 19, 20, 30, 33, 35, 36, 37, 39, 45, 46, 47, 48, 49, 51, 52, 55, 56, 58, 70, 89, 102, 109, 112, 116, 141, 146, 149, 164, 198, 199, 201, 207, 208, 209, 212, 213, 214, 215, 216, 231, 234, 235, 236, 250, 253, 255, 262, 263, 275, 277, 278, 279, 280, 281, 282, 285, 286, 291, 295, 296, 302, 303, 305, 320, 324, 326, 342, 354, 357, 358, 359, 360, 361

Breschi, Fiamma 122

Bristow, Chris 37, 38–39

Broadley, Eric 138, 179, 202, 226, 343, 354

Brock, Peter 255

Brooks, Tony 6, 15, 30, 32, 34, 36, 58, 70, 71, 89, 295

Bucknum, Ronnie 242, 278, 286, 291, 320, 327, 328, 331, 333, 334, 358, 360

Bulgari, Gianni 190

Buzzonetti, Daniele 206

Cabianca, Giulio 12, 27, 28, 60, 62, 70

Cabral, Mario 303

Cahier, Bernard 6, 49, 64, 119, 136, 161, 174, 175, 234, 296, 316, 337

Campari, Giuseppe 178

Canestrini, Giovanni 126

Cannon, John 181

Cantrell, Ed 181, 226

Caracciola, Rudolf 113, 324

Casner, Lloyd 'Lucky' 17, 42, 76, 89, 90, 92, 113, 114, 202, 310

Casoni, Mario 335

Castellotti, Eugenio 59, 69, 207

Causey, Dave 21

Cella, Leo 319

Chapman, Colin 21, 36, 52, 138, 169, 179, 201, 217, 234, 264, 292, 324

Charles, Maurice 158

Chemin, Henri 179

Chinetti, Luigi 21, 64, 65, 66, 67, 93, 129, 174, 206, 336, 343, 346, 357, 363

Chiron, Louis 149, 327

Chiti, Carlo 12, 13, 74, 75, 82, 88, 99, 116, 117, 121, 122, 123, 126, 173, 201

Clark, Jim 6, 28, 29, 34, 36, 40, 42, 49, 52, 55, 56, 58, 81, 82, 87, 88, 89, 90, 94, 97, 101, 102, 116, 117, 132, 133, 134, 138, 143, 144, 146, 147, 149, 150, 153, 161, 164, 166, 169, 172, 174, 176, 190, 191, 195, 197, 198, 200, 201, 207, 208, 209, 210, 212, 214, 215, 216, 217, 218, 219, 220, 221, 222, 225, 231, 232, 234, 235, 236, 250, 251, 253, 255, 256, 257, 262, 264, 269, 270, 271, 275, 276, 277, 278, 279, 280, 281, 282, 284, 285, 286, 291, 292, 295, 296, 297, 298, 299, 300, 302, 303, 304, 310, 313, 319, 324, 327, 329, 330, 339, 340, 342, 347, 348, 349, 350, 351, 352, 353, 354, 355, 356, 357, 358, 360, 361

Clarke, Peter 305

Coco, Vito 248

Cole, Tom 65

Collins, Peter 6, 68, 69, 70, 119, 141

Colombo, Gioacchino 12

Connell, Alan 40, 131, 132

Consten, Bernard 162

Coombs, John 222

Cooper, Gary 64

Cooper, John 282

Coundley, John 158

Crawford, Ed 21, 22, 23

Crombac, Gérard 'Jabby' 74, 138, 153

Cunningham, Briggs 21, 42, 76, 94, 97, 131, 158, 202

Daigh, Chuck 21, 22, 23, 33, 42, 70

Dal Monte, Luca 195, 331

Dallara, Giampaolo 158

Davis, Colin 28, 30, 134, 137, 155, 174, 250, 294, 316, 319, 322

de Beaufort, Carel Godin 33, 166, 245

de Bourbon-Parme, Michel 289

de Luca, Marcello 144

de Palma, Ralph 62

de Portago, Alfonso 12, 66, 67, 69, 120, 141, 226

de Saint-Aubin, Bernard 287, 289

Dei, Guglielmo 'Mimmo' 114, 195

Della Casa, Ermanno 122

Dernier, Léon 43, 158, 161, 202

Deserti, Bruno 316

Dewes, Jacques 158, 206

Dickson, Tom 159

Digby, Harry 322

Donner, Bob 180

Donohue, Mark 307

Dragoni, Eugenio 123, 134, 137, 141, 142, 149, 151, 153, 166, 178, 180, 183, 184, 185, 186, 191, 193, 199, 215, 223, 240, 259, 262, 264, 276, 302, 310, 352, 357, 360, 361

Dubois, Claude 288, 294

Dumay, Pierre 40, 43, 44, 45, 202, 258, 272, 273, 331, 336, 337, 343

Dumpitt, Bob 234

Dupeyron, Maurice 226, 289

Einsiedel, Wittigo 27

'Elde' — see 'Dernier, Léon'

Etancelin, Philippe 206

Facetti, Carlo 249, 250

Fairman, Jack 40, 42, 43, 106, 159

Fangio, Juan Manuel 6, 23, 47, 69, 104, 113, 201, 212, 231, 324, 354

Fantuzzi, Medardo 12, 75

Farina, Giuseppe 66

Farina, Pinin 12, 126

Ferlaino, Corrado 249, 250

Ferrari, Alfredino 'Dino' 12, 121

Ferrari, Enzo 10, 11, 12, 15, 18, 21, 39, 42, 59, 60, 63, 66, 69, 74, 75, 97, 98, 108, 113, 114, 116, 119, 120, 121, 122, 123, 126, 127, 128, 129, 132, 134, 155, 162, 169, 173, 175, 178, 179, 185, 191, 194, 195, 210, 237, 240, 248, 264, 284, 290, 302, 306, 309, 310, 313, 315, 319, 331, 354, 357, 362, 363

Ferrari, Laura 97, 109, 120, 121, 122

Ferraro, Pietro 134, 137, 143, 144

Filipinetti, Georges 210, 311

Finance, Jacques 126, 158

Fitch, John 42

Flockhart, Ron 40, 42, 43, 94

Ford, Cristina 333

Ford, Henry II 179, 194, 195, 333, 363

Forghieri, Mauro 123, 129, 132, 135, 138, 139, 142, 159, 161, 166, 167, 168, 173, 175, 179, 191, 200, 201, 207, 223, 233, 234, 243, 246, 248, 262, 276, 277, 284, 304, 305, 331, 335, 347, 357

Forghieri, Reclus 123

Fossati, Guido 229

Fowler, Howard 21

Foyt, A.J. 180, 241

'Franc' — see 'Dewes, Jacques'

Francolini, Ariberto 229

Frère, Paul 8, 36, 40, 42, 43, 265, 269

Fulp, John 'Buck' 129, 155, 180, 181, 242, 305, 306, 308

Gable, Clark 64

Galassi, Fausto 122

Gammino, Mike 242, 244, 307

Gardini, Girolamo 121, 122, 173

Gardner, Frank 276, 322, 343

Gauld, Graham 120, 121

Gavin, Bill 296, 324

'Geki' — see 'Russo, Giacomo'

Gendebien, Marie-Claire 90
Gendebien, Olivier 8, 12, 13, 17, 21, 23, 24, 25, 26, 27, 28, 30, 36, 38, 39, 40, 42, 43, 47, 51, 69, 70, 75, 76, 77, 78, 79, 80, 81, 88, 89, 90, 91, 92, 94, 95, 96, 97, 98, 99, 100, 101, 126, 129, 130, 131, 132, 134, 135, 136, 137, 141, 142, 144, 146, 155, 156, 157, 158, 159, 161, 206, 226, 290, 292
Giberti, Fedrico 122
Ginther, Richie 6, 16, 17, 18, 21, 22, 23, 24, 27, 28, 29, 30, 31, 33, 34, 35, 36, 40, 42, 44, 45, 59, 60, 63, 64, 65, 66, 75, 76, 78, 81, 82, 84, 85, 86, 87, 88, 89, 90, 91, 92, 93, 94, 95, 97, 98, 100, 101, 102, 104, 105, 106, 107, 108, 109, 110, 113, 114, 116, 117, 120, 123, 134, 138, 149, 158, 164, 172, 173, 181, 184, 191, 195, 197, 198, 208, 209, 214, 216, 218, 219, 220, 221, 222, 225, 231, 234, 235, 236, 242, 253, 258, 262, 264, 265, 266, 270, 272, 273, 278, 280, 281, 282, 286, 305, 307, 327, 328, 329, 330, 340, 347, 348, 349, 350, 351, 358, 360, 361, 362
Goldschmidt, Erwin 66
González, José Froilán 17, 18, 21
Gosselin, Gustave 294, 336, 337, 343
Grana, Maurizio 190
Grant Allen 305, 312, 314, 315, 336
Grant, Jerry 248, 250, 305, 307, 333, 335, 336
Greene, Keith 105
Greger, Sepp 27, 30
Gregory, Masten 6, 12, 16, 18, 21, 23, 28, 29, 30, 42, 49, 76, 89, 90, 92, 162, 170, 202, 248, 265, 272, 333, 336, 337, 338
Gretener, Jean 229
Grossman, Bob 42, 97, 131, 132, 155, 158, 159, 161, 164, 202, 226, 241, 269, 272, 273, 305, 306, 308, 309
Guiberson, Allen 64, 65, 66
Guichet, Jean 97, 158, 161, 162, 192, 193, 194, 202, 228, 229, 230, 240, 241, 242, 243, 244, 249, 250, 253, 254, 255, 258, 259, 261, 264, 265, 266, 267, 268, 269, 287, 288, 289, 290, 292, 294, 302, 312, 313, 315, 316, 318, 320, 321, 323, 333, 334, 335, 336, 338, 343, 344, 345
Gurney, Dan 15, 16, 18, 21, 22, 23, 27, 28, 29, 30, 35, 36, 40, 42, 43, 44, 49, 51, 55, 56, 58, 70, 76, 78, 88, 89, 90, 101, 102, 103, 104, 109, 110, 112, 116, 128, 129, 134, 137, 142, 143, 144, 149, 155, 157, 161, 166, 172, 173, 180, 198, 201, 202, 209, 212, 214, 215, 216, 222, 225, 226, 231, 234, 235, 236, 241, 242, 248, 250, 253, 255, 256, 257, 262, 264, 265, 266, 268, 269, 270, 271, 272, 273, 275, 276, 278, 279, 280, 281, 282, 285, 286, 291, 292, 295, 296, 297, 298, 299, 300, 302, 303, 304, 305, 307, 310, 319, 324, 327, 328, 329, 333, 335, 336, 340, 342, 350, 352, 354, 356, 357, 358, 359, 360, 361, 362

Halford, Bruce 40, 42, 43
Hall, Jim 128, 180, 202, 242, 244, 306, 307
Hansgen, Walt 21, 22, 23, 40, 43, 76, 131, 158, 202, 226, 241, 305, 307
Harper, Peter 336
Hawkins, Paul 162, 258
Hawthorn, Mike 6, 14, 15, 47, 49, 69, 70, 80, 104, 141, 158, 212, 295
Hayes, Charlie 164, 226, 244, 305
Hedges, Andrew 186
Hegbourne, Tony 214
Heins, Christian 18
Herrmann, Hans 17, 18, 21, 23, 24, 25, 26, 27, 28, 40, 42, 51, 52, 55, 60, 62, 69, 76, 78, 90, 109, 134, 137, 143, 146, 319
Heuer, Harry 180, 181
Hill Graham, 6, 17, 18, 21, 24, 27, 30, 32–33, 35, 36, 38, 39, 40, 42, 44, 47, 49, 51, 55, 58, 76, 78, 81, 88, 89, 90, 92, 94, 100, 110, 112, 116, 132, 133, 134, 137, 138, 143, 144, 146, 147, 149, 150, 153, 161, 162, 164, 166, 169, 172, 173, 180, 182, 184, 190, 195, 196, 197, 198, 200, 201, 202, 207, 208, 209, 210, 212, 214, 216, 218, 219, 221, 222, 225, 230, 231, 234, 235, 236, 242, 244, 250, 251, 252, 253, 255, 256, 257, 258, 259, 260, 262, 263, 264, 265, 266, 267, 269, 270, 272, 273, 274, 275, 276, 277, 278, 279, 280, 281, 282, 284, 285, 286, 291, 292, 293, 294, 295, 296, 297, 298, 299, 300, 302, 303, 304, 306, 307, 309, 316, 319, 320, 322, 323, 324, 325, 326, 327, 329, 342, 343, 344, 345, 347, 348, 349, 350, 352, 354, 356, 357, 358, 359, 360, 361
Hill, Phil 6, 8, 15, 16, 17, 18, 19, 20, 24, 25, 26, 27, 28, 29, 30, 31, 32, 33, 34, 35, 36, 37, 38, 39, 40, 42, 45, 46, 47, 48, 49, 50, 51, 52, 53, 55, 56, 58, 59, 60, 62, 63, 64–71, 72, 74, 75, 76, 77, 78, 80, 81, 85, 86, 87, 88, 89, 90, 94, 95, 97, 98, 99, 100, 101, 102, 104, 105, 106, 107, 108, 109, 110, 112, 113, 114, 116, 117, 120, 121, 122, 123, 126, 128, 129, 130, 131, 132, 134, 135, 136, 137, 138, 139, 141, 142, 143, 144, 146, 148, 149, 150, 151, 152, 153, 155, 156, 157, 158, 159, 161, 164, 165, 166, 167, 168, 169, 172, 173, 178, 180, 192, 194, 198, 201, 202, 206, 230, 240, 241, 242, 244, 248, 250, 252, 253, 254, 255, 258, 259, 265, 266, 272, 273, 279, 281, 282, 295, 307, 320, 322, 323, 333, 360
Hissom, Ronnie 180, 307
Hitchcock, Tommy 240, 258
Hoare, Colonel Ronnie 259, 273, 275, 343
Hobbs, David 202, 206, 316
Holbert, Bob 15, 21, 240, 241, 242, 244
Howe, Earl 206
Hudson, Skip 179, 265, 267, 272, 273, 306, 308, 309

Hugus, Ed 23, 45, 155, 164, 206, 306, 336
Hulme, Denny 6, 316, 324, 339, 341, 342, 350, 351, 354, 357
Hurt, Bob 305

Ireland, Innes 6, 20, 30, 33, 35, 36, 38, 47, 49, 51, 52, 55, 102, 112, 116, 129, 132, 138, 146, 149, 150, 164, 169, 181, 190, 202, 206, 209, 216, 219, 220, 222, 230, 248, 253, 258, 259, 260, 268, 269, 271, 272, 273, 277, 282, 286, 314, 335, 343, 358

Jano, Vittorio 12, 126, 201
Jeffords, Jim 42
Jenkinson, Denis 6, 29, 33, 63, 85, 109, 153, 167, 234, 319, 331, 357
Jennings, Bruce 307
Johnson, Bob 241, 242, 305, 336
Jopp, Peter 206

Kamm, Wunibald 75
Keck, Harold 305
Kerguen, Jean 158, 206
Kerrison, Chris 229
Kimberly, Bill 76, 158, 202, 206
Klass, Günther 316, 319, 322
Koch, Gerhard 258, 322
Köchert, Gotfrid 142, 143
Kolb, Charlie 226, 241, 242, 306, 308
Kurtz, Charles 77

Lampinen, Simo 334
Lanfranchi, Tony 282
Langlois van Ophem, Gérald 202, 203, 205, 206, 258, 259, 272, 273, 294, 295, 343
Leguezec, Claude 158, 227, 229
Leslie, Ed 305
Leston, Les 88
Levegh, Pierre 12
Lewis, Jackie 134
Ligier, Guy 292, 320, 333
Lindner, Peter 192, 258, 260, 294, 295
Linge, Herbert 27, 30, 42, 134, 137, 185, 190, 192, 194, 202, 250, 258, 316, 319, 322
'Loustel' — see 'Dumay, Pierre'
Love, John 282
Lovely, Pete 21, 23, 24
Lowther, Ed 184
Lualdi, Edoardo 27, 186
Lumsden, Peter 155, 158, 161, 184, 258
Lunn, Roy 226

MacDonald, Dave 240, 242, 244
Maggs, Tony 6, 94, 97, 143, 162, 164, 166, 172, 197, 208, 212, 214, 218, 268, 269, 272, 273, 274, 282, 292, 294, 295, 307, 308, 309, 320
Maglioli, Umberto 24, 25, 66, 67, 78, 89, 92, 142, 143, 146, 185, 186, 194, 202, 204, 240, 242, 243, 244, 245, 246, 250, 258, 259, 265, 266, 306, 307, 312, 313, 316, 319, 322, 331, 332, 333

Mairesse, Willy 24, 27, 28, 29, 30, 36, 38, 39, 40, 42, 45, 47, 59, 60, 62, 75, 76, 78, 89, 90, 94, 96, 97, 109, 110, 113, 126, 127, 129, 132, 133, 134, 135, 136, 137, 141, 143, 144, 146, 147, 148, 149, 150, 151, 153, 155, 169, 170, 171, 172, 173, 174, 178, 180, 183, 184, 185, 186, 188, 189, 190, 191, 192, 193, 194, 195, 196, 198, 199, 201, 202, 203, 206, 207, 214, 219, 220, 226, 240, 292, 294, 307, 312, 313, 314, 320, 322, 323, 334, 335, 336, 339, 343, 345
Mann, Alan 315
Mantia, Sergio 79
Manzon, Robert 69
Marsh, Tony 134
Martin, Marcel 289
Massimino, Alberto 12
May, Michael 190
Mays, Raymond 280
McLaren, Bruce 6, 20, 21, 30, 32, 33, 35, 36, 38, 39, 47, 48, 49, 51, 55, 56, 58, 89, 90, 92, 131, 134, 138, 143, 148, 149, 150, 153, 158, 164, 166, 172, 173, 197, 198, 201, 202, 206, 207, 208, 212, 213, 215, 216, 218, 220, 221, 231, 232, 235, 236, 253, 255, 257, 258, 262, 264, 265, 266, 269, 271, 272, 273, 277, 278, 281, 282, 285, 286, 296, 302, 307, 309, 312, 314, 315, 320, 320, 323, 333, 353, 354, 357, 358, 360, 362
Merlin, Olivier 174
Miles, Ken 180, 226, 242, 289, 305, 307, 309, 312, 314, 315, 333, 335
Miomandre, Raymond 10, 15, 18, 81, 302
Mitter, Gerhard 258, 316, 319, 322
Moity, Christian 69, 76, 94, 230, 294
Morolli, Olinto 12
Morton, John 242
Moss, Stirling 20, 21, 22, 23, 27, 28, 29, 30, 32, 33, 35, 36, 40, 49, 51, 55, 56, 58, 70, 76, 78, 81, 82, 84, 85, 87, 88, 89, 90, 92, 94, 97, 100, 101, 102, 104, 105, 106, 109, 112, 113, 116, 128, 129, 131, 132, 133, 134, 138, 166, 207, 291, 295, 324
Müller, Charly 229
Müller, Herbert 143, 294, 311, 312, 313, 314, 331, 333, 334
Munaron, Gino 13, 28, 29, 30, 42
Murphy, Jimmy 62, 63
Musso, Luigi 6, 13, 49, 69, 70, 79, 120, 122, 141, 207
Muther, Rick 305

Napoli, Giovanni 79
Nazzaro, Felice 178
Neerpasch, Jochen 258, 259, 260, 265, 266, 272, 273, 284, 286, 287, 288, 289, 322, 324, 332
Nelson, Ed 12, 120, 226
Nethercutt, Jack 21, 23, 24
Nixon, Chris 121
Noaille, Jean 267
Noble, Jed 142

Noblet, Pierre 28, 43, 97, 158, 161, 192, 193, 194, 202, 254
Nöcker, Peter 146, 258, 294, 322
Nolan, William F. 33, 36, 69, 98, 116
Norinder, Ulf 222
Nuvolari, Tazio 104, 113, 206
Nye, Doug 336

O'Brien, Tom 242, 244, 307
Ohlsen, John 241
Olthoff, Bob 155, 258, 282
Ortiz-Patiño, Jaime 173

Pabst, Augie 23, 45, 97, 98, 181, 184, 202
Parkes, Michael 30, 94, 95, 96, 97, 126, 143, 144, 146, 155, 158, 174, 175, 178, 180, 182, 183, 184, 185, 186, 187, 191, 192, 202, 204, 210, 211, 212, 217, 222, 240, 242, 243, 244, 245, 246, 247, 248, 253, 254, 255, 258, 259, 261, 264, 265, 266, 272, 273, 274, 275, 286, 292, 302, 310, 312, 313, 315, 316, 317, 320, 321, 322, 323, 324, 333, 334, 335, 336, 338, 343, 344
Parnell, Reg 52
Patria, Franco 295
Payne, Tom 305, 336
Pease, Al 245
Penske, Roger 131, 179, 181, 184, 202, 242, 244
Phipps, David 300, 331
Pilette, André 36, 40, 42, 43, 97
Piper, David 181, 202, 212, 214, 222, 240, 241, 242, 244, 253, 255, 272, 273, 274, 282, 289, 292, 294, 295, 305, 307, 308, 309, 312, 314, 320, 333, 335, 343, 344, 345, 357
Pon, Ben 194, 253, 258, 322
Pritchard, Anthony 120
Protheroe, Dick 253, 254
Pucci, Antonio 78, 134, 185, 250, 316, 319

Rancati, Gino 119
Raphael, Peter 229
Reed, George 155
Rees, Alan 162
Reiber, William 179
Remington, Phil 255
Reventlow, Lance 33, 45
Revson, Peter 252, 262
Ricci, Mario 66
Richards, Paul 202
Rindt, Jochen 258, 302, 304, 322, 323, 330, 333, 336, 337, 338, 352, 353, 358, 359
Ripley, Millard 77
Rives, Johnny 264, 265
Roberts, Glenn 'Fireball' 155, 158, 159, 161
Roche, Raymond 103, 104, 211, 346
Rodríguez, Pedro 8, 21, 22, 24, 26, 28, 29, 30, 40, 42, 76, 77, 78, 89, 90, 91, 92, 93, 94, 95, 97, 126, 129, 131, 132, 134, 142, 143, 144, 155, 156, 158, 159, 164, 173, 174, 179, 180,

182, 184, 202, 230, 240, 241, 242, 244, 265, 266, 267, 272, 273, 292, 294, 295, 296, 298, 305, 306, 307, 309, 324, 335, 336, 339, 343, 344, 345, 357, 358, 359, 360, 361, 362
Rodríguez, Ricardo 6, 15, 21, 22, 24, 25, 26, 28, 29, 30, 40, 42, 43, 76, 77, 78, 79, 81, 89, 90, 91, 92, 93, 94, 95, 96, 97, 114, 115, 116, 126, 128, 129, 131, 134, 135, 136, 137, 138, 140, 141, 143, 146, 149, 150, 152, 153, 155, 156, 158, 159, 166, 169, 171, 172, 173, 174, 292
Rosati, Raffaello 113
Ruby, Lloyd 305
Rudd, Tony 201
Russo, Giacomo 334
Ryan, Pete 129, 155, 159

Salamano, Carlo 178
Salmon, Mike 158, 202, 204, 240–241, 314, 332, 335
Salvadori, Roy 28, 30, 42, 56, 94, 97, 146, 158, 164, 202, 212, 217, 222, 241, 247, 282
Salviati, Forese 66
Sanderson, Ninian 202
Sargent, Peter 155, 158, 161, 258, 260
Scaglietti, Sergio 12, 128
Scarfiotti, Ludovico 8, 17, 24, 26, 27, 28, 40, 42, 70, 89, 137, 155, 158, 161, 174, 178, 180, 181, 183, 184, 185, 186, 188, 189, 192, 202, 205, 206, 207, 208, 209, 210, 214, 221, 240, 242, 244, 248, 258, 259, 264, 265, 266, 272, 273, 274, 275, 282, 283, 284, 285, 286, 292, 293, 294, 310, 312, 313, 315, 316, 317, 320, 321, 323, 331, 333, 335, 336, 346, 357, 360, 361
Scarlatti, Giorgio 25, 27, 28, 29, 30, 42, 70, 78, 113, 114, 134, 137, 143, 144, 195
Schechter, Roy 21
Schell, Harry 49, 118
Schlesser, Jo 6, 28, 30, 202, 206, 210, 211, 212, 227, 229, 241, 242, 244, 247, 248, 253, 258, 260, 265, 266, 272, 273, 284, 294, 295, 305, 307, 309, 322, 336, 343, 345, 346
Schulze, Helmut 27
Scotuzzi, Giuseppe 65
Sculati, Eraldo 69
Sears, Jack 202, 204, 266, 282, 312, 314, 315, 322, 334, 335, 336, 339, 343, 345
Seidel, Wolfgang 13, 40, 42, 106, 146
Selmi, Enzo 122
Senna, Ayrton 236
Sharp, Hap 180, 306, 307
Shaw, Graham 244
Shelby, Carroll 21, 23, 69, 179, 248, 250, 253, 305, 309, 310, 358
Siffert, Jo 6, 276, 278, 286, 289, 292, 310, 329, 330, 332, 358, 360
Simon, André 69, 158, 161, 162, 202, 203, 211, 212, 226, 287, 288, 289, 294, 322, 323

Simone, Colonel John 158, 202
Smith, Carroll 323
Soisbault, Annie 287, 292, 343
Solana, Moisés 358
Sommer, Raymond 206
Spear, Bill 64
Spence, Mike 247, 286, 292, 296, 298, 300, 302, 303, 304, 310, 324, 327, 348, 349, 350, 351, 352, 353, 355, 360
Spencer, Lew 180, 242, 244
Spinedi, Aghdass 228, 229, 230
Spinedi, Gérard 228, 229, 230
Spoerry, Dieter 339
Spychiger, Tommy 310, 311, 312, 313, 314
Stacey, Alan 30, 35, 36, 39, 52
Stagnoli, Antonio 65
Stear, Luke 21
Stewart, Jackie 272, 273, 292, 293, 294, 302, 320, 324, 326, 327, 329, 330, 339, 340, 342, 347, 348, 349, 350, 352, 354, 355, 356, 357, 358, 360, 362
Strähle, Paul Ernst 27, 78, 185
Strudwick, Anne 134
Stubbs, Arnold 64
Sudan, Pierre 284
Surtees, John 6, 30, 49, 51, 52, 55, 56, 58, 89, 98, 101, 134, 138, 146, 147, 148, 149, 164, 166, 169, 172, 174, 175, 176, 178, 180, 181, 183, 184, 185, 186, 187, 190, 191, 192, 193, 194, 196, 197, 198, 199, 200, 201, 202, 203, 207, 209, 209, 210, 212, 213, 214, 215, 216, 217, 218, 219, 220, 221, 222, 223, 224, 225, 230, 231, 232, 234, 235, 236, 237, 239, 240, 242, 244, 245, 246, 247, 248, 250, 251, 252, 253, 255, 256, 257, 258, 259, 262, 263, 264, 265, 266, 267, 269, 270, 271, 272, 273, 274, 275, 276, 277, 278, 279, 280, 281, 282, 284, 285, 286, 290, 291, 292, 295, 296, 297, 298, 299, 300, 302, 303, 304, 305, 310, 311, 312, 313, 315, 316, 319, 320, 321, 322, 323, 324, 325, 326, 327, 328, 329, 330, 331, 332, 333, 335, 336, 339, 340, 341, 342, 343, 344, 345, 347, 348, 349, 350, 351, 352, 353, 354, 355, 356, 357, 360, 363
Surtees, Pat 192, 215, 247, 262
Sutcliffe, Peter 253, 254, 322, 336
Swaters, Jacques 36

Taramazzo, Luigi 249, 250
Taruffi, Piero 28, 29, 66, 102, 119, 134
Tauranac, Ron 328
Tavano, Fernand 40, 43, 44, 45, 94, 97, 158, 161, 202, 203, 227, 229, 269, 289
Tavoni, Romolo 24, 30, 42, 60, 69, 76, 90, 97, 101, 102, 104, 120, 121, 122, 123, 173, 312
Taylor, Henry 34, 40, 58
Taylor, Mike 36

Taylor, Trevor 138, 141, 143, 149, 150, 151, 153, 169, 172, 201, 213, 235
Tchkotoua, Zourab 240
Thépenier, Jean 158
Thiel, Günter 258
Thompson, Dick 43, 97, 98, 131, 158, 184, 334, 335, 336, 339
Thuner, Jean-Jacques 334
Timanus, John 305
Trintignant, Maurice 12, 17, 18, 20, 27, 28, 30, 40, 42, 47, 49, 51, 56, 68, 69, 78, 89, 134, 146, 149, 158, 213, 214, 250, 252, 278, 287, 288, 289, 294, 320, 322, 323, 333
Tyrrell, Ken 342

Ugolini, Nello 229

Vaccarella, Nino 24, 25, 26, 27, 78, 89, 113, 114, 128, 131, 134, 137, 142, 143, 180, 183, 184, 185, 194, 240, 242, 244, 258, 259, 264, 265, 267, 268, 269, 272, 273, 292, 294, 310, 312, 316, 317, 319, 320, 322, 323, 335, 336, 339, 354, 356, 357
van Dyle, Louis 64
Vandervell, Tony 52
Varzi, Achille 104, 113
Vecchi, Ener 219, 233
Volpi, Count Giovanni 129, 173
von Csazy, Kalman 186
von Frankenberg, Richard 119
von Hanstein, Huschke 142
von Neumann, Eleanor 63
von Trips, Wolfgang 6, 8, 12, 14, 16, 17, 18, 19, 20, 24, 25, 26, 27, 28, 29, 30, 31, 33, 34, 35, 36, 37, 38, 39, 40, 42, 45, 46, 47, 48, 49, 50, 51, 52, 53, 55, 56, 58, 59, 60, 62, 63, 69, 70, 72, 75, 76, 78, 79, 80, 81, 82, 84, 86, 87, 88, 89, 90, 91, 92, 94, 95, 97, 98, 99, 100, 101, 105, 106, 107, 108, 109, 110, 112, 113, 114, 115, 116, 117, 118–119, 120, 141, 207, 292

Wacker, Fred 65
Walker, Rob 20, 30, 33, 51, 134, 175, 252, 282, 286, 292, 327, 331
Walter, Hans 42, 143, 194
Walter, Heini 229
Walters, Phil 69
Ward, Rodger 230
Watts, Nicholas 212
Weslake, Harry 358
Whitehead, Graham 40
Whitmore, John 155, 174, 312, 314, 315, 316, 320, 322, 323, 335, 343, 345
Wilkins, Gordon 225
Williams, Richard 195
Willment, John 339
Wimpffen, János L. 336
Windridge, Fred 43
Wyer, John 202, 226, 310

Zeccoli, Teodoro 332
Zuccoli, Carlo 334